# Everyone's Country Estate

*Roy W. ⟨signature⟩*

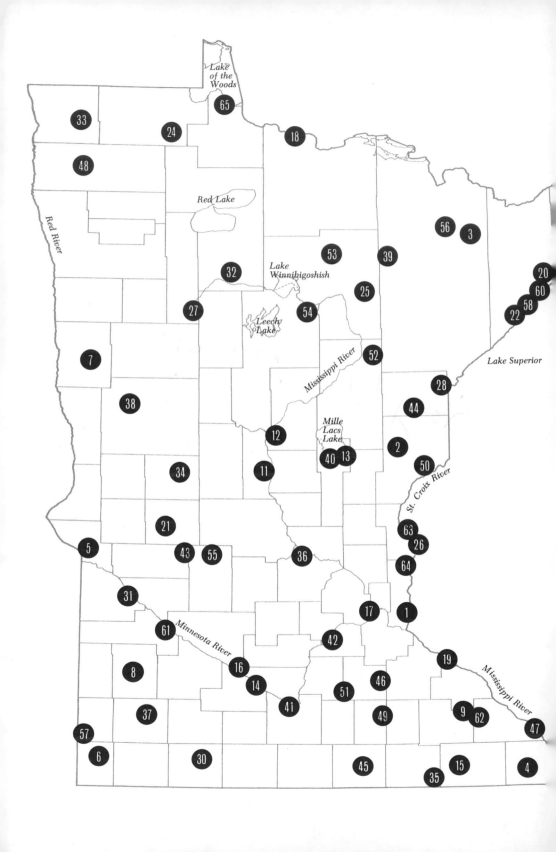

# Minnesota's State Park System, 1991

1. Afton
2. Banning
3. Bear Head Lake
4. Beaver Creek Valley
5. Big Stone Lake
6. Blue Mounds
7. Buffalo River
8. Camden
9. Carley
10. Cascade River
11. Charles A. Lindbergh
12. Crow Wing
13. Father Hennepin
14. Flandreau
15. Forestville and Mystery Cave
16. Fort Ridgely
17. Fort Snelling
18. Franz Jevne
19. Frontenac
20. George H. Crosby Manitou
21. Glacial Lakes
22. Gooseberry Falls
23. Grand Portage
24. Hayes Lake
25. Hill Annex Mine
26. Interstate
27. Itasca
28. Jay Cooke
29. Judge C. R. Magney
30. Kilen Woods
31. Lac qui Parle
32. Lake Bemidji
33. Lake Bronson
34. Lake Carlos
35. Lake Louise
36. Lake Maria
37. Lake Shetek
38. Maplewood
39. McCarthy Beach
40. Mille Lacs Kathio
41. Minneopa
42. Minnesota Valley
43. Monson Lake
44. Moose Lake
45. Myre-Big Island
46. Nerstrand Big Woods
47. O. L. Kipp
48. Old Mill
49. Rice Lake
50. St. Croix
51. Sakatah Lake
52. Savanna Portage
53. Scenic
54. Schoolcraft
55. Sibley
56. Soudan Underground Mine
57. Split Rock Creek
58. Split Rock Lighthouse
59. Temperance River
60. Tettagouche
61. Upper Sioux Agency
62. Whitewater
63. Wild River
64. William O'Brien
65. Zippel Bay

*At the Dalles of the St. Croix River, Interstate State Park, about 1900*

ROY W. MEYER

# Everyone's Country Estate

A HISTORY OF

MINNESOTA'S

STATE PARKS

MINNESOTA HISTORICAL SOCIETY PRESS
ST. PAUL

Minnesota Historical Society Press
St. Paul 55101

Manufactured in the United States of America
10 9 8 7 6 5 4 3 2 1

♾ The paper used in this publication meets
the minimum requirements of the American
National Standard for Information Sciences —
Permanence for Printed Library Materials,
ANSI Z39.48–1984
International Standard Book Number
0-87351-265-0 Cloth
0-87351-266-9 Paper

*Library of Congress Cataloging-in-Publication
Data*
Meyer, Roy Willard, 1925-
    Everyone's country estate : a history of Min-
nesota's state parks / Roy W. Meyer.
        p. cm.
    Includes bibliographical references and index.
    ISBN 0-87351-265-0 : $34.95. — ISBN 0-
87351-266-9 (pbk.) : $19.95
        1. Parks — Minnesota — History.  2.  Parks —
Minnesota — Management — History. I. Title.
    SB482.M6M49      1991
    333.78'3'09776 — dc20                91-14407

*Judge C. R. Magney . . . was most anxious*
*that the river above Taylor's Falls*
*become a park and thus, in his favorite phrase,*
*serve as a part of everyman's country estate.*

SAMUEL H. MORGAN

# Contents

# *Preface*

EVERY BOOK has a beginning. If I wished to follow the example of those colonial historians who began their histories of New England towns by going back to the creation of the earth, I could claim that this book had its inception on Sunday, July 18, 1937, when I attended a family picnic at Whitewater State Park and, together with other children, ran wild climbing the bluffs of that topographically varied spot. More realistically, I can trace my interest in Minnesota's state parks back to 1968, when I first visited the Forestville State Park and became curious about the tangled history of that much more recent addition to the system. My curiosity led to research, which in turn produced an article, "Forestville: The Making of a State Park," published in the Fall 1974 issue of *Minnesota History*.

The history of one state park is linked with that of the state park system, and in studying Forestville I learned much about how the system evolved in Minnesota. It seemed to me that there was need for a history of that system, so that users of our parks — perhaps inclined to take them for granted — could see the amounts of money, effort, and imagination that went into creating the park system that we have today. I was familiar with John Ise's *Our National Park Policy: A Critical History*, and while it would be inaccurate to say that I used it as a model, it did provide me with some ideas that I thought could be adapted to the smaller scale of the state scene.

Although in a sense the park system has its own history, in large part its story is that of the individual units that compose it. Hence this book is primarily a series of individual park histories, arranged chronologically. At an early stage in my thinking, I conceived of the book as a series of articles like the one I had done on Forestville, but I soon realized that such an approach would lead to a book of monstrous proportions. Even though few of Minnesota's parks have so complex a history as Forestville does, a vast amount of information is available on most of them.

The problem thus became one of selection — choosing the most significant features in the story of each park. Since many parks' development followed similar lines, in order to minimize repetition it seemed desirable to concentrate on certain aspects of development in the case of a particular park, even though many other parks might illustrate the same aspects. Thus in treating one park I might emphasize the role of the work-relief agencies of the 1930s; in another, the growth of an interpretive program; in yet another, the problems of land acquisition and relations with the park's neighbors.

Because these sketches of individual parks have to be brief, there is room for many more studies like the one on Forestville. In some cases, master's theses or newspaper articles have been written about single parks. I have availed myself of these whenever I learned of them. No doubt I have missed some, but many parks have not been the subjects of serious, detailed studies. With the growth of programs and courses that focus on parks, recreation, and leisure services, students will have a wealth of opportunities to fill in the gaps by doing research on parks not yet thoroughly investigated.

If some readers feel that their favorite parks have been treated only sketchily in this book, others may detect errors of omission of a different sort. Not much is said here about the role of politics in the establishment, retention, and management of the state parks. Little attention is given to the problems involved in their day-to-day operation, including contact with park users. Nor have I seen fit to analyze the much-publicized crisis of overuse and underfinancing that surfaced (not for the first time) in the 1980s. These and other topics warrant investigation, but not necessarily in a book intended mainly to present a chronological survey of the Minnesota state park system and the individual parks that comprise that system.

I began this project with the encouragement and assistance of the late June Drenning Holmquist. After her death in 1982, the help she had begun was continued by Jean A. Brookins, who invited me to apply for a research grant from the Minnesota Historical Society. This grant, which I received in 1982, enabled me to put in several stints of research at the Society and at the offices of the Parks and Recreation Division, Minnesota Department of Natural Resources, to visit the regional offices of the DNR, and to revisit many of the parks. In the course of this research, I have incurred many debts. At the parks division offices, which are after all not designed to be research centers, I was given unlimited access to records, a place where my wife and I could go through them and take notes, and answers to the many questions that these records inevitably raised. Ruth Husom and Helen Fix were especially helpful in facilitating our research. The number of people who answered my questions is too great for me to list them all here. Including managers, assistant managers, and other personnel at individual parks, it must at least run into the dozens.

The entire manuscript, in a longer form, was read by U. W. Hella, for twenty years director of the Division of Parks and Recreation, and by Samuel H. Morgan, one of the founders, and long an active member, of the Minnesota Council of State Parks and of the Minnesota Parks Foundation, which are now combined as the Minnesota Parks and Trails Council. Others at the Division of Parks and Recreation have read all or part of the manuscript, and, like Mr. Hella and Mr. Morgan, have given me the benefit of their seasoned judgment and encyclopedic knowledge of the park system. Although they have enabled me to reduce the number of factual errors, I must accept responsibility for those that remain or that have crept in after their reading of the manuscript.

Throughout this project I have been aided in a variety of ways by my wife Betty, who shared in the research, accompanied me on visits to the parks, and proofread the manuscript at various stages. Our daughter Annette has also been a participant in the project and has developed an acquaintance with the parks, beginning when at the age of two months she was taken along on a picnic at Lac qui Parle.

*Roy W. Meyer*

# A Note to Readers

THE OVERALL ORGANIZATION of this book is chronological, with each park treated in the order of its establishment. Since it is necessary in the individual park histories to mention legislative acts, persons, and other subjects not yet discussed in the general history of the park system, the reader may find it helpful to have the major pieces of legislation affecting the parks and the names and terms of office of the successive directors presented in chart form in a location where they can be conveniently referred to from time to time.

*Major milestones in Minnesota state park history*

1885 — "Minnehaha State Park" authorized.

1889 — Camp Release monument authorized.

1891 — Itasca, first true state park, established.

1923 — Minnesota state park system legislatively initiated.

1925 — Department of Conservation created, under supervision of three-member commission.

1931 — Five-member Conservation Commission replaced old body; parks placed under Division of Forestry.

1935 — Division of State Parks created.

1937 — Eleven state parks, most of them developed by work-relief agencies, given legal status.

1939 — *The Minnesota State Park and Recreational Area Plan* issued.

1953 — First "park sticker" act passed. Modified in 1961, 1969, 1976, 1981, and 1986.

1954 — Minnesota Council of State Parks organized.

1963 — Omnibus Natural Resources and Recreation Act passed. Fourteen new parks created and seventeen others expanded.

1964 — Land and Water Conservation Fund Act passed by U.S. Congress.

1965 — Minnesota Outdoor Recreation Resources Commission study published.

1967 — Minnesota Parks Foundation formed.

1969 — "Project 80" study authorized. (Published in 1971.)

1971 — "Department of Conservation" changed to "Department of Natural Resources." (Name change authorized by 1969 legislature, to take effect first Monday in January 1971.)

1975 — Outdoor Recreation Act passed. Mandated classification of units as "natural" and "recreational" state parks.

*Directors*, de facto *and* de jure, *of the state park system:*

Ray P. Chase, state auditor, 1921–1931.

Grover P. Conzet, commissioner of forestry and fire prevention, 1924–1937.

Harold W. Lathrop, 1935–1946. First to hold title of "director."

Lew E. Fiero, 1946–1953.

U. W. Hella, 1953–1973.

Donald D. Davison, 1973–1987.

William Morrissey, 1987–

# CHAPTER ONE

# The Beginnings
# 1885-1895

MINNESOTA had parks long before it had an officially designated park system — as did the nation. Although Yellowstone National Park was established in 1872, it was not until 1916 that the National Park Service was created and given jurisdiction over the dozen or so rather loosely administered parks that by then existed. Likewise, Minnesota had no agency exclusively responsible for managing the parks until 1935 — roughly half a century after its first parks came into being. Since important precedents were established and major units of the system authorized during this half-century, a historical survey appropriately begins with the creation of the first parks, treating them and their early successors as members of a system even though they were in fact managed quite independently of one another for many years.

## Minnehaha Falls

In deciding on the date for the beginning of Minnesota's park system, one has a choice of three years: 1885, 1889, and 1891. The claim of 1885 rests on an act of the legislature, signed into law on March 9 of that year, intended to set up a state park at Minnehaha Falls. Such a park was apparently proposed as early as 1867, but nothing came of the idea until it was revived in 1884 by Minneapolis park board president Charles M. Loring. In a letter to the *St. Paul Pioneer Press* later in 1884, John De Laittre, a St. Paul lumberman and banker, asked the rhetorical question, "Is not there just as good reason for the state to own and preserve the beautiful Falls of Minnehaha and adjacent grounds as for the national government to retain ownership of and preserve Yellowstone park?"[1]

The 1885 law instructed the governor to appoint five "Commissioners of the State Park at Minnehaha Falls," who were empowered to select and locate a tract of land in Hennepin County, not to exceed 200 acres, embracing the falls. The commissioners were to prepare a map, notify the affected landowners that the state intended to acquire the lands for inclusion in a state park, and appoint appraisers to do the actual work of determining the value of the lands. An appropriation of $1,000 was made to cover the expenses of the commission.[2]

In the next few months a tract of 173 acres was selected, at an appraised valuation of $88,736.52. Dissatisfied with this appraisal, the property owners appealed to district court, which confirmed the appraisers' action, as did the state supreme court on further appeal. These appeals dragged on through the 1887 session of the legislature, which therefore took no action. The report of the commissioners was finally presented to the legislature in 1889, but by then there was insufficient money to purchase the lands.[3]

At that point the Minneapolis Board of Park Commissioners intervened, promising that if the legislature would confirm the appraisal the city would advance the necessary funds — $92,283.16, including the cost of the appraisal and the interest on deferred payments — and maintain the lands as "Minnehaha State Park." The legislature passed an act accepting the award of the appraisers, appropriating $100,000, and turning the lands over to the city, contingent upon its reimbursing the state.[4]

It is unfortunate, in at least two respects, that Minnehaha Falls did not become a state park as originally intended. Although situated in the Twin Cities metropolitan area, the falls are as much a part of the heritage of all Minnesotans as, for example, Fort Snelling, which much later did become a state park. Moreover, had Minnehaha State Park been established as a state park in fact as well as in name, it would have placed Minnesota in the vanguard of the state park movement. Apart from California, to which the federal government retroceded Yosemite Valley in 1864 for use as a state park, New York is generally credited with initiating the movement in 1885 when it reserved for public use Niagara Falls and a forest preserve in the Catskills and the Adirondacks, part of which became Adirondack State Park.[5]

The Minnehaha State Park episode would be of antiquarian interest only but for the fact that it may have set an unfortunate precedent. In later years the complaint was heard that there were few state parks in or near the Twin Cities metropolitan area. No doubt high land valuations largely accounted for this deficiency. But one wonders if the Minnehaha experience did not persuade outstate legislators that the state's largest cities were better able to acquire and develop parklands than the state itself. If they did hold this view, they were partly right. Minneapolis and St. Paul have fine city park systems, and the Hennepin County Park Reserve District has demonstrated a highly urbanized area's ability to preserve wild lands for its people. Nevertheless, there is at least a possibility that if Minnehaha Falls had been retained as a true state park, it would have been easier for the state to establish other parks in the metropolitan area.

## Camp Release

Minnesota had to wait another four years before action was taken to establish what was subsequently considered (although not quite correctly) its first state park, supporting the claim of 1889 as the system's beginning. On April 24, 1889, the legislature passed an act appropriating $500 for the purchase of not less than 10 acres of land in the Minnesota River valley, on the site west of Montevideo where Colonel Henry H. Sibley had released 269 white and mixed-blood captives at the end of the Dakota War (also known as the Sioux Uprising) of 1862. This modest sum was also to be used for fencing the site, known as Camp Release, and preparing it for the erection of a monument. A committee was appointed to select the appropriate lands, obtain an abstract, and perform other legal functions in connection with their acquisition. Five years later, after an appropriation of $2,500 had been made for the purpose, a fifty-two-foot granite obelisk was erected on the highest point at the site, which eventually embraced 17.8 acres. On July 4, 1894, in the presence of such dignitaries as former governor Alexander Ramsey and some of the survivors of the conflict, this marker was formally dedicated.[6]

After the 1893 appropriation the legislature took no notice of Camp Release for several sessions, but when the site received its attention again, in 1901, it was treated as a state park. The appropriations granted then and for years thereafter were very small — usually $100 each biennium, to be expended for "improvement, maintenance and beautification," until the 1920s, when the amount was increased to $150.[7]

By the late 1920s Camp Release had become a popular picnic site, patronized by local people and by tourists. In 1928 its facilities consisted of two tables, with a fire grate near each one, and two toilets. In order to provide a water supply, the legislature increased the appropriation to $555 for the fiscal year 1930 and to $235 for fiscal 1931. For the rest of that decade Camp Release received sums varying from $200 to $400 per year.[8]

When the nineteenth annual meeting of the National Conference of State Parks was held at Lake Itasca in 1939, Minnesota had been chosen, it was said, to commemorate the fiftieth anniversary of the beginnings of the state's park system — thereby explicitly recognizing Camp Release as the state's first park. Yet, though long a part of the state park system, it was never officially designated a state park. For many years it was the Camp Release State Memorial Wayside; later "Memorial" was eliminated from the name. Since an 18-acre tract can scarcely be regarded as a state park, "wayside" was a more appropriate designation.[9]

Moreover, Camp Release, like most of the other Dakota War sites later acquired by the state, was essentially a monument rather than a park. The granite shaft alone distinguishes it from any other pleasant picnic area along a Minnesota highway. The developed portion of the site occupies the highest ground; the remainder is undeveloped — too large to be kept manicured like the picnic grounds but too small to be laid out with a trail system. With the general reorganization of the state park system in the 1970s, those portions of *Minnesota Statutes* granting the parks division authority over Camp Release and the various state monuments were repealed, and the sites were transferred to other jurisdictions. So the claim of 1889 as the birth year of Minnesota's state park system, resting as it does on the legislation authorizing the acquisition of the Camp Release site that year, would seem to be somewhat shaky.[10]

## *Itasca*

A much stronger case can be made for 1891, the year that Itasca State Park was established. Itasca, containing the source of the Mississippi River, was a true state park in every sense of the term and remains the gem of Minnesota's park system, attracting more visitors annually than some of the national parks. The origins and early history of the park are associated with one man: Jacob V. Brower. Not only did Brower play a central role in getting the park established and in guiding it through its first difficult years, but he wrote an account of the creation and early days of the park that remains our most important primary source.[11]

In the fall of 1888 Brower and two companions camped in an abandoned settler's cabin on Lake Itasca. The next spring he returned to conduct a survey for the Minnesota Historical Society. While it was in progress, Alfred J. Hill, an archaeologist who mapped the prehistoric mounds of Minnesota, wrote a letter to the *St. Paul Dispatch* in which he argued for the establishment of a park at the source of the Mississippi. After commenting on the lack of public support for a proposed park on the river between Fort Snelling and Minneapolis, he asked, "Why cannot we, however, have a real wild park, one far from the hum and bustle of large cities, like the National Park of the Yellowstone, and that once proposed, I believe, for the Adirondack region in New York?" A few months later, Joseph A. Wheelock, editor of the *St. Paul Pioneer Press*, published an editorial to much the same effect, though with a more utilitarian slant. Just as the people of New York had moved to protect the headwaters of the Hudson River, on which their industry and commerce depended, so the people of the Twin Cities, argued Wheelock, ought to be concerned about protecting the sources of the water power that served their mills.[12]

A third plea for the establishment of a park at Lake Itasca, one more in the mainstream of later arguments in favor of parks and other preserves, came from Newton H. Winchell, geologist and archaeologist, who in 1889 stressed the scientific and recreational

*A classic photograph: crossing the Mississippi at its source, about 1955. The man at right records the moment in a home movie.*

values of a large public park. Because Minnesota lies on "that border land which exhibits the transition of the forested area into the prairie," wrote Winchell, it preserves "the faunal and floral characteristics of both" and thus is of special interest to science. Moreover, he added, the state should have a large public park "because of the healthful resort that it would afford for those living in cities" and for tourists from farther south. After weighing the respective merits of a park somewhere in northeastern Minnesota along the Canadian border and one at the source of the Mississippi, he concluded that the latter site would be preferable, partly because of its historical associations and partly because the area would illustrate the topography of glacial moraines.[13]

Thus Winchell in a sense anticipated the potential conflict, still very much alive, between preservation and recreation as proper functions of state parks. The issue had been unconsciously expressed in the legislation establishing Yellowstone National Park, which was set up as a "public park and pleasuring ground" but in which the unique natural features were to be left "in their natural condition" for future generations.. Winchell saw, perhaps more clearly than the architects of the Yellowstone Park bill, the dual purpose of a park, but it is unlikely that even he recognized the problems inherent in any attempt to reconcile these goals.[14]

If these men individually helped generate public sentiment in favor of a park, the Minnesota Historical Society took the initiative in getting the park established. The society first passed a resolution on January 12, 1891, proposing that the park idea be presented to the legislature, and then commissioned Brower to draft a bill to carry the proposal into effect. Senator John B. Sanborn introduced the bill on March 2, 1891, and immediately saw it run into opposition from interests sympathetic to the lumber companies that wished to exploit the area's timber resources. Sanborn pushed it through the senate by a narrow margin, however, at the cost of a crippling amendment that limited to sixty days per year the payment of the five-dollar-a-day salary authorized for the commissioner who was to be appointed to manage the park. The bill also passed the house and was signed into law on April 20 by Governor William R. Merriam.[15]

As was to be the case many times in later years, the legislature's passage of an act authorizing a park did not mean that a park existed. The state of Minnesota owned only a fraction of the land within the external boundaries as defined by the act. Most of the park, a rectangle seven miles north and south by five miles east and west, was the property of the federal government, two railroad companies, and several lumber companies. The federal lands presented no problem. At the request of state officials, Congress passed a law on August 3, 1892, providing for transferring federally owned lands to the state for park purposes; the grant was accepted by the 1893 legislature. Brower, who had been appointed park commissioner, at once opened negotiations with the railroads, which set reasonable prices on their lands, and with the lumber companies, which asked far more than the state was at that time prepared to pay. In his second report, made late in 1892, Brower said he had acquired or expected to acquire 14,174.61 acres, leaving 5,527.08 acres on which negotiations had been unsuccessful.[16]

*Fishing at Lake Itasca, 1902*

The next few years were frustrating ones for Brower and others who wanted to see the park truly established by the acquisition of the bulk of the land included within the legal boundaries. The 1893 legislature did appropriate $1,326.48 for the purchase of lands owned by the Northern Pacific railroad; these lands, together with those transferred by the federal government and those already owned by the state, constituted the nucleus of a respectable park. But at its next session, though authorizing the attorney general to obtain lands by purchase or condemnation, the legislature provided no funds with which to carry out such an acquisition. Worse yet, a change of administration that year resulted in Brower's replacement as commissioner by Adelbert A. Whitney, whom Brower characterized as "an unprogressive, indigent person who received the favors of political friends whom he had variously served." Whitney held the job for the next four years.[17]

Things began to improve in 1899, however, when the legislature appropriated $21,000 for the purchase of the more than 8,000 acres still in private hands. If this should not prove to be enough, the act also provided that the state should obtain a two-year option on the remaining lands. The 1901 session of the legislature passed an act providing an annual appropriation of $5,000 until all of the desired lands were acquired. Another law passed at that session authorized the purchase of 152.8 acres, including the area around the outlet of Lake Itasca, which had been omitted from the park when the original boundaries were delineated. This outlet, usually referred to as the source of the Mississippi, is undoubtedly the most popular spot in the park today, and its acquisition sooner or later was essential. Besides this tract, by the time of Brower's death in 1905 the state owned 16,117.17 acres; the rest of the park was still in the hands of the lumber companies.[18]

Certain administrative changes took place early in the twentieth century. In 1907 the forestry board took over management of the park from the state auditor, who had previously had jurisdiction over it (as he was to continue to have over most of the state parks until 1925). Then, in 1911, the Minnesota Forest Service was created, and the state forester took over the park the following year. A legislative act passed in 1909 made the park officially a state forest, to be managed like any other, with the important exception that no timber was to be cut, except for dead, down, or diseased trees.[19]

No such restrictions applied, of course, to the land still in the hands of private owners, and the history of the park until about 1920 was a story of the state's struggle to acquire land before it was logged. In 1909, for example, the Pine Tree Lumber Company and the state made a deal under which the company donated the land, together with all trees of less than eight inches in diameter. The state could purchase the larger trees, but with limited funds available, the state acquired mainly those of twelve to fourteen inches or less in diameter. The real giants went down before the ax and saw. Gradually, however, the lands were acquired, with or without mature trees, and the park finally took shape. In 1919 the legislature authorized an addition, a strip two miles wide that had already been logged over, along the western border of the park. Large-scale logging ended by 1920, and the last large land purchases, made in 1919 and 1921 from interests associated with the

Weyerhaeuser Timber Company, totaled 8,976.66 acres. Except for minor adjustments, Itasca State Park was complete.[20]

Itasca was not, in its early days, typical of the state's parks. Not only was it administered as a state forest, whereas all but one of the other parks established before 1925 were under the control of the state auditor, but it was remote, isolated, almost inaccessible in comparison to the others. With one exception, all the other early parks were located adjacent to cities or towns or in well-settled farming country; they were easily accessible to the people who had been mainly responsible for their establishment. By contrast, until the automobile came into widespread use and suitable roads were built, Itasca was hard for the general public to reach. Except for logging tracks, no railroad came near its boundaries. Therefore, despite all the talk by Winchell and others about its recreational potential, Itasca was not heavily used by tourists.

Itasca was a large park compared to those that followed it, and hence difficult to administer effectively. To the problem of sheer size was added that of the checkerboard pattern of land ownership that prevailed until the private inholdings had been acquired. Though the park was relatively inaccessible to visitors from distant cities, it was not so to poachers, and the successive commissioners and foresters found it practically impossible to patrol so large an area or to distinguish between private and public lands. A few poachers were apprehended and convicted, but whether these cases served as deterrents to other would-be malefactors is doubtful.

Forest fires also presented a problem. They seem to have been kept out of the park in the early years, but there were bad fires in 1913 and 1917. Since considerable logging was going on at that time, the slash left by the loggers aggravated the problem. Continued logging menaced the park in other ways as well. The lumber companies had to remove their timber from the park, and however they managed the operation, it had adverse effects on the area's pristine beauty. One device was to build a temporary dam on the Mississippi and then blow it up when the reservoir behind it was filled with logs. Such dams raised the water level in Lake Itasca and flooded state-owned lands.[21]

Although Itasca State Park was comparatively remote, it did attract a few visitors. Three hundred sixty-four people were said to have visited it in 1900. For these and future users some accommo-

*Nicollet Cabin, Itasca State Park, 1931*

dations had to be provided. The first real development came in 1899, when Governor John Lind, after a summer tour of the park, had a saddle trail cut through the woods at his own expense. Four years later the legislature appropriated $5,000 for the construction of a "state house" for the accommodation of the park commissioners and visitors. A contract was awarded in March 1904, and construction was completed the next year. The building was named Douglas Lodge for former attorney general Wallace B. Douglas, who had long interested himself in Itasca.[22]

When the park was turned over to the state forestry board, the legislation stipulated that the University of Minnesota might use portions of it for demonstration work in forestry. This was the origin of the forestry school campus, maintained there ever since. A biological station was added in 1935. The forest service also built overnight cabins at various points, connected by roads for use in fire detection and prevention. Other roads, intended more for use by the general public, were gradually added. The scenic drive around the park was built in 1925, and five years later the state forester had a crew reopen the Lind Saddle Trail, which had become overgrown with brush. The Boy Scouts of America laid out several trails, since also overgrown, in the southern section.[23]

Itasca's status as a state forest as well as a state park may account in part for the preferential treatment the legislature accorded it. To be sure, in the early years appropriations were meager enough — $600 a year or even a biennium — but in 1909 Itasca was granted $5,000 for the following biennium, and in 1911 $6,000 for each of the next two years. Aside from special appropriations used for land acquisitions, the amount remained at or near this level until after World War I, when it was increased still further; in 1927 a total appropriation of more than $29,000 was made. In 1929, on the eve of the Great Depression, the legislature blessed Itasca State Park to the extent of more than $31,000. These appropriations were largely for "care and maintenance," mostly having to do with fire protection. Miscellaneous sums were provided from year to year for such purposes as additions to Douglas Lodge, an electric light plant, and other improvements not closely related to the promotion of forestry.[24]

In the difficult 1930s, appropriations were somewhat reduced, but the loss of state funds was more than offset by benefits received from the federal government through the various relief agencies. In an effort to put men and women usefully to work, President Franklin D. Roosevelt and Congress established the Civilian Conservation Corps (CCC) and the Works Progress Administration (WPA). CCC camps were set up just outside the park, and a transient labor camp was constructed at Elk Lake. The CCC and the WPA did an immense amount of work and left the park with a legacy of buildings, roads, trails, signs, picnic and camping facilities, and other conveniences, many of which are still in use. Forest Inn, a part of the Douglas Lodge complex, was rebuilt of stone and logs in 1939 with CCC labor, even though the lodge was run by a concessionaire until 1943 and was not, technically speaking, park property. From the creation of the CCC in 1933 until 1941, when its work in Minnesota ceased, the government provided about $140,000 a year for conservation work. In the seven years that the WPA operated at Itasca, it spent $245,774.28 there.[25]

The federal largess ended with United States entry into World War II, and after the war the improvements made during the 1930s began to deteriorate. The passage in 1953 of the "park sticker" act (discussed in chapter seven) provided a new source of revenue for the state parks, and the CCC and WPA projects were restored or replaced to meet the steadily growing rise in park visitation. Perhaps the most important addition made in the early 1970s was an interpretive center, designed to show the visitor the park's botanical, zoological, geological, archaeological, and historical significance.[26]

Improved facilities were not the only development during the 1930s and 1940s. In 1932, on the centennial of Henry Rowe Schoolcraft's discovery of the source of the Mississippi, a pageant depicting that event was held at the park, with Indians and others in full costume. It proved so successful that another was presented the next year; the tradition continued until 1948, though with diminishing financial success in the later years. Even when expenses far exceeded receipts, the parks division people thought that the pageants justified themselves in terms of the publicity they brought the park, for at that time the success of a park, national or state, was measured by the number of visitors it could attract.[27]

In the years that Itasca enjoyed its double role as park and forest, it was an article of faith among professional foresters that total fire protection was a desirable goal. So successful was fire prevention at Itasca that in time it led to a decrease in the number of jack and red pine seedlings, which depend on occasional fires to create open areas for their growth. At the same time poachers were eliminated from the park and timber wolves dwindled in numbers, so the deer herd expanded beyond the capacity of the park and vicinity to accommodate it. The large herd reduced the number of white pine seedlings, as the deer browsed them off as fast as they could sprout. Beaver also became too numerous, gnawed off all the poplars near lakes and streams, and then starved or froze during the severe winter of 1935–36.[28]

Foresters' changed attitudes led to a reversal of policy after World War II. Controlled hunting brought the deer herd within bounds, and there was some regeneration of the young pine growth. But the ecological problem of Itasca was not solved, nor is it likely ever to be completely solved. The park is only a small remnant of a much larger community whose balance was irretrievably disrupted by European settlement in the nineteenth century. An entire ecosystem cannot be restored or maintained within the limited area of the park. For example, the predator-prey relationship that existed at the time of Schoolcraft's visit would not work,

*Raccoons at Itasca State Park, 1931*

even if it could be reestablished, for neither predator nor prey would respect the park's boundaries, and there would be complaints from surrounding farmers and other residents. Some degree of manipulation is necessary to maintain an artificial balance and create an illusion of pristine wilderness that will meet the expectations of visitors.[29]

Fortunately, this problem does not greatly concern the majority of those who come to Itasca in ever-increasing numbers. Itasca is Minnesota's best-known park, the most heavily used park, and probably the one with the greatest diversity. People can satisfy interests in such fields as geology, zoology, archaeology, and history, as well as pursue the more obvious forms of recreation. The casual summer visitor who touches down only at the main points of interest may feel that the park is overcrowded. Certainly the campgrounds seem always to be filled, the picnic areas are heavily used, and the headwaters area is usually crawling with people, the small fry leaping nimbly from rock to rock while their elders photograph them "crossing the Mississippi" on foot. But as in most of our national parks, the crowds are concentrated in certain places. The person willing to brave the seasonal annoyance of mosquitoes and deer flies can get away from the crowds by exploring some of the thirty-three miles of foot trails that lead into the back country, where more than one hundred lakes enhance the character of the remote areas.

The ten-mile Wilderness Drive, blacktopped in 1984, provides vehicle access to a large area west of Lake Itasca and follows the west and south boundaries of the 2,000-acre Wilderness Sanctuary. This tract of undisturbed forest, its interior accessible only by foot trail, was designated a Registered Natural Landmark in 1965. On the opposite side of the one-way Wilderness Drive, short trails lead to the state's record red (Norway) pine and white pine, as well as other points of interest. For those willing to forgo the amenities of the large, heavily used Bear Paw and Pine Ridge campgrounds, there are remote campsites for backpackers on Hernando DeSoto Lake, reached only by trail.[30]

Itasca is a large park with many resources. It contains a variety of wildlife and wildflowers, including the showy lady-slipper, Minnesota's state flower, and its forests range from the isolated tracts of virgin timber through a whole range of woodlands in various stages of recovery from the lumbering operations of earlier times. The people of Minnesota can be deeply grateful to those foresighted individuals who worked to have the area preserved while there was still something to preserve.

---

## Birch Coulee

After the establishment of Itasca, four years elapsed before another true state park was authorized. In the meantime, however, the legislature laid the foundations for what eventually became a minor unit of the park system. At its 1893 session it appropriated $2,500 for the acquisition of a tract of land, not to exceed 5 acres, embracing the site of the battle of Birch Coulee, where a costly and somewhat indecisive conflict had occurred during the Dakota War, and for the erection there of a suitable monument. A commission was named, to serve without compensation, and authorized to employ the power of condemnation, if necessary, to obtain the desired land.[31]

Although the act was explicit, the commissioners chose to interpret its instructions more liberally than they had any right to do. Instead of the actual battlefield site, they purchased 1.75 acres of land nearly two miles to the south, on a bluff overlooking the Minnesota River valley and the town of Morton, and there raised a forty-six-foot granite marker similar to that at Camp Release. Their departure from the legislative mandate did not go unnoticed. The dedication of the monument on September 3, 1894, became something of a fiasco when one of the speakers, former governor William R. Marshall, launched into an attack on the commissioners, not only for incorrectly placing the monument but also for crediting Captain Hiram P. Grant, instead of Major Joseph R. Brown, with the doubtful honor of commanding the troops at the battle of Birch Coulee. Others shared Marshall's concern, and in 1895 the legislature, miffed at the commissioners for disregarding their instructions, appropriated $1,200 for the purchase of from 5 to 10 acres of land on the site where the battle "was actually fought" and for the removal of the monument to this location. The inscription was also to be changed so as to show Brown as commander of the troops.[32]

No action was ever taken, however, to carry out the terms of this act, and the appropriation went unspent. Although no further appropriations were made for its maintenance, the tract on which the monument stood remained state property and was sometimes referred to as "Birch Coulee park." The Morton village council agreed in 1894 to maintain the site, but it failed to carry out its promise. In 1899 the Minnesota Valley Historical Society erected near the first monument a slightly taller one in honor of certain full-blood Dakotas who had saved the lives of whites during the conflict.[33]

In 1926 supporters formed the Renville County Birch Cooley Association and began agitating for the improvement and enlargement of the park. At least 40 acres, they thought, should be obtained. Nothing was done immediately, but in 1929 the legislature appropriated $7,500 for the purchase of 80 acres, including the battlefield site, to be known as Birch Cooley Battle Field State Memorial Park. Part of the land was to be platted as a cemetery for Minnesota's war dead. This time the commission appointed by the governor did its job, and the proper tract was acquired. The problem of the misplaced monument remained, however. Two years later an appropriation of $1,500 was provided for the removal of the two granite shafts. Again no action was taken. In 1935 the legislature reappropriated the sum but specified that it be used for maintenance of the park over the next biennium.[34]

Similar small appropriations were made in subsequent years, but in 1936 the director of parks complained that the park was not used extensively owing to the lack of facilities. Moreover, only one veteran had been buried in the cemetery, which occupied a considerable part of the park's area. Workers from the WPA made a number of improvements over the next few years: they graded and seeded some of the land; built four erosion dams and a footbridge, a stone arch, roads, and a parking area; and laid out trails through the wooded section of the park. A rather extensive picnic area became the principal attraction, used mainly by local people. Meanwhile, the monument erected in 1894 continued to look out over the Minnesota valley from its scenic but inappropriate site. Finally, in 1976, a legislative act renamed the site Birch Coulee Battlefield State Historic Site and transferred it to the Minnesota Historical Society, which has not thus far made any notable changes.[35]

## Interstate

Minnesota's next state park of real merit, now called Interstate, was originally designated the State Park of the Dalles of St. Croix. The rugged gorge cut by the ancestral St. Croix River through the ancient basaltic rock at the village of Taylors Falls had long been recognized for its scenic beauty. John Sanborn, the sponsor of the Itasca State Park bill, had visited the locality in 1854. Over the years many others followed, establishing a town, and the land adjacent to the river passed into private ownership. The townspeople erected houses and outbuildings, "unsightly, defacing, desecrating and marring the landscape and view," as one observer commented. Several people, including William H. C. Folsom, who was a lumberman, legislator, and historian of the St. Croix valley, and George H. Hazzard of St. Paul, who had first seen the site in 1857, became concerned about what was happening to the Dalles and began enlisting public support for the creation of a park. Hazzard at-

*Rock climbers, Interstate State Park*

tempted some lobbying to this end in the 1893 legislative session, but his efforts produced no immediate results.[36]

The newspapers, certain commercial groups, and other interested parties took up the cause, however, and in March 1895 Representative August J. Anderson of Taylors Falls introduced a bill, drafted by Sanborn, authorizing the governor to acquire title to certain described lands in and adjoining the village and to "confer and cooperate" with the governor of Wisconsin if, as expected, that state should acquire an equal or larger area of land on the east bank of the river. The original bill provided no appropriation for land acquisition, but when it reached the committee on public parks this omission was remedied. The bill encountered little opposition and was approved April 25, 1895, with an appropriation of $6,000. A commission of three, one of whom had to be a resident of Taylors Falls, was to be appointed and charged with the task of examining and appraising the land proposed for inclusion in the park. Once the land had been obtained, the governor might appoint a commissioner, or superintendent, at a salary of not more than $300 a year, to have supervision over the park. Penalties were provided for vandalism.[37]

Even though the specified land was platted into more than three hundred lots, the state bought the first 110 acres, the core of the park, almost at once, at a cost of $4,502.61. Oscar Roos donated his land to the state. Smaller tracts were acquired in 1897, 1913, 1915, and later, to bring the total acreage to 167.5 — an area that included nearly all of the important geological features on the Minnesota side of the river but that would prove insufficient to accommodate all the visitors the park would have in later years. The Wisconsin legislature also created a commission in 1895 to ascertain the probable cost of land on the east side, and in 1899 and 1901 it passed acts for the purchase of these lands. Although the most spectacular features were on the Minnesota side, the Wisconsin park was from the beginning much larger. By 1991 it amounted to about 1,300 acres.[38]

The establishment of the "Inter-State Park," as it was already being called by 1897, was widely hailed. Journalist Henry A. Castle, who had first visited the area in 1868, wrote Hazzard in 1903 that he had been much disturbed by the "desecration" of the rock formations but was pleased to note that this had now ceased. The historian William Watts Folwell, former president of the University of Minnesota, wrote, "The rescue of the Dalles of the St. Croix from neglect and vandalism was a most creditable proceeding of the legislature of 1895." The rejoicing was somewhat premature, however, for the problem of vandalism in the park has never been wholly solved. It is apparently too tempting to throw trash into the potholes or carve one's initials on the rocks, and there is no way to police the entire area.[39]

Besides occasional sums for land acquisition, Interstate Park received comparatively generous appropriations down through the years, though substantially less than Itasca. Early in its history the amounts provided annually for care and maintenance varied from $500 to $1,500, which usually included the superintendent's salary. By 1913 the superintendent was receiving $800, a figure increased to $1,200 the next legislative session, and $2,500 was being appropriated for maintenance for the biennium. As elsewhere, appropriations increased in the 1920s, until Interstate was being granted $4,500 a year, on an average, for maintenance. This figure was reduced during the depression, but Interstate, like the other parks, benefited from work-relief labor.[40]

In an effort to maintain the interstate character of the park, the 1909 legislature attempted to purchase the toll bridge over the St. Croix. So many conditions were attached, including one requiring the Wisconsin legislature to appropriate a similar amount, that nothing came of the attempt. Eventually all toll bridges between Minnesota and Wisconsin became free to the traveling public, and this barrier between the two parks was eliminated.[41]

Interstate was a worthy addition to Minnesota's embryonic park system. The language of the act establishing it may have exaggerated in saying that the Dalles of the St. Croix comprised "the most picturesque and attractive scenery in the state of Minnesota," but there is no doubt that the area is of state park quality. The sheer rock palisades, rising from the turbulent river, the remarkable potholes (one sixty feet deep), and the variety of vegetation to be found in such small compass all add up to a place of unusual interest.[42]

Although the geological formations have always attracted the most attention, from the first there was widespread interest in the park as a "natural botanic garden," as Professor Conway MacMillan of the University of Minnesota called it. He noted that on the rocks were white and red pines (chiefly in inaccessible spots), arborvitae, red cedar, and creeping juniper; on the edge of boggy places were red oak, pin cherry, hawthorn, aspen, bur oak, butternut, white hickory, and sugar maple; and on the tops of the bluffs were black oak, red maple, white oak, canoe birch, aspen, and shadbush. Although prairie species were scarce, southern trees such as box elder and the ashes had "crept up the river and gained a foothold." The assemblage of wild flower species was equally impressive, and the number of bird and animal species was as great as could reasonably be expected in so small an area.[43]

Unfortunately, Interstate Park has been plagued by problems peculiar to it. A boat rental concession grew up at the north end of the park and developed into what amounted to an amusement park, complete by 1931 with a dance pavilion, a launch livery, concessions, a zoo, and lunch rooms. No one seemed to be aware of the incongruity of such an enterprise in a state park, but the superintendent was concerned about the danger of accidents and the lack of revenue to the state. In time an arrangement was worked out by which the concessionaire paid the state a flat seasonal rental, and in 1945 that was replaced by a payment of 10 percent of the receipts. This involved too much bookkeeping for the concessionaire, who also complained that he was unable to make a profit. Eventually, all that remained was the excursion boat operation, and finally it was separated from the park proper. It continued to complicate the traffic problem around the park entrance, however.[44]

Another and more serious problem arose from the small size of the park and its proximity to the Twin Cities, which led to gross overuse, especially on weekends. By the middle 1930s, as many as 10,000 people might descend on the park on a Sunday. Today, even with the establishment of other parks within reasonable driving distance of the Twin Cities, Interstate continues to attract its throngs, with the inevitable damage to vegetation and geological formations. The problem is especially acute in the northern section of the park — the so-called Glacial Gardens, where the principal attractions are found; the more recently developed southern section, which contains picnic areas and campgrounds, is less crowded.[45]

With the opening in 1978 of St. Croix Wild River State Park, about twelve miles up the river, the parks people hoped that use of the family campground at Interstate would diminish and that the campground could be phased out in four or five years. Use remained high, however, perhaps because, as the park manager suggested, the newer park appeals to a "different clientele from that of Interstate." The 1977 legislature expanded the park boundaries to include an additional 125 acres. When this land has all been acquired, new trails can be laid out on the bluffs and on an old railroad grade.[46]

The full potential of the park's interstate character has not yet been fully realized. In 1970 the Minnesota-Wisconsin Boundary Area Commission passed a resolution asking that the park authorities of the two states explore the possibility of establishing a system of reciprocity so that vehicles bearing valid permits from one state could enter the other state's park without payment of an additional fee. Nothing came of the proposal then, but in 1987 a reciprocity agreement was finally negotiated. Minnesota residents can now enter the Wisconsin park from Sunday through Thursday, if they display a Minnesota vehicle permit, and vice versa. Of course it has always been possible to avoid purchasing a permit for the other state simply by walking across the bridge between Taylors Falls and St. Croix Falls.[47]

Despite these problems, Interstate is a park well worth visiting. Most of the natural features that led to its establishment are still substantially intact. One can follow the trail through the Glacial Gardens section, heeding the "Danger" signs and staying on the safe side of the railings installed for the protection of formations and visitors alike. Farther south, one can hike along the St. Croix from the picnic area, where the landforms are more subdued. The most strenuous trail in the park crosses the highway and climbs to an overlook in the western section, where one can see a long stretch of the St. Croix to the south. From there the trail goes on to Curtain Falls, on a small, unnamed creek that is often dry, and then returns to the picnic grounds, recrossing the highway via an underpass that enables the hiker to escape the usual heavy traffic.[48]

Although another two decades would pass before the collection of units could even loosely be termed a system, by 1895 Minnesota had two parks and two monuments under state administration. The parks were both definitely of state park calibre, worthy precedents for those to follow. Since most states had no parks at all at that time, Minnesota was off to a good start.

CHAPTER TWO

# Slow Expansion
# 1895–1915

AFTER INTERSTATE, no new parks were established until 1905. In the meantime, however, the legislature authorized two state monuments, the first of which was later expanded into a park.

## Fort Ridgely

The widespread interest in the Dakota War of 1862, reflected in the acts marking the Camp Release and Birch Coulee sites, led in 1895 to legislation to acquire and similarly identify the site of Fort Ridgely, where two important battles had occurred on August 20 and 22, 1862. Established in 1853 on an open plain 150 feet above the Minnesota River — a setting "ideal for a state park but not for defense against Indian attack," as a recent parks division map points out — it had been abandoned a decade after the conflict. Most of the buildings had been torn down and the materials used by settlers in the surrounding area.[1]

A bill calling for the erection of a monument at Fort Ridgely was introduced in the state senate in March 1895, passed by both houses, and signed by Governor David M. Clough on April 25. It provided for an appropriation of $3,000 for the purchase of a tract of land, not to exceed 10 acres, embracing the site of the buildings and parade ground of the fort, and for the erection of a monument of stone and bronze. On August 20, 1896, a fifty-two-foot granite shaft was dedicated, with the customary speechmaking but with-

*Dedication of Fort Ridgely monument, August 20, 1896*

out any such contention as had marked the dedication of the Birch Coulee monument two years earlier.[2]

The moving force behind the Fort Ridgely monument bill was the Fort Ridgely State Park and Historical Association, of which the first president was Charles E. Flandrau, distinguished lawyer, political figure, Indian agent, and military commander, who aided in the defense of New Ulm during the Dakota War. The first secretary was Colonel Charles H. Hopkins, a Civil War veteran who would be largely responsible for the establishment and early development of Fort Ridgely State Park. The 1895 act did not create a park, however, and the promoters of Fort Ridgely would not be satisfied until they had a true state park.[3]

This goal was achieved in 1911 with passage of a bill introduced in the Minnesota house on February 3 by five sponsors, one of whom was Frank H. Hopkins, son of Charles Hopkins. The bill, as finally approved, appropriated $5,000 for the purchase of certain described lands and specified that they should be set aside as Fort Ridgely State Park. Only 50 acres were acquired immediately, but a further appropriation in 1913 enabled the state to buy an additional 62 acres. More land was added from time to time thereafter, until by 1923 the park comprised 155 acres. State Auditor Ray P. Chase, addressing the legislature that year, saw Fort Ridgely as a site "of wonderful possibilities" but in need of considerable development. His suggested improvements included at least partly reconstructing the old fort, installing a campground, laying out an athletic field, enlarging the amphitheater, and adding an artificial lake. He also favored acquiring about 115 additional acres of land.[4]

Three years after Chase's report, the Fort Ridgely Association, under the leadership of Charles Hopkins, undertook a concerted effort to promote the park. Hopkins led a delegation to St. Paul to confer with Charles M. Babcock, state highway commissioner, and to urge, among other things, the routing of a new state highway through the park. The earth removed by road construction, they suggested, could be used to dam up one of the ravines, presumably to create the artificial lake Chase had recommended.[5]

As it grew, the park included several features besides land. The wooden buildings of the fort had long since vanished, but enough of the stone commissary remained to be worth preserving and, later, reconstructing. The fort's log powder magazine had been moved and transformed into a house; this building was moved back to the fort site and protected from further damage. A large cemetery, virtually surrounded by the park but excluded from its statutory boundaries, held two monuments erected with state funds in the 1870s, commemorating people who had played conspicuous roles on the white settlers' side in the Dakota War. A house and a church that had no connection with the events of 1862 were eventually removed, despite some local opposition; but a more incongruous element, a golf course, was laid out in 1927.[6]

Aside from funds provided for land acquisition, legislative appropriations for the park were meager — usually $500 or less for care and maintenance over a two-year period. The superintendent might or might not receive a salary; if he did, he could be sure it would be small. As with the other parks nominally under the jurisdiction of the state auditor, the actual management of Fort Ridgely was left largely to the local advisory committee, of which Charles Hopkins was the moving spirit. Upon his death in 1928, a Fort Ridgely Park Board — successor to the old Fort Ridgely State Park and Historical Association — was organized, and Charles W. Heimann of Fairfax was appointed superintendent.[7]

In 1931 the first in a series of pageants was presented at Fort Ridgely. The subject was Dakota War battles and related historical episodes, such as the Treaty of Traverse des Sioux, by which the Sisseton and Wahpeton signed away their rights to most of southern Minnesota and the stage was set for the conflict eleven years later. As the years passed, the pageants at Fort Ridgely became quite successful; in fact, in 1939 the pageant there was the only one presented in the state parks that biennium, and it was said to have drawn the largest attendance on record on Labor Day of that year.[8]

As part of the 1930s work-relief programs, with the aid of CCC labor the Minnesota Historical Society conducted an archaeological survey of the fort site and ascertained the locations of eight buildings. Workers restored the old commissary and housed a small museum in it, which was operated by the park. They also made improvements to the park's recreational facilities, adding parking areas, sanitary facilities, a water system, and a combination refectory and shelter to the existing campground and two picnic areas.[9]

By the end of the 1930s the park contained about 225 acres. It remained that size until 1963, when 80 acres were added. In 1969 an addition of more than 200 acres was authorized, enabling the park to expand on three sides. Together with minor additions from time to time, this authorization gave it a statutory area of 584 acres, of which only a small portion remains to be acquired.[10]

Fort Ridgely State Park may be said to have a double identity.

Established for its historical significance, it includes recreational facilities comparable to those of other state parks. One picnic area adjoins the cemetery and the site of the old fort; the other lies in the valley of Fort Ridgely Creek. Farther up the creek the campground extends along a dead-end road; a footbridge connects the campground with a system of trails that ascend the bluffs to the east and give access to the prairie section of the park. Fort Ridgely has some botanical interest, including as it does both prairie and woodland flora.

As part of the Dakota War centennial observance in 1962, new and more detailed markers were placed near the monument to give visitors a clear picture of the action that had taken place there in August 1862. In 1969 the 20 acres embracing the actual site of the fort were transferred to the Minnesota Historical Society, which transformed the old commissary building from a museum into an interpretive center. Opened on June 1, 1975, this center contains exhibits that tell the story of Dakota-white conflict in the Minnesota River valley, with special reference to the part played by Fort Ridgely.[11]

For several seasons, beginning in the summer of 1978, Fort Ridgely's amphitheater was the setting for "Theater at the Fort," a semiprofessional acting company that presented well-known plays on weekends in July and August. In 1979, for example, it performed *Barefoot in the Park* and *Oklahoma!*, while in 1982 it offered *A Streetcar Named Desire* and *Annie Get Your Gun*. Sometimes old-time melodrama was produced, and audience participation in the form of hisses and boos for the villain was solicited. At least once during the season fiddle and bluegrass competitions were held. These performances were discontinued in the middle 1980s. In more recent years a two-day festival has been held, featuring folk singers, country western groups, cloggers, a German band, arts and crafts exhibits, and special speakers.[12]

Fort Ridgely was the earliest in the chain of parks that now stretch up the Minnesota River valley from Fort Snelling to Big Stone Lake. Smallest of the lot, it also lacks frontage on the river or any other significant body of water and thus affords none of the usual water-based types of recreation. Perhaps for this reason, neither the campsites nor the picnic areas seem to be heavily used, except possibly on certain holidays. The area of the old fort itself, most of which is now administered by the Minnesota Historical Society, is of statewide significance, but otherwise the park serves an essentially regional clientele and perhaps might appropriately be administered by a regional authority.

## Hinckley, Brook Park, and Moose Lake

The Dakota War was not the only tragic event in Minnesota's history that the legislature chose to commemorate by means of monuments erected at public expense. Two disastrous forest fires received similar attention. The first of these was the Hinckley fire of September 1, 1894, which swept over a large area in east-central Minnesota and took the lives of more than four hundred people. At its 1899 session the legislature passed an act appropriating $2,500 for the erection of the monument, a granite shaft, that now marks the trenches in which 248 victims of the fire were buried. In 1915 the legislature appropriated $1,500 for the removal of the remains of twenty-three victims of the Hinckley fire and their reburial in the Brook Park cemetery. A granite monument, dedicated October 1 of that year, was placed on the site.[13]

The fire of October 12, 1918, that devastated an area around Moose Lake, in Carlton County, was commemorated by a similar monument. In 1929 a marker was erected in Riverside Cemetery, Moose Lake, to the memory of the 183 casualties of the second of these most catastrophic of Minnesota's forest fires.[14]

The point of including such monuments as these in the state's park system is unclear, especially since several other monuments erected with state funds were not so included. None of the monuments in the system can by any stretch of the imagination be regarded as parks, but on the rare occasions when any funds were appropriated for their upkeep, they were grouped with the state parks. In 1937, when the various units of the park system were classified, they and the smaller Dakota War sites were designated as "monuments," a title changed to "state monuments" when another general reclassification took place in 1969. Finally, however, in 1975 they were eliminated from the system.[15]

## *Traverse des Sioux*

In 1905 the legislature acted to create one park and the nucleus of another. The bill concerning the latter, which ultimately became Traverse des Sioux State Park, was passed first.

Of the many sites associated with Indian-white contact in Minnesota, none is more significant historically than Traverse des Sioux. Used from aboriginal times as a crossing of the Minnesota River, it was the location of a trading post run by Louis Provençalle in the 1820s and of an Indian mission established in 1843 by the Reverend Stephen R. Riggs. In 1851 it was chosen as the site for an important treaty, by which the Sisseton and Wahpeton bands of Dakota ceded nearly 24 million acres of land in southern Minnesota and adjacent portions of Iowa and South Dakota. As soon as the area was open to white settlement, a town called Traverse des Sioux was platted; it served briefly as Nicollet County seat until it was overshadowed by St. Peter, only two miles away.[16]

In recognition of the treaty's historic significance, on January 31, 1905, Charles A. Johnson of St. Peter introduced a bill in the state senate that called for the appointment of a three-member commission to ascertain and survey the site of the 1851 treaty council. Nowhere in the act is the name "Traverse des Sioux" mentioned, nor was there apparently any intention of establishing a park. A decade later, however, when the first appropriation was made for maintenance of the 2.27-acre tract of land, it was referred to as the Traverse des Sioux Treaty Site Park and included with the other state parks.[17]

The commission's task in determining the treaty site was made easier by the earlier research of Mankato judge Thomas Hughes, who had pretty definitely ascertained the exact spot where had stood the brush arbor under which the treaty negotiations took place. The site having been established, however, nothing was done to mark it until 1913, when the local chapter of the Daughters of the American Revolution set about commemorating the treaty with a tangible monument. Members found a large rock on which, according to tradition, the whites had placed trinkets for the Dakotas. They dug it up, set it on concrete, attached a bronze plaque to it, and held a formal dedication on July 17, 1914.[18]

Despite its historical importance, Traverse des Sioux got little attention from the legislature in the early years. Until 1927 the biennial appropriation never exceeded $250 and averaged $150. For the fiscal year ending June 30, 1929, however, $650 was appropriated for "maintenance and permanent improvement." The 1929 session reduced the amount to $300 for the next biennium, and in 1931 nothing was appropriated. As it happened, money was needed that year. Shortly before the eightieth anniversary of the treaty signing, a log cabin was discovered nearby. Although it had no connection with the events of 1851, it was thought to sufficiently resemble the Provençalle trading post so that Judge Henry Moll of St. Peter bought it, moved it to the park, made some repairs, and placed it on a concrete block in time for the commemoration. That affair, held July 23, attracted more than a thousand people, including a few Dakota from the Lower Sioux community near Morton.[19]

Traverse des Sioux continued to receive small appropriations from year to year, but nothing was done to expand it. Its status as something less than a park was recognized in 1937, when it was reclassified as a state historic wayside along U.S. Highway 169. In the early 1960s, about the time that highway was made four-lane, various groups in St. Peter, led by the Nicollet County Historical Society, opened a campaign to have the park enlarged and given full state park status. The plan was to acquire the old townsite and some bottomland along the Minnesota River, east of the highway. Nearly 300 acres belonged to a single farm, owned by Joseph J. Daun, and, though it had been used as pasture, it had never been broken by the plow. Many of the old building foundations were still visible, and the layout of the streets could be discerned. Supporters thought that if this farm could be obtained, along with some smaller tracts, the historically significant sites could be preserved, and there would be room for some recreational development near the river. With the assistance of local members of the legislature and at least moral support from the Minnesota Historical Society, advocates of the expanded park were able to outline a specific proposal in time for the 1963 legislative session.[20]

That session produced an important piece of parks legislation, the Omnibus Natural Resources and Recreation Act (discussed in chapter eight), which established several new parks and authorized additions to others. The Traverse des Sioux proposal did not appear in the original bill, but it was tacked on later — not as an expansion of an existing park but as a new one. Apparently the drafters of the bill felt that the tiny wayside did not qualify as even the nucleus of a park. The legislature also provided an appropriation of $35,000 for land acquisition, and an option was taken on the Daun property. When members of the Minnesota Outdoor Recreation Resources Commission (MORRC), established by the Omnibus Act, visited Traverse des Sioux in May 1964, they agreed with local proponents of the new park that an area of 550 acres, including what was called Roberts' Glen, north and west of the treaty site, should be added to the approximately 300 acres authorized by the legislature.[21]

The Roberts' Glen area was never formally added, and after the Daun property had been acquired, the development of Traverse des Sioux State Park ground to a halt. In part this inactivity was due, said Russell W. Fridley of the Minnesota Historical Society, to the competition for funds among all the parks created or enlarged by the Omnibus Act. In addition, however, the hopes of those who wished to develop the recreational potential of the riverfront area were dealt a severe blow by the floods of 1965, when the Minnesota River rose higher than it had done since 1881 and temporarily created a lake where a campground and a picnic area had been projected on the MORRC planning map.[22]

Although some planning continued at the parks division and the 1969 legislature authorized a further expansion, the only real development carried out after this consisted of marking the sites of the various buildings in the old town and placing a few picnic tables nearby. Early in 1976 park planner Milton E. Krona and Donn Coddington of the Minnesota Historical Society met with the members of the Traverse des Sioux Association and explained that any further development would be carried out by the historical society. Thereafter the parks division worked to gain legislative support for the removal of Traverse des Sioux from the system, which occurred in the 1980 legislative session. Under the terms of a bill that became law on April 7, the greater portion of the park was transferred to the city of St. Peter; the townsite, wayside, and surrounding area came under the jurisdiction of the Minnesota Historical Society. The actual transfer occurred in June 1981. Thus, after more than seventy-five years as a unit of the state park system, Traverse des Sioux State Park passed out of existence.[23]

## Minneopa

The other park established in 1905 was Minneopa, located about five miles west of Mankato. Minneopa is notable chiefly for two waterfalls: the upper falls are six or seven feet high, the lower, about thirty; the amount of water going over varies greatly from season to season, depending on how much precipitation there has been in the area drained by Minneopa Creek.

A band of Dakota Indians had long had a semipermanent village in the vicinity, and the early white settlers were struck by the beauty of the falls and the glen below them. The park's historian, Thomas Hughes, says that Miner Porter built a summer resort near the Dakota village in the spring of 1858, complete with "winding, artistic walks and arbors," swings, and other playground equipment, the whole surrounded by a board fence with three arched gates.[24]

In 1859 the *Mankato Record* waxed eloquent over the beauty of the spot: "The dark frowning rocks over head, the smiling flowers, the spray, the tinny [sic] rainbows, and the incessant roar of the falling waters can only be appreciated by being seen." They were evidently seen, for that very year artists and photographers, including the well-known Joel E. Whitney of St. Paul, visited Minneopa and depicted the falls. About a decade later, when the St. Paul and Sioux City railroad was built southwest from Mankato, a local resident, David C. Evans, and an official of the railroad, Elias F. Drake, laid out a townsite named Minneopa on land Evans owned. Evans also made various "improvements," including footbridges over the creek and a wooden staircase into the glen. The town had a short career, but Evans's property became a popular gathering place for religious and other organizations.[25]

The kind of development deemed appropriate at that time was beyond Evans's personal means, and in 1882 he advanced a proposition to organize a joint stock corporation of fifty or more shareholders, each to have a lot of a half-acre or more. The area immediately around the falls would be held in common. Nothing came of

*Minneopa Falls, about 1860*

this project, and three years later Evans advertised the property for sale. Evans's advertisement stressed the commercial potential of the falls in terms of their waterpower, which could readily turn a mill. He had kept count of the visitors on three successive Sundays in May and noted that 72, 113, and 150 people had visited the falls. If each of them had been charged a ten-cent admission fee, remarked the *Mankato Review*, the owner would have realized a tidy little revenue — perhaps enough to finance extensive development of the area.[26]

Evans sold most of his property to Perry Zimmerman, who planned to develop it as a public resort, but nothing of the kind happened while the property remained in private hands. Later it came into the possession of Orange Little, a farmer and grain elevator operator, who had even more utilitarian views. About 1903 he mentioned to Joseph E. Reynolds of the *Mankato Free Press* that he was thinking of clearing off the timber and pasturing his cattle along the creek, below the falls. Reynolds urged him to wait a while; perhaps the state could be induced to buy the area around the falls. Several businessmen formed a committee and kindled the enthusiasm of Ezra W. Gates, who represented the district in the state house of representatives. In January 1905 Gates introduced a bill to create a state park at Minneopa. With the aid of some lobbying by Mankato business owners, both houses passed the bill and it became law on April 19, despite some opposition on grounds that the park "would be practically a Mankato affair, and that the people of that vicinity should not expect the state to supply and maintain a park for their benefit."[27]

The language of the act resembled that of the one establishing Dalles of the St. Croix State Park a decade earlier, but there were some differences. The act vested care of the park in the state auditor, in the capacity of state lands commissioner, and made provision for acquiring land by condemnation if necessary. As did the earlier state park bill, this act provided penalties for vandalism. It also included an appropriation of $5,000 for land acquisition and development.[28]

Before the state could acquire the land, Little sold it to a land speculator, who talked of building a country estate there, with a deer park and other amenities. Finally, however, when the state auditor threatened to use eminent domain proceedings, the owner relented and sold 25 acres late in 1906. Four years later the state acquired another tract from him. By that time the legislature had extended the boundaries to include additional lands, which were purchased in 1916 and 1917 with the help of contributions from the

Mankato Commercial Club. With these acquisitions, the park embraced an area of about 105 acres.[29]

The manner of administering Minneopa provided a precedent for parks established in the next couple of decades. As at Interstate, immediate control was vested in a superintendent (or "commissioner," as the person was originally called), typically a local resident who did not find it necessary to live in the park. The first superintendent at Minneopa was the depot agent at the Minneopa station. Appointed early in 1907, he was authorized to go ahead with improvements, such as cement steps (to replace the wooden ones), an iron railing and netting around the falls at the top, a new footbridge, and picnic tables. Although the state auditor nominally held authority, a local committee, or advisory board, actually exercised it. At Minneopa, as at later parks, this body consisted principally of the people who had been active in getting the park established, or their successors, and they had a proprietary interest in it.[30]

This proprietary interest is well illustrated in a letter written by George M. Palmer, head of the Minneopa advisory board, to forestry commissioner Grover M. Conzet in 1927. Palmer had planted 2 acres of the park to walnut trees, he said, which he saw as "a source of income to the park in the next generation." Since he and the others who had helped set up the park saw it essentially as *their* park, they felt justified in doing with it as they pleased, so long as the public interest, as they perceived it, was served. Minneopa, then, from the start had many of the attributes of a city park. In this respect Minneopa and Interstate differed sharply from Itasca, which the state managed directly, through its own appointees, as part of the state forest system. Minneopa's and Interstate's proximity to towns, as well as their relatively small size, accounts for this difference. So well established did this feeling of local proprietorship become that it persisted well beyond the creation of the Division of State Parks in 1935; to a degree, it still survives.[31]

Despite the fears that Minneopa would be little more than a city park maintained by the state, it quite soon attracted the attention of people from outside the Mankato vicinity. Three years after the first land was purchased, the *St. Paul Pioneer Press* carried a laudatory article about the park, stressing its value to all Minnesotans. "The chief attraction of the place is that it is as nature made it," said the writer, showing greater understanding of its merits than some of the local supporters, who wanted all sorts of improvements made. What if Little had carried out his plans, the writer asked, or what if some "mercenary" had undertaken to develop the water power? "Such a fate would have been little short of a crime against nature and posterity, and yet it was but narrowly averted."[32]

By 1915 Minneopa was attracting visitors not only from elsewhere in Minnesota but also from other states. Although most users were from the Mankato vicinity and arrived by train, loaded down with picnic baskets and other "accessories" for a pleasant afternoon, an increasing number of automobiles brought people from farther away. Since there were no provisions for parking space, the automobiles were parked beside the road, where they constituted a traffic hazard.[33]

For several years after the park was established, the legislature treated it fairly well. During World War I, however, it was allowed to become run down, especially when Governor Joseph A. A. Burnquist vetoed the appropriation in 1917. Two years later the legislature appropriated $3,000 for the biennium, and some rehabilitation got under way. Besides the usual items coming under the head of maintenance and improvements, Minneopa had certain special needs: its waterfalls were gradually eroding the limestone ledge under them. In 1928 a rock-and-cement wall was constructed under the upper falls, and in 1935 the legislature provided $3,000 for a similar wall under the lower falls, which were reported to be washing away the limestone cap.[34]

Work-relief laborers built the retaining wall under Minneopa's lower falls, along with a parking area, a kitchen shelter, a concession building, and foot trails. They also realigned some of the park roads, refaced the masonry supporting the upper falls, and rebuilt the steps leading into the glen below the falls. A second picnic area was developed to accommodate the steadily increasing crowds that came to the park.[35]

In 1931 the park acquired an addition in the form of an old stone windmill and the 1.24 acres of land on which it stood, more than a mile from the main park. Louis Seppman had completed the mill in 1864 and had operated it, with some interruptions, until 1890. Forty years of deterioration had left little but the sturdy shell

*Seppman mill, about 1890. The smallest child is William Seppman, grandson of Louis, who built the mill.*

and some of the machinery when Seppman's son donated it to the Blue Earth County Historical Society, which carried out some repairs before turning it over to the state. With the addition of the mill and 6 acres acquired in 1932, Minneopa State Park reached 110.24 acres, at which level it remained for the next two decades.[36]

Although another 23.9 acres were acquired in 1961, the park was still too small to meet parks division criteria, which since the 1930s had expressed a preference for parks of at least 500 acres. Besides, the heavily local patronage raised questions as to what agency might most properly be responsible for its management. In 1959 U. W. ("Judge") Hella, director of the parks division, suggested that Minneopa either be expanded to the Minnesota River or be taken over by the county. Local sentiment, often articulated by the Mankato newspaper, developed in favor of expansion.[37]

At first nothing tangible came of this public sentiment, nor did Minneopa benefit from the Omnibus Act of 1963. A year or two later Milt Krona recommended expansion of the park to the MORRC, which included in its 1965 park plan a map of Minneopa that showed a large expansion in all directions, especially to the north, between Trunk Highway 68 and the river. The proposed addition would give the park control over both banks of Minneopa Creek all the way to its mouth, some three miles of frontage on the river, and a pasture strewn with glacial erratics. The Seppman mill would no longer be isolated from the rest of the park, for the new land would surround it. The acreage, then given as 116.24, would be increased to more than 1,100.[38]

After a vigorous campaign by local groups, the 1967 legislature authorized the expansion and appropriated $102,000 for land acquisition within the new boundaries. Most of this land was owned by the Seppman heirs, who were willing to sell it, though not altogether happy to find people trespassing on the property in the mistaken notion that it was already part of the park. Bureaucratic delays followed, but in December 1968 the U.S. Department of the Interior announced a grant of $92,250, and on December 30 the Seppmans were paid $184,500 for the greater part of their land. Another ten months passed, during which the legislature appropriated more funds and the interior department approved another grant, before the entire tract of 867 acres was acquired and the Minneopa expansion was substantially complete.[39]

Even before all the new land had been acquired, planning for development got under way. First priority went to a campground, to be laid out on an oak savanna on the bluffs overlooking the river and the creek. The park had not had a real campground at all, though camping was permitted on a small plot of ground near the picnic area. In the early summer of 1969, following a California visitor's complaints that Minneopa lacked electrical hookups, hot water, flush toilets, showers, and the other amenities he had come to expect, the park manager forbade further camping except in emergencies. Before the new campground could be completed,

people were illegally driving onto the flats beside the creek and setting up tents.[40]

Among the other additions made to the "new" Minneopa in the
three years following the last major land purchase were a new picnic area (designed to take some of the pressure off the overused picnic grounds near the falls), an internal road system providing access
to the Seppman mill, and several new or extended trails. Not all of
the planned improvements materialized, however. The parks people had intended to provide a road connecting the old and new sections, including a "rustic wood overpass" at the crossing of Trunk
Highway 68, but this was not constructed. Many local supporters
of the recent expansion had expected a swimming pool to be created
upstream from the falls, but this plan never got very far. For several
years there was talk of bringing from Blue Mounds State Park the
buffalo that had been removed from Mankato's Sibley Park at the
time of the 1965 flood; but in the absence of any agreement as to
where the animals would be placed, the move was never made.[41]

When the new Minneopa State Park was dedicated on June 25,
1972, most of the improvements were in place or nearing completion. A great deal of effort had been lavished on the Seppman mill,
and more was to follow, until by 1976 the Department of Natural
Resources (DNR) had spent $65,000 on the project. An adjacent
granary was rebuilt out of the same kind of stone as the mill itself,
and other improvements were made, mostly to protect the mill
from further deterioration. Since the mill had been originally built
according to unsound engineering principles, it could not be rebuilt
to the original specifications. Its machinery was housed in a former
refectory building, where it shared limited space with a nature
center.[42]

The naturalist program, launched with scheduled hikes in
1969, was expanded over the next few years to include weekly
campfire talks and weekend films. By early 1977 a four-mile hiking
and cross-country skiing trail had been laid out, without state
funds, by park manager Walt Benson, students from Mankato State
University, and a local skiers' club. It started at the new picnic
area, descended to Minneopa Creek, followed that stream to its
mouth, and then paralleled the Minnesota River through the bottomlands. At its western end, it climbed out of the valley onto the
bluffs and returned across the "stone field."[43]

By the spring of 1976 a major problem had arisen. The previous year the legislature had passed the Outdoor Recreation Act of 1975, which mandated that each unit of the system be classified as a "natural" or a "recreational" state park and that those units that failed to meet the criteria for inclusion in either category be dropped from the system. On its intrinsic merits, Minneopa qualified as a "natural" state park, but a network of county and township roads, not to mention U.S. Highway 169 and Trunk Highway 68, divided it up and made controlling access to its separate parts difficult. As parks planner Dennis Thompson said, it was a question of "how best to fit the parts of the park together." The parks people wanted to close off certain roads, but this solution would inconvenience several users, particularly the Minneopa Concrete Products Company, Inc., whose trucks made fifteen round trips through the park each day.[44]

When the first public meeting was called to discuss Minneopa's future, in April 1976, it was apparently given insufficient advance publicity, and some local people felt that the DNR was trying to exclude possible opponents of its proposals from the planning process. But when another, better publicized, meeting was held in mid-October, it was attended by only about twenty local people. At this time the DNR representatives revealed their plans for closing several roads. Strong opposition came from the county board of commissioners, which had the authority to close the roads but whose members were more responsive to their constituents' wishes than to the DNR's.[45]

The DNR presented its draft management plan at another public meeting on May 31, 1977. The plan called for a phased closing and ultimate abandonment of the disputed roads and added, ominously, "If no mutually acceptable way can be found to close these roads this park should be reclassified as something other than a state park. . . . No development monies will be spent in this park until an acceptable road closing arrangement can be agreed upon." The sixty or so people present at the meeting were sharply divided over the future of the park, though Lloyd Vollmer, who had spearheaded the expansion drive, expressed the belief that compromise was still possible. To the DNR people, the simplest solution to the road issue would be to acquire the Minneopa Concrete property, but since it lay outside the park's statutory boundaries, legislative action to include it would be required, and such action was not forthcoming.[46]

That is essentially where the park stood in 1990. The DNR has relented to the extent of carrying out some improvements, such as installing new footbridges on the river trail and placing "You Are Here" signs at intervals; but it still holds to its position that unless enough roads can be closed to enable it to manage the park as one unit, with a single contact station, no major development should take place. The DNR is used to thinking in long terms, however. Even though Minneopa Concrete has been where it is for many years, it will not remain there forever; perhaps some future legislature will authorize the acquisition of the property.

Meanwhile, the park continues to function in spite of the inconvenience caused by the presence of the roads, just as it has learned to live with two railroads, neither likely to be abandoned in the near future, crossing both the old and new sections. In the light of its history one can understand the position of those who worked for its enlargement in the 1960s but disapproved of the DNR's plans as they emerged in the next decade. The old feeling that it is "their" park is still very much alive, but those holding this view also want Minneopa to remain a *state* park. Use of Minneopa is predominantly local, however, simply because it is near Mankato. If it were located miles from any town, it would be more widely recognized for what it is: a park of better than average quality.

In spring and in seasons of heavy rainfall, its twin waterfalls are still as beautiful as they were in the 1860s. From the picnic area a trail follows the edge of the ravine to where steps lead down to the footbridge over the creek; more steps lead up on the other side, to a trail that returns to the picnic grounds. A spur follows the creek downstream to the south end of a large culvert that carries the stream under the road and the railroad track. In the new section of the park one can picnic in an open oak-birch savanna or follow the trail down to the creek, past oaks that flame in October, and perhaps along the Minnesota, where one may hear the rattle of a kingfisher, the strident call of a pileated woodpecker, or the "Who-cooks-for-you-all?" of a barred owl.

With the aid of proper interpretive devices, the Seppman mill could be an attraction of even greater interest than it is now. Someday, perhaps, the working gear of the mill can be restored, complete with the huge fan with which Louis Seppman caught the wind to grind his grain. Along the road to the mill the parks people plan to establish two gardens, one containing the vegetables raised by the agricultural Indians, the other showing what the early white settlers raised.

All in all, Minneopa is a park that the people of Minnesota can be proud of, one that should remain in state ownership and be managed for the benefit of the whole state.

## Wood Lake, Acton, and Schwandt

After the establishment of Minneopa, the state legislature created no more parks until 1911. In the interval, however, it authorized two monuments of the Camp Release variety to commemorate events associated with the Dakota War — the first and last conflicts. In 1907 the legislature appropriated $500 to locate, survey, and mark the site of the battle of Wood Lake, where Henry Sibley's forces defeated the Dakota late in September 1862. Two years later the legislature appropriated $2,000 for re-interring the remains of four soldiers killed at Wood Lake and for erecting a monument on the one-acre site. The customary granite shaft was dedicated on October 18, 1910.[47]

By another act passed in 1909, the legislature provided $250 for locating, surveying, and marking the place where the Dakota killed several members of the the the Jones family of Acton Township, Meeker County, on August 17, 1862. The Acton Incident (called the Acton massacre at the time the marker was placed) is generally regarded as the starting point of the Dakota War, which broke in full fury a day later. A small granite monument at the site was dedicated on August 22, 1909. In 1967 the Minnesota Historical Society added another marker nearby that gives a more detailed (and presumably more balanced) account and puts the whole affair in historical perspective.[48]

Another Dakota War site was acquired by the state in 1915. The legislature passed an act providing $200 for the purchase of a parcel of land, not to exceed ten feet square, and the placement of a granite monument to honor six members of the Johann Schwandt family who had been killed by the Dakota. The marker was dedi-

cated on August 18, 1915; in keeping with the prevailing white attitudes of the time, the inscription refers to these otherwise obscure
people as "martyrs for civilization."[49]

---

## Alexander Ramsey and Horace Austin

The anomaly of a state park's being used primarily by the people of a nearby community, referred to in the discussion of Minneopa, appeared even more conspicuously in the case of two parks
established in 1911 and 1913. Although both were ultimately transferred to the cities whose residents provided most of their patronage, they were for many years state parks and are the best examples
of a problem that occurred in connection with several other units
of the park system down through the years.

In language much like that used in establishing Minneopa, the
1911 session of the legislature created a state park on the Redwood
River, adjacent to Redwood Falls. It was named Alexander Ramsey
in honor of Minnesota's first territorial governor. The park had considerable scenic beauty, including the rugged gorge of the lower
Redwood River, the wooded hills enclosing it, and a waterfall on
Ramsey Creek comparable to Minneopa Falls. Only 60 acres in size
as originally established, the park gradually expanded until it had
an area of 185.38 acres — more than any of its predecessors except
Itasca.[50]

After an initial appropriation of $6,000 for land acquisition,
the legislature treated Alexander Ramsey State Park rather gener-
ously during the first two decades of the park's existence. In 1921,
for example, the park received a total of $6,425, of which $5,000
was earmarked for roads and a bridge. Eventually the park had
nine miles of roads — much more than the limited area required —
and during the 1930s one of the WPA projects there was the obliter-
ation of unneeded stretches of road. Other improvements made in
the 1930s were of the same sort as in other parks: a parking area,
a new bridge, and a combination shelter and refectory.[51]

In nearly every respect, Alexander Ramsey resembled the other
parks created during this early period; it had the usual camping and
picnicking facilities and had hiking trails through the woodland
along the Redwood. It also had a zoo, something few other state

parks could boast. Its one major defect, in the eyes of the parks people, was that it attracted mainly a local crowd of visitors and lacked the wider appeal that a state park ought to have. As Redwood Falls expanded to the north and west, the city came up to the park boundaries, and thus the park came to seem more and more like a city park. In 1957 Alexander Ramsey was finally turned over to the city, which has since maintained and operated it as a city park.[52]

The same destiny awaited Horace Austin State Park, established in 1913 within the city limits of Austin and named in honor of Minnesota's sixth governor. The area for which the legislature appropriated $5,000 consisted of 50 acres of partly wooded land, including some islands, on the Cedar River. It had a measure of historic significance: Companies B, H, and I of the First U.S. Dragoons camped there in 1835, and the following year a party of hunters from Fort Snelling, including Indian agent Lawrence Taliaferro, camped there. Four years later it was used in similar fashion by Henry Sibley, Alexander Faribault, John C. Frémont, and a number of others, white and Indian. Besides these historical associations, the park area also had its share of natural beauty, though its scenery was not really striking — nothing to justify making a state park of it.[53]

The stake local people had in Horace Austin State Park was recognized early in its history. When the legislature appropriated $5,000 for its maintenance in 1915, it did so on condition that the citizens of Austin or of Mower County would raise an equal amount. In later years the state's contribution — sometimes as high as $7,500 for a two-year period — had no such strings attached, but the reduction of appropriations in the 1920s to $2,500 for a biennium suggests that significant sums were being contributed by local agencies. In the 1930s the park was operated jointly by the state and the city; the state maintained the camp and picnic grounds, and the city operated the swimming facilities. The park received little or no benefit from the work-relief programs during that decade.[54]

As early as 1930 Alfred L. Nelson, a public relations assistant for the state forestry and fire prevention department, was arguing that Horace Austin and certain other parks should be transferred to the cities that mainly used them, or at least that they should be recognized as state parks in name only and responsibility for their management should be handed over to the local authorities. Others expressed the same view in later years. Horace Austin was reclassified in 1937 as a scenic wayside, and finally, in 1949, it was removed from the list of state parks and transferred to the city of Austin.[55]

## *Jay Cooke*

In general, the parks established between 1895 and 1915 were small. None of those so far discussed could be compared with Itasca in size. In 1915, however, the state had an opportunity to acquire a much larger tract of land, which contained notable scenery yet was near the state's third-largest city.

In 1870 the Lake Superior and Mississippi railroad, backed by the resources of financier Jay Cooke, had built a line of track along the bank of the St. Louis River west of Duluth. The track was later abandoned, but in the meantime the St. Louis River Water Power Company, through Cooke's efforts, had bought up nearly all the land between Carlton and Fond du Lac. When it was discovered that the power company did not need the land, the Cooke heirs offered to donate it to the state, subject to certain conditions allowing them to retain the right, among others, to build transmission lines across any part of the lands.[56]

The appropriations act of 1915 contained $15,000 to be used for the purchase of lands, up to a maximum of 4,000 acres, adjoining the tract owned by the power company. The money was not, however, to be available until the power company had donated the 2,350 acres it owned. The park thus created was to be named for Jay Cooke, who had died in 1905. The power company's donation was duly made, but the state bought only 925 additional acres.[57]

F. Rodney Paine, a graduate of the Yale School of Forestry, was appointed superintendent and took up his duties on November 1, 1916. Except for a time during World War I when no one was in charge, the park remained under his supervision until 1931. The first task he faced, in the fall of 1916, was to open a road into the park from the west, following the old railroad right-of-way. It was slow work. By 1920 there were only two and a half miles of road, which had cost $9,000 to build, and in the next three years only a half-mile was added. In 1923 and 1924 the legislature appropriated

*Suspension bridge, Jay Cooke State Park, about 1950*

$10,000 each year for roads, and progress was somewhat more rapid. The city of Duluth, at considerable expense, acquired some right-of-way and constructed an approach road from the east. Nonetheless, by June 30, 1925, there was still a 1.6-mile gap between the two segments.[58]

The age of the automobile was well under way by that time and use of Jay Cooke State Park was increasing steadily, with the result that the inadequate road system created problems. As Paine said in his report for the two years ending in mid-1925, "The fact that there is no through road and that all cars must double back the way they came over what is at best only a narrow one-way road, doubles the amount of traffic and makes a dangerous congestion." Although vast improvements were to be made in the next several decades, traffic is still a problem at Jay Cooke. Trunk Highway 210 runs the length of the park. Since both through traffic and park visitors use it, there is no way of making sure that the latter have vehicle permits.[59]

Besides the road-building project, several other improvements were made under Paine's administration. Almost from the day he became superintendent, he began laying out trails; within a few months the park had four miles of them, and by 1928 the trail system had expanded to about ten miles. Some time in the early 1920s Paine installed the first in a succession of suspension bridges to give access to trails south of the St. Louis River; it proved very popular. The first picnic tables were provided through the generosity of the Northwest Paper Company.[60]

Like the parks previously mentioned, Jay Cooke enjoyed strong local support. Business owners in Cloquet and Carlton had paid $18,017 in back taxes on the donated land to get the park started. An advisory commission made up of local park supporters administered it in the early years. The commission was chaired for a time by Henry Oldenburg, who aided the park in various ways and whose name was bestowed on a scenic overlook from which the valley of the St. Louis can be seen for several miles; Paine served as the commission's "Secretary and Supervising Forester." Another member was Judge Clarence R. Magney, who later worked for the establishment of several North Shore parks, one of which was to be named for him.[61]

In 1928 and 1929 Jay Cooke State Park was the center of a swirl of litigation involving the Minnesota Power and Light Company (successor to the St. Louis River Water Power Company), which decided that it wished to build a transmission line through the park. The company could have built without special authorization on the south side of the St. Louis River, where it had retained that right, but to do so would have been more expensive than to build on the north side, where the state had acquired lands through purchase. According to Paine, the local advisory committee recommended that the company be permitted to build on the north side, where less timber would have to be removed, but the conservation commission did not concur and denied permission. The power company then sued in district court to obtain a right-of-way, and won. The decision, however, was appealed by the state and overturned in the state supreme court.[62]

The supreme court's decision is of some interest because of the point of view expressed concerning conflicts between different kinds of public service. When the park was established, the legislation contained provisions specifying penalties for willful damage to trees and other vegetation. It would surely be a violation of the in-

tent of this law, thought the court, for the power company to remove all trees, shrubs, and brush from a strip fifty feet wide, build
four or five towers along this strip, and provide road access to the
towers for their construction and maintenance. The court agreed
with the state's argument that "in a park such as this, chosen because of its natural beauty, intended to be kept in its primitive
state, the running of a high tension electric line such as this through
the middle of the park territory is essentially and necessarily an im-
pairment of the state's use." Noting that the park already had two
railroads, a highway, and five power lines within its boundaries,
the justices said that to add further intrusions "might well lead to
its final extinction as a public park."[63]

In the 1930s Jay Cooke underwent a period of massive expansion and development. One hundred acres were donated in 1930,
and a master plan drawn up in 1933 envisaged a park of some 4,150
acres. Much of that acreage was then owned by the power company, the Northern Pacific railroad, and private owners. The
work-relief agencies were active; several small picnic areas were
developed by the Emergency Conservation Work force (predecessor to the CCC) along the highway that traverses the park, and under CCC auspices, a new suspension bridge was constructed across
the St. Louis River. (As the years passed, the bridge's floor and railing mesh had to be replaced annually. In 1940 the bridge was re-
modeled and the deck elevation set at one and a half feet above the
highest water known, at a cost of $2,029.04. Several times since
then it has been temporarily closed for repairs.) Among other
projects either the CCC or the WPA carried out were a trail system,
some of it along the route followed by the fur traders, a large picnic
area near the bridge, and road construction and surfacing.[64]

The park continued growing. A great deal of land was acquired, mainly through tax-forfeiture, so that by 1948 the acreage
amounted to 8,366.7, about double that of fifteen years earlier. In
the 1951 session of the legislature funds were appropriated to purchase about 550 acres of additional land, and in 1967 the statutory
boundaries were redefined so as to include an area of 11,316 acres.
When all this land has been acquired, Jay Cooke will rank as the
state's fourth-largest park. At the time of the public hearings on the
management plan mandated by the Outdoor Recreation Act of

1975 (discussed in chapter nine), some local people expressed concern over a report that the DNR was planning to close Trunk Highway 210 and prohibit snowmobiling in the park. DNR representatives denied that there were any such plans, but indicated that Jay Cooke would probably be classified as a natural rather than a recreational state park.[65]

Besides being one of the largest parks in the system, Jay Cooke is scenically impressive. It includes the most spectacular stretch of the St. Louis River, where the swift waters have cut through the ancient rocks known as the Thomson formation. This area, called the Dalles of the St. Louis, consists of a mass of jagged rocks over which the river tumbles and swirls in a continuous series of rapids. The best views of the spectacle are afforded from the swinging bridge and vicinity. Unfortunately, the diversion of water into the Thomson reservoir reduces the amount flowing in the river at this point, especially at times of low water.[66]

Jay Cooke is also historically important. It includes much of the trail known to fur traders in the late eighteenth and early nineteenth centuries as the Grand Portage of the St. Louis, where the voyageurs had to leave the unnavigable stream and bypass the most difficult section, on their way west to the Big Sandy Lake trading posts in modern Aitkin County. The stretch of trail within the park has been marked and can be hiked.[67]

The visitor to Jay Cooke can explore some fifty miles of hiking trails, including an extensive system on the south side of the river, accessible only via the footbridge. Other trails lead to overlooks from which the lower valley of the St. Louis may be seen from a distance. Trunk Highway 210 parallels the river on the north side and provides the motorist traveling between Carlton and Duluth with an opportunity to see much of the park en route. Picnic areas and a campground are located along this highway.

One of Jay Cooke's principal advantages is its proximity to the Duluth-Superior metropolitan area. Minnesota's state park system has been faulted for failing to provide an adequate number of parks within easy driving distance of most of the state's population. So far as the Twin Cities metropolitan area is concerned, this complaint is to some extent still justified; but since 1915 the people of Duluth have had a large recreation area available to them.

## Summary

Minnesota did not have a state park system in 1915. Rather, it had a miscellaneous collection of parks and monuments varying greatly in size and quality. In size they ranged from Itasca, which would eventually embrace an area of more than 30,000 acres, to the Schwandt monument, which stood on a few square feet. Of the fifteen units created before 1915 that would be absorbed into the park system when it was established in 1935, seven were monuments commemorating events associated with either the Dakota War or the Hinckley fire. Of the remaining eight, one (Traverse des Sioux) was as yet only a site and would not become a park for nearly half a century — and then only briefly; two (Alexander Ramsey and Horace Austin) were essentially city parks and would finally be recognized as such and dropped from the park system. Only the remaining five would be considered true state parks, and even they varied greatly in merit. Itasca and Jay Cooke were definitely the best of the lot; Interstate, though small, was clearly of state park calibre; the same might be said of Minneopa, though it attracted mainly local visitors; Fort Ridgely, though historically important, was naturally and scenically less significant than the other four. When all allowances are made, however, Minnesota had created the foundation on which a park system might be built. In the next decade a number of units of true park quality were to be added, so that by 1925 the state would have a park system in fact, if not yet in name.

# CHAPTER THREE

# The Rudiments of a Park System 1915-1925

IN THE DECADE from 1915 to 1925 eight additions were made to what was beginning to take on some of the contours of a state park system. Five of these were of state park calibre and remain members of the system; the other three were of lesser merit and have been turned over to local agencies. For all of the six established by the legislature (two were acquired by donation), the essential action was taken during the 1919 and 1921 sessions, in which several other park proposals were introduced but not passed.

## Toqua Lakes

The 1919 legislative session was responsible for the creation of three parks — or perhaps two and a half would be more accurate, since one of them was not of true park stature and later proved an embarrassment to the people in charge. Two of the proposals had been advanced in the 1917 session without success. The first of these would have established Toqua Lakes State Park a half-mile south of Graceville, in Big Stone County. This region, near the South Dakota border, was deficient in lakes and woodland, both of which were found at the location of the proposed park.[1]

Unsuccessful that year, the bill was revived two years later, only to meet with failure again. Its language, however, was incorporated in the appropriations bill for that session, and it passed in that way. Five thousand dollars was provided and a commission, consisting of the state auditor, the secretary of state, and R. A. Costello of Graceville, was appointed to acquire the necessary land. Perhaps feeling that there was some irregularity in the way the park proposal had been inserted in the appropriations bill, the senator responsible for the original bill in 1919 introduced another in the 1921 legislature to reconfirm the provisions of the earlier act. The bill was passed, along with another to extend the powers of the commission and the time in which the $5,000 might be expended; it also specified that the land might be acquired by "gift, purchase or condemnation."[2]

Toqua Lakes State Park having been duly established, the state began acquiring land. Estates donated a couple of parcels and the state bought other tracts, but the park never achieved an area of more than 40 acres. More serious for its value to the state, it suffered severely from the drought of the 1930s, when more than half the trees died and the lakes largely dried up. Nevertheless, WPA labor was employed to erect several small buildings, obliterate certain unnecessary roads, and put in parking lots. The lakes recovered when seasons of heavier rainfall returned, but the park remained something of a white elephant. As early as 1930 its transfer to a local agency had been recommended, and later in the decade it had been downgraded to a state scenic wayside. Finally, in 1965, legislation was passed authorizing its transfer to Big Stone County.[3]

---

## Whitewater

Thirty years after the establishment of Camp Release, the state still had no parks in the scenic southeastern counties. Referred to as a "stream-dissected" area, the region tributary to the Mississippi is traversed by such rivers as the Root, the Whitewater, and the Zumbro, which have eroded deep valleys through the otherwise level or gently rolling farm countryside. This area attracted white farmers early in the history of the state, but it was still essentially rural, though becoming steadily more urbanized. It clearly had both the need and the potential for state parks.

As with Toqua Lakes, the first attempt to establish Whitewater State Park was made during the 1917 legislative session, but the bill died in committee. Before the next session, Ludvig A. Warming of

*Campground, Whitewater State Park, about 1960. After problems with persistent flooding, the area was made into a picnic ground.*

St. Charles published an attractive pamphlet of photographs of the Whitewater valley under the title *The Paradise of Minnesota: The Proposed Whitewater State Park* and offered it for sale at $1.50 a copy to raise funds for the state park project. Two years later the proposal surfaced once more as part of the appropriations bill. In this form it called for an appropriation of $10,000 and the appointment of a commission, to consist of the governor, the state auditor, and state Senator Arthur C. Gooding of Rochester, which was empowered to acquire "by gift, purchase, or condemnation" such tracts in four specified sections as they might deem necessary for park purposes.[4]

Here, too, there appears to have been a sense that the vehicle used to effect the intentions of the earlier bill was slightly inappropriate, and in 1921 Senator Gooding introduced a bill to "ratify and confirm" all acts performed pursuant to the provisions of the 1919 bill. This was duly passed, including provisions authorizing the attorney general to acquire land and providing penalties for vandalism. The commission immediately purchased 435 acres; smaller tracts were bought over the next three years, so that by 1923 482.62 acres had been acquired. In 1926 a sizable parcel of 191.3 acres was donated by John A. Latsch, a Winona wholesale grocery merchant and patron of the state parks who later donated land for a park named for him.[5]

The bill creating Whitewater State Park had one interesting sidelight. Although it merely specified that the lands to be acquired should be *within* four certain sections in Elba Township, the people administering the park later took these four sections to *be* the statutory area of the park. Such an area — 2,560 acres — would have made Whitewater the largest park in the southern half of the state. As a matter of fact, not all this land has yet been acquired — nor does the parks division even want it — but adjacent tracts have from time to time been added to the statutory area.

Apparently the park facilities provided in the first years were minimal — a "pavilion" or picnic shelter and a few other bare essentials — but this did not prevent large numbers of people from using the area. In 1926, for example, it had 40,000 visitors. Although many of these must have come from Winona and Rochester, the town of St. Charles, nine miles away, took the sort of proprietary interest in Whitewater that Mankato residents displayed toward Minneopa. The local American Legion club maintained a cabin in the park until 1934; in 1928 St. Charles people were able to get a golf course laid out, which remained for almost fifty years. In the late 1920s the St. Charles chapter of the Izaak Walton League of America tried to influence the selection of a superintendent, ultimately with success.[6]

Besides several minor problems, Whitewater had one major problem, which cropped up early and has plagued the park ever since: the periodic flooding of the Whitewater River. The source of the park's beauty — the deep, nearly level valley hemmed in by sheer limestone bluffs — is also the cause of its chronic trouble with spring and summer floods. Unwise farming practices in the surrounding countryside in the early days aggravated the problem, but the valley undoubtedly suffered floods in presettlement days as well. Although various proposals have been advanced down through the years to control flooding on the Whitewater and its tributaries, none of them has ever worked, and competent engineers believe that there is no practicable way to prevent floodwaters from periodically inundating most of the valley.[7]

Before this fact was recognized, however, a great deal of money was spent on the construction of inappropriate structures and their replacement or repair when the inevitable floods came. During the 1930s work-relief agencies carried out several projects, some of them intended to come to grips with this problem. A CCC camp was established at Whitewater in June 1934; it was later replaced by a transient labor camp under the direction of the National Park Service (NPS). The two agencies, with some WPA labor help, constructed such improvements as a picnic shelter and kitchen, sanitation facilities, trails, bridges (including a three-arch limestone bridge of considerable architectural distinction), a parking area, several cabins for a group camp, a sewage system, and campgrounds. The workers also relocated the highway through the park and did some landscaping. For years users of the park had complained about the lack of swimming facilities, and proposals had been advanced and rejected for a swimming pool. Finally a pool was constructed, only to have the diversion dam washed out. The dam was later rebuilt, and a bathhouse and beach were added.[8]

Apart from flooding, Whitewater's chief problem, as in so many parks, has been overuse. As the earliest park in southeastern Minnesota, it became the mecca of picnickers and campers from Rochester, Winona, and smaller towns, and the establishment of several other parks since World War II has not appreciably relieved the pressure on Whitewater. Excessive use is most evident on the trails, where constant work by park personnel has not been able to keep up with the erosion caused by the unfortunate combination of human use, running water, and steep slopes.[9]

In the 1970s Whitewater State Park became the scene of conflict between the Department of Natural Resources and the local population. Although such clashes erupted over many existing and proposed parks, they seldom reached the intensity of the one at Whitewater. The dispute centered on three major issues: the golf course, the road (Trunk Highway 74) through the park, and land acquisition. A different group of people was involved in each of the three, but all seemed to perceive the DNR as the enemy. Fundamental to the controversy was a change in the constituency the DNR served in its management of the park. According to one local resident, as late as the 1950s, a majority of park users lived within a fifty-mile radius, whereas twenty years later those residents constituted only 20 percent of the patrons; the DNR was more responsive to the wishes of the majority, who came from farther away.[10]

Conflicting wishes regarding the golf course aroused tempers when park officials proposed phasing it out. As far back as the 1930s, when a local resident had submitted a resolution calling for improvement of the golf course, Grover Conzet, director of the forestry division, had replied that projects supported by the NPS would not permit such use of funds, "as they claim that is not a proper use of state parks." Forty years later the golf course was still there, but the parks people decided to close it in 1977 — partly as a result of floods in 1974 and 1975, which did a great deal of damage — and allow the land to return to its natural state.[11]

After a year of what the DNR regarded as benign neglect, some local people were distressed by the results. As St. Charles's mayor, Harold D. McCready, and his family drove through one Sunday evening, he was "totally shocked" by what they saw. "I became so upset that I literally became sick," he wrote Governor Wendell R. Anderson. He had heard that the area was to become a nature center for the handicapped, but he was unable to imagine anyone wanting to visit such a place; as weed inspector in St. Charles, he would have ordered such a mess cut. Park manager Harold Becker explained that time would be needed to accomplish the goal parks people had in mind, the restoration of the original prairie vegetation on this land. As funds became available, it would be made more accessible to people with physical handicaps. But his words did not mollify the locals, one of whom saw the episode as another case of St. Paul people deciding how St. Charles and Elba residents should conduct themselves.[12]

The parks people got their way in respect to the golf course, but they were forced to back off or compromise on the other issues, which were more vital to the local people. Like Jay Cooke, Whitewater is bisected by a state highway, and users of the road are pretty much on their honor to buy a permit if they stop in the park. Moreover, the highway, though not heavily traveled, does constitute somewhat of a hazard to pedestrians in the park. Proposed in a management plan drawn up in 1977, the rerouting of Trunk Highway 74 around the park was bitterly resisted by local people. At a public meeting held that summer at Plainview, several speakers, most of them farmers, showed great hostility toward the parks division, which they saw as an alien force trying to disrupt their lives for the benefit of a few "outsiders," that is, park users. By 1990 no changes in the highway had been made; if the DNR had not abandoned its proposal, it was at least not pushing it.[13]

The issue of land acquisition also came up at the Plainview meeting, where, reported the *St. Charles Press*, the DNR "played its latest act" to a standing-room-only crowd. Despite DNR representatives' promises that tillable land would be excluded from further additions to the park, the landowners were not satisfied with what they heard. Some went so far as to assert that they derived no benefit from the park and that they would like to see it abolished and absorbed into the adjoining Whitewater Wildlife Management Area, which is open to hunting. Far from seeing Whitewater as "their" park, as the St. Charles people did, the speakers looked upon it as a nuisance and upon the parks division and park users alike as the enemy.[14]

About a year after the Plainview meeting, an advisory task force was appointed, composed of representatives of such diverse interests as the Whitewater Sportsmen's Club, a snowmobile and cycle group, horseback-trail riders, adjacent landowners, education (two divisions: college and elementary-secondary), mechanized camping, nonmechanized camping, the Sierra Club, senior citizens, the St. Charles Chamber of Commerce, the soil conservation district, Winona County, the town of Elgin, and Elba Township. Although progress at the first few meetings was slow, there was agreement that some of the DNR's goals could be achieved through the use of easements rather than outright ownership. Most landowners in the area were said to be favorable to the idea.[15]

Early in 1979 the task force agreed to recommend that the legislature change the statutory boundaries so as to restrict the park to the wooded ravines and bluffs and use visual easements as buffers. A bill embodying these conditions was introduced too late for passage at the 1979 session, but after public hearings that fall, it came up for consideration in the 1980 session. After more hearings and some amendments, it emerged as Chapter 489 of the 1980 laws. Though described as a compromise, the bill gave the DNR very little of what it wanted. The statutory boundaries were changed so as to exclude all land not yet acquired, except for 110 scattered acres, some of them representing enclaves within the park. As a condition for exclusion, landowners were required to grant scenic easements on their property; this provision did not apply to any tract more than thirty feet back from the top of the bluffs that could not be seen from any point on Trunk Highway 74. About all the DNR salvaged was a provision that the state might buy from willing sellers in the excluded area; park boundaries would then be changed to include such purchases.[16]

Although supposedly settled by the 1980 legislation, the conflict between park supporters and local residents has served to further complicate the problem that topography imposed on Whitewater State Park. Whitewater is one of the most attractive parks in the system, containing the most picturesque portions of the generally scenic Whitewater valley. From the overlook lamely denominated "Inspiration Point" one enjoys a view suggestive of the Southern Appalachians — a vista of wooded hills, without a trace of human intrusion, stretching off to the horizon. Whitewater's twelve miles of hiking trails, its opportunities for fishing, the beauty of its landscape, and its scientific importance as a classic example of stream-dissected topography, together with the flora and fauna that it shares with the other southeastern parks, make it an area deserving — and requiring — the most careful protection if it is to continue serving the people of Minnesota.

## Sibley

The third park established in 1919 was Sibley, named for Minnesota's first elected governor, Henry Hastings Sibley, who had hunted in the part of west-central Minnesota later included in Kandiyohi County. Still earlier, Dakota Indians had camped and held councils on the summit of Mount Tom, a glacial moraine that rises 150 feet above the level of Lake Andrew, about a mile distant. Because of the protection afforded by numerous lakes, the slopes of Mount Tom had not suffered from prairie fires as the surrounding countryside had, and a considerable forest had grown up there. After settlers had suppressed the fires, the wooded area had spread over the nearby hills. By the early years of the twentieth century it had become a popular picnic spot.[17]

About 1916 Peter Broberg, sole survivor of his family at the time of the Dakota War, began talking up the idea of a state park in the Lake Andrew–Mount Tom area. He and other proponents adopted the strategy of first having the area declared a game preserve and then persuading the legislature that it was really better suited to a park. Landowners' signatures were obtained at a meeting held in January 1917 in New London and presided over by Broberg. The Monongalia Game Preserve was established the following October, and a few months later Carlos Avery, game and fish commissioner, visited it and was reportedly impressed with the area's state park potential. Land was available for purchase, and local sentiment strongly favored the establishment of a park. So, on March 19, 1919, identical bills were introduced in the state house and senate calling for the creation of Sibley State Park.[18]

Although neither of these bills passed, their intent was accomplished, as in the cases of Toqua Lakes and Whitewater, by incorporating their language in the appropriations bill, which provided $25,000 for the purchase of so much of section 35, Colfax Township, and section 2, Lake Andrew Township, as the game and fish commissioner might deem "desirable and necessary" for state park purposes. The act contained two unusual provisions. In the first place, care and supervision of the new park were vested, "until otherwise provided for," in the game and fish commissioner, rather than in the state auditor, as had been the policy with all other parks except Itasca. More important — and ultimately more pernicious

*Top of Mount Tom, Sibley State Park, August 22, 1920*

— was the proviso that the park should "forever be maintained by the County of Kandiyohi under the terms of the resolution of the county commissioners of said county dated March 26, 1919 . . . which is a proposal on the part of said county to perpetually maintain said park." Local park supporters accepted this clause, reluctantly, as the price they had to pay to get the park established.[19]

Dedicated on June 26, 1920, the park as originally constituted covered an area of 356 acres and included about a mile of shoreline on Lake Andrew, with an extension to the north to include Mount Tom. The legislative appropriation had been used wholly for land acquisition, but $2,300 provided by the county, plus over $500 in individual contributions, made possible the construction of a road from Lake Andrew, past Mount Tom, to the Colfax Road (the present Trunk Highway 9), where the official entrance was located. For the protection of the park, the county board appointed four

wardens. As a source of income, hay land was leased for $70 a year.[20]

As the years passed, however, local interest waned, and the county failed to maintain the park, which fell into neglect. By 1929 the local game warden wrote that the roads were in poor shape. Without an appropriation from any governmental agency, the park's only income the previous year had been $130 from the sale of hay. To replace the old advisory committee, which had long since become defunct, in July 1929 the county board appointed a "Sibley State Park Committee." The committee immediately set about urging the legislature to delete the clause in the 1919 act making the county responsible for the maintenance of the park. A bill to do so was introduced that year by state Senator Victor E. Lawson, whose rationale for state support was that, although the park's patronage in 1919 was largely local, by 1929 people from all over the state were using it, and it seemed only fair to give it a broader financial base. The bill failed to pass, however, perhaps because it called for an appropriation of $2,651.42. Lawson had better success in 1931, and two years later the first state appropriation — $100 for each year of the next biennium — was authorized for Sibley State Park. Similar appropriations were made in 1935 and 1937.[21]

The appropriations made in the 1930s were too small to accomplish much more than to keep the park roads from deteriorating further. No funds were made available to buy up the enclaves of private land, some of which, according to the secretary of the New London chapter of the Izaak Walton League, had "unsightly shacks" on them, visible from the public road. Fortunately, Sibley benefited from the work-relief programs launched by the federal government in 1933 and later. In 1935, after an NPS inspection, a two-hundred-man CCC contingent composed of World War I veterans was authorized. They arrived on May 3, in the midst of a spring snowstorm.[22]

Local newspapers displayed a lively interest in the camp and provided a running account of its accomplishments. By July 10 the veterans had cleaned 1,200 feet of beach (Lake Andrew had receded during the drought years, leaving a fringe of debris), planted 5,000 trees, and constructed ten permanent buildings, latrines (not "cheap out house style," boasted the *Willmar Daily Tribune*, but real flush toilets), and a water system. Under way or planned were five miles of foot trails, a tourist camp building, three parking areas, a floating dock in the lake, completion of the picnic grounds, and the planting of another 5,000 trees. New roads were also being built — straight rather than winding, in line with the preference of the era.[23]

Although the *Tribune* writer apparently preferred straight roads and lamented the fact that thickets and woods had in the past prevented people from going to Mount Tom, others recognized the dangers of commercialism and understood the diversity of tastes that a state park needed to satisfy. In an article titled "Imagining Sibley Park in 1960," published in 1935, Senator Lawson expressed the fear that if current "improvements" adjacent to the park should continue, twenty-five years hence it might have a merry-go-round, a dance hall, or a beer parlor near the foot of Mount Tom.[24]

*"Chicken dinner coming up" at Sibley State Park CCC camp, about 1935*

Senator Lawson also emphasized the need to plan parks for different types of users. Certain conveniences, such as camp and picnic grounds, had to be provided for one kind of visitor — the person who was there for an outing. But, he added, "Then there is the 'wilder' portion [of the park], oftentimes thickets and woods thru which trails are blazed for those who wish to 'leave the crowd' and wander, studying trees, bird life, etc." Thanks in part to Lawson's own efforts, public interest in the park manifested itself in the reactivation of the dormant advisory committee. In October 1935 the Sibley State Park Improvement Association was formed and a constitution and bylaws were adopted.[25]

The CCC workers completed their project in the summer of 1938 and the NPS turned it over to the state. The veterans left a legacy of sturdy and aesthetically pleasing buildings, as well as a network of roads and trails. As in other parks, many of the stone structures (at Sibley they were made from waste rock obtained from the quarries at Cold Spring and Rockville) remain in use a half-century later. The last structure the CCC built was a stone shelter on the summit of Mount Tom, to which a road was also built. By today's park-planning standards, it can be argued that neither shelter nor road ought to have been built, but they are there and do not detract seriously from the atmosphere of the park.[26]

Although Sibley State Park underwent major improvement in the 1930s, it was not greatly enlarged at that time. The original purchase of 356 acres was shaped roughly like an hourglass, most of the land concentrated on Lake Andrew and around Mount Tom, with a corridor connecting the two. In 1933 and 1934 there were proposals to acquire a half-section to the east, where tenant farmers were unsuccessfully trying to make a living on marginal land that should not have been under cultivation, but lack of funds prevented any action at that time. Except for two tracts of privately owned land, no additions were made, and as late as 1948 the park had an area of only 378.83 acres, all in the original two sections.[27]

In 1957, however, a gradual expansion began. Every legislative session but one from then until 1973 saw additions authorized. Most of these were small, but in 1969 a considerable area on the north and south sides of the original park was added. Much of this and some of the other additions were outside the original two sections. Then in 1973 the legislature authorized massive additions to the park and almost doubled its size.[28]

As early as 1929 interest had been shown in a wooded area to the west, adjacent to Middle Lake, Norway Lake, and Games Lake, but the price of this land was substantially higher than that of the land on the east side of the park, so attention shifted to the latter. The idea had not been given up, however, and was revived in 1971. Despite some local opposition, a bill authorizing the major expansion was introduced in the Minnesota house on April 4, 1973. It moved surprisingly fast through the appropriate committees and was passed by a 124 to 0 vote in the lower chamber. In the senate a strongly worded amendment was tacked on: "No land described in this section may be acquired by eminent domain, notwithstanding any provision of Minnesota Statutes . . . as now enacted or hereafter amended, nor any other law, to the contrary." With this provision, it passed the senate, 59 to 0, and was subsequently repassed by the house, 130 to 0, and signed by Governor Wendell Anderson on May 23, 1973. In 1975 the cost of acquiring all private lands in the enlarged park — 135 individual tracts — and relocating sixty-two owners was estimated to be $1,692,790. Legislation passed in 1980 excluded from the park certain highly developed lakeshore parcels that the state would have found extremely difficult to acquire. Even so, it will be a while before all the lands within the statutory boundaries are incorporated into the park. When that is accomplished, it will have an area of more than 3,000 acres.[29]

The self-study mandated by the Outdoor Recreation Act of 1975 led to a careful appraisal of Sibley's place in the state park system. Because of its heavy recreational use, particularly at the beach on Lake Andrew, it was classified as a recreational rather than a natural state park, though it has many of the qualifications for consideration as the latter. In order to capitalize on Sibley's natural features, a fine new interpretive center has been built and an ambitious program of nature hikes and evening programs instituted. To relieve congestion at the campground near the lake, a second campground has been laid out well away from the center of most of the activity in the park; but it has not proved as popular as the old one.

Sibley State Park receives heavy patronage by people from Willmar and smaller nearby towns, but its campgrounds are popular also among motorists headed north or south on U. S. 71, which parallels its eastern boundary. In an area where most desirable lakeshore property is in private hands, its frontage on Lake Andrew has considerable public value. For this reason, that part of the park is overdeveloped and overused. Any day of the week in summer the beach may be crowded, and the adjoining picnic ground is likely to be in use. Far fewer park visitors find their way to Mount Tom, even though a road takes them to within a short distance of the summit.

Apart from water-oriented activities on Lake Andrew, hiking and horseback riding are the principal forms of summer recreation at Sibley. Yet on the eighteen miles of foot trails (five of which may be used also by horseback riders), it is unusual at any time to encounter other hikers, and almost unknown in the off-season. One trail follows the bluff overlooking the lake, while another parallels the road to the top of Mount Tom and then returns along another route. In the northern section of the park a horse trail leads through hardwood forest and open grassland, much of it once used for farming. In winter many of the trails are used by snowmobilers and cross-country skiers. Since Sibley is near the western edge of the Big Woods and the prairie is not far off, vegetation and wildlife represent both environments. Depending on the season, it is possible to see an impressive display of wildflowers and a variety of birds and small mammals. After fifty years' absence, the deer began returning about 1931, and now visitors frequently see them.

Back in 1923 State Auditor Ray Chase complained that Minnesota's parks, by and large, were not located where the greatest number of people could use them. He saw Sibley as an exception to this generalization, however, because it was situated near what was then the state's population center. Kandiyohi County is less centrally located now, with the population shift to the Twin Cities area, but Sibley still serves Minnesotans from a large area, not to mention travelers passing through the state. It fills a niche in the state's park system that needs to be filled. Not so environmentally fragile as some of the parks in the southeast and the northeast, it can stand relatively heavy recreational use without serious damage, and yet it offers the visitor much that cannot be found elsewhere on public land in the west central part of the state.[30]

## Scenic

If the 1919 legislative session was a fruitful one for the development of Minnesota's park system, that of 1921 was almost as much so. It produced one major and one minor park and saw the introduction of several other park bills, one of which was enacted into law at the next session. The process began on February 3, when state Senator Patrick H. McGarry of Walker introduced a bill to establish Sandwick Lake State Park in Itasca County. As was customary, the bill was referred to the committee on public domain, which reported it back some three weeks later with the recommendation that the name be changed to Scenic State Park. This amendment, which was adopted by the full senate, was unfortunate. Except for those whose significance is solely historical, all state parks are almost by definition "scenic," and to single out one park by attaching the word to its name is misleading. "Sandwick" might have had a hard time avoiding corruption into "Sandwich," but the name would at least have been distinctive.[31]

McGarry's bill, as amended, was passed by the senate and in due course by the house as well, with minor amendments, and

*Trailer camping, Scenic State Park, about 1935*

signed by Governor Jacob A. O. Preus on April 19. The act set apart certain described lands totaling 2,422 acres, much of which was already owned by the state, including school and swamp lands. It provided that the forest should be kept intact except for "weak, deceased [*sic*] or insect-infested trees or dead and down timber." The act empowered the state auditor to acquire privately owned lands within the statutory boundaries of the park, but it included no provision for the exercise of eminent domain.[32]

Although the act establishing Scenic State Park contained no appropriation for land acquisition, state-owned lands provided a nucleus of 847 acres — not, however, in a continuous block. The 1923 legislature appropriated $8,300 for additional land purchases, and 197.25 acres were added. Since the privately owned lands within the park boundaries were not occupied or developed, at least 820 acres of such lands were being used for park purposes by 1935. In that year the legislature appropriated $15,600 for the acquisition of just over 600 acres, and the process of filling in the statutory limits of the park moved ahead.[33]

Dedicated in 1922, Scenic State Park, remote from population centers, underwent only minimal development in the early years. In lieu of a state appropriation, Itasca County provided funds, and local people contributed labor. A picnic area was laid out on Chase

Point, the long, narrow spit of land that separates Coon and Sandwick lakes, and in 1925 the first building was erected there. Once
they began, legislative appropriations were fairly generous, ranging from $1,540 to $2,800 annually for the fiscal years 1928 through
1931; with the onset of the economic crisis, the sums appropriated
dropped to $2,500 for the 1932–33 biennium and to $1,200 a year
thereafter. Apparently these funds were used mainly for fire protection and other purposes more characteristic of state forests.[34]

The real development of the park began in the 1930s, with the
advent of work-relief programs. A CCC camp was established
there in the summer of 1933. Hugo Zaiser, who had been in charge
of the park since its inception, acted as camp superintendent and
headed a staff of eleven technical and supervisory personnel under
the direction of the NPS. For most of the two and a half years of
its existence, the camp was located in the extreme southern end of
the park, on Lake of the Isles, the site of the present primitive group
camp.[35]

CCC workers obliterated the old picnic ground, located in a
fragile area, and constructed new picnicking and camping facilities
on the west side of Coon Lake. The lodge in which interpretive programs are presented is part of the legacy of the CCC, as are the
murals on the walls, which depict a woodland scene before, during, and after a forest fire. Crews built several overnight cabins, an
icehouse and a fish-cleaning house, and the predecessor of the present park road. Unlike Whitewater and Sibley, Scenic does not have
a public road crossing its most heavily used area. Instead it has a
dead-end road extending from Itasca County 7 to the Lodge campground. Since all traffic has to pass the entrance station, the problem of control is much simplified.[36]

Not all problems faced by park superintendents in the earlier
years concerned relations with visitors; some grew out of bureaucratic practices. Until 1939 it was customary for the legislature not
only to appropriate specific sums of money for each park but also
to earmark these funds for specific purposes. This policy placed the
park superintendents in something of a straitjacket, as is illustrated
by what happened at Scenic in 1925. The legislature had appropriated $1,000 for a caretaker's cabin and $750 for firebreaks and
trails. The building, which the superintendent had started without
submitting the plans to the Commissioner of Administration and

Finance or the Conservation Commission, was far from completed when the $1,000 ran out; it still lacked flooring, partitions, a chimney, doors, and other necessary features. When asked whether the money earmarked for firebreaks and trails could be used to complete work on the cabin, State Comptroller Henry Rines replied emphatically that it could not be so diverted.[37]

Because of its size, remoteness, and complexity, Scenic is not an easy park to get to know. It covers nearly 3,000 acres, and it will be even larger when additions authorized in 1980 have all been acquired. Scenic has been repeatedly referred to in parks division leaflets as one of the state's most primitive parks. The term is appropriate if it refers to the wilderness character of the backcountry, including some fine tracts of virgin white and red (Norway) pine. Its visitor facilities, however, are less primitive than those of many other parks. As early as 1940, for example, the campground combination building had showers. But the park is still well off the beaten path, not likely to be used by motorists merely passing through the state on a major highway. Away from the developed areas on the west side of Coon Lake, it is wild enough to satisfy most tastes. A trail partly circles the two major lakes and approaches Pine Lake, in the northern end of the park. Campsites for backpackers and canoeists are scattered along the east shores of Sandwick and Coon lakes and on Pine Lake, in an authentic wilderness setting. On an elevation between Coon and Pine lakes a forestry lookout tower provides a vantage point from which to view the park. For those who prefer less extended hikes, there is the Chase Point Trail. Chase Point is an esker, a slender ridge created by a stream flowing through a tunnel in a glacier and depositing sand and gravel.[38]

Scenic does not have the intimacy of the smaller southern parks, with their reminders of long human occupancy and use. Although portions of it were logged over and even briefly settled by homesteaders, these reverted rather quickly to wilderness. Together with the tracts of virgin pine, they today make up a park where one can get more than a hint of what northern Minnesota was like before the loggers came. With the Chippewa National Forest on the west and the George Washington State Forest on the east to serve as buffers, Scenic State Park should retain its atmosphere of remoteness and primitive beauty for a long time to come.

## Sleepy Eye

If the 1921 legislature can take credit for establishing Scenic, it must also accept the blame for making the state responsible for what was in fact a city park in the town of Sleepy Eye in Brown County. The bill creating the park was passed with little opposition. Although it carried no appropriation, the attorney general was authorized to acquire certain described lands, by condemnation if necessary. Each of the next three legislatures appropriated $2,000 for land acquisition and other purposes — rather liberal treatment, considering that the park never encompassed more than 40 acres. It was ignored by the 1929, 1931, and 1933 legislatures, but then small appropriations of $500 a year (in 1935) and $250 a year (in 1937) were made.[39]

Sleepy Eye State Park was used almost entirely by local residents. As early as 1930 there were calls for its return to the city, and later in the decade it was downgraded from a park to a wayside. Nevertheless, a campground was laid out as part of a WPA project in 1936; the city of Sleepy Eye also wanted a project to divert water to keep the lake at its normal level during the drought years, but it did not get its way. Not until 1965 did the legislature authorize the transfer of the park to the city.[40]

## Lake Bemidji

Parks were popular with the 1921 legislature. In addition to those that reached fruition, at least five other park proposals were introduced during the session. One of these, calling for a Mille Lacs State Park, had been first advanced in 1919. Although it had considerable support in both years, it did not pass, and Mille Lacs Lake was not to acquire a state park until 1941. Other bills introduced in 1921 called for the establishment of a North Shore State Park, a Carlton Lake Park, an East Chain Lake Park, and a Lake Bemidji State Park. Some of these died in committee, while others were simply lost in the shuffle at the end of the session.[41]

The Lake Bemidji bill failed to pass in 1921, but the next July State Auditor Chase visited the area north of the city of Bemidji and was reported to be favorably inclined toward the park proposal. He

*Park naturalist conducting tour of spruce tamarack bog area, Lake Bemidji State Park, about 1984*

mentioned it, along with many other potential sites for state parks, in his biennial report to the legislature early in 1923. At that session companion bills calling for establishment of a Lake Bemidji State Park were introduced, but both died in committee. Their substance, however, was incorporated in the general appropriations bill for state parks and forests. In its original form, the Lake Bemidji clause of this bill authorized the purchase of 160.04 acres of land for a state park. It was later amended to read "not to exceed 421.05 acres." Passed by both houses, the act was signed by Governor Preus on April 21.[42]

Besides an appropriation of $45,000 for land acquisition, the law contained a provision, similar to that in the Sibley State Park act four years earlier, for county maintenance. It specified that the park should "forever be maintained by the County of Beltrami," whose board of commissioners was "authorized and empowered to make such appropriations of county funds and to levy such taxes as may be necessary to maintain said park." No doubt this proviso assisted with the passage of the bill, but, as in the case of Sibley, it ultimately retarded the development of the park. It presumably reflected strong local interest at the time the park was established; the Bemidji Civic and Commerce Association promoted the bill as a means of preserving a tract of virgin red pine.[43]

The two-year delay in getting the park authorized partly frustrated this intention, however. Charles F. Ruggles, a Michigan lumberman, owned most of the pine around the lake, and the Civic and Commerce Association apparently persuaded him in 1921 to sell certain tracts to the state. When the bill failed to pass that year, he sold much of the property to the Crookston Lumber Company, which paid a high price for the stumpage and harvested a great deal of the standing timber. By the time the park was authorized in 1923, only a little over 200 acres could be found in pristine condition, instead of the more than 400 acres specified in the legislation. The owner rejected the state's offer, and condemnation had to be used, as provided in the law. The court fixed a price of $36,486.71 for the land and timber on a 163.8-acre tract on the north shore of Lake Bemidji and $6,569.83 for a smaller parcel of 41.68 acres some five miles distant, on the east side of the lake.[44]

For a number of years after its establishment, Lake Bemidji was plagued by the consequences of the provision leaving responsibility for its maintenance to the county. As at Sibley, local enthusiasm waned, and the county failed to adhere to its promises. In 1926 the superintendent of the city of Bemidji's park board wrote to forestry commissioner Grover Conzet, asking whether the state governmental reorganization act passed in 1925, creating a Department of Conservation, might not take precedence over the now undesired proviso in the 1923 law. Conzet replied that it did not and suggested the formation of a local advisory committee, to consist of the game warden, the forest ranger, one of the timber cruisers, a city park board member, a county commissioner, and anyone else who might be interested in serving and qualified to do so. A volunteer force, he thought, might be recruited to clear some firebreaks, provide campgrounds, and otherwise develop the park.[45]

Nothing much came of Conzet's suggestions. During the later 1920s John H. Nelson, district ranger for the Bemidji area, functioned as *de facto* park manager, and early in 1932 he was officially appointed superintendent, an extension of his duties for which he showed little enthusiasm. He was uncertain as to how far his jurisdiction extended and reluctant to risk offending local park supporters by adopting too aggressive a stance in managing the park. As a result, he did very little, a course of action that earned him a reprimand from his superior, Commissioner Conzet. A few months after Nelson's appointment as superintendent, Conzet wrote him that a "rather vigorous complaint" about his inaction had come from some Bemidji people. Although there was no money for use in the park, said Conzet, the five men at the Bemidji ranger station could all put some *time* into park maintenance. They could do some brushing out and cleaning up; so far the park had "looked like just so much wild timber to most people." Conzet added a comment that revealed his forestry-oriented attitude toward parks. "You cannot do any harm," he wrote, "by cutting out underbrush if you leave any species that might grow up to good merchantable timber." He urged Nelson to build a few picnic tables and make "a good showing" that might induce the legislature to appropriate some funds for the park.[46]

When in 1931 legislation was passed relieving Kandiyohi County of the care of Sibley State Park, there was sentiment in favor of similar legislation for Lake Bemidji, but it does not appear that any such bill was even introduced, let alone passed. The clause specifying the county's responsibility was not finally repealed until 1955. Nevertheless, the legislature in 1933 began appropriating $250 a year for the upkeep of the park.[47]

As in so many other parks, work-relief labor in the 1930s gave Lake Bemidji a much-needed face-lifting. Besides the CCC, the Civil Works Administration and the National Youth Administration were involved in the development of the park. To supplement the very limited facilities already existing, these agencies built a new park road, a kitchen and shelter, sanitary facilities, and a bathhouse, and put in two parking areas, additional campsites, and a number of picnic tables. The NYA also developed the natural beach on Lake Bemidji. The biennial reports submitted by the newly appointed parks director, Harold W. Lathrop, for 1936, 1938, and 1940 record steady progress toward bringing Lake Bemidji State Park up to the level of the parks that had not been handicapped by the provision making the county responsible for their upkeep.[48]

Like other state parks, Lake Bemidji suffered from a lack of maintenance during World War II and emerged from the war years in somewhat poorer shape than it had entered them. Then, a few weeks before the end of the war, a threat developed to the very existence of the park: a veterans' hospital was proposed for the site. On April 16, 1945, the legislature passed and the governor approved a bill authorizing the commissioner of conservation to convey to the United States certain described lands squarely in the heart of the park. The transfer was not to be executed until the board of county commissioners (still nominally responsible for the park at that time) had approved "dismantling and moving to another state park all buildings and improvements." This provision was evidently based on the assumption that Lake Bemidji State Park would be doomed if the hospital were built. Fortunately for the park and its admirers, the hospital was never constructed.[49]

One reason the park was so vulnerable to such threats was that it was still very small. A pamphlet published in 1948 credited it with 205.48 acres — precisely the acreage that had been purchased in the mid-1920s. Once the 1955 legislation was passed, specifying that "this park shall forever be maintained and conducted by the state as a state park," however, Lake Bemidji began to grow. By 1964 it had increased to 285.45 acres. The first big increase came in 1971, when the legislature authorized the addition of a quarter-section — 160 acres — just east of the existing park; this acquisition included a biologically important bog area. An even larger expansion, one that more than doubled the size of the park, came in 1977, followed by a smaller increase in 1979. With these additions, Lake Bemidji, one of the more heavily used parks in the state, increased not only in size but also in biological and topographical diversity.[50]

Legislative authorization to expand a park's statutory boundaries, however, is only one of the earlier steps toward acquisition of additional land. The later steps often generate local or regional opposition on the part of one or another of the constituencies the DNR serves. A couple of years after the first of the three big expansions at Lake Bemidji, Philip R. Sauer, spokesman for the Bemidji chapter of the Izaak Walton League, wrote to newly appointed parks director Donald D. Davison to express his group's feelings about certain matters. He believed that Lake Bemidji should have a full-time naturalist and should provide more trail maps and other interpretive devices. He thought there should be less junk and more authentic crafts in the park store, and he represented his organization as opposed to any increase in the number of campsites. In the spirit of the early citizens' advisory groups, he assured Davison that the members of the Izaak Walton League were always available to assist the park professionals in an advisory capacity.[51]

Not all expressions of public opinion were that moderate, however, nor were the contacts between DNR staff and segments of the public as friendly as either party might have preferred. In 1977 — the year of the big expansion — there was a complex controversy that brought the DNR into conflict with the Beltrami County Board of Commissioners. Although the board members supported expansion of the park (or said they did), they wanted the state to pay for 500 acres of tax-forfeit land in the area proposed for addition to the park. The DNR representatives took the position, long sanctioned by custom and, according to them, by law, that tax-forfeit land belonged to the state, with the county having only custodial control.[52]

In the same year the first series of management plans mandated by the Outdoor Recreation Act of 1975 were drawn up. Lake Bemidji was one of twenty parks for which such plans were immediately made, and the process included a series of public meetings at which interested persons could voice their opinions and ask questions of the DNR representatives. The land acquisition issue seemed to have top priority in the minds of many who attended the final public information meeting on February 21, though some were also concerned about what they saw as competition with private enterprise in the development of campground and cross-country skiing facilities.[53]

Another element was introduced in 1978, when the Minnesota Parks Foundation, formed in 1967 to assist the state in acquiring land, agreed to purchase, on behalf of the state, 96 acres between the park boundary and a golf course owned by the Bemidji Town and Country Club. This was tax-forfeit land and had been appraised at $59,925.90. At the public auction held in midsummer, the only bidders were Wesley Libbey, representing the foundation, and a man from Blackduck. Libbey's bid of $90,000 was accepted, and the foundation was owner of a tract of land that it would sell to the state if the legislature agreed to expand the park boundary, which it did in 1979. The episode aroused a great deal of local hostility to the DNR. Thus, although the state obtained its desired land, it appeared that the DNR would have to do some fence mending if it hoped to enjoy any degree of popularity around Bemidji.[54]

Though a small park until the 1970s, Lake Bemidji has been an important link in the state park system since the 1930s. Heavily used by local people, it has also attracted summer visitors from a greater distance. With most of the lakeshore in private hands, the park's stretch of public beach has been much appreciated. Its network of trails, long limited by the park's small size, has recently been expanded to fifteen miles. Along these trails the hiker can see a wide variety of northern trees and wildflowers. Besides the towering red pines, many other conifers grow in the park, including the tamarack, especially colorful in the autumn before its needles fall. Bunchberry, twinflower, wild sarsaparilla, wintergreen, Labrador tea, and the carnivorous pitcher plant — the last two in a bog east of the developed area — all can be found by the enterprising explorer. The park offers guided nature trails, naturalist programs for overnight visitors, and an interpretive center with natural history displays, all to make a visit to the park an educational as well as a recreational experience.[55]

## Garvin Heights and John A. Latsch

All the parks thus far discussed were created by legislative act. Two parks, both in Winona County, that came into being in the early 1920s were donated to the state. (Much of Jay Cooke had been donated, too, but legislative action was required to add necessary lands to those given by the Cooke executors.) In 1922 Herbert C. Garvin, vice-president of the Bay State Milling Company of Winona, gave the city a tract of 12 acres (later enlarged to 17), mostly on the bluffs overlooking the Mississippi River valley on the southern edge of the town. The city transferred the land to the Winona State Teachers College (later Winona State University), which in turn offered it to the state, retaining certain vestiges of control.[56]

Aside from providing splendid views up and down the river and across the city to Wisconsin, Garvin Heights State Park had no special merit and might better have remained what Garvin apparently intended it to be, a city park. He built two small shelters for the benefit of picnickers, but otherwise there was practically no

*John A. Latsch State Park*

development. No CCC or WPA labor was employed there; by 1940 the only employee was one part-time laborer. In 1935 and 1937 the legislature did provide an appropriation of $200 annually, to be expended on the recommendation of the local director of the teachers college. Long considered by park personnel to be in a class with Horace Austin and Sleepy Eye, Garvin Heights was turned back to the city of Winona in 1961.[57]

The other park acquired by the state through donation was more important. A well-to-do Winona businessman, John A. Latsch, who has been mentioned in connection with Whitewater State Park, became interested in an area some fourteen miles northwest of Winona, along the Mississippi. He bought land from several owners and then donated to the state a narrow rectangle comprising about 350 acres. Separated from the river by a highway and a major railroad line, the park consisted mainly of three towering bluffs, known as Faith, Hope, and Charity. Unofficially called "Scenic Highway State Park" at first, it was given the name of its donor when the first appropriation was made by the legislature in 1929.[58]

No development of consequence occurred until that appropriation, which amounted to only $750 for the next fiscal year. Frank J. Fugina of Winona was appointed superintendent. Fugina, described by the Winona newspaper as a "veteran riverman," received little or nothing for his services in the early years, and when he began being paid $300 a year for the summer months, he spent part of his salary on improvements. In the late summer of 1929 he cleared about nine acres at two locations, brushed out a road, built two toilets, put up some signs, and cleaned out a spring. Later he had a well drilled and added four picnic tables. Latsch often paid for improvements himself, expecting to be repaid by the state. Ordinarily such an expectation would have been unfounded, but his good will was valued — Fugina wrote that the state's refusal to reimburse him would amount to killing the goose that laid the golden egg — and the 1933 legislature stipulated that he might be paid $400 out of the $1,000 appropriation voted two years earlier.[59]

During the summer of 1933 CCC labor was used to construct trails to the bluff top, and subsequently WPA workers built pit toilets and did some landscaping. In addition, the Department of Highways, which took part of the land in widening its right-of-way, assisted in improving the facilities. There was no campground as such, but the picnic area was used for limited camping. In 1936 the parks director proposed building some overnight cabins and putting in an entrance station; neither of these improvements was carried out.[60]

As a matter of fact, after the flurry of activity during the 1930s, John A. Latsch State Park had no further development for many years. The chief reason for its failure to realize the hopes of its donor and others was that the peculiar configuration of the park restricted its development. The only sites that could be developed were small areas at the mouths of the ravines that separated the three bluffs. It had apparently been Latsch's intention to acquire and donate more land; the 1925 *Legislative Manual* spoke, prematurely, of a park of 600 acres. About a month before his death in 1934, Latsch told an NPS inspector that he could have got more land at the time he bought the tracts that he later donated to the state. He believed, however, that the owners of that adjacent land still would be willing to sell; but in this expectation he was mistaken. In fact, the park actually lost acreage in the early 1960s as a result of highway construction, which, according to park planner Bernard A. Halver, took the most valuable land and reduced the park to a roadside picnic area. Some sources give it an area of only 322 acres after this loss.[61]

In an effort to expand John A. Latsch into a full-sized park, the conservation department in 1963 proposed to increase it to 1,467 acres through the purchase of lands extending well back from the bluff tops. Halver outlined the plan in a meeting with the tourist committee of the Winona Chamber of Commerce in January, and later in the legislative session the proposal was incorporated into the Omnibus Recreation and Natural Resources Act of 1963. The idea was to have the camping and picnic areas on the bluffs, reached by a road leaving U.S. Highway 61 at the north end of the park.[62]

Since that time, however, only a few small parcels have been added to the park, bringing the size to approximately 389 acres. Funds have apparently not been available for buying up the desired lands, and in any case the owners have been reluctant to sell. In 1969 John A. Latsch was reclassified as a wayside (though that may have resulted from a clerical error), and a parks study issued two years later recommended that it be designated a scientific and natural area — one of the categories into which park lands might be classified according to the Outdoor Recreation Act of 1975 — since its recreational possibilities seemed limited.[63]

For a time in the early 1970s the park had an air of neglect about it. The grass had not been mown in the picnic grounds, and the eight campsites that had been squeezed into the limited area showed little sign of use. There was not even a sign along the highway identifying the park. But during the summer and fall of 1972 it received a general sprucing-up, and since then the campground has been replaced by walk-in sites, which occupy less space than conventional sites. Although the park lands do not directly abut on the river, a boat access was constructed by means of large culverts passing under the highway and railway.[64]

But these efforts are palliative at best and do not get at the heart of the problem, which is that John A. Latsch is too small, given its topography, to be a satisfactory state park. A few people can camp there; a larger number can picnic; and boaters can make use of the boat access. But beyond that there is not much one can do. The only trail, which leads to an overlook atop one of the bluffs, is steeper than most hikers like and is eroding badly. Moreover, vehicles entering and leaving the park constitute a traffic hazard on busy U.S. Highway 61, now a four-lane highway. If the expansion envisaged in the Omnibus Act could be realized, these problems would be largely obviated, but that seems unlikely.

Preservation rather than recreational development may be the most appropriate goal for such rugged terrain. Certainly there is much to preserve. The forest cover alone is a valuable biological resource. The steep slopes precluded logging as long as other timber was more readily accessible, and the protection afforded the area as a state park has ensured the survival of the mixed hardwood forest. An inventory taken in 1932 revealed a rich variety of tree species: white, black, bur, and red oak, sugar and silver maple, black, white, and prickly ash, black walnut, butternut, bitternut hickory, basswood, ironwood, birch, poplar, slippery and rock elm, and many shrubs among the hardwoods, not to mention red cedar and white cedar (arborvitae) among the conifers. In spring the amateur botanist can find the comparatively rare shooting star on the bluff tops, along with commoner flowers like puccoons and false Solomon's seal.[65]

Whatever its future, as a conventional park with a certain amount of development or as a scientific and natural area, John A. Latsch should definitely be retained in the park system. Though its bluff-top views of the Mississippi are duplicated to some degree by the newer O. L. Kipp State Park, it has its own unique qualities. With imaginative management and the acquisition of more land, these qualities could be made available to the segment of the public most likely to appreciate them.

## Summary

By 1925 the outlines of a state park system had emerged. The eight additions since 1915 brought the total to twenty-three parks and monuments. More significant than the number of units, however, was the improvement in quality represented by the additions made during the last decade. The chief weaknesses of the system as it existed in 1925 stemmed from the haphazard manner in which it had grown and the absence of any philosophy governing the acquisition and development of parks. State Auditor Ray Chase had called the legislature's attention to these faults in 1923. The parks had been created, he wrote, as a result of individual effort and local demand. Although some had been worthy of state park status, others were "of comparatively slight merit." He considered this method of establishing state parks "thoroughly bad."[66]

Chase argued that if a state park system was a good thing, "it should be developed sanely and carefully by expert park men." This had not been done in Minnesota, and as a consequence there was, he said, no *system* of state parks in the state. Placing them under the direction of the state auditor was unfortunate, because his duties did not give him much time to devote to the parks. They should be placed under the supervision of an expert commission or commissioner, as had been done in Wisconsin and several eastern states. Besides defects in the overall administration of the parks, Chase saw faults in the management of individual units. Most were too small, and their boundaries followed section lines or subdivisions thereof. Some of the smaller units should be transferred to the counties, he thought, and the others should be expanded.[67]

One consequence of the lack of overall planning and direction was a geographic imbalance in the system. Chase complained that the parks were not located where they could serve the largest number of people, either Minnesota residents or out-of-state visitors. The nine counties along the Iowa border had only one park, Horace Austin; the thirteen counties along the state's western boundary had only one, Toqua Lakes. Except for a couple of monuments, there were no parks in the southwestern part of the state, apart from the Minnesota River valley. Nor were there any in the western and northwestern sections, west of Itasca. More serious, there were no parks on the North Shore of Lake Superior, the most scenic region of the state. Except for Interstate, there were no parks in or near the Minneapolis–St. Paul metropolitan area. Finally, the southeastern counties were underrepresented in the system. By contrast, the Minnesota River valley was, if anything, overrepresented, though several of the units there were merely monuments commemorating the Dakota War. Elsewhere the parks were reasonably well spaced with reference to scenic attractions, if not to the needs of the population.[68]

In his proposals for additional parks, Chase spotted many of the areas subsequently acquired for inclusion in the state or national park system. Among his suggestions for future park sites were Albert Lea Lake, realized in 1947 by Helmer Myre State Park; Blue Mound, in extreme southwestern Minnesota, created in 1937; the Pipestone quarry, which became a national monument in 1937; Lake Shetek, where a state monument was expanded into a park in the 1930s; the Camden Hills, established in 1935; Ortonville, realized as Big Stone Lake State Park in 1961; Inspiration Peak and Lake Lida in Otter Tail County, which became parks in 1931 and 1963, respectively; Mille Lacs Lake, where two state parks were later created; and Grand Portage, made a national monument in 1960.[69]

Perhaps as a result of Chase's suggestions for reform of the system, the legislature made an effort in 1923 to rationalize the administration of the parks and to lay down ground rules for the future. In what might be considered the official beginning of the state park *system*, a detailed piece of legislation was passed that year. It classified the various units that had been acquired and that might be acquired in the future as state parks, state public camp grounds, state monuments, and state monument sites. All except Itasca were to be under the administration of the state auditor. The law contained provisions governing how land might be acquired, specifying that gifts, donations, or bequests could be accepted by the state treasurer only upon the approval of the governor, the auditor, and the treasurer. Two provisions that had to be modified in later years related to the public's free access to the parks: one stated that "State parks shall be preserved and maintained for the free use and enjoyment of the general public," and the other stipulated that no fees should be charged for transient camping. This act, which would be in part supplemented and in part superseded two years later by the establishment of the Department of Conservation and the transfer of the state parks to that agency, brought a measure of order to a system that had been evolving for nearly forty years.[70]

Despite Chase's criticisms, Minnesota's park system was nothing to be ashamed of. In comparison to the systems of neighboring states, it was respectable in both quality and quantity. If a disproportionate number of the units were monuments commemorating two events in the state's history, the system also included some extremely desirable acquisitions. Few states could boast anything better than Itasca — and Jay Cooke, Interstate, Whitewater, Scenic, and some of the others were well worth the effort and money expended in adding them. It was perhaps enough that the lands within these parks were protected; too much development, of the kind in favor then, would have proved inimical to the long-range needs of the state and its people. The parks were there; they needed only development of an enlightened sort, with some kind of professional body to determine its direction, to make them what people like Jacob Brower and Newton Winchell had hoped to see when they advocated the establishment of Itasca State Park.

# CHAPTER FOUR

# Under the
# Conservation Commission
# 1925–1935

THE YEARS from 1925 to 1935 may be regarded as a fallow period in the history of Minnesota's state park system, preceded by a time of comparatively swift growth and followed by one of the two greatest periods of expansion the system has ever experienced. Of nine units added during the decade, most of them by the 1929 and 1931 legislatures, only two remained in 1990 as full-fledged state parks. These ten years were less significant for the number and quality of parks created than for certain administrative changes in state government that influenced the management of the parks.

Until 1925 the state parks (except for Itasca and Sibley) had been under the jurisdiction of the state auditor, who was in charge of the state land department. Their actual protection and management, however, were in the hands of local advisory committees. Some auditors, such as Ray Chase, took an active interest in the parks, though other responsibilities of their office had a higher priority; some local committees performed their tasks conscientiously, if not always in the best long-term interests of the parks. But the system, if it can be called that, was haphazard, as was the manner of establishing parks. What was lacking was what might be called professionalism — a dedicated and disciplined effort by trained people to manage the parks as the national park system was beginning to be managed.

Such true professionalism did not come to Minnesota's parks until 1935; but a step in the right direction was made in 1925, when, as part of a massive reorganization of state government, the

*Grover M. Conzet, 1918*

legislature created the Department of Conservation and placed parks under its jurisdiction. The new department was to be supervised and controlled by a commission consisting of the commissioner of forestry and fire prevention and the commissioner of game and fish, both appointed by the governor, and the state auditor, who served as ex officio commissioner of lands and timber. The commissioner of forestry and fire prevention was to serve as chairman of the commission and exercise the duties hitherto vested in the state forester and the state forestry board.[1]

Although the act did not specifically place the parks within the forestry section of the conservation department, the forestry commissioner's role as chairman made him, in effect, director of parks, though that title did not emerge for another ten years. For that entire period the commissioner of forestry and fire prevention (and after 1931 director of forestry) was Grover M. Conzet. People with an interest in the parks — field personnel under his direction, members of local committees, legislators, and the general public — addressed their inquiries, suggestions, and reports to him. Hence it is from Conzet's correspondence that much information on the parks during the decade comes. From this correspondence one gets not only a running history of the parks but also an indication, now and then, of an evolving park philosophy.

Born in Todd County in 1886, Conzet had worked in sawmill and logging operations before entering the University of Minnesota to study forestry, receiving a bachelor of science degree in 1912 and a master of science degree in 1913. From 1914 on he was connected in some way with the state forest service, and on July 1, 1924, he was appointed state forester. With the reorganization the following year, he became effective head of the new conservation commission, one of his duties being the overall surveillance of the state parks. Although his primary interest was presumably forestry, he also took an interest in the parks and was more actively involved in their management than most of the successive state auditors had been.[2]

The 1931 legislature effected a major change in the makeup and governance of the conservation department. The three-member Conservation Commission was replaced by a five-member body, to be appointed by the governor with the advice and consent of the state senate. This new commission was to employ, at an annual salary of $5,000, a conservation commissioner, who was to serve for a six-year term and exercise the powers then vested in the various commissioners who had comprised the commission set up in 1925. Their offices were abolished and replaced by four divisions — forestry and fire prevention, waters and drainage, game and fish, and lands and minerals — each under its own director. The division of forestry, which remained under the directorship of Grover Conzet, was now specifically mandated authority over state parks and monuments.[3]

The 1931 act did not basically alter the status of the parks, except that instead of floating in limbo within the Department of Conservation they were now legally within the division of forestry. Conzet's continuing tenure as head of the forest service meant that he would also continue to direct their operation. The commissioner of conservation, William T. Cox, also a forestry graduate of the University of Minnesota, was Conzet's superior and therefore nominally in charge of the parks. In practice, however, Conzet's authority remained pretty much what it had been, and correspondence continued to be directed mainly to him, with Cox being involved only in major policy decisions.[4]

Soon after becoming president of the United States in 1933, Franklin D. Roosevelt persuaded Congress to establish the Civilian Conservation Corps, one of the first of the many alphabetical agencies spawned by the New Deal. The CCC and other work-relief agencies soon became involved in the development of state parks, both those already existing and those created as a result of these activities. The National Park Service also played an important role in the planning and execution of the massive improvements that took place all across the country, wherever there were state parks.

The NPS and other agencies preferred to deal with professionally trained parks people rather than with foresters, game-and-fish men, or other administrators who might have little real knowledge of or interest in parks. In fact, the federal government insisted on channeling its aid and expertise through such professionals. In order to benefit from the largess being dispensed by the federal government, therefore, the state of Minnesota was obliged to amend the 1931 legislation so as to create a division of state parks within the Department of Conservation. The law establishing this division, passed in 1935, defined the duties of the director of parks to include the acquisition and maintenance of park lands; the renting, leasing, and operating of public service privileges and facilities; and the performance of a great number of other functions. The only important restriction on these powers was that the director was not permitted to take any land or property, by purchase or condemnation, for an amount more than had been approved by the conservation commission.[5]

## Milford and Sam Brown

After unsuccessful attempts in 1925 and 1927, the legislature in 1929 passed a bill creating a monument to honor the fifty-two settlers of Milford Township, Brown County, who were killed during the Dakota War of 1862. The act set up an Indian Outbreak Monument Commission of three persons, who would acquire a suitable site in Milford Township and erect a monument there. An appropriation of $2,500 was made to carry out the terms of the act.[6]

The commission obtained an acre of land, and then deviated from the custom of erecting a tall granite obelisk, placing instead a monument consisting of a cross and a figure said to symbolize Memory. (Tradition holds that the statuary was originally intended for a Catholic cemetery.) The land was fenced in, trees were planted, and a few picnic tables were installed. The legislature provided $100 annually for the years 1934 through 1937 and $50 annually for the following two years for the maintenance of the site. As with the other monuments, there came to be some question in later years of the appropriateness of state control and management of a site of largely local significance. Eventually, in 1975, it was transferred to local control.[7]

A second monument established in 1929 was intended to honor Samuel J. Brown, who on the night of April 19, 1866, had ridden 120 miles through a storm to warn settlers of what was thought to be an impending Indian attack. Although his ride earned him the sobriquet of the "Paul Revere of the northwestern frontier" (and damaged his health for life), the expected attack failed to materialize, a fact that rendered Brown's service less patriotic in effect than in intent. Nevertheless, Brown, a son of the prominent trader, Indian agent, and politician Joseph R. Brown, remained something of a regional hero, and after his death in 1925 at the age of eighty, some citizens of the western border community of Browns Valley wished to honor him.[8]

The first attempt to accomplish this end, in 1927, failed, but in the 1929 session of the legislature a bill was passed creating a "Sam Brown Memorial Park Commission." The commission was to repair a log cabin associated with Brown, place a suitable tablet on it, and erect a monument to Brown. For these purposes the legislature allocated $6,500, but the maintenance of the site was to be the responsibility of the village of Browns Valley.[9]

The inclusion of Sam Brown Memorial Park in the state park system was questionable from the first, though as long as the people of Browns Valley were willing to pay for its upkeep, there was no strong sentiment for getting rid of it. The six-acre tract later acquired a marker providing some information about Samuel Brown. Then in 1966 a rural school building was added through the efforts of William L. Paul, a member of the original commission. U. W. Hella, the parks director at that time, was distinctly cool to Paul's ideas. Even though the village assumed the cost of moving the school to the site, Hella warned Paul that "we have consistently maintained a policy of not permitting the moving in of buildings foreign to a park site" and suggested that he ask his state senator and representative to draw up a bill transferring the park to the village. No such bill has been passed, and Sam Brown, a community park in all but name, remains under the nominal jurisdiction of the parks and recreation division.[10]

The 1929 legislative session also authorized the Moose Lake Monument, which is discussed in chapter two with the similar Hinckley and Brook Park monuments.

## Lake Shetek

One of Minnesota's parks grew by bits and pieces of legislation over a period of years, but 1929 will serve as well as any other date for its establishment, for it was then that the term "state park" was first applied to it in official documents. The 1905 legislature had appropriated $400 for the reburial of the bodies of twelve white people killed by Indians near Lake Shetek during the Dakota War, and for the erection of a suitable monument on the site. The selection of the site was to be left to the Murray County board of commissioners. Though the bodies were reinterred, no monument was erected at that time. So in 1921 the legislature acted again, appropriating $1,000 for that purpose.[11]

Once again no action was taken, and two years later state Senator Louis P. Johnson of Ivanhoe introduced a bill to consolidate the funds appropriated on the two previous occasions and use them for a monument. The bill was enacted into law, and a granite monument twenty-five feet high was placed on the site and dedicated August 3, 1925. In 1929 Johnson again introduced a bill, this time for the acquisition of additional land and a right-of-way through private property to the monument. Although neither his bill nor a companion measure introduced in the house successfully passed through the entire legislative process, the essential elements found their way into the appropriations bill, which provided $1,000 for the purchase of a tract not to exceed 10 acres. Such lands, stated the law, were "hereby declared to be a state park." Thus was created the nucleus of Lake Shetek State Park.[12]

The park as it exists today is largely the product of the work-relief activities of the mid-1930s. As an outlet for relief labor, the state's Executive Council acquired lands totaling 180.62 acres, adjoining the original tract on which the monument stood and including parts of two islands in the lake. Over the next few years laborers from both the WPA and an NPS-directed transient camp built a picnic area, an entrance road, a sewage system, a parking area, a water system, a bathhouse and beach, a campground, a group camp with its own mess hall, a council ring, and a causeway to Loon Island.[13]

By 1936 so much had been accomplished at Lake Shetek that parks director Harold Lathrop recommended that it be legally established as a state park. (Technically, it already had that status under the 1929 law, but apparently Lathrop felt that the newly acquired areas did not properly fall under the old classification.) The 1937 legislature took action to this effect, as it did in the case of nine other new parks developed by work-relief agencies. In the years that followed, Lake Shetek State Park gradually increased in size, though in 1947 a portion of it was withdrawn and sold to a church organization, leaving the park with only 155.82 acres. An addition authorized in 1963 brought it to 396.74 acres, and further additions authorized in 1965 and 1967 gave it a statutory area of 1,175 acres. By 1971 the actual size was 708 acres. Since then several tracts have been acquired, but there are still privately owned lands within the statutory boundaries.[14]

Lake Shetek has had its share of problems. For one thing, the lake level tends to fall in periods of extended drought, with the result that a strong stench pervades such areas of shoreline as the causeway. Efforts to control the water level by means of dams have not been entirely successful. Deer have also been a problem, crossing the park boundaries to feast on corn in neighboring fields. Establishing small food plots on recently purchased land has partially alleviated the difficulty by giving the animals an incentive to stay in the park. Another problem arose in connection with a proposal to find a log cabin and move it to the park as a point of historical interest. The first cabin considered had been located on the lake and had some associations with the events of 1862, but in 1955 a ent cabin, with no such significance, was moved in from the Murray County fairgrounds. This cabin, the Andrew Koch dwelling, now stands along the main park road; a sign identifies it as the last surviving pioneer cabin in Murray County, built before the Dakota War.[15]

On the centennial of that conflict 1,500 people gathered at Lake Shetek, where several white people had been killed by Dakotas a century earlier. During the ceremony a high wind toppled a battery of flags, which struck Wray A. Eastlick on the head, inflicting injuries serious enough to require a doctor's attention. As Joseph Ludwig, of the parks division, reported to director Hella, "Eastlick blood was again spilled at Lake Shetek." In general, however, the historical associations are much less in evidence here than they are at Fort Ridgely or Birch Coulee. The monument stands at the end of a side road, and few park visitors bother to drive down for a closer look than is possible from the entrance road.[16]

Lake Shetek's importance has always been that it includes much of the shoreline of southwestern Minnesota's largest lake. It originally provided the only water-based recreational opportunities in the area; when other parks were established in that region, artificial lakes had to be created to provide such recreation. Not surprisingly, Lake Shetek's patronage has been largely regional — so much so that recommendations have been made that it be changed from a state park to a regional park. Yet, as an oasis in the prairie, it includes a biotic community quite different from that of the surrounding countryside. The trail that encircles Loon Island, the most popular hike in the park, affords a glimpse of hardwood forest far removed from its typical setting. Although development has been primarily along recreational lines, such trails and a seasonal naturalist program offer the interested park visitor more than just a place to boat and fish. The recreational and biological values of Lake Shetek State Park have far overshadowed its historic significance, which led to its establishment in the first place.[17]

## Charles A. Lindbergh

The 1931 session of the legislature established three "parks," only one of which is still called a state park. The first and most im-

*Swimming in Pike Creek, Charles A. Lindbergh State Park, about 1937*

portant of the three was created to preserve the boyhood home and farm of the famous flier Charles A. Lindbergh, Jr. His father had acquired 110.42 acres of land on the west bank of the Mississippi south of Little Falls, in central Minnesota, in 1898. A few years later he built a large house, which burned in 1905 and was replaced by a smaller dwelling the next year. Since Charles A. Lindbergh, Sr., served in the U.S. House of Representatives from 1907 until 1917 (after his unsuccessful 1916 campaign for the Senate), the family spent most of the year in Washington and used the farm only during the summers. In his later teens the younger Lindbergh tried farming the land for a couple of years but abandoned the effort and entered the University of Wisconsin. Thereafter, to all practical purposes, the place was unoccupied, especially after the father's death in 1924.[18]

In May 1927 Charles A. Lindbergh, Jr., flew the *Spirit of St. Louis* from New York to Paris and became a national hero. Souvenir hunters then descended upon the house and left it a "wreck," in the words of the first superintendent of the park. Local people, wishing to preserve what was left of the house, prevailed upon the family to offer it and the farm to any agency willing and able to care for it. On January 15, 1931, Christian Rosenmeier of Little Falls introduced a bill in the state senate, authorizing the state auditor to accept the gift of the Lindbergh estate and to designate it as Charles A. Lindbergh State Park. The bill passed the senate with only one dissenting vote, and after passage by the house it was signed into law on March 12 by Governor Floyd B. Olson. An appropriation of $5,000 was included for repairs to the buildings and grounds and for their subsequent maintenance.[19]

By the end of September of the same year Superintendent Martin A. Engstrom had spent $3,235 of the appropriation in carrying out the necessary repairs. Later in the decade the Minnesota Historical Society, with the aid of WPA labor, continued the work of restoration. The Lindbergh family generously contributed furniture and other articles, some of which had once been in the house or its predecessor. The house and the immediate grounds, which are the main attraction of the park, were transferred to the Minnesota Historical Society in 1969, and an interpretive center was opened in 1973 adjacent to the main building. Lindbergh was guest speaker at the dedication.[20]

The rest of the park is essentially like any other small state park. A bridge over Pike Creek has been built to replace one constructed by the youthful Lindbergh during his years on the farm, but otherwise there are few reminders of the family in the area that remains under the jurisdiction of the parks division. A campground and a picnic area serve the public, and there are hiking trails through the woodlands that occupy most of the park. It, like Fort Ridgely, is basically a historic site rather than a natural or recreational park.

## *Chippewa Mission, Inspiration Peak, and Old Crossing Treaty*

The second unit added to the park system in 1931 embraced one of the state's major historic sites, the Williamson mission at the foot of Lac qui Parle in western Minnesota. Nearly a century earlier, in 1835, Dr. Thomas S. Williamson, a Presbyterian minister and practicing physician, opened a mission to the Dakota at the point where the Minnesota River flows out of the lake. For the next eleven years he and other missionaries labored at this remote outpost, protected and assisted by Joseph Renville, mixed-blood trader with the American Fur Company. After the missionaries' departure following Renville's death in 1846, the mission buildings fell into disrepair and ultimately vanished. In 1910 a missionary society from Montevideo placed a marker on the site, but nothing else was done then.[21]

On March 13, 1931, Nels A. Pederson of Milan introduced a bill in the Minnesota senate calling for the establishment of a "Lac-qui-Parle Mission Park." The bill did not pass, but it was revived as part of the general appropriations act for that year. The legislature provided $2,000 for the acquisition of the necessary land and appointed a commission made up of the state auditor, Jacob F. Jacobson of Madison, and Oluf Gjerset of Montevideo to obtain title to it by negotiation or condemnation. Unfortunately, in the shuffle the name of the park had been altered to Chippewa–Lac qui Parle Indian Mission Park, apparently in deference to the wishes of the people of Chippewa County, in which the site was located. The result has been misleading, especially when the name was shortened to Chippewa Mission Memorial State Wayside, since it suggested that the Indians among whom the missionaries worked were Ojibway (Chippewa) rather than Dakota.[22]

After the first 17 acres of land had been acquired, limited development of the site commenced. From 1934 through 1939 the legislature provided $500 annually for maintenance, and a small picnic area was created. Archaeological work begun in 1940 under the auspices of the WPA, the Chippewa County Historical Society, and the Minnesota Historical Society revealed the locations of the chapel, built in 1841, and of most of the missionaries' houses, and these sites were appropriately marked. In 1941 the state acquired 2.2 acres, including the site of Renville's trading post. In 1941–42 the county historical society, with the help of state funds and WPA labor, built a reproduction of the original mission, as accurately as circumstances and the limited knowledge available permitted. The reconstructed mission, dedicated on July 12, 1942, serves mainly as a repository for artifacts representative of the mission and early settler period.[23]

By the 1940s a 438-acre recreation area had been developed on the opposite side of Lac qui Parle, and the original park came to be a kind of satellite to the larger unit, though most parks division publications continued to list it separately, as a wayside. In 1973 the wayside and the Renville fort site were transferred to the Minnesota Historical Society, while the recreation area (discussed in chapter five) continued under the jurisdiction of the parks and recreation division. The historical society moved the artifacts from the reconstructed mission to safer storage and installed new exhibits; its long-range plans call for a fully developed interpretive program to emphasize the role of the early missionary activities in Minnesota's history. No better location could be found for such a project than the site of the Lac qui Parle mission, where the first church bell in Minnesota is supposed to have rung. The original bell, cracked during its years of service, is preserved in the reconstructed mission.[24]

The third park created by the 1931 legislature was of scenic rather than historic interest. On March 20 state Senator Edward D. Smith of Glenwood introduced a bill calling for the establishment of "a new state park" and the appropriation of money for that purpose. The bill, which was passed by the senate but was not acted on by the house, was ultimately embodied in the appropriations act, which referred to "Inspiration Peak Park" and provided the sum of $2,000 for the purchase of 82 acres of land — an 80-acre tract and a narrow strip containing an access road.[25]

This newest acquisition of the state park system consisted of a densely wooded area in Otter Tail County, in west-central Minnesota. Its most prominent feature was a hill, somewhat higher than Mount Tom in Sibley State Park and nearly three hundred feet above the surrounding countryside. From this elevation parts of three counties could be seen, a vista of lakes and farmlands. Part of the glacial moraine called the Leaf Hills, the hill itself was in Leaf Mountain Township; but it had long been known simply as Inspiration Peak. The idea of making it into a park dated back to the early 1920s. Once the legislation had been passed, people began using the land as a public picnic area, even though it was not formally conveyed to the state until August 11, 1932.[26]

As Conzet wrote to conservation commissioner William Cox, Inspiration Peak had no great merit as a park, but he thought that it would serve as a good public camping place. The 1933 and 1935 legislatures appropriated $750 for the 1934 fiscal year, $300 for fiscal 1935, and $250 for each of the following years. With these modest sums, the conservation department put in a water supply, toilets, picnic tables, and fireplaces, and later added a picnic shelter; trails to the summit apparently already existed. Although other projects were proposed, they were not carried out, except for a parking lot. Facilities were fairly spartan at first. In the spring of 1935 Conzet's assistant, Harold Ostergaard, wrote the caretaker, "I believe it is unwise to purchase toilet paper and suggest that you supply some newspaper instead." Garbage cans should be bought, however; they would probably be stolen, but they could be replaced for a little more than a dollar. In his report for 1936, parks director Lathrop observed that Inspiration Peak was not extensively used. Although he attributed the lack of use to the constricted space available for picnicking, the park's remote location may have been as much of a factor. No large towns were nearby, and Lake Carlos State Park, established in the middle 1930s, proved a more attractive setting for picnics and other outdoor activities.[27]

Although Inspiration Peak State Wayside, as it is now designated, remains one of the system's least known and least visited units — a candidate for transfer to the county — it is not altogether unworthy of potential state park status. The hardwood forest and "goat prairies" that cover the slopes of the peak are botanically significant, including, among other trees, the northern pin oak, or jack oak. Moreover, it is surrounded by wooded countryside and many lakes. Like virtually every other unit in the park system, it is, in the final analysis, a unique biotic unit and ought to be preserved by an agency competent to give it the necessary protection.

Although not established by the legislature, another unit of the park system had its origins in 1931. Old Crossing Treaty Historic Wayside, located in Red Lake County, in northwestern Minnesota, was a historically significant site for two reasons: first, one of the early oxcart trails from St. Paul to Winnipeg crossed the Red Lake River there; second, in 1863 whites and Ojibways negotiated a treaty there by which the United States obtained much of northwestern Minnesota and part of eastern North Dakota. As early as 1914 local authorities had acquired the site, and in 1931 the Red Lake County Board presented 6 acres to the state. With the aid of a congressional appropriation, a statue of an Ojibway was erected as a monument and was dedicated on June 25, 1933. A picnic area

*A Minnesota Historical Society tour group at Old Crossing Treaty Historic Wayside, 1955*

already existed, and, although the legislature neglected to appropriate any funds for maintenance or improvement, National Youth Administration labor was employed to clean up and generally develop the site.[28]

Old Crossing Treaty was greatly enlarged in 1947, when more than 100 acres were added, to bring the total area to 111 acres, later increased to 122 acres. It remained off the beaten path, however, and despite its historic importance it received comparatively few visitors. In 1987 the legislature formally abolished the wayside and divided the land, like Traverse des Sioux, among three agencies. Red Lake County acquired 35 acres for use as a county park; the University of Minnesota Technical College, Crookston, received 28.5 acres; and the rest was made part of the adjacent Huot Wildlife Management Area.[29]

---

## Kaplan Woods

No new parks emerged from the 1933 session of the legislature, but two years later the system was enlarged by the addition of Kaplan Woods State Park, a 180-acre tract of hardwood forest in Steele County, in south-central Minnesota. Located on the south edge of Owatonna, the area included a stretch of the Straight River and several tributary streams, which made for rather varied topography in a landscape otherwise characterized mainly by level prairies. The Kaplan family, prominent in the city's business life, had owned and preserved the woods, which had received some local recreational use. The legislature now appropriated $16,000 for the purchase of the tract. Despite the unsatisfactory results such provisions had produced in the cases of Sibley and Lake Bemidji state parks, the act contained the condition that the park should be forever maintained by Steele County, "and no request for additional funds from the state shall be made."[30]

As might have been predicted, the county offered no financial aid for the development of the parks during the depression years, and Kaplan Woods remained undeveloped for several years. By the time of the parks director's fifth biennial report in 1940, however, the state had put in a well and some picnic tables and had laid out trails through the woods. A parking area, latrines, expansion of the picnic area, and reforestation were on the docket for future action. Most of these projects were carried out, but that is as far as development of the park ever went. In 1946 retiring parks director Lathrop wrote his successor that it was used mainly for picnicking, though now and then someone camped there.[31]

Kaplan Woods remained part of the state park system for less than thirty years. Besides its proximity to Owatonna, which gave it some of the characteristics of a city park, its integrity was impaired by the construction of a four-lane highway designed to bypass Owatonna on the south. In 1963 Kaplan Woods was, by act of the legislature, transferred to the city. Although it was not truly of state park quality, it is unfortunate that Kaplan Woods could not in some way have been protected by a state agency. Today it is a good example of a wooded area, on the edge of a city, that is essentially unprotected. Although it no longer has picnic facilities, it is heavily used by local people, and there has been a proliferation of trails that have largely spoiled the semiwilderness quality of the area.[32]

## *Other Proposals*

Between 1925 and 1935, other parks were proposed but did not survive the legislative winnowing. In 1925 and 1927 the earlier Carlton Lake proposal was revived but did not receive favorable action. Since the site was in Chippewa County, and since the partisans of a park in that county received recognition in the establishment of the Lac qui Parle Mission Park in 1931, nothing further was heard about Carlton Lake. A bill for the establishment of a park in Crow Wing County was introduced in the 1925 session, and the old Mille Lacs Lake proposal was advanced in both 1927 and 1929. All of these efforts failed.[33]

In 1927 an Ignatius Donnelly Memorial Park was proposed but not passed. If the park was intended to include the old home of Donnelly, one of Minnesota's most colorful political figures, it is unfortunate that the bill failed of passage. Years later the house was razed, over the protests of many history-minded Minnesotans; if it had been in a state park, it would almost certainly have been preserved. Also in 1927, Herbert Garvin, who had donated the area that became Garvin Heights State Park, gave the state another tract of land near the headwaters of Garvin Brook, in Winona County. Although a joint resolution accepting the donation was passed by both houses and signed by Governor Theodore Christianson, for some obscure reason the proposed state park was never formally established.[34]

And then there was "Pipestone State Park." An area of more than statewide significance, Pipestone had first been suggested as a national park about 1890. As the site where Indians had quarried stone for their ceremonial pipes from time immemorial, it had received publicity in Henry Wadsworth Longfellow's *The Song of Hiawatha*, and a body of legend had grown up about it. The Yankton Dakota, who had been the last to use the quarries extensively, claimed title to the land; the federal government opened an Indian school there in 1893 but did not settle the Yanktons' claim until 1929. In the meantime white squatters had settled on some of the land, a railroad had been built across it, and the city of Pipestone had launched a move to create a city park out of part of it.[35]

City officials in 1923 and 1924 had recommended establishing a state park, and in January 1925 identical bills were introduced in the state senate and house. The bill, as it finally emerged, called for the establishment of Pipestone State Park out of such land in a specified section as the state already owned or might acquire from the United States, which was assumed to have title to the reservation claimed by the Dakota. Apparently a tract was acquired that included a small lake, Winnewissa Falls, and the rock on which John C. Frémont and others had carved their names in 1838. The 1927 *Legislative Manual* spoke of "Pipestone State Park, so called," as "a tract of 22 acres . . . which Congress will be asked to set aside for a park to perpetuate the historical points therein contained."[36]

"Pipestone State Park," though mentioned in successive *Legislative Manuals*, never had any existence as an actual state park. After the Yankton title was extinguished in 1929, following protracted litigation, efforts were made over a period of years to have the area declared a national park. Finally, in 1937, Congress passed a bill creating a national monument, and on August 25 of that year Pipestone National Monument came into being.[37]

## Summary

At the same time that the park system was undergoing major administrative changes and new units were being added, a more sophisticated view of what a state park ought to be was evolving. It would be unfair as well as inaccurate to assert that no one in earlier decades had given any thought to this question. The arguments of Newton Winchell and Jacob Brower in favor of the preservation of Itasca would belie such a claim. And State Auditor Chase in his statement to the 1923 legislature had set forth some criteria that were in advance of most thinking at that time. But it is nevertheless true that most people, including many who were intimately associated with the parks, saw them almost exclusively as playgrounds and made no distinction between city and state parks in this respect. Such a view is implied by the types of areas proposed for inclusion in the system, and it is clearly evident in the kind of development favored for the parks that had been established.

In the late 1920s and early 1930s, however, a more enlightened view began to be voiced occasionally. Two statements, one by a man outside the administrative system of the parks, the other by one within the system, can be cited to show the altered point of view that was emerging. In 1927, when confronted by the proposed budget for the development of Sleepy Eye State Park, State Comptroller Henry Rines expressed his disapproval of the plans that had been drawn up. His comment on the general subject of what a state park should be deserves to be quoted at length:

> There should be a distinct difference between the manner of improving state parks and those maintained by cities and villages. It is perfectly proper to beautify local parks by the planting of shrubbery, flower beds, etc., but it is our view that the legislature had a different purpose in view when it acquired the state parks. It was to preserve and perpetuate certain historic and scenic spots in their natural state. For that reason state parks should be kept as nature made [them] in so far as it is practicable to do so.[38]

Although one may question Rines's interpretation of the legislature's purposes in establishing the parks, his distinction between city and state parks points ahead to the modern view of state parks as natural sanctuaries as well as, or even instead of, playgrounds.

Similar sentiments are found in a remark by Alfred Nelson, a public relations assistant for the Department of Forestry and Fire Prevention, less than three years later. After listing certain parks that he thought ought to be transferred to the cities whose residents were their principal users, he added, "The state parks should be places of outstanding scenery, of historical interest or unique attraction that cannot be duplicated elsewhere. The primary attraction or reason for people visiting the park should not be because there is a baseball field, tennis court, or golf course there." Noteworthy here is Nelson's belief that each park should have something unique about it, some feature that could not be found in any other park. Years later, after much discussion and experimentation, this idea was to reassert itself in the concept that each park ought to represent a particular landscape type (later called a biocultural region), so that the system as a whole could encompass all the state's landscape regions.[39]

The people of Minnesota were not ready for such advanced ideas in 1930, but in the following decade, as the NPS came to be involved in park planning, the people responsible for developing existing parks and establishing new ones started thinking in different terms. No longer confined to private correspondence, the ideas found expression in published programs, where they were presented in far greater detail. The result was that in the last half of the decade of the 1930s Minnesota came to have a true park system, with a rationale governing the acquisition and development of the units that composed that system. A decade of marking time had ended in 1935; a shorter period of tremendous growth had begun.

CHAPTER FIVE

# *Professionalism and Expansion*
# *1935-1945*

EVEN BEFORE the Minnesota legislature created the Division of State Parks in 1935, the state had begun to benefit from the federal government's efforts to provide work for the unemployed. As early as June 1933, the Emergency Conservation Work program, predecessor to the CCC, was launched with the establishment of three ECW camps. Two more were added in April 1934. In July of that year a supervisor of state park ECW was appointed, and five more camps were allotted to Minnesota. By April 1935 the state had fifteen such camps operating: nine in state parks, three in highway waysides, two in city-owned areas, and one in a federal recreation area.[1]

Although the number of ECW camps fluctuated from year to year and was soon cut nearly in half, several projects were also initiated under the Federal Emergency Relief Administration and later taken over by the WPA. Initially, five transient camps were assigned to the parks division, with National Park Service personnel providing technical supervision. Although some of these were closed in the next few years, others were established, so that nearly all the existing parks benefited and several new parks were created.[2]

The state and federal governments cooperated closely in the management of these programs. The 1925 reorganization of state government had set up the Executive Council, consisting of the governor, the attorney general, the state auditor, the treasurer, and the secretary of state. In the 1930s this body allocated state funds for the purchase of lands, which were then developed by the federal relief agencies. The state's monetary contribution was normally much smaller than the federal government's.[3]

Besides money, the federal government provided advice and expertise. In 1934 President Franklin D. Roosevelt appointed a National Resources Board (NRB) to study the nation's recreational needs, including existing and potential park areas. In its report the NRB proposed working definitions of state parks, state recreational reserves, state monuments, and state waysides, and thus laid the groundwork for a system of classifying the various units administered by the parks division. The report stressed that a large portion of every park should be left in its natural condition, with cleanup restricted to areas where disease or insect infestation existed. According to the NRB criteria, Minnesota should have had from 100,000 to 120,000 acres of parkland. The state's acreage as of July 1, 1934, was 38,519.90.[4]

Some of the NRB's recommendations proved impracticable to implement. For example, the report had stated that "since use and enjoyment of state parks, monuments and recreation reserves is not and probably never will be on such a completely equitable basis as to provide actual equality of opportunity for all the people, it is recommended that a part of their cost of operation be borne by those who use them, through payment of reasonable fees." In line with this suggestion, in March 1935 the Conservation Commission adopted a resolution setting up a fee system: a parking charge of 25¢ a day for Saturdays, Sundays, and holidays in the ten largest parks, 25¢ a day for camping, and 25¢ a day for each boat used in a park, together with various charges for the operation of refectories, commissaries, and concessions. So much opposition developed to the parking fees, mainly from residents of nearby communities, that this part of the fee system had to be rescinded in all but one park, for which the legislature had made no appropriation.[5]

The people in the parks division agreed with the NRB report that Minnesota had insufficient space devoted to parks. Moreover, the parks people believed that the existing parks were badly distributed geographically. The apparent consensus was that forty miles was the maximum distance a Minnesotan should have to travel to reach a park. It was true that 1.5 million of the state's roughly 2.6 million inhabitants lived within forty miles of a park.

But the only one that close to the Twin Cities was Interstate, small, heavily used, and in some respects fragile. As noted in chapter four, several other regions of the state were inadequately provided with parks. The obvious solution was to expand existing parks and establish new ones, giving special attention to those areas of the state where people had to drive more than forty miles to reach a state park.[6]

---

## Camden

The first of the new parks to be formally established was Camden, in southwestern Minnesota. In Lyon County the level or gently rolling prairie, intensively cultivated, is gashed by the Redwood River, whose wooded valley lies 150 feet or more below the enclosing hills. Like three other major southwestern Minnesota rivers, the Lac qui Parle, the Yellow Medicine, and the Cottonwood — each of which now flows through a state park — the Redwood begins on the Coteau des Prairies, the divide separating the Missouri River drainage from the Mississippi drainage system. To Indians and white settlers alike, this spot on the upper reaches of the Redwood was a place of refuge, providing three necessities: wood, water, and shelter. The Eastern Dakota had long camped there in winter, after hunting buffalo and pronghorn on the open prairies during the warmer months. There is evidence of three semipermanent villages within the park.[7]

The first Europeans to use the Camden Woods, as they came to be called, were fur traders and explorers. After the treaties of Traverse des Sioux and Mendota had been signed and the Dakota were confined to a reservation along the Minnesota River, James W. Lynd in 1855 opened a trading post in a log building, located not far west of the present swimming pool. White settlement did not begin in earnest until after the Dakota War of 1862. Three successive towns named Lynd were started, and in 1874 the village of Camden was laid out within the present park boundaries. The Marshall newspaper, the *Prairie Schooner*, described Camden in December of that year: "It is snugly tucked away between two ranges of hills which afford a safe retreat from the winds of winter, and furnish beautiful and refreshing scenery during other portions

*Parking lot, Camden State Park, about 1934*

of the year." It had a short career. When the railroad came through
in 1888 and located its depot at the third and final Lynd, Camden
faded away.[8]

The Camden Woods remained an important source of wood for
the farmers on the surrounding prairie and provided a popular picnic spot for them and for residents of the nearby villages. Interest
in developing the wooded area as a public park began about 1920,
and in the mid-1920s State Auditor Ray Chase investigated the site
and recommended its acquisition. Governor Theodore Christianson was said to favor the project, but since he had been elected on
an economy platform, he was unwilling to recommend any action
that would necessitate expenditures by the state. About 1930 the

Camden Park Association was organized by several prominent citizens of Marshall, Lynd, and other towns in the vicinity.[9]

In the early 1930s the construction of a new highway southwest from Marshall, together with government efforts to relieve unemployment, led to a revival of interest in the park idea. The local association issued an appeal to the conservation commission in 1932, and early the next year Joseph W. Whitney, a Marshall newspaperman and sparkplug of the group, invited Grover Conzet to visit the site. His invitation led to visits over the next two years by Harold Ostergaard, a member of Conzet's staff; Reuben A. Skogland, an NPS landscape architect; E. V. Willard, the conservation commissioner; and Harold Lathrop, soon to be named the director of parks. All were impressed by the area's park potential. They may also have been influenced by the infectious enthusiasm of Whitney, who wrote in the *Marshall Messenger:* "Very few people of this section realize the beauty of this new park, for it has not been readily accessible from roads and only those who are venturesome enough to climb and scale wire fences, have gained the edges of this three hundred foot [*sic*] chasm to gaze at its vastness of beauty."[10]

The executive council bought 469.96 acres of land in the heart of what is now Camden State Park, and in the summer of 1934 an ECW camp composed of World War I veterans was placed there. The men worked under army supervision, with technical assistance provided by the NPS. Between July 1934 and December 1936 the men removed thousands of dead and damaged trees. The master plan called for construction of a custodian's cabin, a warehouse and garage, a picnic shelter, a refectory, a bathhouse, several modern sanitation buildings, and two water systems. The program also called for laying out several miles of hiking trails and replanting the cutover areas. Local people donated many young trees for the reforestation project.[11]

Most of the planned improvements were completed on schedule, and the park, which had been formally established in 1935, was heavily used long before the work was finished. On a single day, July 4, 1936, more than 6,000 people had entered the park gates by 3:00 P.M. Over the next few years further construction was carried on by the WPA, which continued its work almost up to the eve of World War II. By that time the park had (besides the facilities already mentioned) a group camp with mess hall and crafts building, a lifeguard cabin, an icehouse-woodshed, a couple of bridges, and several parking areas. Much of the physical plant provided by the work-relief programs remains in use, though it has deteriorated with the passage of time.[12]

Located in a narrow valley, Camden has been subject to occasional flooding, especially in June 1957, July 1969, and June 1977. Damage by the 1969 storms raised questions about the future of the park, over half of which was unusable after the road had been washed out. By that time expansions in 1963, 1965, and 1967 had more than tripled the park's original area, though much of the newly authorized land was still in private ownership. The original park had been confined to parts of one section in Lynd Township and two in Lyons Township, all in the valley of the Redwood River. The proposed additions would bring into the park a great deal of upland prairie, desirable partly because a buffer was needed between adjacent farms and the park proper and partly because the prairie environment had intrinsic merits.[13]

Although Camden grew in size during the 1960s, its status as a state park was questioned early in the next decade. In 1971 a mass of data on the various units in the state park system was collected and subjected to computer analysis. The result, called Project 80, recommended reducing the number of state parks to twenty and reclassifying the other units, some of which would be turned over to local or regional agencies. Camden, it was decided, was not truly of statewide significance and, like many other units, ought not to be retained as a full-fledged member of the system. Despite disclaimers from the parks division, whose personnel disagreed with much of Project 80, many supporters of Camden feared that the park was about to be transferred to the county, whether or not the county wanted that responsibility.[14]

To forestall such an eventuality, Camden's users in Lyon County and elsewhere deluged the parks division and local newspapers with letters, demanding that the state retain control of the park. The Marshall city council passed a resolution on May 1, 1972, "strenuously opposing" the transfer of the park to the county "as being detrimental to the taxpayers of Lyon County." U. W. Hella, then director of the parks division, assured the mayor of Marshall that any change would have to be authorized by the legislature, adding: "I believe that the park is worthy of its present state park classification and . . . a responsibility of the state."[15]

Camden weathered this storm, and a bill embodying much of the substance of Project 80 was defeated in the 1973 legislature. By 1975 the state had invested in a new park entrance and other improvements, and local people were inclined to think the danger was over. Their confidence was not shared, however, by everyone in the vicinity. Camden was vulnerable to the charge of being used chiefly by a local clientele. According to a 1974 park-user survey, out of nine parks in the southwestern region, Camden had the highest proportion of visitors — 81 percent — from within a fifty-mile radius. Gone were the days when park planners thought there should be a park within forty or even thirty miles of every citizen! To deserve *state* park status, a park had to draw visitors from outside its locality, preferably from outside the state.[16]

Visitation statistics do not, of course, tell the whole story of a park's importance. In the case of Camden, its special merits warranted continued state management. In 1971 a joint survey by the Minnesota Academy of Science and The Nature Conservancy concluded that Camden was of scientific interest chiefly because it contained one of the westernmost natural occurrences of the sugar maple in North America — a phenomenon that gave it more brilliant autumn color than is to be found for many miles around. It also contained 70 acres of unbroken grassland, which, though not the best surviving prairie in Lyon County, was at that time by far the largest, with only two others approaching it in size.[17]

Camden's standing as a state park came through another close examination in 1977. As required by the Outdoor Recreation Act of 1975, a management plan for Camden was submitted to the public at a series of hearings. It was classified as a natural state park, meaning that its development would emphasize its natural values rather than its recreational potential, though it would continue to be used for recreation as well.[18]

Several problems remained to plague Camden State Park, however. One of these, lack of a convenient entrance, was remedied in 1975 with construction of a new entrance road leading directly off Trunk Highway 23. With the addition more recently of a contact station and an impressive entrance sign, the new approach to the park is a vast improvement over the old. The most serious remaining problem is the presence of an active railroad line extending the length of the park (which even with recent additions is relatively long and narrow), following the course of the Redwood River. Although the dangers of a grade crossing have been eliminated by means of an overpass on the new entrance road, park users still have to put up with freight trains passing through at all hours of the day and night.

Since the campground at Camden was crowded and the site had been in use too long, a new campground was constructed in the early 1980s near the south end of the park. A combination interpretive and trail center is planned, together with a new group campground and another for horseback riders. Changes in the trail system take place almost constantly, in order to give heavily used trails a chance to recover.[19]

Camden is a good park, one well worth keeping in the state's system. Like their predecessors, travelers crossing the plains of southwestern Minnesota today find welcome relief in this oasis on the Redwood. Besides the river itself, almost the only trout stream in that part of the state, the park has several intermittent streams, one of which is dammed to create the swimming pool. In a year of normal or above-normal rainfall, hikers can follow a rushing stream up to the overlook called Sioux Lookout and imagine they are somewhere in the Southern Appalachians. Camden is primarily a summer park, but a visit in late September or October can be rewarding for the striking colors. And in recent years, it has been receiving heavy winter use, mainly by cross-country skiers. The decision to establish a park here, though motivated in part by economic considerations unrelated to its natural beauty, was a wise one; the development since then has been, on the whole, enlightened. With careful management in the future, Camden can continue to serve the people of southwestern Minnesota and also to attract visitors from elsewhere.

## Gooseberry Falls

At almost the same time that Camden was being developed, another park was taking shape in the opposite corner of the state, along the North Shore of Lake Superior. So long as the North Shore

*Gooseberry Falls State Park, about 1955*

was relatively inaccessible, its lack of parks was not serious. With the construction of U.S. Highway 61 in the mid-1920s, however, interest began to develop in this most scenic region of Minnesota. The first park to be established on the North Shore was Gooseberry Falls, embracing the lower reaches of the Gooseberry River, where the stream plunges more than a hundred feet in a series of waterfalls.

A French map dating from 1670 shows a "Rivière des Groseilliers," which may have been named for Médard Chouart, sieur des Groseilliers, who, with his companion, Pierre Esprit, sieur de

Radisson, explored the western end of Lake Superior about a decade earlier. The name, translated into English as "Gooseberries," had become firmly attached to the river by the early nineteenth century, when Major Stephen H. Long, Joseph N. Nicollet, and other explorers referred to it. In 1870 a photographer from Ishpeming, Michigan, toured the North Shore in a sailboat and took several pictures of the region around the mouth of the Gooseberry. Late in the century it became known to well-to-do fishermen, who found good fishing in this almost untouched stream.[20]

After some sporadic logging in the 1880s, the Gooseberry drainage basin attracted serious attention from lumber companies in the following decade. Several exploited the timber resources of the region and built logging railroads into the interior, so that pine logs could be hauled to the lakeshore and then rafted to Ashland, Wisconsin, and Baraga, Michigan. One entrepreneur, Joe Pernoval, is credited with getting out many million feet of square timbers and logs in the years 1900 to 1906. By the early 1920s most of the timber was gone, and with it the loggers, and the area around the Gooseberry was just another tract of cutover land.[21]

In 1933 the Conservation Commission and the state Department of Highways jointly acquired 637.83 acres of land, including the lower stretch of the river and its major waterfalls. The highway department primarily needed a right-of-way for improvements on U.S. Highway 61, while the Conservation Commission at that time wanted to establish a "scenic game preserve." Representatives of the NPS recognized the park potential of this tract of land, however, and an ECW camp was moved in during the spring of 1934. The camp was closed on September 30, but by then a second one had been operating for nearly two months. From then until 1942, some kind of work-relief camp was maintained at Gooseberry Falls, and much of the construction still in evidence at the park was carried out.[22]

Private enterprise had anticipated the government's activity. A concessionaire had held a lease for several years and had built a few tourist cabins, which were not wholly in keeping with the development plan envisaged by the NPS people. Particularly offensive were a couple of diners in old streetcars, which were eventually removed. Long before that, laborers had begun laying out four miles of hiking trails and a mile of park road. By the end of 1936 Gooseberry Falls was a well-equipped state park (though not yet one in name): besides a custodian's cabin, it boasted a complete picnic ground, a parking area, a water supply, toilets, a kitchen shelter, and a refectory. Over the next few years concourses were laid out at both ends of the highway bridge, the picnic area was enlarged, and a campground was added, complete with a kitchen shelter, showers, and laundry facilities.[23]

Since Gooseberry Falls received no legislative appropriations, the fee system that had been initiated in 1935 and abandoned almost everywhere else was continued there. It appears that for a time the state operated the refectory, and profits from the enterprise helped defray costs of the park. But in 1940 apparently a private party operated the refectory. By then development of the park was virtually complete; among the recent undertakings were realignment of the park road and a certain amount of landscaping.[24]

Gooseberry Falls met all the requirements for state park status, and it was incorporated into the system as part of omnibus legislation signed into law April 26, 1937. This law established ten new parks, all of them developed over the previous two or three years by CCC and WPA labor under NPS supervision. The law lists the other nine parks in alphabetical order, with Gooseberry Falls tacked on at the end, suggesting that Gooseberry Falls was an afterthought or that in its inception and growth it had been somewhat different from the others.[25]

The subsequent history of Gooseberry Falls has been largely uneventful. It remained its original size until 1955, when 2.6 acres were added. Then in 1967, during the massive parks expansion of that decade, an addition of 920 acres more than doubled its size. A smaller addition, somewhat over 100 acres, was authorized in 1971. All but an insignificant part of the park is in state ownership, so development of such features as winter trails has proceeded without the delays suffered by parks whose statutory boundaries included privately held land. Another kind of problem threatened late in 1972, however, when Lake County proposed to relocate three solid-waste disposal sites on land within the park boundaries. The next year the county board of commissioners and the county zoning and planning office ruled out these sites because of unfavorable soil conditions and "because of [their] proximity to the park."[26]

The main problem Gooseberry Falls faces today is the same one that has plagued it throughout its history: it is too popular. For years it was the only state park on the North Shore, and even now it is the first one travelers encounter in driving northeast from Duluth on U.S. Highway 61. Its campgrounds are always crowded in summer, and there is a continual traffic problem near the park, as motorists decide to break their drive at a place with memorable scenery. In seasons of good rainfall the falls of the Gooseberry are impressive, as the water cascades over huge ancient rocks before entering Lake Superior. The Gooseberry is one of the smaller streams along this shoreline, however, draining an area of only 97 square miles (as compared to the Brule's 282 square miles) and losing much of its water by seepage into the bedrock before it reaches the park.[27]

This park of 1,662 acres offers more to see than the waterfalls immediately below and above the highway bridge. A trail system penetrates an extensive backcountry, where the venturesome hiker may encounter deer, bears, woodchucks, raccoons, snowshoe hares, beavers, ruffed grouse, loons, pileated woodpeckers, and other wildlife. Along the lake shore are gulls, mergansers, and other waterbirds. For those unwilling to hike considerable distances over rugged terrain, Gooseberry Falls offers more readily accessible attractions than the other major North Shore parks, newer and larger though they may be. Whatever one's tastes, Gooseberry Falls State Park provides something of interest.

## Flandrau

Another park given official standing by the 1937 omnibus legislation was Flandrau, originally called Cottonwood River. As a site for work-relief activities, 836.48 acres on the outskirts of New Ulm were purchased by the state's Executive Council. Between the wooded bluffs lay an expanse of low "wasteland," occasionally inundated by the river, here very close to its confluence with the Minnesota. Throughout the 1920s there had been talk of flood-control measures, including possibly a dam on the Minnesota just above the mouth of the Cottonwood. When the idea resurfaced in the early

1930s, it included a dam on the Cottonwood. Although the main objective was still flood control, the plan also called for development of water-related recreational facilities near the shoreline of the artificial lake that would be created. Such facilities might at least partly replace those on the natural lakes that had dried up or receded in the drought years.[28]

In 1935 a group of World War I veterans arrived, to be replaced the following year by a CCC camp, which stayed until 1942; a transient (WPA) camp was located in a secluded area south of the river. The dam was completed early in 1937, and a 209-acre lake soon took shape behind it. Simultaneously with its construction came a water system and a camp entrance road; soon afterward followed a combination bathhouse-refectory-picnic shelter, a parking lot, a picnic area, a beach, a boat dock, and other facilities. By the end of the 1930s all the usual appurtenances of a state park were in evidence, and the new park was drawing a large, if chiefly local clientele.[29]

Although "Cottonwood River" was an appropriate name for the park, sentiment developed in favor of renaming it to honor one of Minnesota's illustrious pioneers, Charles E. Flandrau. A New Yorker by birth, Flandrau arrived in Minnesota in 1853 and set up as a lawyer, first in St. Paul and later at Traverse des Sioux, where he built a fine house. He served briefly as government agent to the Dakota and then was appointed to the territorial supreme court. While serving in the latter capacity he presided over the first term of court held in Brown County, of which New Ulm is the seat. A more significant tie with New Ulm was his service in organizing the town's defense during the Dakota War of 1862. On March 8, 1945, the park's name was officially changed to Flandrau State Park.[30]

From its beginning, Flandrau State Park has had two problems: it is too close to town and it is at the mercy of the Cottonwood River. Portions of the park lie within the city limits, and the rest is immediately adjacent to the city. Its geographical position therefore creates jurisdictional problems when the park manager or a park employee has to deal with an offense committed within the park — a situation of frequent occurrence in any park located so near a town or city. Moreover, because park use tends to be heavily local, questions have occasionally been raised about the legitimacy of its status as a state park.

Presumably the Cottonwood River occasionally overflowed its banks before the dam was built. It has done so several times since 1937, and on three occasions it has carried major portions of the dam with it. In July 1947 the north dike was washed out; it was reconstructed at considerable expense. In April 1965, when streams throughout Minnesota went on a rampage, part of the dam was again destroyed. Efforts to rebuild it were partially frustrated by difficulties in raising the necessary funds. On grounds that the dam had been built mainly for recreational purposes rather than for flood control, the federal authorities denied a request for $40,000. Despite considerable local sentiment in favor of rebuilding the dam to its original height, such state funds as became available were used to reconstruct it to a height four feet lower and to build a separate swimming pool — a suggestion made by parks director Hella.[31]

Then, on April 9, 1969, following "the heaviest snowfall in the history of the State . . . during the late winter months plus heavy rainfall immediately before and during the period of the disaster," the dam went out again, this time for good. After weighing the alternatives, Hella recommended that the dam not be rebuilt. Instead, he proposed removing all of the superstructure above the spillway, redesigning the river channel, and replanting the former lake bed to native cover. This is substantially what was done — and thereby the essential character of Flandrau State Park was changed. Originally oriented toward water-based recreation on a large artificial lake, it now has two swimming pools, one adjacent to the main picnic area, the other at the group camp on the south side of the river, inaccessible from the main part of the park. Flandrau is now primarily a picnic area for New Ulm people, a camping place for travelers on U.S. Highway 14, and a setting for some seven miles of hiking trails.[32]

These trails are perhaps Flandrau's most attractive feature now. The park staff designed a self-guiding nature trail called the Oxbow Crossing trail, which traverses portions of the former lake bed and what was once an island. Although vandalism has somewhat reduced its value, there is still much to be seen along this trail and those on the hillsides above. By following these hillsides far enough on the north side of the river, one will eventually emerge on a New Ulm street; indeed, some of the best overlooks are most readily accessible from the streets.

The south side of the park is less used, partly because the road leading to the group camp is usually closed and the gate padlocked. From near the group camp (which was used to house German prisoners of war in World War II), a fine trail formerly followed the bluff, at various levels, to the county road that marks the western edge of the park, affording an especially good view of the entire valley. In summer, when the leaves concealed buildings, scarcely anything of New Ulm was visible from this overlook, and it was easy to imagine that one was looking out over a wilderness valley. Unfortunately, portions of this trail were washed out in 1983, and the trail was closed; so far it has not been reopened.

## Blue Mounds

Together with the expansion of Lake Shetek State Park, the establishment of Camden and Flandrau relieved the dearth of parks in southwestern Minnesota. For people in the extreme southwestern corner, however, a more important event was the creation and development of what was at first called Mound Springs Recreational Reserve, located four miles north of Luverne, in Rock County.

The rock for which the county was named is a huge mass of Sioux quartzite that rises above the glacial till of which most of the surface is composed, to form a cliff a mile long and as much as one hundred feet high. This formation looked bluish to the early settlers, who named it Blue Mound. Because the soil on top of the "mound" is thin and littered with boulders, most of it has never been plowed. Thus it preserves a sizable fragment of the original prairie, with much of the native flora that has elsewhere been destroyed by farming.

Preservation of the prairie was not the main consideration that led to the establishment of the reserve, which became Blue Mounds State Park in 1961. Like the other parks created in the 1930s, it was intended to provide work for the unemployed and water-related recreation for people living in an area devoid of natural lakes. Although State Auditor Chase had recommended its inclusion in the park system as early as 1923, it was not until 1934 that a more effective attempt to preserve the area began. In May of that year mem-

*View from Blue Mounds State Park looking east, 1940*

bers of the conservation commission, at the invitation of state Senator Frank J. Sell, toured the vicinity. The next year they prevailed on the executive council to allocate $9,109 in Emergency Relief Administration funds for the purchase of 194.9 acres north of the mound proper. There, where a small stream called Mound Creek flowed over the red quartzite, two dams were built, impounding two artificial lakes, of 18 and 28 acres respectively.[33]

The early development of Mound Springs Recreational Reserve paralleled that of other parks established in the 1930s. WPA labor provided landscaping, picnic facilities, a parking area, toilets, a water supply, a beach and bathhouse, and the necessary service facilities. The original reserve embraced little more than the two lakes and a segment of the stream that passed through them, but with small additions in 1955 and 1961 and much larger ones in 1963 and 1965, the last some 1,100 acres, the park expanded southward to include the entire mound and a buffer to the east and south.[34]

When the 1965 additions were authorized, the statutory boundaries of the park included the home of Minnesota author Frederick Manfred, who had built a house on the rock overlooking Luverne and the lower country to the south. The state bought the land in 1972, intending to use the house as an interpretive center, but Manfred was permitted to occupy the property for another three years. No road connected the proposed interpretive center with the previously developed portion of the park, some two miles away across the mound. Manfred had reached the house from a county road by way of a narrow, primitive trail up the south face of the mound. It had given him plenty of trouble, he said; one winter he had to carry his food supplies up to the house from late December until near the end of April. He opposed widening the lane, however, because of the damage it would do to the mound.[35]

Local people were concerned about potential damage to the virgin prairie when, in June 1974, they learned that the park planners had surveyed a road across the top of the mound and driven stakes in along the route. A public meeting on July 17 drew about forty-five people, nearly all of whom opposed building the road. Both flora and fauna would be disturbed, they argued; prairie plants would be damaged, and several species of birds, uncommon elsewhere in the locality, would suffer from this intrusion on their home ground. According to Josephine Blanich, secretary of the Minnesota Ornithologists' Union, Henslow's sparrows, Smith's and chestnut-collared longspurs, Sprague's pipits, blue grosbeaks, and yellow-breasted chats were known to nest in the area. She thought that a road would give people too easy access to the prairie, to the detriment of the birds.[36]

Various solutions to the problem were offered. None met with general approval, however, and when the interpretive center was formally opened in July 1976, it still was not directly accessible from the main part of the park. The controversy surfaced again the next year, with another round of meetings at which sentiment was overwhelmingly against a road. The *Worthington Globe* cautioned against "fitting the park to the frame." The house might be gone in time, but the prairie could last forever. In the face of such determined opposition, the parks division announced in April 1977 that it had abandoned its plans for a road, at least for the time. An advisory committee of area residents would be formed to assist in drawing up a plan for the future of the park, and public hearings would be held before any final decisions were made. Finally, in 1986, a blacktop road was built, roughly paralleling Manfred's old track, leading in from the county road that forms the southern boundary of the park, leaving the interpretive center without direct access from the developed portion of the park.[37]

The center is accessible by trail, of course, as is every other major feature of the park. The most popular trail is a loop that circles the lakes, crossing on the lower dam and on a footbridge over Mound Creek above the upper lake. A much longer trail goes south from the developed area and makes a wide loop near the southern face of the mound, passing near the interpretive center along the way. It passes a fenced-in enclosure containing a small herd of bison. The nucleus of the herd, a bull and two cows, was obtained in November 1961 from the Fort Niobrara National Wildlife Refuge in Nebraska. In order to keep the herd to manageable size, excess animals are auctioned off periodically.[38]

Bison are appropriate residents at Blue Mounds, for according to tradition, the sheer cliff was used by Indians as a *pishkun*, or buffalo jump, as far back as prehistoric times, though archaeologists who conducted surveys in 1968 and 1969 found no surviving evidence of kills. Another feature of interest on the mound is a wall of stones extending for some 1,250 feet, presumably prehistoric in origin. Manfred has suggested that it might be a sort of American Stonehenge. He noted that the wall was lined up with the sun as seen at sunrise about the time of the vernal and autumnal equinoxes.[39]

When the Project 80 study was made, Blue Mounds was one of the twenty units in the system deemed worthy of continued state park status. It represented, better than any other park in the system, a particular landscape: the tallgrass prairie of southwestern Minnesota. With statutory boundaries now enclosing an area of 1,380 acres, Blue Mounds is not likely to undergo any extensive recreational development. Emphasis probably will be on preservation rather than on accessibility to the public. It is a good place to see such wildflowers as pasqueflowers, wild four-o'clocks, prairie smoke, wild roses, prairie clover, evening primrose, downy gentians, vervain, and a great variety of composites, including the compass plant and the rough blazing star. It is one of the few places in Minnesota where prickly pear and other cacti are found, and it is almost the only place in the state where one is likely to see a blue grosbeak.[40]

## Split Rock Creek, Monson Lake, and Pomme de Terre

The 1937 legislation brought into being three inferior parks, two of which are still members of the system. In the same manner and for much the same reasons as the Mound Springs Recreational Reserve was created, a similar outlet for relief labor was developed in Pipestone County, to the north of Rock. Near the village of Ihlen, the Executive Council purchased 227.64 acres of land on Split Rock Creek and set WPA labor to building a dam that would impound a 140-acre artificial lake. Unlike Mound Springs, however, this site had no special biological or geological features to justify its becoming a state park.[41]

Split Rock Recreational Reserve (renamed Split Rock Creek State Recreation Area in 1969) was developed in much the same manner as other parks started during the 1930s. It has not, however, been expanded or otherwise developed to any great extent since then. In fact, the parks division has sought its transfer to a local agency. Except for visitors to Pipestone National Monument, Split Rock Creek is used mainly by local people, who prefer to have it maintained by the state and have so far been able to head off any serious effort to transfer the area.[42]

A management plan drawn up in 1981 suggested that land be added, on which prairie vegetation might be restored. Some desire was also expressed for the acquisition of private land fronting the lake, so that a trail could be laid out to circle that body of water. Only a short trail exists now, along the west side of the lake, where both the campground and the picnic area are located. As a result of these proposals, the 1982 legislature authorized a small expansion along the eastern boundary. Although Split Rock Creek is, more than most other units of the system, essentially a human artifact rather than a natural setting in need of preservation, the recent expansion makes a transfer to a local unit of government unlikely.[43]

Another unit that the parks division has been trying to get rid of is Monson Lake State Park. Although it, too, is a product of the work-relief programs of the 1930s, its roots go back somewhat further. In 1927 the Lake Monson Memorial Association was organized to commemorate the killing of thirteen white settlers from the Swift-Kandiyohi counties area of west-central Minnesota during the Dakota War. After purchasing 2 acres of land, in 1935 the group appealed to the State Emergency Relief Administration to acquire a larger tract and establish a park. In response, the Executive Council bought 198.95 acres, including considerable frontage on Monson and West Sunburg lakes. After some delay owing to lack of funds, the usual facilities were eventually constructed.[44]

The Monson Lake project provided work for a few unemployed people, but the results of their work, which still constitute the core of the park's buildings, have never been given a great deal of use. As early as 1940 the conservation department reported that the park had been only partly maintained because of its limited use. Despite local sentiment in favor of expansion, the parks division has been markedly unenthusiastic about retaining the park. Legislation passed in 1965 provided for its transfer to a local agency, but such action has not been carried out. Monson Lake is a good place for a quiet picnic, a few hours of fishing, or a short hike on the mile or two of trails that extend from one lake to the other, but it is not really worthy of state park status.[45]

Recognizing the need for recreational facilities near the Stevens County seat of Morris, in west-central Minnesota, the Executive Council also acquired 363.51 acres of land on the Pomme de Terre River, employed WPA labor to construct a dam that impounded a lake of 120 acres, and thus created Pomme de Terre Recreational Reserve, which also received official standing in 1937. All the standard facilities were installed, plus a diving tower and an outdoor amphitheater. As at Split Rock Creek, the landscape was originally treeless, so the WPA workers planted some 5,000 trees. Only a mile from Morris and patronized chiefly by local people, it was a city park in everything but name. In 1965 it was included in the legislation that transferred Toqua Lakes and Sleepy Eye to local jurisdiction, and thus the parks division disposed of another of its minor units.[46]

## Lake Bronson

In the far northwestern part of the state the first park to take shape was located in Kittson County and came about more or less as a spin-off from a water-control project. During the drought of

*Dam construction, Lake Bronson State Park, 1936*

the 1930s several towns and rural areas in this region suffered from insufficient water as wells dried up. Hallock, the county seat, was one of those towns. Unable to sink deeper wells because of a layer of salt, Hallock residents thought that the solution to their problem lay in the creation of an artificial body of water in the vicinity. The county engineer had long advocated the construction of a dam on the South Fork of Two Rivers, which would impound a reservoir from which Hallock could get its water. It was believed that such a reservoir would also help control flooding on the level Red River valley plain.[47]

After a political struggle that went on for a year and a half, a dam was authorized, and construction began at the point where the river had cut through Glacial Lake Agassiz's Lower McCauleyville beach, lowest of several beaches left as terraces when the huge lake gradually drained. Technical problems caused by the presence of one hundred feet of quicksand beneath the damsite threatened the whole project. An engineer was hired, who solved the problem with a dam that remains in use more than fifty years after its construction. As elsewhere, WPA labor built recreational facilities, including a combination water and observation tower and a bathhouse and beach.[48]

When the job was completed, the dam and its associated facilities were turned over to the county. Soon afterward, a former mayor of Hallock, then in the state legislature, arranged to have the state assume management of the dam and park; the 1937 law that officially designated so many parks included "Two Rivers State Park." The reservoir was named for the nearby town of Bronson, whose post office was changed to Lake Bronson on January 2, 1939. The park became Lake Bronson State Park in 1945, through the same legislation that changed Cottonwood River to Flandrau.[49]

Lake Bronson has always been a fairly large park. Its original acreage was 711.76 — second only to Flandrau among the parks established in 1937 — and several additions have been made since then. By 1977, when a management plan was drawn up, it had a statutory acreage of 2,983. Only 1,654 acres were in state ownership, however, and some of the privately owned land was not considered suitable for park purposes. The chief attraction has always been the lake itself, which serves an important recreational purpose in an area without natural lakes. Considering its remote location, Lake Bronson attracts an extraordinary number of visitors. Besides drawing people from northwestern Minnesota, it has visitors in increasing numbers from North Dakota and Manitoba, especially from Winnipeg.[50]

When the Outdoor Recreation Act of 1975 mandated the classification of all parks according to their primary purpose, Lake Bronson was designated a recreational state park. It does, however, possess features not exclusively recreational in the narrow sense. Its present boundaries enclose a considerable area upstream from the lake and on both sides of the South Fork of Two Rivers. Much of this land is forested with cottonwood, bur oak, box elder, poplar, elm, ash, and basswood. Two pioneer cemeteries and a couple of river crossings used by early travelers give it some historical significance, and the Arvilla Indian mounds, an important prehistoric site, lie just outside the park boundaries. Future development of the park will probably give greater emphasis to these features. Although Project 80 would have reclassified Lake Bronson as a recreation area and transferred it to a regional authority, this disposition seems unlikely.[51]

## Buffalo River

The next park created in the Red River valley was Buffalo River, thirteen miles east of Moorhead. Said to have been the brain-child of the Moorhead Rod and Gun Club and mentioned as a possible addition to the system by parks director Harold Lathrop in his first report, it got off to a somewhat later start than the parks just discussed. By the end of 1938, however, the WPA had built a swimming pool, an entrance road, toilets, a water supply, a parking area, and two small diversion dams. It was dedicated on Memorial Day in 1939 and immediately became popular with residents of the Fargo-Moorhead area.[52]

Although Buffalo River began with only 122 acres, it was soon increased to 247 acres, and additions in the 1960s enlarged it to about 1,240 acres, much of it relatively undisturbed prairie. Its botanical importance had long been recognized; even before it became a park, classes from schools and colleges in Fargo and Moorhead made field trips there. It includes both high and low prairie, as well as a limited amount of woodland along the river and on higher ground. Immediately adjacent to the park is the 1,360-acre Bluestem Prairie preserve, owned by The Nature Conservancy. Together the park and preserve provide a sizable sample of tallgrass prairie, an ecosystem all too rare in Minnesota.[53]

The existence of this virgin prairie presumably enabled Buffalo River to survive the Project 80 elimination contest. It lacks exceptional scenery, and it is close to U.S. Highway 10 and the Burlington Northern's main line. Together with the high rate of local use that results from its proximity to the Fargo-Moorhead community, these factors do not add up to an ideal state park.

Most park users congregate in the developed area, especially around the swimming pool, leaving the grasslands unvisited. Just east of the developed area, however, several trails provide access to one section of the prairie. The trail names, Prairie Smoke, Wide Sky, and Savannah Cutoff, suggest their character. Although some of this land was once cultivated, it produces a rich display of native wildflowers, especially in late summer, when the composites come into bloom. The major undisturbed grassland lies on the south side of the river. A footbridge connects it with the developed portion of the park and leads to a long loop trail that parallels the river in one direction and follows the boundary of the Bluestem Prairie preserve in the other. Except for its importance as a remnant of native prairie, Buffalo River is not likely to have much statewide appeal, but it serves an area deficient in parks and hence has considerable value.[54]

## Beaver Creek Valley

Last to be developed of the parks established in 1937 was Beaver Creek Valley, about four miles west of Caledonia, in Houston County, in Minnesota's southeast corner. In the driftless, or unglaciated, region, it affords a good example of stream-dissected topography. East Beaver Creek flows through a deep, narrow valley cutting its way through the rolling farmlands. The creek originates in the Big Spring, which pours from the limestone wall of the valley, and joins West Beaver Creek near the north end of the park.[55]

Although the area was privately owned, much of it divided into woodlots, it had been used for picnics long before the state took an interest in it. State Representative John R. Trisch of Caledonia has been credited with bringing Beaver Creek Valley to the attention of state officials about 1934. In June 1935 the Executive Council allocated $45,000 to a project there as part of an $8.5 million flood-control project to provide work for the unemployed. Actual work did not begin for another three years, but people began talking about the "park" almost at once, even before any land had been acquired. The Houston County Rod and Gun Club began holding its annual picnic there in 1935, and two years later parks director Lathrop addressed the group there.[56]

Land acquisition began in 1936 and continued over the next few years, until the park had an acreage of 325.17. At the time of the first purchases, state WPA administrator Victor A. Christgau had not released the necessary funds to begin development, but in July 1938 work got under way. The local newspaper reported that the project, which would employ up to ten men, consisted of building a dam, two bridges, and a road to the tract that was to be developed for recreation. Work must have proceeded very slowly, for by

*Beaver Creek Valley State Park*

1940 the only facility constructed by WPA workers was the entrance road. Picnic grounds followed, and a few trails were laid
out. Not until after World War II were campgrounds added,
however.[57]

In time the park's small size became a matter of concern. Despite a minor expansion authorized by the legislature in 1955, by
the late 1950s the parks people were becoming concerned that the
owners of land on the bluffs above the park might cut the timber
and thereby damage the park by encouraging erosion. They
thought that the park ought to be expanded to at least 1,000 acres,
including a buffer to protect the valley itself. The 1963 legislature
authorized an expansion to 1,025 acres, and further increases were

provided for in 1967 and 1969. As in so many other parks, however, landowner opposition prevented the acquisition of most of this additional land. By 1980 only 617 acres out of 1,214 within the statutory boundaries was state-owned, and no additions have been made since then.[58]

Opponents of park expansion claimed that much of the land within the statutory boundaries was perfectly good farmland and of little value for park purposes. The boundaries, they said, had been drawn along section lines and with slight regard for actual topography. These and other complaints were aired at a series of public meetings in 1977 and 1978. Although some of these objections had substance, they were rooted in a growing antipark bias that surfaced in connection with proposed expansions at Whitewater and elsewhere during the 1970s and early 1980s. Some of the exchanges reported by the *Caledonia Argus* became quite heated. One farmer asked what "DNR" stood for, then answered his own question: "Damned Near Russia." At a meeting in October 1978 some farmers questioned the DNR's credibility and complained of being asked to provide a playground for outsiders.[59]

The upshot of these discussions was a compromise similar to that reached at Whitewater. The statutory boundaries would be redrawn to include only state-owned lands. Then the DNR would be authorized to acquire, on a willing-seller basis, up to 800 acres of land with outstanding resource and recreation development value outside these boundaries. Unlike the Whitewater settlement, however, this formula has not been embodied in law and probably never will be. So in respect to acreage, Beaver Creek Valley remains just where it was in 1977.[60]

Beaver Creek Valley is perhaps the finest small park in the system. When the Project 80 planners ran their computer analysis, they divided all units in the system into four quartiles, on the basis of twenty-nine criteria, and they identified those parks that fell into the top 10 percent of the first quartile. There were only four: Itasca, St. Croix, Banning, and Beaver Creek Valley. Since the other three are much larger, a fact that counts heavily in their favor, it is evident that Beaver Creek Valley has some special qualities or combination of qualities to recommend it.[61]

These special qualities fall largely under the general headings of landforms and vegetation. Not only does the park provide an excellent example of stream-dissected topography, but it contains some of the most striking scenery in southern Minnesota. Like Whitewater, it affords welcome relief from the intensively cultivated countryside around it. The botanical range is great; some species of flowers found here, including at least two classified as "threatened," do not exist elsewhere in Minnesota's park system. Geologically and biologically, Beaver Creek Valley has much to offer.[62]

On one of the tracts desired for addition to the north end of the park stands the old Schech mill. Built in 1876, it is one of only three water-powered mills in Minnesota now operating, the only one still using the original millstones. Most of its machinery is still operational. The present owner was quoted as saying, at one of the public meetings in 1977, that when he is no longer able to take care of the mill, he would just as soon let the state take over. Its acquisition, though desired by the DNR, would present some administrative problems, since the mill is not accessible by road from the main park area, where the entrance station is located. The mill can be reached from the picnic area, however, by a trail that parallels the creek and crosses it three times on small footbridges and once on a former township road bridge. Because of the linear shape of the park, this is the only trail that remains in the valley; several others ascend the steep bluffs and afford occasional views of the scene below.[63]

Hiking and fishing are the principal recreational options available in Beaver Creek Valley. About 20 percent of park users go there to fish in the natural production trout stream, one of the best in the state. On summer weekends the long, narrow campground is often filled, especially on holidays. The picnic grounds receive less use, but there is usually a family or two picnicking on any given day in summer. A nature center of modest size, usually staffed by volunteers from nearby communities, has been started in part of the picnic shelter. The park is too far from major transportation routes to attract the transient camper who might readily spend a night at Blue Mounds or Buffalo River. Beaver Creek Valley appeals to more of a regional clientele — people who have been coming there for years, or their friends, trying out the park on the veterans' recommendation.[64]

## Oronoco

Except for Camden, all of the state parks so far discussed in this chapter were legally established by a single bill, approved April 26, 1937. A separate piece of legislation, approved the same day, created Oronoco Park and appropriated $7,500 for its development. It was located on 105 acres of land at the village of Oronoco, in Olmsted County, about ten miles north of Rochester. A dam below the confluence of two branches of the Zumbro River impounded an irregular body of water called Shady Lake. WPA labor provided the standard facilities: picnic grounds, a parking lot, toilets, a swimming beach, and a bathhouse. The park came to be heavily used, mainly by Rochester people. Because no land was available for expansion, Oronoco could not attain state park status (preferably 500 acres or more) and was reclassified as a state scenic reserve, along with Toqua Lakes, Sleepy Eye, Horace Austin, and others. Finally, in 1965, it was transferred to Olmsted County.[65]

## Lake Carlos

Besides the newly developed areas officially admitted to the state park system in the 1930s, there were several others whose development began at roughly the same time but that were not then legally designated as state parks or recreational reserves. At least one, Lake Carlos, never was so designated by act of the legislature. It was established as a state park by resolution of the Executive Council and by the director of state parks, who acted on the authority vested in him by the act of April 29, 1935, which set up the Division of State Parks.[66]

Extending in a great arc from near Willmar, in Kandiyohi County, through west-central Minnesota, to Lake Itasca, a veritable Milky Way of lakes appears on the map. Produced for the most part by glacial action, these lakes comprise what is sometimes called Minnesota's Lake Region. In the mid-1930s Sibley was the only sizable park in this whole area. Parks director Lathrop and others recognized the need for at least one more in the Lake Region and chose a tract of rolling, wooded land on the north shore of Lake Carlos, said to be the deepest and cleanest lake in the immediate area. In 1936 an Alexandria lawyer, Constant Larson, assisted by political allies of Governor Floyd B. Olson, persuaded the governor to help them "save those trees," as Larson expressed it. Late the next year, after Lathrop and conservation commissioner Herman C. Wenzel had investigated the tract and approved its purchase, land acquisition began. Originally only 140 acres, the land sought for park purposes was increased to slightly over 400 before acquisition began.[67]

On October 6, 1937, the Executive Council allocated $12,900 for land acquisition. The county was asked to provide $1,013 to sponsor the WPA project, which would cost a total of $43,000. In the next two weeks all but $100 of this amount was raised, $40.84 of it in pennies contributed by schoolchildren. The land purchases were largely completed by the end of the year, and on January 24, 1938, a crew of fourteen WPA laborers began working. Development was ambitious, probably because the park promised to be highly popular. Before WPA projects came to an end with U.S. entry into World War II, the park had been equipped with an entrance road, a parking lot, a picnic ground, a water system, a tourist campground, a bathing beach, and a group camp with a recreation building.[68]

Some early boosters intended that the initial land purchases should be in the range of 640 acres and hoped that eventually much more would be added, to "make this park second only to Itasca State Park in a recreational and conservation project," as a local newspaper reported. Although the expansion was a long time in coming — in 1948 Lake Carlos still had only 403.56 acres of land — and the park never has approached Itasca, it has grown to nearly three times its original size. Beginning with a 343.44-acre expansion authorized in 1961, it was enlarged over the years, mainly in 1963 and 1967. By the early 1980s, it embraced an area of 1,118 acres, including some private land yet to be acquired.[69]

Project 80 would have relegated Lake Carlos to the status of a recreation area, but it would have remained under state rather than regional management. Actually, it is more than the typical recreation area oriented toward swimming and boating. Its twelve miles of foot trails take the hiker into various ecosystems, from the hardwood forest, chiefly maple and basswood, to a tamarack bog, to open grassland with prairie vegetation. Plenty of wildlife can be

seen and heard, and geologically the area provides a good example
of the glaciated terrain so familiar to Minnesotans. In short, Lake
Carlos State Park, while lacking in spectacular scenery or unique
features, has much to offer besides a swimming beach, though a visitor on a summer weekend might think everyone for miles around
had congregated there.

## Old Mill

Another park with its roots in the 1930s, though not officially
established under its present name until 1951, is Old Mill. Located
seventeen miles northeast of Warren, in Marshall County, it
represents another effort to provide the northwestern corner of
Minnesota with recreational facilities. The initiative seems to have
come from local people, who had long used the area for picnics,
pageants, and public meetings. The park was formally proposed in
June 1934 at a picnic of the Marshall County Historical Society.
About a month later Governor Floyd Olson expressed himself as being "sold on the idea" and promised to help acquire the necessary
land.[70]

Despite such an auspicious beginning, the park proposal made
little progress until the following winter, when a well-orchestrated
publicity campaign got underway and the Executive Council was
deluged with letters and petitions from individuals and organizations in favor of the park. Even this effort yielded no immediate
results, for parks director Lathrop and an NPS representative
decided, after visiting the site, that it was better suited to development as a county park than as a state park. Lathrop apparently
changed his mind later, however, for when a local committee had
taken options on the most essential parcels of land, he sent engineers
from the parks division to make surveys and estimate the cost of the
various facilities that would be needed. Late in November 1936 it
was announced that the federal government had allocated $35,000
and the executive council $9,235 for a WPA project at what was to
be called Middle River State Park. Most of the state contribution
was used to purchase 287 acres of land, valued at $9,200 at the time
the options were taken.[71]

*Minnesota Historical Society tour at Old Mill State Park, 1958*

Although most of the early development was intended to meet the need for recreational facilities, parks people had from the beginning recognized the historical value of an old mill on the site. Still in operation when the state bought it in 1937, the mill had been built about 1896 by John Larson, whose father had previously operated, successively, a water-powered mill and a windmill in the vicinity. Originally steam-powered, the Larson mill was run by a gasoline engine in its later years.[72]

Except for feasibility studies, nothing was done to restore the mill until after World War II, by which time the building was in poor condition. Then an Old Mill Restoration Committee was formed, and the name of the park was changed to reflect the growing interest in the mill as its central feature. Supported partly by local contributions of money and labor, with technical assistance from the parks division, rehabilitation went on from 1952 to 1958. Finally, on June 1, 1958, the restored mill was dedicated at a ceremony attended by about 7,500 people. Since then there have been mechanical problems and difficulties caused by the periodic flooding of the river, but the mill is operated a few weekends each summer, when on "grinding days" it turns out flour for the tourist trade.[73]

Besides the attractions of the mill itself, the park has continued to serve a recreational function in its region. Its main limitation is that it has remained small. Although Project 80 recommended that it be enlarged by 2,900 acres, Old Mill State Park is still the same size it was to begin with: 287 acres. The picnic area, campgrounds, a swimming pool, the mill, a log cabin, and service facilities are all crowded into this limited space, leaving little room for anything else. Surrounded by farmland, the park would be difficult to expand. One solution that has been suggested is to acquire a corridor that would connect it with a 400-acre wildlife management area to the east. The legislature has not acted on this suggestion, so Old Mill remains too small to meet current definitions of a state park, yet worth keeping in the system.[74]

---

## Joseph R. Brown, Lac qui Parle, and Watson

The interest in preserving sites associated with the Dakota War of 1862 had pretty well spent itself by the 1930s, but one more historic place remained to be incorporated into the park system: the ruined walls of Joseph R. Brown's nineteen-room mansion overlooking the Minnesota River in Renville County, south of Sacred Heart. Brown was a colorful politician, businessman, land speculator, inventor, editor, founder of Henderson and several other towns, Indian trader, and Indian agent; he had dabbled in nearly everything. When a change of administration deprived him of his job as agent in 1861, he built this house — facetiously called Farther and Gay Castle — and settled down there with his mixed-blood wife and their twelve children.[75]

Brown was absent when the fighting broke out, but his family was taken captive and the house burned. The Browns chose not to

*Excavations at Joseph R. Brown Memorial Park, June 1938*

rebuild after the war, and when white settlement resumed, the site was homesteaded. It is likely that some of the stones from the house found their way into farm buildings. By the 1930s little remained visible but part of the external walls. Through the efforts of Andrew A. Davidson of Renville, the owners of the land donated 3 acres to the state, and on July 23, 1937, Joseph R. Brown Memorial Park was established.[76]

With the aid of WPA labor, the Minnesota Historical Society carried out excavations on the site and found many articles that had been used by the Brown family, including parts of a grand piano. The act creating the park (later renamed Joseph R. Brown State Wayside) included an appropriation of $500 toward the restoration of the mansion. When estimates of the probable cost of restoring the structure ran to more than $25,000, however, the idea was abandoned and the $500 allowed to revert to the general fund. No further appropriations were made until 1955, when funds were made available to widen the access road and install fireplaces and picnic tables. Some attempt was also made to stabilize the ruins, which had suffered from vandalism.[77]

When the parks division began to divest itself of some of the smaller, more strictly historical sites in the system, it was proposed to turn the Joseph R. Brown Wayside over to the Minnesota Historical Society. No such transfer has occurred, and the site remains in the park system. It is not heavily used, though vandals still seem to be able to find it. Whatever agency owns them, the remains of Brown's pretentious mansion are going to be difficult to protect and impossible to restore.[78]

Several units of the park system developed during the 1930s occupied a somewhat anomalous position because of the involvement of two or more governmental agencies in them. Among these were the Lac qui Parle State Recreation Area and its satellite, the Watson State Wayside, which came into being as a result of a joint federal-state flood control project on the upper Minnesota River. Discussed as early as 1909, the proposal remained just that until the 1930s, when the need to find work for the unemployed provided an added justification for it. The Flood Control Act of 1936 included the Lac qui Parle project, estimated to cost $464,000, plus $974,000 for lands and damages. It was supplemented in 1937 by the Pittman-Robertson Act, which set up a fund to aid states in wildlife restoration programs.[79]

Although parks director Lathrop had suggested at the beginning of the project that it include recreational facilities, no development took place until 1938, when a WPA camp began work at the Watson site. By the time that site was unofficially dedicated with a Boy Scout picnic in June 1939, considerable progress had also been made at Lac qui Parle, across the river from the so-called

*Lac qui Parle Park, about 1935*

Chippewa Mission State Wayside. Early that month the commissioners of three neighboring counties toured what was already being called Lac qui Parle State Park and were much impressed by some of the artwork in stone that had been done by the WPA. By the summer of 1940 the park was being regularly used for picnics. The following year the Executive Council, which had assumed jurisdiction over the recreational facilities from the U.S. Army Corps of Engineers, designated Lac qui Parle as a state park and Watson as a state wayside. By that time the park had a combination picnic shelter and kitchen, toilets, a well, an entrance road, and a parking area; the Watson site had picnic grounds.[80]

In 1957 the legislature transferred all the lands in the Lac qui Parle project to the commissioner of conservation, to be managed as a game refuge and public hunting grounds. Although there was probably no intent to turn the park over to the Game and Fish Division, that is what the legislation in fact did. So two years later the

lands previously included in the state park were specifically established as a state recreational reserve. Watson State Wayside, near
the village of Watson, was leased by the municipality and the Watson Lions Club, which have since maintained it.[81]

Lac qui Parle, which now encompasses 529 acres adjacent to
the 27,000-acre Lac qui Parle Wildlife Management Area, is overshadowed by that entity. To all practical purposes, they are part of
a single unit, whose chief function is the protection and management of waterfowl, pheasants, and other game; during the hunting
season, sections of the recreation area are off limits to other users.
Shaped something like a bulky, short-handled spoon, the recreation
area lies within the delta of the Lac qui Parle River where it enters
the Minnesota, and oxbow lakes and former channels cut through
the dense bottomland forest. The trail system threads its way
through the timber, leading the hiker from one body of water to another. The area is vulnerable to flooding; the recreation area was
closed to the public a good share of the summers of 1984 and 1985
because of high water in the spring. Still, Lac qui Parle has a certain beauty, especially the shoreline at the picnic grounds, where
rocks rise from the shallow waters.[82]

---

## Cascade River and Temperance River

While the Corps of Engineers was developing recreation sites in
far western Minnesota, the state highway department was doing
much the same thing on the North Shore, where it acquired land
in two places. After completing U.S. Highway 61, the department
purchased some 2,300 acres of land near the mouth of the Cascade
River, about sixty miles up the lakeshore from Gooseberry Falls
State Park. An ECW camp moved in on July 1, 1934, and erected
ten barracks, which were intended for use as tourist cabins when
the park was in operation. A picnic area and a few foot trails were
developed, but the main thrust of the highway department's work
was to eliminate the scars left by road construction.[83]

From the beginning Cascade River was thought of as a state
park — the WPA guide to Minnesota, published in 1938, so desig-
nates it — but it was to be more than twenty years before the lands
were transferred to the Department of Conservation. In the mean-

*Temperance River, about 1905*

time there was comparatively little development, since the highway department was not legally permitted to operate parks. Finally, in 1957 the legislature officially placed Cascade River in the state park system. Most of the development now visible, such as a thirty-eight-site campground, has taken place since the transfer.[84]

Cascade River is an oddly shaped park. Originally acquired to protect the area along the highway from "private encroachments of undesirable nature," the lands consist of a noncontiguous strip along the Lake Superior shoreline, state lands interspersed with private lands. At no point does the park extend very far inland, though adjacent forest lands permit the extension of trails beyond the park. The main attractions are the falls of the Cascade River, which are as impressive as any on the North Shore. It is possible to go up one side of the river, cross on a footbridge, and return along the other side. However one does it, a hike here is no leisurely stroll; as elsewhere on the North Shore, much climbing is required if one is to see anything not visible from the highway or the campground.[85]

The Project 80 planners did not envision much of a future for Cascade River. They proposed to transform it into a scenic wayside, despite its size (2,813 statutory acres by 1990) and its waterfalls. The parks division, however, has not changed the park's status. Despite the number of individual units acquired on the North

Shore since World War II, there is not enough public land to meet the recreational needs of the traveling public, and it makes sense for the state to hold onto every bit that it has.[86]

During the 1930s the highway department acquired a much smaller piece of land at the mouth of the Temperance River, which was also transferred to the parks division in 1957. Temperance River, with only 200 acres, is the third smallest unit in the system officially designated a state park. Two sizable camping areas, with a total of fifty-one sites, take up much space on both sides of the river. (The Temperance, by the way, is supposed to have been so named because, unlike other North Shore streams, it has no bar at its mouth. This legend is weakened, however, by the facts that sometimes it does have a bar and that there are other rivers that do not.) Along the Cauldron Trail the hiker sees potholes formed by the rushing waters of the Temperance. The scenery here compares favorably with that elsewhere on the North Shore.[87]

Project 80 would have relegated Temperance River to the status of a highway rest area, presumably because of its small size. Admittedly space is a problem, but fortunately the largely undeveloped Cross River State Wayside, with a statutory area of 2,620 acres, is near enough so that the two units can be administered together. If the two could be combined by the acquisition of the land between them, the result would be another fine North Shore park.

## St. Croix

One more state park developed initially by an agency other than the Department of Conservation is St. Croix, a large area fronting on the river of that name, northeast of Pine City in east-central Minnesota. Originally covered with white pine, it was logged over in the late nineteenth century. When its rich forest cover had been removed, settlers moved in, misled into thinking that its soil would be equally successful for growing crops. By the time of the Great Depression they had learned otherwise and were willing to sell their homesteads to the federal government, which developed the St. Croix Recreational Demonstration Area in an effort to show that such submarginal agricultural lands could be put to use in a way that would benefit the public. By 1938, 27,000

*St. Croix State Park, 1984*

acres had been acquired, and the site had been provided with a
public-use area and two organization camps.[88]

From the beginning it was expected that the area would eventually be transferred to the state and become a state park. The
transfer was completed in 1943, and since then St. Croix has vied
with Itasca for the honor of being the state's largest park. Each has
somewhat over 30,000 acres, and their boundaries frequently
change, so that either one may be ahead at any given time. In the
late 1970s Itasca had a thousand-acre edge, but figures given by the
parks and recreation division in its 1990 guide to Minnesota state
parks credit St. Croix with 34,037 acres, Itasca with 32,000.[89]

As might be expected of so large a park, St. Croix has nearly
everything. Besides the usual appurtenances, it has several boat

landings, a fire lookout tower, the most extensive trail system of any Minnesota park (127 miles, including a segment of the Minnesota-Wisconsin Boundary Trail), and considerable variety of scenery. The part of the St. Croix River that forms the park's southern boundary has been designated a National Wild and Scenic River; the Kettle River, which flows through the western section of the park, is a Minnesota Wild and Scenic River. The Kettle River overlook is perhaps the most popular scenic attraction in the park, but almost any prospect along the St. Croix would rival it. It is one of Minnesota's major parks, both in size and in the wealth of experiences it offers the visitor.[90]

## *Summary*

The decade of the 1930s, especially the years 1934 to 1937, constituted a seminal period in the history of the Minnesota state park system. The situation at the end of the decade was quite different from what it had been ten years earlier. A Division of State Parks had been set up, with a full-time director and a salaried staff, plus superintendents or custodians at most of the parks. Harold W. Lathrop, who was appointed director of state parks on July 1, 1935, was a native of Wisconsin who had grown up in Minneapolis. After serving in the U.S. Navy in World War I, he attended the William Hood Dunwoody Industrial Institute and the University of Minnesota, both in Minneapolis, before going to work for the Minneapolis park board. In May 1934 he was called from that job to serve as park consultant for State Emergency Relief Administration projects. About two months later he was appointed supervisor of ECW work in the state parks. He occupied that post until his appointment as director the following year, and remained in the latter capacity until 1946.[91]

The number of units in the park system increased from thirty in 1934 to forty-seven in 1940. If the eight state monuments are omitted from the enumeration and the areas already developed but not yet included in the system are added, the increase was 95 percent. Mainly because of the great size of one of the old parks, Itasca, the growth in terms of acreage does not look quite so impressive. In 1934 the system embraced 38,519.9 acres; six years later the total was 45,711 acres. Park use was also up. Attendance rose from 450,000 in 1935 to 1,350,000 in 1941, the last year before gasoline rationing cut into park visitation.[92]

These were impressive gains. They were not, however, sufficient grounds for complacency. The many new parks (and some of the old ones) had been developed with the aid of federal money, which totaled $7,441,323.27 by 1940. These funds had been provided with the understanding that the state would assume the burden of maintaining the parks afterward. The legislature did not, however, fulfill this promise. As early as 1938 director Lathrop complained that it had been necessary during the preceding biennium to operate ten new parks for which no maintenance funds had been provided. Two years later he observed that federal support was becoming more difficult to obtain. Recent regulations called upon "sponsors" (that is, states) to supply at least 25 percent of the costs of WPA programs. As a result, these programs had become a hand-to-mouth affair, "with no assurance of how long work on any one unit may be continued."[93]

Things were improving by 1940, however. Whereas the 1937 legislature had appropriated sums ranging from $50 to $12,000 for twenty-three units of the system — a total of $33,040 for each year of the biennium — the 1939 legislature chose to appropriate a lump sum of $70,000 annually for the maintenance and improvement of the parks, leaving its allocation up to the director. Still, Lathrop was not satisfied. In his 1940 report he tried to shame the legislature into making larger appropriations by comparing the amount spent per acre in the Minnesota parks with the expenditures in other states. Announcing that $204,000 would be requested for the next biennium, he pointed out that this would come to only $2.22 per acre, at a time when Michigan was spending $2.63 per acre, Pennsylvania, $2.68, Wisconsin, $5.44, Indiana, $6.90, New York, $6.32, Iowa, $7.65, and Illinois, $13.80.[94]

Lathrop had obtained ammunition for his demands from a study of the Minnesota park system that had been carried out with NPS assistance between May 1937 and March 1939. The published report that followed this study is interesting both for its statements about the system as it then existed and for its recommendations for the future. It called for an appropriation of $252,076.37 for fiscal 1940. Added to receipts (from camping fees, concession leases, etc.)

of $56,049.63, this appropriation would have provided a fund of $308,126, of which $173,126 would be used for the maintenance of existing parks, $100,000 for land purchases, and $35,000 for the central office. The report recommended expansion of the existing parks by 13,045.08 acres and acquisition of 11,815 acres for new parks. These additions would give the system a total of 70,309.57 acres.[95]

The 1939 report also had things to say about park philosophy. The people who drew up the report were fully aware of the potential conflict between preservation and use. "The development of state parks," they said, "should be based on demands by the public weighed against the values of conservation of the wilderness." The authors of the report cautioned that care should be exercised in selecting lands for development as parks and recreation areas. Tracts should be large enough — at least 500 acres for parks and 400 for recreation areas — so that they could stand heavy use without serious damage.[96]

The report warned that development of a park system should not be a haphazard affair. Those in charge should make sure that "lands unsuitable or not properly located will not be shouldered upon the state merely because of the desires of a small group or because someone wishes to turn certain lands over to the state, to avoid payment of taxes." The report specifically called for the elimination of Horace Austin, Sleepy Eye, and Garvin Heights from the system and for only limited development of other parks that served mainly the locality in which they were situated.[97]

Besides these general recommendations, the report held many specific suggestions. Historic sites should be approved by the Minnesota Historical Society, and no reconstruction should be attempted except on the basis of true authenticity. Forests should be preserved as much as possible in their natural state. A park should have only one entrance. Entrance and park roads should intrude as little as possible on the scenery. Buildings should be in harmony with their surroundings and be of native materials. Trails should be constructed in the form of a loop wherever possible. Refectories should be state-operated. The report also offered recommendations for the design of campgrounds, picnic areas, and other facilities.[98]

In 1934 Grover Conzet had written, echoing what State Auditor Ray Chase had said more than a decade earlier, "Management of state parks has never been given serious consideration by the state. Parks and monuments have been created from time to time without much thought having been given to their development." If the recommendations contained in the 1939 report were followed, in substance if not in detail, such a criticism would never have to be made again.[99]

In many respects the report is strikingly modern. Interpretation, today perceived as a major function of the parks staff, was at least not totally ignored. The report did say that conservation education was needed, both to increase the visitors' enjoyment and to protect the natural features.[100]

With the 1935 creation of a separate parks division and the appointment of Harold Lathrop as its director, the Minnesota state park system took a giant step forward. The 1939 report gave to the new professionalism a needed ideological buttressing. Between the two events the number of parks had greatly increased, and their capacity to accommodate growing numbers of people had been strengthened. Legislative support had improved by the end of the decade, so that it seemed likely that the new facilities would be properly maintained and new ones added as the need developed. Just then, however, something happened thousands of miles away that had a profound effect on Minnesota's parks: the Japanese bombed Pearl Harbor.

# CHAPTER SIX

# Years of Slow Growth
# 1942–1952

WORLD WAR II had a great impact on Minnesota's parks, as it did on almost every other aspect of American life. Three parks came in for direct use as part of the war effort. Flandrau and Whitewater were transformed into prisoner-of-war camps; interned men worked on farms or at nearby canneries. Camouflage maneuvers were carried out at Blue Mounds, or, as it was then still called, Mound Springs.[1]

For the rest of the parks, the chief effect of the war was a change in attendance patterns as a result of gasoline rationing. Those located near urban centers had almost as many visitors as before the war, but the more remote parks experienced decreases ranging from 40 to 76 percent. Conditions varied from year to year during the four summers that the United States was at war, and managers found it difficult to estimate probable park use. They also shared with managers in business and industry the problem of finding workers to do the necessary maintenance and operation, since most men and many women were more directly involved in the war effort.[2]

The war ended late in the summer of 1945. When the next park season got under way eight or nine months later, attendance shot up, and managers were faced with the problem of how to accommodate greatly increased numbers of visitors with facilities that had been neglected during the war years. The roads, picnic shelters, dams, and other structures built by the CCC and WPA were now a decade old and needed rehabilitation. Unfortunately, not until 1953 was the legislature to pass a law — the so-called park-sticker law — that provided something like an adequate source of revenue. In the meantime, the parks had to make do with what they had.

Two important administrative changes occurred in the conservation department during and shortly after the war. In 1943 Chester S. Wilson replaced William L. Strunk as commissioner. Strunk, who had assumed the post in 1940, had previously been a medical doctor and college administrator; Wilson was a lawyer who had served in the state attorney general's office. Both had a deep commitment to conservation. Strunk had been associated with conservation work in Iowa for ten years before becoming commissioner; Wilson, a native of Stillwater, had a special interest in the St. Croix valley.[3]

On August 31, 1946, Harold W. Lathrop stepped down as director of the Division of State Parks after eleven years and one month in that post and nearly another year as *de facto* parks director before the division was created. Because he was the first to hold the office and because he held it for so many years, his influence on Minnesota's park system was incalculable. He had guided the system through the years of rapid expansion and through the trying war years. Lathrop was replaced by Lew Elton Fiero, who took over on September 1, 1946. Born and educated in Mankato, Fiero had had a varied career. Besides being in business in Mankato, St. Peter, and St. Paul, he had been athletic coach at a military academy in Kansas, had served as an officer in the field artillery in both world wars, and had worked with the Farm Security Administration and the Soil Conservation Service during the 1930s. In 1940 he had been named director of the game and fish division of the conservation department.[4]

As he was about to leave his post, Lathrop wrote his successor a long letter, describing the park system as it then existed and suggesting improvements he thought would be needed in the years to come. Besides providing a great deal of factual information useful to historians, the letter reveals the attention to detail that characterized Lathrop's administration; he knew every park and knew it well. So far as may be inferred from his public statements, Fiero seems to have shared Lathrop's underlying philosophy, and he generally continued his predecessor's policies, within the constraints of legislative frugality. In his second biennial report he deplored, as Lathrop had, the haphazard way in which the park system had evolved. "Too often," Fiero wrote, "state parks are established through the efforts of well-meaning individuals and groups by offering for purchase or gift for state park development purposes, tracts of land that have little value as a source of income from other uses." Management, too, had been careless in the early days. Before 1935, he said, "it was not unusual to permit local committees using legislative appropriations to manage state parks located in their immediate vicinities with only nominal control by the division of forestry."[5]

Other changes were taking place in the park system during these years. The 1941 legislature had authorized the establishment of a State Parks Working Capital Fund, which made it possible for the state to assume operation of various special services and facilities, such as concessions. During the 1930s this issue had received considerable discussion but not much action, but by 1946, with the new fund, all concessions were state-operated except two excursion boats. Another development in the postwar years was the emergence of what we know today as "interpretation," though the word was not then used in park officials' published remarks. In his report for 1947–48 Fiero mentioned that in some parks nature trails were being developed, either with trained naturalists to guide visitors or with tags to identify plant species. Initiated at Itasca and extended during the next two years to Whitewater, Interstate, St. Croix, Scenic, Gooseberry Falls, and Camden, nature trails were such a new idea that Fiero felt impelled to make note of the innovation:

> This type of recreation is a departure from the generally accepted and prevailing practices of emphasizing the purely amusement types . . . by introducing what is developing into an enjoyable educational diversion to complement other pastimes.[6]

Not all the innovations of the later 1940s were so innocuous as interpretation, nor did they all lend themselves so well to expansion in later years. For example, in 1948 Fiero reported remarkable success in the use of DDT to control mosquitoes at St. Croix State Park. He added that the program was being extended to other parks.

When the undesirable effects of DDT were discovered and it was gradually taken off the market, this mosquito-control program was abandoned. Today the more heavily used areas of the park are sprayed with an accepted chemical, but mosquitoes still efficiently extract blood from park visitors.[7]

Although sixteen new parks, waysides, and monuments were established during the years 1942–52, the legislature continued to be stingy in its support of both old and new parks. Moreover, in its efforts to find a way of financing land acquisition for parks without making direct appropriations, the legislature embarked on a land-exchange program that failed so miserably that two of the parks never got off the ground and had to be reestablished in the 1960s. The others grew more slowly than they would have done if sufficient funds had been available to purchase the needed lands and develop the necessary facilities.

### Father Hennepin

One park started in this period was actually established before the United States entered World War II, but its development did not really get under way until after the war. As early as the 1920s State Auditor Ray Chase and others had recommended the purchase of lands for a park on Mille Lacs Lake. In 1938, when a 129-acre parcel near the village of Isle came onto the market, a resident of the town notified the deputy commissioner of conservation of its availability. Nothing came of the proposal then, but three years later enough local support, as well as support from Catholic groups elsewhere, had been generated so that a bill was introduced in the legislature establishing Father Hennepin State Memorial Park on this land. Hennepin was the Catholic priest who, in 1680, named the Falls of St. Anthony and spent eight months living near Mille Lacs with a band of Dakota.[8]

Since most of the land was forfeited for nonpayment of taxes, its purchase did not require the state to spend much money. The bill establishing the new park contained a provision, inserted by the house appropriations committee, that "no funds of the state of Minnesota shall be expended upon the maintenance of said park for a period of five years." Clearly some members of the legislature, which had created no new parks since 1937, did not wish to see the state enter over-hastily into the business of park making. Since the bill authorized the parks director to accept any funds or services donated for the improvement of the lands, the burden of development fell on local government units and private citizens.[9]

The early history of Father Hennepin closely resembles that of the other parks established with a proviso that the state would not have to foot the bill for their development. Although there was talk of improvements being carried out under county and local sponsorship soon after the park bill was approved, by the time of Lathrop's 1946 valedictory letter to Fiero nothing had been done. In the next two years, however, the access road was improved through local effort, and the bare necessities of a picnic ground were installed. After passage of the park-sticker act in 1953, serious development, under state auspices, got under way.[10]

Most of Father Hennepin's problems stem from its small size. Although minor additions were authorized in 1955, 1961, 1963, 1965, and 1967, and the power of eminent domain was granted in 1971 so that a small but strategic tract of land could be acquired, the park still contained only 316 acres, including some 50 acres in private hands, in 1987. In less than half a square mile of land are crowded two picnic areas, a sixty-two-site campground, two boat docks, a bathing beach, a fish-cleaning house, and the necessary service facilities, plus four miles of trails. The park's small size also renders it vulnerable to natural or human damage. A violent windstorm in the summer of 1975 blew down many trees and made the hiking trails nearly impassable.[11]

Park use, as measured in visitor-days, grew from 15,000 in 1954 to 95,085 in 1975. The 1957 establishment of Mille Lacs Kathio, a large park on the west side of the lake, did not take the pressure off Father Hennepin. Some expansion seems necessary, or the park will simply wear out; the park manager and the DNR people would like to see Father Hennepin at least double in size, perhaps to about 700 acres. But when the suggestion of expansion was broached at the public meeting on the park's future in 1977, so much opposition was voiced that the idea was dropped. The future of the small park remains clouded, though it seems likely to continue within the state park system.[12]

## Nerstrand Big Woods

In the closing months of World War II, when victory was clearly in sight, the 1945 legislature, showing that it was looking ahead to the peacetime recreational needs of Minnesota's people, added six units to the system. The first of these was Nerstrand Woods, a sizable block of hardwood forest in Rice County, about forty miles south of the Twin Cities.

It is difficult to say just when the idea of preserving the Nerstrand Woods was first advanced. The possibility may have been discussed as early as the mid-1920s. Certainly by 1934, when the first serious drive for a park got under way, a newspaper in nearby Kenyon spoke of the "long, weary fight" that had been waged by the local Junior Chamber of Commerce to achieve park status for the woods. In response to a letter from the Jaycees, conservation commissioner E. V. Willard visited the area in the fall of 1934 and reported that it had "outstanding possibilities as a park to be set aside for recreational and education purposes." His report led to the full conservation commission's endorsement of the project, followed by a visit the next January from parks director Lathrop and two NPS inspectors. They were much impressed, and they were also concerned about some recent cutting, which suggested that no time should be lost in buying up the lands.[13]

One problem they faced was that ownership was divided among 169 landholders who owned more than 170 parcels; except for one tract of nearly 125 acres, none of these woodlots embraced more than 19.95 acres, and they ranged down to .02 acre. The owners were scattered from California to France, and some titles were clouded. Nevertheless, about a month after Lathrop's visit a land appraiser with the State Emergency Relief Administration began taking options on 480 acres, for which the owners were asking a total of $23,012. Eventually he got options on 1,027.54 acres, and there the process stopped.[14]

Bureaucratic delays, failure to get a CCC camp, a lack of legislative action, and perhaps some waning of the local backers' initial enthusiasm for the project combined to bring a premature end to this first concerted effort to make a state park of the Nerstrand Woods. When the project surfaced again in 1938, Lathrop enlisted the aid of Carl L. Weicht, editor of the *Northfield News* and one

*Nerstrand Woods State Park, 1960*

of the most vocal supporters of the park. Weicht's ideas about state parks were quite modern, in that they played down the recreational angle in favor of other possible uses. After commenting on the careless way parks had been established in the past, he went on:

> The ideal park, both national and state, is not only a place for recreation, a public playground on a large scale, but also has distinct character in preserving some site because of its historical interest or because it is unique from a natural history point of view. The Nerstrand Woods meets both these requirements.[15]

This time a Nerstrand Woods Committee was formed, Commissioner Wenzel tried to persuade a lumber company to defer cutting 50 acres, and companion bills were introduced in both houses of the legislature in 1939. The result was much the same as in 1935. Neither bill passed, the local committee lapsed into inactivity, and the momentum was lost once more. Although bills were introduced again in 1941 and the house bill passed that body, the senate bill failed to make its way out of committee.[16]

But about this time a new approach was tried. A constitutional amendment adopted in 1938 permitted the state to exchange lands with the federal government. A scheme was now devised by which the U.S. Forest Service (USFS) would acquire lands in the Nerstrand Woods and exchange them for state-owned lands of equal value within the boundaries of the Superior National Forest. Although this strategy met with only partial success at Nerstrand Woods and failed completely in the case of two other parks established in the 1940s, it did have the effect of getting the park proposal off dead center and moving again.[17]

Once more the laborious process of getting options from scattered owners was undertaken. By the end of fiscal 1944 the USFS had acquired more than seventy woodlots covering 460 acres. Although the land exchange program bogged down after that because of clouded titles to some of the tracts and the USFS's unwillingness to use condemnation to acquire others, the 460 acres already acquired were enough to induce the legislature to pass a bill establishing Nerstrand Woods State Park.[18]

The Nerstrand Woods bill, introduced on February 2, 1945, provided that upon receipt of the lands acquired by the USFS, together with tax-forfeited land, within sections 9 and 16, Wheeling

Township, the area should be established and dedicated as Nerstrand Woods State Park. The commissioner of conservation was empowered to cure defects in the title to such lands as suffered from clouded titles and to acquire other lands by gift or purchase. A special provision stated that suitable portions of the park might be used for forestry experiments and other scientific purposes in cooperation with the University of Minnesota, "reserving at least 100 acres of the best timbered and most scenic portions exclusively for public park purposes." The bill, which included no appropriation, was signed into law on March 28 by Governor Edward J. Thye.[19]

To a greater extent than with most other parks, a long time lapsed between the formal establishment of Nerstrand Woods and its development for the public. To both Harold Lathrop and his successor, obtaining more land had a higher priority than preparing it for the public's use. It was important, they thought, to acquire enclaves of private land to prevent logging and to consolidate state holdings within a closed boundary. Aided now and then by legislative appropriations, land acquisition progressed slowly. By 1968 the acreage was up to 563.[20]

In 1971 the legislature granted the right of eminent domain for the acquisition of "all land remaining in private ownership within the park boundaries." After this legislation, land acquisition moved a little faster. By 1976 the park embraced an area of 896 acres, and it was hoped that the remaining 384 acres could be acquired with the aid of the Land and Water Conservation Fund (LAWCON), a federal source for financing land purchases for recreational purposes. In 1990 the name was changed to Nerstrand Big Woods State Park; a few small parcels remained to be incorporated into the park, but they did not seriously impair its integrity.[21]

Long before Nerstrand Big Woods had reached even half its statutory dimensions, it had taken on some of the attributes of a state park. Trails and picnic facilities came first, and they were in place by the early 1950s; a campground followed in the next decade. Not much more in the way of development has taken place or is likely to take place. Nerstrand Big Woods is not adapted to intensive recreational use. Its primary value lies in its botanical significance as a remnant of the Big Woods. The planners of Project 80, who proposed to reclassify the park as a scientific and natural area, recognized that fact. Their proposal has not been adopted by the DNR, but the legislative fiat that much of the park should be available to the University of Minnesota as a hardwood forest experimental area has been accepted. The southern half of the park — everything south of the county road that bisects it — was chosen to serve this function, though it is laced with trails and even used by snowmobiles.[22]

The developed part of Nerstrand Big Woods is probably overused. Trails in the vicinity of the campground and the picnic area became so eroded that some were closed in 1983, and a couple of years later a new route was found for the popular trail to a small waterfall on a tributary of Prairie Creek. Yet a hiker seldom encounters anyone else on the more remote trails. If activity can be dispersed over the entire park, rather than concentrated in one area, the park can probably stand the traffic. Some local park use of a strictly recreational sort has been diverted to the Rice County parks, especially the Cannon River Wilderness Area. But from its inception Nerstrand Big Woods has been a popular destination for Twin Cities people, and even though they now have other more readily accessible parks, they continue to use it.

Nerstrand Big Woods has an important role to play in the state park system: that of a botanic reserve where the ecology of the Big Woods can be studied better than elsewhere because the area is larger than in other parks where bits of the hardwood forest have been preserved. The statutory boundaries, following section lines, do not enable it to fulfill this purpose as well as it might if the boundaries enclosed the whole woods and nothing else. But even with its rigidly rectangular shape, Nerstrand Big Woods consists chiefly of forest and encompasses most of this particular forest. In that respect it serves and will continue to serve the purposes envisioned by its early supporters in the 1930s.

## Baptism River and Split Rock Lighthouse

Two weeks after he approved the Nerstrand Woods bill, Governor Thye signed a bill creating two more parks on the North Shore of Lake Superior. In 1889 Newton Winchell had suggested a park in the Arrowhead region of Minnesota; with the completion of the highway up the shoreline from Two Harbors in the 1920s, that area had become more accessible. Yet, except for the Cascade River and Temperance River waysides, managed by the state highway department, Gooseberry Falls remained the only park along the North Shore at the beginning of 1945. What the state needed was a person of means and influence with a deep interest in the North Shore. It found such a person in Judge Clarence R. Magney, who had been instrumental in the establishment of Gooseberry Falls State Park and, even earlier, had taken a part in the expansion of Jay Cooke. A lawyer, jurist, and former mayor of Duluth, Judge Magney was in 1945 an associate justice of the Minnesota Supreme Court.[23]

According to his own statement, in 1944 Judge Magney had seen a sign near the Baptism River bridge saying, "Lake and River Frontages for Sale." Accessibility meant commercial development, and with the war evidently approaching its end, such development was bound to occur on the North Shore. The Baptism River Club had owned this area from 1886 to 1921 and had protected it against intrusion, but now the land was in danger. Magney put up option money to hold it until the legislature could act; he also promoted the bill, introduced February 2, 1945, to establish Baptism River State Park and Split Rock State Scenic Wayside. The bill passed easily, even though it contained an appropriation of $15,200 for the purchase of 506 acres at Baptism River and 35 acres near the Split Rock lighthouse.[24]

Baptism River State Park included frontage on Lake Superior at Shovel Point, from which Palisade Head can be seen down the lake; Baptism, or High, Falls, highest in the state; and two lesser waterfalls. Two hundred acres were added to the park later, but except for trails to the major attractions, it received no development in its thirty-four years as a state park. In 1979, when Tettegouche State Park was established, Baptism River was incorporated into the new and much larger park.[25]

The other park created by the 1945 act consisted of a hill southeast of U.S. Highway 61, seventeen miles up the lake from Two Harbors, that offered a commanding view of the Split Rock lighthouse, long a tourist attraction on the North Shore. No development took place during the time it remained a wayside. An NPS study in 1958 recommended that it be expanded to include the land around the lighthouse, and in 1967 legislation to this effect was

*Split Rock Lighthouse, about 1925*

passed. At that time the name was changed to Split Rock Light-house State Park and the statutory limits were expanded to include 996 acres, later increased to 1,872 acres.[26]

The Split Rock lighthouse was built by the federal government in 1909–10 in hopes of minimizing the danger to ships plying the waters of Lake Superior along this rocky shore. In 1939 the U.S. Coast Guard took over management of the station from the U.S. Lighthouse Service, but left the service's civilian operators in place; the following year, electricity replaced the kerosene used to power the light at the top of the tower. In 1961, when the last civilian operator retired, Coast Guard operators took over. A report cir-culating in 1967 that the government was about to close down the lighthouse led to the Minnesota legislature's action creating the park. Before the bill was approved, the Coast Guard made known its intention of continuing to staff the lighthouse, but less than two years later it was abandoned, made obsolete by radar.[27]

There was general agreement that the lighthouse should be

preserved, and parks director U. W. Hella believed that it could be acquired under the Historic Sites Act, at no cost to the state. Early in January 1970 the General Services Administration declared the structure and 7.63 acres of land surrounding it surplus government property. The state applied for its transfer, and on May 2, 1971, the property was deeded to the state at a formal dedication ceremony. The previous August the state had acquired an adjacent 112-acre tract containing, among other things, a gift shop. In 1976 the fifty-four-foot tower and the other buildings immediately around it were transferred to the Minnesota Historical Society, which assumed responsibility for the restoration, maintenance, and interpretation of the historic light station and the surrounding 25 acres. The parks division retained the rest of the property, including the contact station, picnic grounds, roads, and trails that it had developed; no provision for camping was made at that time.[28]

In the summer of 1984 a $555,000 development program began at Split Rock Lighthouse State Park, intended to provide recreational facilities comparable to those of other major North Shore parks. These included a new access road into the interior, parking lots, a new picnic area, a trail shelter building for year-around use by hikers and skiers, and a "cart-in" campground where users would leave their cars at the parking lot and haul their equipment to twenty remote campsites in two-wheel garden carts furnished by the park. All these facilities were in place by the summer of 1990, along with an expanded trail system. In 1986 the historical society opened a $1.2 million history center at Split Rock and completed restoration on many of the historic buildings. Together with the development of facilities at the new Tettegouche State Park, also begun in 1984, these improvements substantially increased the recreational capacity of the North Shore parks.[29]

## Kilen Woods

On April 21, 1945, Governor Thye signed into law two bills creating state parks in widely separated parts of the state. The bill establishing Kilen Woods State Park, in Jackson County, had been introduced first, on February 8. It called for the acquisition of 258 acres in sections 16 and 17, Belmont Township, and appropriated

$15,000 for the purchase of these lands. Like the other park bills in 1945, this one generated no significant opposition, passing both houses with scarcely a dissenting vote.[30]

As usual, the legislative act came as the culmination of a long campaign waged by local supporters of a park in what was called the Kilen Hills. About three weeks before the park bill was introduced, parks director Lathrop toured the area in the company of about twenty-five local citizens. In the expectation that a bill would be introduced and passed, the Windom newspaper commented: "After many years of dreaming and hoping, it now seems quite possible that this part of the state may be able, in the near future, to boast a State Park, one which will be located in the beautiful Kilen Hills a few miles south of Windom."[31]

Approximately 178 acres of land, much of it in woodlots, was acquired almost at once. Further appropriations in 1951 and 1955 enabled the parks division to buy another 21.6 acres, bringing the total area to just under 200 acres, where it has remained. The county built a road in from the west, but no funds were provided for development for several years. That lack might be fortunate, for if funds had been available in any large amount, the new park might have been overdeveloped. One of the parks division's plans called for a swimming pool, a bathhouse, a playground, and a two-hundred-car parking lot. Had this been carried out, it would have changed the character of the park and shifted the emphasis toward recreation.[32]

Beginning with the 1950–51 biennium, when the modest sum of $41,000 was appropriated, the parks division was able gradually to provide the necessary facilities: a picnic ground (complete with a shelter that later came to be used also as a nature center), a campground, and a network of trails. In 1957 an elevated wooden platform was erected adjacent to the picnic grounds so that visitors could get a good view of the Des Moines River valley.[33]

For the next twenty years Kilen Woods remained much the same — a quiet park, off the main routes of travel and therefore not heavily used. On a typical Fourth of July weekend, when the campground at Lake Shetek would be filled to capacity, there might be sites available at Kilen Woods until late in the day. The pace began to pick up after passage of the Outdoor Recreation Act of 1975, which mandated detailed studies of each park, classification of each park into one of several categories, and the preparation of a management plan to guide future development. In the summer of 1976 local supporters of the park formed the Committee of Concerned and Interested Citizens for the Preservation and Expansion of Kilen Woods State Park, which two years later became the Kilen Woods Advisory Committee. As with many other small units of the system, Kilen Woods had to grow or die — that is, either it had to be expanded to minimum state park size or it might be dropped from the system.[34]

Recommended figures for expansion — 660 acres as a recreational park, 1,700 acres as a natural park — were advanced by the parks people, but they seem also to have had considerable local support. Early in 1977 twenty-three members of the Friendly Garden Club of Lakefield wrote to the DNR, expressing concern over the possibility that the area adjacent to Kilen Woods might soon be developed for homesites and urging expansion of the park. When the question of expansion came up, both the DNR and the local advisory committee were inclined to think big. The latter had investigated an area of 7,040 acres, of which 2,680 were considered to be of state park quality. The members invited DNR representatives to tour the area and presented them with a map showing the proposed park boundaries. The first specific proposal for expansion, however, presented at a workshop held at Lakefield on July 11, 1978, called for increase of only 791.2 acres.[35]

Another workshop and another tour of the area followed. Discussion with DNR representatives then led to a proposal for an expansion of 3,926 acres. When a map showing the suggested park boundaries was distributed at a third meeting, held December 12, it drew fire from the affected landowners. They formed an organization to oppose expansion, circulated a petition, contacted government officials, and in general did all they could to counter the proposals, which were now definitely associated with the DNR. At the final workshop, held June 12, 1979, a scaled-down proposal for a 1,700-acre expansion was presented, to meet the same uncompromising opposition from landowners that the earlier one had. They now hired an attorney to prepare a landowners' agreement not to sell land to the state.[36]

The DNR's further efforts to arrive at an acceptable compromise were met by the landowners' absolute refusal to consider any expansion whatever. Unmoved by the argument that only nine landowners would be affected, they responded with comments like, "I think we have enough parks," or "I don't see why we have to provide recreation for the whole Midwest." As park planner Greg Rosenow saw the issue, a small group of local farmers had misrepresented the DNR's proposals and by intimidation and manipulation had made it impossible to implement any proposal for park expansion. He did not, however, advocate disposing of the park, an option that was not really practicable in any case. Jackson County had already indicated that it would not accept the land, and areas developed with LAWCON funding were required to remain available for recreational use.[37]

The conflict reached a sort of climax in the summer of 1980, when a couple of the angry farmers plowed up a garden belonging to park manager Lowell Jaeger. They probably did their cause more harm than good by this gesture, if one may judge from the adverse publicity it received and the response from at least one person far from the scene. A Stillwater man wrote to one of the farmers and sent copies of his letter to Jaeger and to the *Worthington Globe*. He found the farmers' act "disgusting and reprehensible behavior" and sarcastically suggested some even more extreme forms of violence "in keeping with red-necked, KKK principles," — perhaps even a necktie party.[38]

Things have been quieter around Kilen Woods since this episode, but the basic issue remains unresolved. Originally established to preserve a small wooded area surrounded by farms — an oasis in the prairie — the park would not be large enough to meet state park criteria even if it were expanded to include the remaining woodland along the Des Moines River. In recent years more emphasis has been given to the prairie portions of the park; seeds from forbs and grasses have been collected for reintroduction into former cultivated fields, and controlled burning has been used as a management tool to prevent the spread of trees and brush into the prairie areas.[39]

Kilen Woods is a good park for hiking in the summer or skiing in winter. Most of its trails (which are perhaps too numerous for the space) traverse the wooded sections, though some are on the prairie. Several footbridges cross Rock Creek, a pleasant woodland stream in years of normal rainfall. Here and there the trails are badly eroded. Between the woods and the river, below the picnic and camping areas, an expanse of open meadow bursts into color when the composites begin blooming in late summer. Like other oases in the prairie, Kilen Woods attracts a wide variety of birds that prefer the forest edge. All in all, it is a park well worth keeping in the system, despite its small size.

## McCarthy Beach

The other bill signed by Governor Thye on April 21, 1945, gave state park status to 135 acres of virgin red and white pine between Side and Sturgeon lakes, in St. Louis County, about twenty miles north of Hibbing. For years this had been a popular picnic and tenting ground for people from the Iron Range, whose use of it was not resented by the owner, "Old Man McCarthy" — John A. McCarthy, described as a "tolerant recluse" — who had homesteaded there. When he died in January 1943 and his daughter, Mary McCarthy Coffin, sold the land to a lumberman, local people became concerned about the fate of the timber — and their own recreational use of it. They were able to persuade the new owner to sell the land — at a 233 percent profit to himself. They then set about raising $50,000 by April 1945. After the American Legion and the Veterans of Foreign Wars of the United States proposed establishing a park as a memorial to the men who had died in World War II, the conservation commissioner, parks director, and various local and state foresters became involved and provided help and advice.[40]

The senate bill to establish McCarthy Beach State Memorial Park, introduced on March 14, did not emerge from committee until two or three days before the session was to end. Through a local person's vigorous efforts, it was pulled from the stack of some six hundred bills yet to be considered and pushed through the upper house, where it met no opposition. Substituted for a companion bill that had been introduced in the house, it passed that body with equal ease. The law is of some interest because it proposed the concept of matching funds for the establishment of a state park: it appropriated $25,000 for land purchases on condition that an equal amount be raised locally. Nearby municipalities (Hibbing and

*McCarthy Beach State Park*

Chisholm) were empowered to tax themselves up to a maximum of
$1.50 per capita for land acquisition and "initial permanent im-
provements" and up to $.50 per capita for subsequent improve-
ments and maintenance. Clearly the legislature was seeking not
only to hold down its own contribution to the cost of land acquisition but also to saddle local municipalities with the responsibility
for maintaining the park when it had been established.[41]

The necessary money was raised and the land purchased in a
few months. In order to put the park into operation as soon as possible, while at the same time to cut costs, the parks people constructed a refectory, bathhouse, toilets, tables, and grills out of
materials salvaged from old CCC buildings in Jay Cooke State
Park. Old CCC mess tables were transferred from Gooseberry
Falls. Local business owners and the city of Hibbing provided labor
and equipment. The job was largely completed by the end of 1947,
so that by the beginning of the 1948 season, the new park was in
full operation.[42]

McCarthy Beach State Park (the "Memorial" was dropped in
1969) has had a history of controversy, some of it stemming from

the provisions of the law that created it. In the early stages of development there was a clash between Frank Robertson, one of the chief promoters of the park, and park manager John Halgerson, who accused Robertson, in effect, of trying to run it with a bulldozer, in gouging out roads and parking lots. Then there were recriminations over who should maintain the park. Local people charged the parks division with neglecting it, while manager Halgerson reminded them that the terms of the law establishing McCarthy Beach had placed the responsibility for maintaining it on the local communities.[43]

A third controversy erupted over the expansion of the park. It had started with only 135 acres, but when it began expanding, it grew by leaps and bounds. Large increases were authorized in 1961, 1965, and 1969, bringing the total acreage to 3,754. This was cut back to 2,605 acres in 1971, but there was a slight increase in 1977. The land actually acquired had not cost the state much. In 1972, when 1,749 acres were state owned, only 219 acres had been purchased; the rest was tax-forfeited and state trust fund land. Regardless of how much or how little it cost the state, however, this expansion disturbed some local people. When the 1977 expansion was authorized, a resident of the area asked, "What 277 acres is destined to be added to this growing and uncontrollable monster?" The boundary has not changed since then, and it may be assumed that the "monster" has reached its natural limits.[44]

Except for trails, practically all the development at McCarthy Beach is in the original 135-acre tract between the two lakes. From there the park extends northwestward in a huge arc to Beatrice Lake, across the line in Itasca County. County and forest roads form the boundaries, but the interior is accessible mainly by trail. The park is practically surrounded by state forest lands; the Superior National Forest is only a short distance to the east. Although the forest lands provide recreational facilities, their chief purpose is the production of timber. Since the timber in a state park is protected, McCarthy Beach serves the public in a way the forest lands do not. Even though it provides swimming for at least 100,000 people annually, McCarthy Beach is not exclusively a recreation area, as Project 80 would have classified it. It is habitat for a variety of plants and animals associated with the northern boreal forest and as such deserves its present status as a state park.[45]

## Count Beltrami and Pine Tree

The last addition to the state park system made in 1945 was something of an anomaly. Years after the vogue of erecting monuments to commemorate historic events had waned, the legislature, at the behest of some Beltrami County residents, established a monument to honor Count Giacomo Constantino Beltrami, an Italian explorer who went in search of the source of the Mississippi and thought he had found it in a small body of water called Lake Julia, a few miles north of Bemidji. An appropriation of $500 was included for the purchase of an acre of land and the erection of such "markers and embellishments" as might be placed there.[46]

On August 22, 1948, the 125th anniversary of Beltrami's arrival, a bronze plaque in the shape of a Minnesota map, mounted on a boulder and engraved with an appropriate inscription, was dedicated. Along a county road, it was visited by few but local people. In the 1960s and early 1970s a dispute arose between the state and Turtle Lake Township, whose town hall occupied part of the site, over whose responsibility it was to maintain the monument. The issue was temporarily resolved in 1974, when a ten-year lease was signed, by which the township agreed to pay a token fee of $1 and to keep the premises in "neat and clean condition." Before two years of the lease had expired, however, the legislature passed an act transferring the entire property to the township on condition that it agree to maintain the monument.[47]

The 1947 legislature did almost as well as its predecessor, in terms of the number of parks it established. Three of the new parks were minor additions, however, and one of the others never materialized in its original form. The first — and least — was Pine Tree State Park, located on 21.55 acres of land fronting on Blackduck Lake, in Beltrami County. The same lawmakers who had initiated the legislation to create Count Beltrami State Monument introduced companion bills in their respective houses on January 23. The land, which belonged to the village of Blackduck, had been developed for recreational purposes in the 1930s, under U.S. Forest Service supervision. Since the village agreed to transfer the land to the state for no consideration except an agreement to maintain it as a state park, there was no opposition to the bill.[48]

Though a pleasant picnic spot, Pine Tree was never really of state park calibre. An attempt was made to raise its status in 1963, when its boundaries were extended to encompass an area of 222.3 acres. Land costs proved to be in excess of estimates, however, and a problem arose involving the adjacent village golf course. As a result, only a small part of the addition was ever acquired. In 1965 Pine Tree was included in the legislation that turned Oronoco, Toqua Lakes, Pomme de Terre, and other parks over to local jurisdiction.[49]

### Caribou Falls and Kodonce River

Largely through Judge Clarence Magney's efforts, two small but scenically valuable tracts of land on the North Shore were brought into the park system in 1947. Almost identical bills were introduced in the Minnesota house on February 10 calling for the establishment of Caribou Falls and Kodonce River state parks. Neither bill encountered any opposition, and Governor Luther W. Youngdahl signed both into law on April 1. Caribou Falls, with an area of 91.62 acres, included a short segment of the Caribou River, a minor North Shore stream with a fine waterfall a half-mile above U.S. Highway 61. It lay entirely north of the highway and so had no frontage on Lake Superior. A parking lot, some picnic tables, and a trail to the falls were all the development it received. Kodonce River (usually known as Kadunce Creek; the stream has also been known as "Diarrhoea Creek," referring to the water's effects) embraced part of the lower gorge of the stream and did include a strip of shoreline. Its statutory boundaries encompassed an area of 128 acres; the development was much the same as that of Caribou Falls.[50]

As suggested by the parks division's reclassification of both units as waysides in 1969, neither is of state park dimensions, and in neither case is there much likelihood of an expansion in the future. The removal of identifying highway signs from both sites in the mid-1970s symbolizes the DNR's partial withdrawal. Perhaps both will eventually come under the jurisdiction of the Department of Transportation as highway waysides. Whatever their disposition, the land should remain in public ownership, so that the scenic values for which the parks were created will be safeguarded.

## William O'Brien

Two of the parks established in 1947 have proved so popular that it is difficult now to see how Minnesota got along without them. One of these was William O'Brien, the first state park readily accessible to the Twin Cities metropolitan area. The lack of such a strategically located park had long been recognized as one of the defects of the system, but no solution to the problem had been apparent until Alice M. O'Brien, daughter of an early lumberman who had died in 1925, offered the state 180 acres of riverfront land on the St. Croix. The site was almost ideal, thought director Lathrop; the riverfront was high enough to be protected from floods but was readily accessible to canoes and other small boats. The land was covered with hardwood timber, with a scattering of pines that had survived logging days.[51]

Although Alice O'Brien's offer was made to Governor Thye and conservation commissioner Wilson in the summer of 1945, and the deed was filed November 1, the park was not formally established until the next session of the legislature. A bill was introduced on March 13, 1947, moved swiftly through both houses, and was signed by Governor Youngdahl on April 7. In keeping with the donor's request, the park was named for her father, William O'Brien.[52]

Like McCarthy Beach, this new park grew far beyond its original dimensions. Alice O'Brien herself contributed another 15 acres in 1951, and in 1958 S. David Greenberg, a St. Paul businessman, donated a 66.01-acre island, formerly known as Berkey Island but now renamed Greenberg Island. Other boundary changes were authorized in 1955, 1959, 1963, 1973, and 1986, as the park's popularity created problems in the form of crowded campgrounds and overuse of the trails. The original park was entirely east of Trunk Highway 95, between the highway and the river. As it expanded, it added lands west of the highway. Because the park is in a metropolitan area, it is in greater danger of incompatible development on adjacent lands than rural parks are. The fear of im-

*William O'Brien State Park*

minent housing developments on the fringe of the park led to the massive and somewhat controversial expansion authorized in 1973, which added to the park a large area of rolling, partly wooded terrain west of the Soo Line railroad tracks. With this increase and a 120-acre addition authorized in 1986, the park had a statutory area of 1,450 acres, of which nearly all had been acquired by 1990.[53]

The reason land has been so important an issue at William O'Brien is that space is needed for the increasing numbers of visitors the park receives every year. By 1969 visitation had surpassed 250,000, and in 1978 the number had increased to 357,765, including 35,084 campers. Outstate tourists camped in the park while visiting St. Paul, and Twin Cities families parked their trailers in the park for ten days at a time while the breadwinners commuted to work. The original campground, along the river, became too small many years ago, and a new one, on lands acquired west of the highway, was constructed to relieve the pressure. That, too, is now crowded. The heavy use also poses disciplinary problems, especially in May and early June when large numbers of young people camp in the park and hold all-night parties.[54]

Because of these and other problems caused by its location, William O'Brien is not everyone's park. To a camper fresh from a remote state or national forest campground, it may come as something of a shock to encounter the congestion that is the normal thing here. Most of the regular visitors seem not to mind this state of affairs.

William O'Brien's beauty is of a placid sort. The St. Croix is not the wilderness river it is at St. Croix State Park or the spectacular rock-bound stream it is at Interstate. Its appeal here is gentler. The far western reaches of the park have not been extensively developed, and they give a sense of space lacking on the beaches of Lake Alice, the artificial lake created by damming up a small watercourse. Above all, William O'Brien is valuable because it offers an outdoor experience for countless city-dwellers. Even with the recent development of county parks, there is never enough open space in and around the Twin Cities.

---

## Myre–Big Island

Another section of the state deficient in park facilities was in Freeborn and Mower counties, including the cities of Albert Lea and Austin, where the 1939 NPS study had recommended a park be established. People in the Albert Lea area had a piece of land in mind that they thought would make a good park: a heavily wooded island, 117.3 acres in size, in Albert Lea Lake, connected with the mainland by a causeway maintained by the county. Divided into small woodlots, with at least seventeen owners, the island had been used for recreational purposes for years. Moreover, artifacts found there suggested a long prehistory of Indian occupancy. Now, just after World War II, the timber was in danger of being logged off. Cutting had actually begun, but a local park committee had persuaded the lumbermen to stop before serious damage was done to the virgin stand, chiefly maple and basswood.[55]

At the request of local people, including state Senator Helmer C. Myre, deputy director John H. Martin of the parks division investigated the island in January 1947 and was favorably impressed with its potential. On the strength of his recommendation, Myre and Representative Irvin M. Talle, both of Albert Lea, introduced companion bills on February 27. The senate bill, which passed without serious difficulty and was signed into law on April 19, authorized the commissioner of conservation to acquire by gift, purchase, or condemnation certain described lands "known as Big Island in Albert Lea Lake." When they had been obtained, they would be dedicated as a state park "to be known by such name as may be designated by the commissioner of conservation." An appropriation of $11,500 was included. Since the land was valued at $18,000 or $19,000, the rest of the purchase price would have to be raised locally.[56]

Supporters of the park organized the Big Island State Park Founders Association of Albert Lea, Minnesota, and during the next two years took donations, secured options on the land, and tracked down the scattered owners. The final certificate was filed with the state auditor on May 6, 1949. When the land had been acquired, local contributions were used to provide fireplaces and two wells, while picnic tables and two pit toilets were financed out of general park maintenance funds, since no appropriations had been made for improvements. Because of limited space on the island, hiking and picnicking were the only activities provided for in the early years; a campground was added in the early 1960s. Although known locally as Big Island, the park did not officially have a name until 1953. Then the legislature formally named it to honor Senator Myre, who had died on October 6, 1951, after a long career of public service that included membership on the Albert Lea police force, a period as county sheriff, and a term as state representative before his election as state senator. In 1990, the legislature renamed the park Myre–Big Island State Park.[57]

Like almost every other state park, Myre–Big Island started out with too little land for the demands that came to be placed on it. When planning began on the interstate highway system and it was learned that Interstates 35 and 90 would both pass near the park, local interest, which had flagged somewhat over the years, revived. The State Park Improvement Association, formed in January 1963, began efforts to have the park expanded to include some of the mainland adjoining Big Island. The proposal was incorporated into the Omnibus Natural Resources and Recreation Act of 1963, which authorized the addition of about 839 acres, including certain land-form types, notably prairie and marsh, that were missing from the original park. After considerable delay owing to rising land costs and a lack of funds, most of the newly authorized land was acquired by the early 1970s, bringing the total acreage of the park to 956.[58]

But the park's expansion was not yet finished. The Interstate Power Company owned a 560-acre tract just north of the park. The land included considerable frontage on the lake, expanses of woodland, prairie, and marsh, and an interesting geological feature: an esker, defined as a long, narrow ridge of coarse gravel deposited by a stream flowing through a tunnel under a decaying glacier. Although the parks people had studied the land in 1967–68 and agreed that it would nicely complement the existing park, Interstate Power was expected to build a power plant there, thus precluding the state from obtaining the land. Late in 1974 the company dropped this plan and placed the land on the market. It was quickly snapped up by an Albert Lea real estate firm, which proposed to develop it for residential use.[59]

A two-year struggle followed between local advocates of expansion, aided by the Department of Natural Resources and the real estate agents. At first the parks people had been at most lukewarm toward the proposal. For one thing, only 40 acres of the tract were within the park's statutory boundaries, and until the legislature could act to extend those boundaries the DNR was powerless to acquire the rest of the land. Moreover, the price tag of $350,000 the realtor placed on it — nearly a third of the division's annual budget for land acquisition — seemed prohibitive. But when the 1975 legislature passed a park expansion bill including a $350,000 appropriation, the DNR became increasingly committed to supporting the plan.[60]

Unfortunately, as the months passed, the asking price of the land rose dramatically, first to $532,875, then to $783,000. The DNR rejected these offers, but when a federal grant of $396,985 for expansion of the park was announced, strong local pressure kept negotiations going. Although the state had commenced eminent domain proceedings (authorized by the expansion bill), the commissioners' award of $673,000, well above what the DNR was prepared to pay, temporarily stalled the process. At that point Samuel H. Morgan, of the Minnesota Council of State Parks, which had interested itself in the affair, suggested that the award be appealed and that contributions be solicited. The upshot was that the district jury reduced the amount of the award to $562,000 and the land was purchased, $21,000 having come from private donations by the end of 1976.[61]

With its approximately 1,648 acres, Myre–Big Island State Park contains several biotic communities besides the maple-basswood forest with which it started — not in quite the condition they were when white settlement began, but susceptible to restoration by modern techniques. The park includes some sixteen miles of hiking trails, about half of which can be used for snowmobiling and cross-country skiing in winter. It boasts the spacious Owen Johnson Interpretive Center, housing what has been called the largest "surface collection" of American Indian artifacts in North America, collected by Johnson over many years and bequeathed to the park in 1972. The park is big enough, has sufficient variety of life space zones, and, with the construction of Interstates 35 and 90, draws people from a large enough area to justify its remaining a full-fledged state park. The investment the DNR has made in it since the mid-1960s probably ensures that it will continue as part of the system.[62]

## Carley

After the sizable additions made to the state park system in 1945 and 1947, it is perhaps not surprising that the 1949 legislature slowed down the pace by creating only one new park. Late in 1948 state Senator James A. Carley, whose roots were in the Whitewater River valley of southeastern Minnesota, donated to the state nearly 200 acres, which he had bought in 1937, along the North Branch of the Whitewater. Long used as a picnic and recreation spot by people from the Plainview vicinity, the area was scenically attractive and included a large stand of virgin white pine, a rarity in that part of Minnesota. The commissioner of conservation promptly accepted the gift, and the 1949 legislature unanimously passed a bill creating Carley State Park. With the addition of a small parcel donated by the Boldt family, the park embraced an area of 211 acres, which has remained its size ever since.[63]

From its beginning, Carley was perceived as a sort of detached overflow campground for Whitewater, long the most heavily used park in southern Minnesota and only ten miles away. Carley had no development until the 1960s, and as late as 1967 the park had a raw, unfinished look about it. It was eventually provided with a picnic area, a small family campground, a group camp, and five miles of trails. The Whitewater River makes a wide, sweeping horseshoe bend here; a trail lies on each side of the river, the longer one located mostly on high ground, well above the river. Two footbridges give access to the higher trail from the picnic ground–campground complex.

Carley's chief appeal is botanical. A severe hailstorm in 1954 destroyed many of the pines that were its principal attraction, but replacements planted soon afterward are gradually maturing. The spring wildflower display is one of the richest in this region of the state, and in autumn the colors of its sugar maples and red oaks contrast with the green of the surviving pines. Carley is more than a lesser Whitewater, as those visitors discover who are sent to Carley when campgrounds in Whitewater are full; it has a subdued charm all its own. Although it probably will not be expanded, and although Project 80 would have relegated it to a trail wayside, Carley has a place in the state park system and ought to be retained.

## Ray Berglund

The last addition made to the state park system during the 1942–52 period was the Ray Berglund State Wayside, conceived as a memorial to a St. Paul businessman, both a lumberman and a conservationist. When he died in 1948, some of his friends contributed to a fund for the purchase of 54 acres of land at the mouth of the Onion River, between Tofte and Lutsen, in Cook County. The land was deeded to the state in 1949, and two years later the legislature established the wayside. Although the parks division planned extensive development of the site, a parking lot and minimum picnic facilities were all that materialized, along with a memorial plaque, dedicated in 1959, honoring Berglund. The remarks made earlier about Caribou Falls and Kodonce River apply equally to Ray Berglund. Though not likely to be expanded into a true state park, the site should remain in state ownership so that the natural features the wayside was created to preserve will continue to enjoy adequate protection. Travelers following U.S. Highway 61 up the North Shore need occasional rest stops, where they can enjoy the view and perhaps eat a picnic lunch. Small units like Ray Berglund serve this purpose well enough to justify the modest cost of maintaining them. [64]

---

## Summary

If the war and immediate postwar years did not witness so dramatic an expansion of the state park system as the mid-1930s did, they did bring significant additions. Nerstrand Woods, McCarthy Beach, William O'Brien, and Helmer Myre were all units of state park calibre. Baptism River and Split Rock later achieved that status in their expanded forms as Tettegouche and Split Rock Lighthouse state parks. Father Hennepin, Kilen Woods, and Carley were potentially of state park quality but were handicapped by their small size. Caribou Falls, Kodonce River, and Ray Berglund were only waysides, but in each case state ownership protected notable features of the North Shore landscape. Only Count Beltrami and Pine Tree were unworthy of inclusion in the state park system, and they were eventually dropped.

The main problems faced by the parks in this period were economic. The division of parks was trying to maintain an enlarged system by the standards adopted during the 1930s, but without the financial resources to do so. The state relied on local contributions for the purchase of land and, in some cases, for the subsequent development and maintenance of the parks thus created. Neither these contributions nor the biennial appropriations were adequate to the task of acquiring sufficient amounts of land or that of maintaining the buildings and roads constructed during the days of work-relief programs and federal funding. By 1952 the parks were approaching a crisis. Director Fiero's published reports, presumably reflecting the views of the staff in the field, told of deteriorating facilities in the older parks and of inability to develop the new ones for public use. Clearly, what was needed was a new source of revenue.

# CHAPTER SEVEN

# A *Time of Change*
## *1953-1962*

THE NEED for a new source of revenue for the parks was met in 1953 by passage of the park-sticker act, as it was generally called, which placed part of the burden of support directly on users of the parks. Such a policy had been considered and rejected several times before. As early as 1923 State Auditor Ray Chase had argued that to charge fees would not provide much revenue, and it would displease the public, who, he said, considered such commercialism "repellent." The legislature apparently agreed, for a law passed that year specifically stated that "state parks shall be preserved and maintained for the free use and enjoyment of the general public." No fees were charged even for transient camping at that time, though later that policy was changed.[1]

In 1933 a law was passed authorizing a charge of twenty-five cents a day for parking space and the same amount for camping, no one to be charged more than a total of twenty-five cents a day. With some modification, this served as the basis for the resolution adopted in 1935, which, as we have seen, aroused so much opposition that it was not enforced in most parks. Parks director Harold Lathrop apparently continued to entertain the idea of an entrance fee, however, for as late as 1940 he remarked that some states charged such a fee, adding that if this was the answer, the legislature should provide the parks division with the necessary authority.[2]

The 1953 law provided that no motor vehicle should enter a park, recreation area, or wayside of more than 50 acres without a permit, valid for one year, costing one dollar. It went on to say, "All fees collected shall be deposited in a State Park Maintenance Fund which . . . shall be used solely for maintenance and operation of state parks." Since the parks needed help immediately, the law also provided for the transfer of $450,000 from the game and fish fund, the money to be repaid out of sticker fees. Governor C. Elmer Anderson allowed the bill to become law without his signature on April 11, 1953.[3]

Despite some grumbling, the sticker law was generally well received by the public. Because of its acceptance and because of inflation, the fees have been raised five times since 1953. At the extra session in 1961 the legislature raised the fee for the annual permit to $2.00 and the two-day permit from 25¢ to 50¢. In 1969 the fees were raised to $3.00 and $1.00, respectively, and in 1976 to $5.00 and $1.50, respectively. The biggest jump came in 1981, when the price of permits was doubled, an annual permit to $10.00 and the two-day sticker to $3.00. By this legislation, Minnesota also temporarily joined the ranks of those states, such as Wisconsin, that discriminate against nonresidents. Vehicles not licensed in Minnesota were now charged $15.00 for an annual permit, $4.00 for a two-day permit. Moreover, people over sixty-five, who had formerly received free permits, were now charged half-price. In 1986 the cost of an annual fee went up to $15.00 (residents and nonresidents being charged the same). When the 1987 legislature extended the sales tax to such items as park entrance fees, another 6 percent was added; in 1988 the fees were rounded off at $16.00 and $3.25, tax included.[4]

The philosophy behind these latest increases apparently was that if charging $5.00 for a sticker brings in X number of dollars, tripling the charge will bring in three times as much revenue. Whether this is a valid assumption remains to be seen. Certainly the escalating cost of using a state park has generated an increasing number of complaints. A frequently encountered type of letter in the DNR's files comes from irate park visitors who believe they have been treated unfairly in the matter of entrance fees. A typical objection is that the writer has paid the entrance fee, expecting to find a campsite available, only to discover that the campground is full and to be obliged to leave the park, without having received anything for the money spent. One may assume that not all of these complaints are legitimate, but some of them surely are. Whatever the effects of the steadily rising fees, however, the original park-sticker law breathed new life into the system by providing a badly needed source of revenue.

A few weeks before the passage of the park-sticker bill, Lew E. Fiero resigned as director of the division of parks, and Udert W. Hella replaced him. Known since youth as "Judge," Hella was a forty-four-year-old civil engineer, a 1931 graduate of the University of Minnesota whose varied career had included many years of work with parks. After two years as draftsman and member of a field survey crew with the state highway department, he had served from 1933 to 1937 with the NPS, starting as an engineering foreman in a CCC camp at Scenic State Park. He had spent some time at the regional office in Omaha and in the state of Wyoming and then had become camp superintendent at Sibley State Park and supervisor of the Minnesota Park, Parkway and Recreational Area Study. From 1937 to 1941 he had been with the Minnesota division of parks as supervisor of the Northern District. During World War II he had worked with Northwest Airlines, and since the war he had held quite different jobs, including one as general manager of production and corporate secretary of Kol, Inc., of St. Paul, manufacturers of tubular steel and sheet metal items. It was from that post that he now moved to the top position in the parks division.[5]

During Hella's twenty years in that post he saw the state park system grow rapidly — 1963 witnessed the biggest increase in the number of parks in any single year — and then abruptly slow down after most of its primary goals had been achieved. Together with assistant director John Martin, he became a repository of information on the parks he supervised and on areas that he hoped to see incorporated into the system.

## George H. Crosby Manitou

The first addition to the system during Hella's term as director was another North Shore park, a donation from George H. Crosby, a mining magnate who had been involved in the development of both the Mesabi and Cuyuna iron ranges. Early in 1954 he wrote to Attorney General Joseph A. A. Burnquist, offering his property

*U. W. ("Judge") Hella, engineering foreman at CCC camp, and Garfield Iverson, CCC worker from Virginia, Scenic State Park, 1933*

on the Manitou River to the state on condition that it be used for a state park to be called George H. Crosby Manitou. The state promptly accepted the offer, and the 3,320-acre tract was formally established as a state park by the 1955 legislature, whose action was signed into law by Governor Orville L. Freeman on March 11.[6]

It seems to have been Crosby's wish, which has been honored by the parks division, to severely limit development of the park, so that it would remain a wilderness. Early on, a decision was made to exclude the usual facilities available to park users who seldom get far from their automobiles. Instead of the customary campground, this park would have primitive campsites scattered through the park, accessible only by foot trail. In the words of park planner Milt Krona, the parks division hoped in this way to "satisfy one kind of camping need." In 1973, two years after the park formally opened, a Twin Cities newspaper columnist sampled it and found that people had discovered it. By midsummer the park manager estimated that 1,300 people had visited it that season, 300 of whom were campers. On weekends the sites were 75 percent filled, he said, though during the week only one or two groups a day appeared. He was pleased to report that there was as yet no garbage problem; park users were packing it out.[7]

For the most part, Crosby Manitou consists of rugged, heavily wooded terrain extending for several miles up the Manitou River from its mouth. The trees are chiefly fir, spruce, cedar, and maple, remnants of the forest that existed there before the days of lumbering. Here and there rise rocky crags from which one can see Lake Superior. Like most of the North Shore streams, the Manitou falls sharply in the last few miles of its course. The most spectacular waterfall, directly into the lake, is on private property, but the Crosby Cascades, a series of rapids, are in the park, reached by trail.[8]

Although not all the land within Crosby Manitou's statutory boundaries has been acquired, hikers have plenty of room to move around in the park; in summer, however, one is not likely to hike very far without encountering someone else doing the same thing. One may also encounter other park users, such as bears. Although some human visitors are less than enthusiastic about the presence of these permanent residents — one wrote to the parks and recreation division demanding that "the bears should be removed or destroyed *immediately*" — reasonable precautions in the storage of food should prevent any unpleasant confrontations.[9]

George H. Crosby Manitou State Park is an experiment, the first park in the system to be designed primarily for backpackers. So far it appears to be a success. Of course, day visitors can hike the trails and even picnic beside Bensen Lake, not far from the parking lot where cars are left. The trails offer plenty to see: a wide range of plants representing the boreal forest vegetation and the wildlife associated with that biotic community. One can obtain a checklist at the manager's residence and see what wildflowers are likely to be in bloom at a particular season. The rugged terrain ensures that hiking is strenuous — as George Crosby doubtless wanted it to be.

## Judge C. R. Magney

The next addition to the system was another large North Shore park. Early in 1957 companion bills were introduced in both houses of the legislature, calling for the establishment of Brule River State Park and the acquisition of 160 acres of land in Cook County. Passed by decisive margins in both chambers, the house bill was signed into law by Governor Freeman on April 24. In its final form it included an appropriation of $5,000 for land acquisition and also provided that any other state-owned lands in sections 22, 27, and 34 should become part of the new park.[10]

The Brule River is the longest North Shore stream entirely in Minnesota, and because it has its source in sizable lakes and swamps its flow remains more uniform throughout the summer than the flow of such rivers as the Gooseberry and the Baptism. It is the only North Shore stream that has a potential for whitewater kayaking in the upper reaches. Like the other rivers, it drops precipitously as it approaches Lake Superior. The 160-acre tract specified in the law creating the park contains three impressive waterfalls: Lower Falls, Upper Falls, and the Devil's Kettle. The last, which is the highest drop, seventy feet in two stages, has the peculiarity that one channel disappears in a pothole at the lip of the falls and does not reappear. The mist generated by the waterfalls creates a microclimate in which certain plants flourish that are not found a short distance away.[11]

*Judge C. R. Magney at Upper Baptism River*

Before the Brule River State Park bill was passed, the Grand Marais newspaper reported that the new entity would be named Magney State Park. The report was premature, but after Judge Clarence Magney's death on May 14, 1962, sentiment developed to have the park renamed in his honor. The 1963 legislature made the necessary change, and on September 27, 1964, a plaque was unveiled at the park honoring the man who, more than anyone else, helped preserve strategically located pieces of land on the North Shore.[12]

Judge C. R. Magney State Park contained 1,030 acres at the time of the name change. The 1965 legislature authorized a 3,470-acre expansion to include a stretch of the Brule upstream from the falls. This gave it a statutory area of 4,500 acres, of which 4,095 was in state ownership by 1987. Only a small part has been developed. Near U.S. Highway 61 there is a forty-two-site rustic campground; for many years that, together with a picnic area, a footbridge, and trails to the falls, constituted all the development that had been carried out. In 1987 a longer trail, on the bluffs overlooking the right bank of the river, was laid out.

Magney has the distinction of being the last Minnesota state park on the highway leading to Thunder Bay, Ontario. Though less used by campers than Gooseberry Falls, Cascade River, or Temperance River, it serves as a good base for trips to Grand Portage National Monument, still farther up the North Shore.[13]

---

## Mille Lacs Kathio

Besides establishing Brule River State Park and bringing Cascade River and Temperance River officially into the system, the 1957 legislature created two parks that had long been sought by local residents and others. One of these was in the Mille Lacs Lake region. Father Hennepin State Park was too small to serve the growing recreational needs of that district, and so interest once more developed in a large park more or less equidistant from the Twin Cities and Duluth. Verner Nelson, editor and publisher of the *Onamia Independent*, claimed to have begun talking to Onamia business owners and others in 1956 and encouraging the idea of a park between that town and the lake. By the time of the 1957 legislative session, they were ready to move. On February 28 companion bills were introduced in the two houses, calling for the establishment of Mille Lacs Kathio State Park. After striking out an amendment that would have allowed travel on park roads without a vehicle permit, both houses passed the bill unanimously, and Governor Freeman signed it on April 15.[14]

The Mille Lacs Kathio bill provided that all state-owned lands in the area already under the jurisdiction of the conservation commissioner, together with tax-forfeited lands then owned or subsequently acquired by the state, should be dedicated for park purposes. The statutory boundaries enclosed an area of nearly 10,000 acres; some 6,500 acres were already tax-delinquent or otherwise in public ownership, so the park was able to begin with a nucleus greater than almost any other park in the system had ever enjoyed. Within a few months the claim was being made that Mille Lacs Kathio was the fourth largest park in the system.[15]

While the park bill was still pending, Russell Fridley, director of the Minnesota Historical Society, wrote parks director Hella about the archaeological and historical importance of the Kathio area. Until the middle of the eighteenth century it was the principal seat of the Dakota. In 1679 Daniel Greysolon, sieur du Luth, visited the great Dakota village of Izatys (later corrupted into Kathio), and Father Louis Hennepin was held captive there the following year. Archaeological evidence suggested a long period of Indian occupancy. When the Dakota vacated the Mille Lacs region, partly because of pressure from the westward-moving Ojibway, the Ojibway's Eastern Woodland culture replaced the Dakota's. The Mille Lacs band still lives just north of the park, in the vicinity of Vineland.[16]

In this historically important area Harry and Janette O. Ayer operated a trading post and collected a virtual museum of Indian artifacts, which in 1959 they donated to the Minnesota Historical Society. The parks division and the historical society thereafter worked cooperatively in interpreting the history and prehistory of the area. Archaeologists had long conducted digs there, and in the summer of 1965 State Archaeologist Elden Johnson began a series of excavations in the park. His idea was to combine scientific study and interpretation. By 1973 he was speaking of "actual controlled excavations at sites in the park for the purpose of demonstrating field archaeology." He had in mind a program similar to that at Dinosaur National Monument, where the process of exposing fossilized dinosaur bones is carried on in full view of visitors to the interpretive center. The camper at Mille Lacs Kathio could walk a short distance along the south shore of Ogechie Lake and see an actual dig not too far from the site of Izatys. Johnson wrote, "Working two to four hours per day over two and one half months each summer, we have enough site areas to last a good one hundred years."[17]

Relations between the park and its modern Ojibway neighbors have not always been harmonious. The statutory boundaries included some land belonging to the Mille Lacs band. The parks division assumed that these could be obtained by exchange for other state-owned lands adjacent to the reservation. Things did not work out that way, and by 1973 conflicts had developed; the Ojibway were concerned about burial sites and hunting and trapping rights on the land. The land question remains an unsettled issue between the Ojibway and the parks division. Ojibway-owned land is shown in red on the official park map, and an accompanying note warns the park user: "Caution 'Indian Tribal Lands' are hunted annually from July 1 through December 31." Considering that one of these tracts extends from immediately behind the interpretive center to the south edge of the campground, the park visitor might well heed the warning.[18]

A visitor finds much to do in Mille Lacs Kathio. Hikers have thirty-six miles of foot trails, portions of which can also be used by skiers, snowmobilers, and horseback riders. The terrain is generally rolling, consisting of a series of hills left by a large terminal moraine. The vegetation is mostly second-growth northern hardwood forest. In fall the sugar maples and red oaks blaze with color, contrasting with an occasional remnant of pine. A lookout tower affords a view of this multicolored carpet, with the blue of the big lake in the distance. Near the entrance station is an outdoor display telling of the prehistory of the area. Mille Lacs Kathio is a big park, a park with a variety of offerings, and a park that can absorb a great deal of use without serious injury to its resources.

## Frontenac

The last park established in 1957 was Frontenac, located about sixty miles from the Twin Cities, on that lovely expansion of the Mississippi called Lake Pepin. Frontenac offers historic, biological, and scenic appeals; it was first suggested for park status perhaps as early as 1925. Here, many believe, was the site of the last French fort on the upper Mississippi, Fort Beauharnois, erected in 1727. In 1853 Evert V. Westervelt began trading here with the Dakota Indians; when they were moved to reservations, he and Israel Garrard platted the town of Westervelt, later renamed Frontenac for Louis de Buade, comte de Frontenac, the governor of New France in the late seventeenth century. Although Israel's three brothers were associated with him in the enterprise, he alone lived out the rest of his life at Frontenac, as a sort of lord of the manor. When the railroad came through in 1870, he gave land for a station well away from the old town so that the town would not be disturbed by commercialization.[19]

The first concrete proposals for a park date from the mid-1930s, when parks director Lathrop tried to interest the Executive Council in appropriating funds for the purchase of lands there. Nothing came of the plan then, mainly because federal officials decided that Goodhue County had insufficient relief labor to warrant a CCC

*Inyan Tiopa, now in Frontenac State Park, about 1890. The name means "Stone Entryway" in the Dakota language.*

camp. Early in 1938 the proposal was revived, and the parks division, with assistance from the NPS, conducted a survey and submitted a detailed report. Although the suggested acreage had been scaled down from 400 to 350 acres, the report recommended the inclusion not only of a fine beach on Sand Point and a forested area inland along Wells Creek, but also of some high land on Garrard Bluff, overlooking the lake.[20]

Again the Frontenac park proposal failed to materialize, and no further efforts were made until 1953, when local enthusiasm, reflected in an editorial in the Red Wing *Republican Eagle*, coincided with Judge Hella's feeling that the time was ripe for another attempt. Conservation commissioner Wilson contacted the owners of some of the desired land, who were said to favor selling it to the state in order to forestall commercial development. After state officials met with local park supporters the next year, the Frontenac State Park Association was formed, with Albert M. Marshall, editor and publisher of the Red Wing newspaper, as acting chairman. Marshall, one of the founders of the Minnesota Council of State Parks, had a special interest in Frontenac, only ten miles down the river from Red Wing.[21]

When the first Frontenac State Park bill was introduced in the 1955 legislature, opposition to the proposal surfaced at the hearings that followed. Many local residents feared littering and wild parties, and some complained that they had not been consulted when plans for a park were formulated. Partly because of these objections but mainly because of the anticipated cost of land acquisition, the bill never came up for a vote at that session. It was becoming evident that local advocates of the park would have to buy at least part of the needed land and hope that the state would match their contributions, as had been done elsewhere.[22]

By December 1955 the Frontenac State Park Association had raised enough money for a down payment on a 160-acre tract in the heart of the proposed park. The plan was to pay for the parcel over a five-year period and then present it to the state. Some land might also be obtained from two other sources: the state highway department owned 110 acres in three parcels and had plans to realign the highway, so the land not needed could be transferred to the conservation department, and Goodhue County owned two small tracts in the Sand Point area.[23]

In the fall of 1955 engineers from the U.S. Bureau of Public Roads made a survey of the Frontenac area and offered some suggestions to enhance the proposed park, including construction of a skyline drive, which would leave U.S. Highway 61 east of Frontenac Station, pass to the west of Old Frontenac, climb to the top of the bluff, and continue westward, eventually to rejoin Highway 61 several miles beyond. To anticipate objections from Old Frontenac residents, they hastened to emphasize that the road would be laid out to "safeguard the privacy and quiet of the quaint, old place," as the Red Wing newspaper expressed it.[24]

In 1956, as the association continued to solicit contributions, it received a windfall donation of 200 acres, including Garrard Bluff, from John H. Hauschild, chairman of the board of the Great

Northern Insurance Company, the land to be turned over to the state as soon as the legislature authorized the park. Local opposition remained strong and vocal, however. When conservation commissioner George A. Selke and parks director Hella met with the association and other interested parties, only one Frontenac resident dared voice support for the park. Besides widespread concern over the loss of tax revenue, many again expressed fears of the impact a park would have on the quiet village. Hella told the group that it was a case of "planned encroachment" versus "unplanned encroachment" and that the park could provide a buffer against undesirable development.[25]

The park association prepared carefully for the 1957 legislative session. More than thirty influential legislators, of both houses, were taken on a tour of the area in January, and the senatorial contingent was entertained at a dinner in Red Wing that evening. When companion bills were introduced in February, their sponsorship included legislators from the Twin Cities and outstate areas, as well as from Goodhue and Wabasha counties, suggesting that the park had wide support. At the hearings held in succeeding weeks, testimony in favor of the park was offered by Commissioner Selke, Minnesota Historical Society director Fridley, and representatives of the Natural History Society of Minnesota, the Izaak Walton League, the University of Minnesota's Museum of Natural History, the Hiawatha Valley Association, and various conservation clubs.[26]

The local residents' opposition largely followed the lines of earlier objections, but some who had previously favored the park now testified against it. Edward S. Hall wrote Hella that the original plans had been so changed in the final bill that the park as now proposed would not accomplish the purposes that had led many to support it. The stress, he complained, seemed to be on making a recreational playground rather than on preserving its natural beauty. "Old Frontenac village," he wrote, "has charms that cannot be added to by surrounding it with a public playground."[27]

The course of the Frontenac State Park bill was more tortuous than almost any other such piece of legislation since the Itasca State Park bill in 1891. Amended substantially in committee, the senate bill finally passed, 47 to 3, though not without a parliamentary battle to defeat it. In the house it was virtually rewritten by the appropriations committee, and in its radically altered form, after a vigorous floor fight, it passed by a margin of only 73 to 35 — a sharp contrast to the all-but-unanimous votes by which most other park bills were approved.[28]

In its final form the bill had features objectionable to both sides in the controversy. Besides limitations on the appraised valuation of donated lands (designed to hold down the amount of matching funds from the state), it contained a restriction not found in any previous park legislation. Further development, it specified, "shall be limited to the preservation of the present natural feature[s] of the area as a wild life and bird sanctuary. Any development shall not exceed the laying out and clearing of footpaths." If followed literally, this clause would have prevented any development whatever in the usual sense of the term. The parks people, who argued that this restriction had been intended to apply only to the Sand Point–Wells Creek area, succeeded in gaining the 1961 legislature's passage of an amendment making the parks people's interpretation explicit.[29]

Meanwhile, land acquisition went forward, with the assistance of the park association and over the objections of some property owners. Hosea Randall, owner of Sand Point, adamantly rejected the state's offer for his land. John Martin, who tried to negotiate with him, remarked, "It appears that Mr. Randall believes that he is carrying out a mandate of General Garrard [whom he professed to have known] in maintaining this area in this state." Eventually the state had to employ eminent domain proceedings to obtain Randall's property and that of some other unwilling sellers. The 1961 legislation extended the statutory boundaries of the park westward and at the same time excluded all land owned by Villa Maria Academy, a Catholic girls' school adjoining the park. The boundary changes effected a net gain of about 200 acres, bringing the park's area to some 1,150 acres.[30]

Even after the restrictions contained in the original legislation were lifted, land acquisition problems delayed actual development until 1964 and 1965, when a long, sweeping, two-mile road was built to the top of Garrard Bluff and the necessary camping and picnicking facilities were installed. The idea of a skyline drive had been abandoned by this time, but the approach road accomplished much the same purpose, at less cost to the setting. Among other benefits, it rendered more accessible a large perforated rock, called Inyan Tiopa, that perches almost on the edge of the cliff overlooking the lake.[31]

Additions authorized in 1965, 1969, and 1971 gave the park a statutory area of 2,689 acres. Some of this land was being actively farmed, however, and the owners were unwilling to part with it. Moreover, by 1977, when the management plan mandated by the Outdoor Recreation Act (ORA) of 1975 was prepared for Frontenac, the park planners had come around to accepting continued private ownership of the land, provided zoning ordinances were enacted to prevent incompatible use of it. The 1977 plan proposed a land exchange, dropping about 750 acres west of Frontenac Station from the park and adding a roughly equivalent area on the bluff, west of the campground. It also outlined proposed development of the Sand Point–Wells Creek area. To many who attended a public meeting in Red Wing on June 20, such development seemed to violate both the letter and the spirit of the original legislation, as amended. In the face of their opposition, the planners modified their proposal to include only a self-guiding trail and a sanitation building. Legislation passed in 1986 effected the land exchange, which changed the shape of the park and brought a greater portion of park-quality land into it.[32]

The animus behind some objections to more extensive development has its origins in Frontenac's reputation as a birders' paradise. On the Mississippi flyway, it has been known since at least 1900 as an excellent place to watch bird migration. Those who favored establishment of the park in order to protect the bottomland forest naturally oppose its recreational development.

Recreational use of Sand Point has not been totally excluded, however, and one wonders if the area would not be better protected from abuse if it were more accessible to park personnel. Boaters use the beach and leave trash around. With only a foot trail leading in on the landward side, it is impossible to police Sand Point with any thoroughness.

Many park users prefer hiking the bluffside trails in spring, when the woodland flowers are in bloom, or the prairie trails in late summer, when the composites reach their peak, rather than explore the marshy lowlands, where the mosquitoes and other insects diminish hikers' pleasure. The bluffside trails are steep and expensive to maintain, but the experience they provide is worth the expense — not to mention the effort required to climb back up after one has descended to the shoreline, a narrow strip of rocks between the foot of the bluff and the water.

Recognized by Project 80 as one of the twenty units deserving continued state park status, Frontenac was classified under the 1975 ORA mandate as a natural state park — meaning that it should be preserved chiefly for the biological values and that recreational development should be held to a minimum. If this is indeed its destiny, then the park will fulfill the intent of those who argued for its establishment in the first place. Since the biological and historical functions do not conflict, Frontenac can continue to serve both interests as a major unit in the Minnesota state park system.[33]

## Zippel Bay and Schoolcraft

Two of the three units of the state park system created in 1959 were what were then called state recreational reserves, later redesignated state recreation areas. The first to enter the legislative hopper resulted from the need for some kind of public access to Lake of the Woods, that great body of water that Minnesota shares with Ontario and Manitoba. Companion bills were introduced in February calling for the establishment of "Lake of the Woods–Zippel Bay [State] Recreation Reserve." The house bill, chosen as the vehicle for this objective, passed both chambers by nearly unanimous votes and was signed into law by Governor Freeman on March 3. Since 2,611 acres of the 2,766 acres within the statutory boundaries were tax-forfeited, no appropriation was included. The 1961 legislature changed the boundaries so as to add 154.75 acres of land deemed essential to the development of the park and provided an appropriation for its purchase. There have been no other additions.[34]

Development got under way at Zippel Bay with unusual alacrity. The 1961, 1963, and 1965 legislatures all appropriated adequate, if modest, sums for capital improvements, such as roads, parking areas, picnic grounds, campgrounds, a seasonal residence, a boat launching ramp, and the necessary water, sewer, and electrical services, as well as landscaping and boundary marking.

*Zippel Bay State Park, 1971*

Within a few years of its establishment, Zippel Bay (as the name came to be unofficially shortened) boasted all the usual facilities of a state park, and by 1990 it had three campgrounds and two picnic areas (one at the beach, the other, a limited facility, at the boat harbor). Appropriations for land acquisition have made it possible to buy up all of the small acreage of privately owned land.[35]

Zippel Bay is not an outstanding unit of the park system, but it serves its intended function as a public recreation area in a part of the state where there are few others. Though the scenery is not exceptional, the beach, with its scattering of driftwood brought perhaps from Canada, has a certain austere beauty. On a chill late-August morning, when the north wind whips up whitecaps on the seemingly limitless expanse of Lake of the Woods, that beach can appear positively forbidding. Zippel Bay's biological significance lies in the beach-front marshes, a rare feature on Lake of the

*Schoolcraft State Park*

Woods, and in sightings of the endangered piping plover and great gray owl. The area is certainly worthy of continued inclusion in the park system.

The other recreational reserve to emerge from the 1959 legislative session was Schoolcraft, located on the Mississippi, mostly in Cass County, west of Grand Rapids. Its inception was at least partly due to local initiative. The North Grange had lost its picnic ground when a resort was built at Day's High Landing. Some of its members interested conservation commissioner Selke and state Representative Robert G. Renner of Walker in another area along the river, and on February 19 Renner introduced a bill calling for the establishment of Schoolcraft State Recreation Reserve. Passed

121 to 0 by the house, it was amended in the senate to omit the word "condemnation" from the ways by which land might be acquired. With that change it passed the senate 65 to 0 and was signed by Governor Freeman on March 23.[36]

Part of the 295 acres within the park's statutory limits consisted of tax-forfeited lands, which were speedily acquired. The remainder consisted of Indian lands, which, as at Mille Lacs Kathio, proved more difficult to obtain. The most recent figures give the park an area of 217 acres. There have been no boundary changes and no appropriations for land acquisition. Although the park was not officially opened until 1964, in 1963 it had 1,328 visitors, a number that shot up to 5,826 the following year. If these figures seem modest, it must be remembered that Schoolcraft is in an out-of-the-way location and serves mainly a local clientele.[37]

The park was named for Henry Rowe Schoolcraft, a self-taught geologist and biologist who accompanied Governor Lewis Cass of Michigan (which included Minnesota east of the Mississippi) in 1820. He returned in 1832, to discover the source of the Mississippi in Lake Itasca, which was named by his companion on the second journey, the Reverend William T. Boutwell. Since Schoolcraft's route took him up the Mississippi, it is likely that he passed the site of the park named for him. It is obvious, however, that if any state park ought to bear his name, it is the one named Itasca, for there he made his chief contribution to Minnesota history. Since that park had been named nearly seventy years earlier, Schoolcraft's memory had to be served by a lesser unit of the system.

Schoolcraft State Recreation Area, as it is now called, is a pleasant spot to spend a few hours. The picnic area is in a grove of pines overlooking the Mississippi, where Indians formerly harvested wild rice. Relics from prehistoric times have been found there, along with bottles, horseshoes, ox shoes, and other mementos of logging days, when the floating cook shacks, or "wannigans," used to tie up at the mouth of the Vermilion River. An interpretive nature trail called the Whisper Trail circles the developed portion of the park and passes the site of the Dobson homestead, taken up in 1898. The campground is seldom crowded, though it is as well equipped as most state park camping areas. With a little effort, one can imagine Henry Schoolcraft, Governor Cass, and the Reverend Boutwell making their way up the Mississippi and perhaps camping in this vicinity.[38]

## Crow Wing

The last park established in 1959 was Crow Wing, located at the confluence of the Crow Wing and Mississippi rivers, mainly in Crow Wing County but spilling over into Cass and Morrison counties, nine miles southwest of Brainerd. It included the site of the ghost town of Old Crow Wing, which had flourished in the 1850s and 1860s at the point where the trail from St. Paul to Pembina crossed the Mississippi. Location of several fur-trading posts and of Catholic, Episcopal, and Lutheran missions, at its peak the town boasted a population of 600 and a full line of business places. Bypassed by the railroad in favor of Brainerd in the 1870s, Old Crow Wing gradually faded away.[39]

The Crow Wing County Historical Society spearheaded the drive for a park in 1957, after archaeological investigation under the direction of Russell Fridley and Arch Grahn of the Minnesota Historical Society had revealed the outlines of the major buildings in the old village. Spurred by the interest shown by the historical societies, the parks division made an official inspection of the area in October 1957. Director Hella recommended the establishment of a park at the confluence of the two rivers. Eventually, he thought, 1,450 acres should be obtained on the east side of the Mississippi.[40]

The legislative history of the park is obscure because it came into being as part of the general appropriations bill rather than through a separate piece of legislation. The act provided $15,000, conditional upon receipt of gifts of cash or land of equal value. Such organizations as the Izaak Walton League, the Brainerd Junior Chamber of Commerce, and the Knights of Columbus were active in soliciting contributions, and by April 1960 the entire sum had been collected and was turned over to the conservation commissioner.[41]

As usual, actual development of the park took much longer. When it was dedicated, on July 8, 1962, only 448 acres of the 1,255 acres authorized had been acquired, and that had taken $27,800 of the funds donated and appropriated. A campground near the Mis-

*Looking southeast at Crow Wing State Park, about 1963. The townsite of Old Crow Wing is at center left.*

sissippi, two picnic areas, and a boat landing were among the earliest developments; interpretive services at the old townsite were added later. The site of a notable battle between the Dakota and the Ojibway in 1768 was identified and marked. The locations of the three missions were also marked, and at the site of the Catholic mission, begun by Father Francis X. Pierz in 1852, the Knights of Columbus built a chapel.[42]

Two controversies have punctuated the history of Crow Wing State Park. The Minnesota branch of the American Civil Liberties Union believed that the erection of a religious edifice in a state park violated the separation of church and state. Their concern seems to have been allayed by the assurance that no public funds were used to build the chapel and that it stood on private land, a small enclave reserved for that purpose when a parcel of land owned by the Catholic bishop of St. Cloud was sold to the state. Another conflict arose when officials at Camp Ripley discovered that the park's statutory boundaries included a portion of the military reservation. Choosing to regard this as an error, they warned that visitors would be in danger if they intruded upon training areas. Parks and recreation director Donald Davison replied that the new edition of the park map would contain a warning that not all land within the park was state owned.[43]

Crow Wing State Park has been expanded three times, in 1963, 1965, and 1971, to encompass an authorized area of 2,198 acres, most of which has been acquired — enough certainly to serve the park's primary purposes, which are to provide public recreation along the Mississippi in central Minnesota and to protect the Old Crow Wing townsite. (The entire park was entered on the National Register of Historic Places on July 28, 1970.) The topography is predominantly glacial moraine, part of the sand plain that stretches across much of central Minnesota. Along the rivers the vegetation consists of typical bottomland hardwoods, while most of the park is covered with prairie and second-growth forest. The rivers contain abundant aquatic vegetation, wild rice, cattails, and pondweeds.[44]

Project 80 was somewhat ambivalent toward Crow Wing, suggesting that it did not possess the qualities necessary to a full-fledged state park and tentatively relegating it to the status of a state water wayside. Yet, besides being of historic interest, it has scenery comparable to that found elsewhere in the system. From the north picnic area one gets a fine view of the Mississippi near where the Crow Wing enters it, and there are trails that closely follow the larger river, here a more impressive stream than at Schoolcraft. South of the main picnic area the trail takes one past the rifle pits dug by the Indians during the 1768 battle. Crow Wing offers enough to do and see to justify its retention in the state park system.[45]

---

## Savanna Portage

The 1961 legislature created four state parks — Savanna Portage, Bear Head Lake, Fort Snelling, and Big Stone Lake — and two waysides — Cross River and Devils Track Falls. This number had not been equaled since 1945 and had been surpassed only in

1937. It marked the penultimate stage of the golden era of park building, which was to end with a flourish two years later.

During the heyday of the fur trade, travel between posts near the west end of Lake Superior and Big Sandy Lake, in the Mississippi drainage, went by way of the East Savanna River, a tributary of the St. Louis, and the westward-flowing West Savanna. Between the headwaters of the two streams was a six-mile portage through swamps and rough terrain. After the decline of the fur trade, the portage fell into disuse and was virtually obliterated by the forces of human and natural change. A more easterly segment of the same route, the Grand Portage of the St. Louis, had been preserved in Jay Cooke State Park, and by 1960 sentiment developed in favor of giving similar protection to the Savanna Portage. A Savanna Portage State Park Association was formed, and on January 16, 1961, companion bills were introduced in the legislature. Both houses unanimously passed the senate bill, and Governor Elmer L. Andersen signed it on April 10. The bill included an appropriation of $3,300, to be expended only as gifts of cash or land of equal value were made available. If this seems a rather small appropriation for land acquisition in a park of over 14,000 acres — third largest in the system — it is explained by the fact that the state-owned Floodwood Game Refuge was incorporated into the new park and there was also considerable tax-forfeited land within the statutory boundaries.[46]

Development got under way almost at once and was greatly accelerated when the 1963 legislature appropriated $265,000 for Savanna Portage. The park was dedicated on September 23, 1967. Its boundaries have been expanded twice, in 1963 and 1967, to bring its statutory area to 15,818 acres. Designed to embrace the portage itself and stretches of the two Savanna rivers, the park is long and narrow — about thirteen and a half miles long and nowhere more than four miles wide, usually much less. It is approached from the southwest, by way of an Aitkin County road that leaves Trunk Highway 65 just south of Big Sandy Lake. The park is nearly surrounded by the Savanna State Forest, with which its recreational facilities are coordinated.[47]

Presumably because it is not on the way to anywhere else, but is at the end of a dead-end road, Savanna Portage receives less use than might be expected of so large a park. Yet its recreational resources and its archaeological and historical importance should make it attractive to a growing number of visitors. The old portage has been marked and can be followed on boardwalks for most of its length; park visitors can also hike twenty-two miles of other foot trails. One of the pleasantest is the trail that circles Loon Lake, where the picnic grounds and swimming beach are located. So far, development has complemented the park's natural beauty without threatening to dominate it. The half-timbered entrance station is one of the handsomest in the system, and the other facilities are also designed to fit in with the natural setting. A large park, Savanna Portage can stand a great deal of use; perhaps eventually it will become known to a wider range of park users.

## Bear Head Lake

One day in the fall of 1959 Edward L. Lawson, director of the division of forestry, and George T. Gaylord, regional forester, were inspecting a road that had been built a year earlier to give access to the territory around Bear Head Lake, in northern St. Louis County. They were struck by the state park potential of the area around the lake, adjacent to Bear Island State Forest and not far from the Boundary Waters Canoe Area (BWCA) of the Superior National Forest. Lawson spoke to conservation commissioner Selke and wrote to parks director Hella about the area. The next year, when a local resident, Oral D. Zaffke, wrote about the possibility of a state park, Hella's reply was encouraging. Over the next few months a good deal of enthusiasm for the proposed park developed. Gaylord must have played an important role in generating local support, for on a plaque in the Bear Head Lake State Park picnic grounds he is credited with being "largely responsible for the establishment of this area as a State Park for the enjoyment of future generations."[48]

On February 3, 1961, two Iron Range representatives introduced a bill calling for the establishment of Bear Head Lake State Park. One may infer from the sponsorship of the bill and its senate counterpart that the park was visualized as a recreation area for people from the Iron Range cities, to serve the eastern Mesabi Range and the Vermilion Range much as McCarthy Beach was serving the western Mesabi. Both chambers passed the house bill by the usual unanimous votes, and Governor Andersen signed it into law on April 14.[49]

Although the bill included no appropriation, it did provide for the use of condemnation in acquiring lands. Neither was really needed, however, for of the somewhat more than 4,000 acres within the park's statutory boundaries, the state already owned 3,386. The necessary lands were speedily acquired, and development got under way at once. By October, slightly more than six months after the bill had become law, roads and picnic and camping areas had been carved out of the brush, and the park was well on the way toward the day when it could be opened to the public. It was dedicated on June 26, 1962; the principal speaker was Conrad L. Wirth, then head of the NPS.[50]

Bear Head Lake State Park has not changed a great deal since development was essentially completed, in its early years. Only one minor boundary change was made, in 1963, when three government lots on the south shore of Bear Head Lake were added. It has a seventy-three-site campground, a picnic area, a group camp, a boat ramp, and a swimming beach. Only a small part of the acreage has been developed; large portions of the park remain inaccessible even by trail.[51]

The area was logged over around 1900 and subsequently burned over, so that most of the forest one sees today is second-growth. A few tall pines, remnants of the original forest, stand in the picnic area. Because of the relatively low human population density and the proximity of state and national forests, the park's wildlife includes such large mammals as bear and moose, along with commoner animals like deer, snowshoe hares, red squirrels, and chipmunks. Bear Head Lake thus offers the interested visitor, besides the usual forms of outdoor recreation, a chance to see something of the northern conifer forest's animal and plant life, which are somewhat more accessible than in the nearby BWCA. That should be its function in the state park system.

---

## Fort Snelling

None of the sites preserved in Minnesota's state parks is of greater significance in the history of white settlement than Fort

Snelling. In 1805 Lieutenant Zebulon M. Pike negotiated a treaty with the local Dakota for the purchase of a tract of land at the confluence of the Minnesota and Mississippi rivers. Under the supervision of Colonel Josiah Snelling, troops who arrived in 1819 began construction of a military post the following year. From its commanding position on the bluff overlooking the rivers, Fort Snelling watched over the development of Minnesota for nearly 126 years, with a brief interruption just before the Civil War. After undergoing a series of physical changes that all but obliterated the original post, in 1946 Fort Snelling was transferred to the Veterans Administration.[52]

Although interest in the preservation and restoration of the fort appeared as early as 1895, nothing was done until the 1930s, when the round tower was made into a museum under WPA auspices, the Minnesota Historical Society providing the exhibits. As the years passed, urban sprawl began to impinge on the environs of Fort Snelling. Bridges were built across the two rivers, and in 1956 the state highway department proposed to build a freeway through the area, with a cloverleaf intersection around the round tower. Protests from the public led to the substitution of a tunnel through the central part of the fort, but the whole episode revealed how vulnerable the fort was to threats of this kind.[53]

Some of those who wished to see Fort Snelling preserved were thinking in terms of a national park or monument. Having conducted several studies of it, however, the NPS did not see Fort Snelling as having national significance. An NPS official to whom Hella had talked early in 1956 thought it would be "a very fine and logical State Park project." Two years later the Minnesota Statehood Centennial Commission granted the Minnesota Historical Society $25,000 for an archaeological investigation of the site. The results led director Fridley to conclude that restoration of the fort was "not only possible but highly favored by the richness and extent of the remains of the post."[54]

In 1960 the state park proposal began to gain momentum. A. R. Nichols, the landscape architect who had been involved in planning at Frontenac, made a study of Fort Snelling and the surrounding area, which he saw as undergoing a transition in function and in the direct line of urban development. He thought a park would serve a recreational as well as a historical purpose. Pike Island

*Snowshoeing at Fort Snelling State Park, about 1987*

(where Zebulon Pike had made his treaty with the Indians) and the right bank of the Minnesota River should be left in their natural state, while the bottomland on the left bank could be developed for recreational use. He suggested that access to the fort itself should be by foot.[55]

Late in 1960 the Veterans Administration declared 320 acres of its land, including the site of the original fort, surplus property. The parks division applied for the land under the Surplus Property Act, which authorized the transfer of historically significant sites to the states without cost. Before the state obtained title to the land, about a year later, the Fort Snelling State Park Association was formed to lobby for the park and solicit funds for land acquisition. Among its leaders were parks director Hella, historical society director Fridley, Samuel H. Morgan, who was a founder of the Minnesota Council of State Parks, and Thomas C. Savage, who was an officer in a St. Paul investment firm. These people were thinking in terms of a large park, to embrace some 2,500 acres, of which 881 acres along the Minnesota River were then privately owned.[56]

Companion bills to authorize the park were introduced in the legislature on January 25. Both bills suffered drastic reductions in the proposed appropriations, and the senate bill never reached a vote. The house bill, after its appropriation had been cut from $675,000 to $65,000, passed both houses handily and was signed by Governor Andersen, a strong supporter of the park system, on April 20.[57]

Land acquisition began immediately and progressed rapidly enough so that the park could be dedicated on June 2, 1962, although relatively little development had taken place. Development finally got under way in 1964 and 1965, when the most essential tracts of land had been acquired. High water on the Minnesota River during the spring of 1965 delayed work until the flood waters had receded, but by the summer of 1965 it was possible to picnic near the old steamboat landing or hike along an abandoned railroad grade. Since the round and hexagonal towers were undergoing restoration, only the exteriors were visible to the public that summer. Pike Island had been acquired by then, and a future interpretive center had been readied for use.[58]

Land acquisition problems plagued Fort Snelling for a time. In 1964 the General Services Administration announced plans to build a federal office building on what had once been the fort's polo field. Opposition from Governor Karl F. Rolvaag, the Minnesota congressional delegation, the officers of the park association, and many private citizens led to a reversal of this plan, conditional on the availability of an alternate site without cost to the federal government. Such a site was found, and its acquisition used up $12,160 of the association's funds. Both the U.S. Department of Defense and the U.S. Post Office Department still had their eyes on the polo field, but it finally became part of Fort Snelling State Park in 1971.[59]

The chapel posed another problem. Although included with the round and hexagonal towers in the first transfer of federal land, it was not properly part of historic Fort Snelling. It had been built in 1926–28 by an organization called the Fort Snelling Chapel and Community Center Association. When the park was established, the advisory committee organized a subcommittee of churchmen, who worked out a system of policies and procedures. The arrangement, never wholly satisfactory, became increasingly awkward when one of the incorporators of the Chapel Foundation, who styled himself the Fort Snelling "chaplain," organized a local residential congregation, for whom he conducted services. Prodded by the American Civil Liberties Union, the parks division finally conceded that the separation of church and state had been violated. After a few more attempts to reach a workable compromise, in 1975 the DNR revoked its policy of reserving the chapel for religious exercises. The chapel, architecturally a distinguished building, is now used frequently for weddings, but is no longer the scene of denominational services.[60]

Meanwhile, the park was being developed. By the beginning of 1969, 1,758 acres had been acquired, the road system was 70 percent complete, and the Minnesota River channel for barge traffic had been relocated to the south side of Pike Island. The park had parking for two hundred cars, a picnic area with forty tables, an entrance road, and seven miles of snowmobile trails. That year legislation was passed transferring the fort proper to the Minnesota Historical Society.[61]

The next year, 1970, was important in the park's brief history. It marked the opening of a swimming beach, and attendance shot up from about 100,000 to 176,393 the following year. That year was also the 150th anniversary of the founding of Fort Snelling. The Post Office marked the occasion by issuing a commemorative postage stamp, and on October 17 the Fort Snelling post office was temporarily reestablished so that first-day covers could be canceled there.[62]

In 1974 the Pike Island interpretive center was opened as the first year-round facility in the system. Several programs were to be implemented there: teacher training in environmental education, slide shows, hikes, special events and workshops, the preparation of maps and similar materials, public relations, and continual updating of the displays. To provide access from the mainland, a causeway had been constructed over the old channel of the Minnesota River. After heavy rains in 1975 rendered it unsafe, it was replaced by a footbridge, which has since served as the approach not only to the interpretive center but to the Pike Island trail system. The trail that circles the island gives the hiker a suggestion of wilderness in the heart of a metropolitan area. The sounds of car, truck, barge, and plane traffic are ever present, but the essentially unspoiled condition of the island, isolated as it is by water, conveys an impression of nature (almost) undisturbed.[63]

Because of its location, Fort Snelling has become immensely popular, second only to Itasca in attendance, despite the absence of the most popular activity in many parks, camping. It is agreed that the park is not suited for the standard variety of automobile camping. The park's eighteen miles of hiking trails and five miles of bicycle trails attract many visitors, but the old fort is also heavily used. Fort Snelling manages to provide recreation for a large number of people and at the same time to protect and interpret the fort where so much of Minnesota's early history was made.

## Big Stone Lake

The last true state park established by the 1961 legislature was Big Stone Lake, on the far western edge of Minnesota, where the long, narrow lake forms the boundary with South Dakota and serves as the source of the Minnesota River. In 1960, when Ortonville business owners became concerned about the rate at which lakeshore development was occurring, they learned from director Hella that a detailed study had already been made of the recreational potential of the lake. It turned out that he, landscape architect A. R. Nichols, and Russell Fridley had visited the area about three years earlier and had concluded that the shores of Big Stone Lake would be a good location for a *county* park, perhaps tied in

*Fishing somewhere on Big Stone Lake, about 1900*

with a skyline parkway along the lake. Hella's reexamination of the area late in 1960 led to a proposal for a state park.[64]

Companion bills were introduced on January 26 and 27, 1961. The senate bill passed both houses decisively and Governor Andersen signed it on April 20, the same day as the Fort Snelling bill. Its $30,000 appropriation for land acquisition, which might be accomplished by condemnation, was conditional upon matching funds from the community; the county was empowered to levy a 3.5-mill tax, to continue until the $30,000 had been collected and deposited with the state treasurer.[65]

The original Big Stone Lake State Park, as provided for by the legislature, was somewhat different from the one that actually developed. The proposed park was to consist of three units. The largest, which turned out much as planned, was called the Meadowbrook area and was six miles up the lake from Ortonville. Some ten miles farther up the lake was a small tract along Trunk Highway 7, offering a spacious view of the lake and the South

Dakota shore. The third, as originally designed, would have been another eight or nine miles up the lake, where the state already owned 90 acres. Either because land at the third site proved difficult to obtain or because another and better site became available, in 1963 an additional area some twelve miles up the lake from Meadowbrook was incorporated into the park, and in 1965 the original third site was deleted. Eventually the second site was transferred to the highway department.[66]

Big Stone Lake State Park today consists of the Meadowbrook unit, where park headquarters, campground, and a picnic area are located, and the Bonanza unit (named for an early town), added in 1963, which contains another picnic area, a swimming beach, and an interpretive center. The Bonanza unit extends farther west than any other Minnesota state park, and thus Big Stone Lake can claim to be the state's most westerly park, just as Zippel Bay can claim to be the most northerly. When all the adding and subtracting had taken place, the park was left with a statutory area of 1,090 acres, of which 1,083 had been acquired by 1981.[67]

The interpretive center was the most ambitious project undertaken at the park. Since the area was archaeologically significant, planners decided to center the displays on the theme of man and the changing face of the Red River valley (loosely defined to include the upper Minnesota drainage). The sequence would begin with the present, proceed to the Dakota with their hunting and farming culture, then go farther back, to the Mississippian and Woodland peoples, and conclude with the hunters who entered the region after the last glacial era. Exhibits staff, responding to the concerns of some Dakota people, removed skeletal remains from the display, but in general the center's exhibits followed these outlines pretty closely. Unfortunately, because of financial exigencies and a low visitation rate, the center has been closed.[68]

The Project 80 planners suggested reclassifying the Meadowbrook unit as a trail wayside with water access and Bonanza as a recreation area. Both would remain in the state park system but would no longer enjoy the status of a state park. Such a change would meet opposition from the local people who worked and taxed themselves to get the park started and who have been its principal users over the past three decades. The present management plan recommends designating Bonanza as a water access site and a scientific and natural area and retaining Meadowbrook as a state park.[69]

Big Stone Lake has certain distinct merits. Besides its archaeological importance, it represents a landscape type not found elsewhere in the state park system: a lake in a setting of vast horizons. The western edge of Minnesota has much in common with the high plains still farther west, but the characteristics of this type of terrain are more evident at Big Stone Lake than at, say, Blue Mounds or Buffalo River. For this reason, the park does have statewide significance, even though its recreational use is predominantly local. The park's future as a recreation center will depend in large part on imponderables such as the availability and cost of gasoline. If Americans continue to enjoy the high degree of mobility they have come to take for granted — admittedly problematical — Big Stone Lake should draw more and more people from other parts of the state, as well as from adjacent parts of South Dakota. In that case its continuance as a state park should be easily justified.

---

## Cross River and Devils Track Falls

In addition to creating four good-sized parks, the 1961 legislature carried on the work of protecting major scenic areas on the North Shore by establishing two wayside-type units in that region. On January 18 identical bills were introduced in the house and senate calling for the establishment of Cross River State Scenic Wayside, at the village of Schroeder and a short distance from Temperance River State Park. The senate bill went the whole way and was signed by Governor Andersen on March 16.[70]

The Cross River was named for a cross erected there in 1843 by missionary priest Father Frederic Baraga in thanksgiving for his deliverance from a storm encountered while crossing Lake Superior in a small boat from La Pointe, in the Apostle Islands. There are five waterfalls in the Cross River's lower reaches, including one visible from U.S. Highway 61. The law establishing the wayside authorized the conservation commissioner to acquire by gift or purchase, "as funds are available," four sections of land on the lower river. If it had all been acquired — all 2,560 acres of it — the wayside would have been larger than most of the units classified as state parks.[71]

Three years after the establishment of Cross River State Wayside, the state owned 640 acres and had detailed plans for a picnic area and a campground, together with the necessary access roads. None of this development has materialized, however, nor has the remaining land been acquired. Identified by no sign such as once notified the traveler of the locations of Caribou Falls and Kodonce River waysides, Cross River has only a small parking area along the highway and a trail that crosses federal lands from Temperance River State Park. It is possible that the two units will be combined and the Cross River portion will be used to take some of the pressure off the small and heavily used park. Cross River's scenery is on a par with that of other North Shore parks and waysides, and it definitely needs the continued protection of state ownership.[72]

The other piece of North Shore legislation passed in 1961 was a bill to establish Devils Track Falls State Park northeast of Grand Marais, inland about a mile from the lake. The house bill was introduced on January 31, passed unanimously by the lower chamber, and tabled by the senate, whose companion bill died in committee. Revived in the extra session, it became law as part of the general appropriations bill approved June 5.[73]

Judge Clarence Magney wished to bring under the umbrella of the state park system a section of the gorge of the Devil Track River, including two waterfalls fifty feet high and a stone face profile on the canyon wall. To accomplish this objective, the park boundaries were drawn to include three separate tracts of land — a quarter section and two 40-acre tracts farther upstream. The Superior National Forest lands adjoin and separate these three parcels. Although no public road leads to the park (renamed a wayside in 1969), it is possible to reach the fringes of the largest unit by way of a primitive track leading in from Croftville, just east of Grand Marais. However, Thomas F. Waters, who has written extensively on Minnesota's waterways, claims that the only means of access to the gorge itself is by hiking up the stream from U.S. Highway 61 or by employing mountain-climbing techniques to descend from the brink.[74]

It is not clear what will be done with Devils Track Falls State Wayside. In its present state it is nearly inaccessible. Its topography

*Artist Birney Quick and children fishing on the Devil Track River, about 1947. The photo is titled, "The kids got tangled."*

is its protection, and it would probably be as safe from unwanted development if it were part of the national forest as it is in its present status. There has been talk of building foot trails into it, perhaps even of providing spartan backpacking facilities; expansion to 600 acres or more has also been discussed. If it could be made more accessible to the dedicated hiker, without making it too easy to get to, it would be a valuable addition to the system of North Shore parks and waysides that now enclose nearly all of the outstanding scenic spots in that region.[75]

---

## Summary

In the years 1953 to 1962 the state park system grew both quantitatively and qualitatively. Thirteen units were added, some of them negligible and some, such as Fort Snelling, Frontenac, and the two major North Shore parks, ranking with the best of the earlier ones. For this accomplishment the people of Minnesota could give credit to U. W. Hella's leadership, to Judge Clarence Magney and the Minnesota Council of State Parks, and to the successive legislatures, each of which authorized more new parks than its predecessor.

When the Big Stone Lake bill was about to be introduced, the *Ortonville Independent* remarked that its chances of passage were good, because "the Legislature is becoming more state park conscious." Yet even though the legislature created more and more parks, close scrutiny of the park bills passed during these years reveals that the legislature was scarcely guilty of open-handed generosity in its appropriations for land acquisition. In some cases there was no appropriation at all; in others it was comparatively small and conditioned upon receipt of an equal sum from local sources. One reason the legislature did not appropriate more money was that the 1953 park-sticker act provided a new source of revenue, at first small but increasingly important as the years passed.[76]

It was no doubt true, as the Ortonville editor said, that legislators were becoming more park-conscious — and, one suspects, so were their constituents. These were, on the whole, prosperous years, and one way for families to spend their increased disposable income was to visit state parks, perhaps camping for a night or two and devoting the days to fishing or swimming. As facilities became increasingly crowded, it was not difficult to justify the expansion of old parks and the establishment of new ones.

The five legislative sessions 1945, 1947, 1957, 1959, and 1961 brought into the system twenty-three new parks; in the whole half-century from 1891 to 1941 only twenty-eight true parks (excluding monuments and units subsequently disposed of to other agencies) had been established, sixteen of them in the middle 1930s. With legislators, reflecting public sentiment, becoming more park-conscious and revenue from motor vehicle permits relieving the legislature of part of the burden of providing money for the park system, the future of that system looked bright.

# CHAPTER EIGHT

# The Omnibus Act
# 1963

THE OMNIBUS Natural Resources and Recreation Act, one of the half-dozen most important pieces of legislation in the history of the Minnesota state park system, was passed in 1963. Although its provisions concerned much besides parks, its effects on the park system were profound. The legislative history of the Omnibus Natural Resources and Recreation Act is complex; it incorporated a large number of separate bills that ranged widely in content and purpose.

In line with recommendations made by the Outdoor Recreation Resources Review Commission established by Congress in 1958, companion bills creating a Minnesota Outdoor Recreation Resources Commission were introduced in the two houses of the Minnesota legislature on January 29 and 30. While these bills were making their way through the appropriate committees, another pair of companion bills was introduced about mid-March; they proposed to initiate a long-term program for the preservation and intelligent use of the state's natural resources. The later legislation would implement the suggestions made by the Minnesota Natural Resources Council, appointed in October 1961 by Governor Elmer L. Andersen in response to the recommendations of the American Forestry Association's study in the later 1950s.[1]

Meanwhile, similar pairs of bills had been introduced calling for the establishment of thirteen new state parks. Two of these were withdrawn because of local opposition, but three others were added later in the session. Near the end of February the first eleven were combined into two companion bills. On March 19, all of the various bills having to do with natural resources and recreation were combined in House File No. 1291, which, after numerous amendments and after consideration by a conference committee, was finally passed by both houses and signed into law by Governor Karl Rolvaag on May 20, 1963.[2]

The act specified fourteen parks, but the result was not fourteen new additions to the system. Lake Maria and Forestville had actually been authorized in the late 1940s, but no land had ever been acquired, and it was thought necessary to go back to square one and establish them all over again. Traverse des Sioux was really not new at all, but the acreage proposed for addition to it was many times the size of the existing park. Grand Mound was never developed by the parks division and was subsequently transferred to the Minnesota Historical Society. Finally, O. L. Kipp was not developed at the location specified in the 1963 law. Several years later it was relocated at a different site, and hence it belongs to a different generation of state parks, to be discussed in chapter nine.[3]

## Lake Maria

Shortly after the establishment of Nerstrand Woods and before it became apparent that exchange with the U.S. Forest Service (USFS) was an inadequate means of acquiring land, the legislature attempted to increase the number of parks within reasonable driving distance of the Twin Cities metropolitan area by authorizing a park in Wright County, a few miles west of Monticello. Late in February 1947 companion bills were introduced calling for the creation of a state park, of no more than 1,000 acres, in sections 3, 4, 9, and 10 of Silver Creek Township. Upon acquisition of the land, the commissioner of conservation was to name the park after consultation with local public officials, organizations, and citizens. The house bill was dropped in favor of its senate companion, which encountered no significant opposition, passed both chambers by lopsided majorities, and was signed on April 19 by Governor Luther Youngdahl.[4]

As at Nerstrand Woods, the USFS was invited to acquire land in the location specified and then exchange it for state-owned land in the Superior National Forest. Also as in the Nerstrand Woods bill, this law provided that "suitable portions" of the park could be used for wildlife, forestry, or other projects, "reserving suitable portions for public park purposes." Like Nerstrand Woods, the Wright County park would protect and make available to the public a remnant of the hardwood forest known as the Big Woods. The terrain, the product of successive glacial invasions, is best described as rolling, though in places the hills are fairly steep. Marshes and small lakes lie between these hills, and on the fringes of the woodland are tracts of prairie, much of it formerly cultivated. More than two hundred species of birds have been seen in the park area, as well as smaller numbers of mammals, amphibians, and reptiles.[5]

One factor that hindered the expansion of Nerstrand Woods, the USFS's unwillingness to use condemnation, also caused the land exchange scheme to fail in Wright County. By 1963 it was evident that if a park were ever going to be established there, the state would have to go about the project in the same way it had created other parks: by officially authorizing the park and appropriating money for land acquisition. Companion bills to effect this purpose were introduced early in February, and subsequently the intent of these bills was incorporated into the Omnibus Act.[6]

The 1963 law was superior in several ways to that of 1947. For one thing, it gave the park a name: Lake Maria. (Southwest of the center of the area to be acquired was a small body of water, inaccessible by road, shown on the maps as Maria Lake. Several years later, however, the DNR renamed it Bjorkland Lake and applied the name "Maria Lake" to a sort of appendage to Silver Lake, which itself lies outside the park boundaries; this Maria Lake fronts on the picnic grounds and is the lake most often seen by park visitors.) Another advantage was that the new legislation created a larger park, with an authorized land area of 1,312 acres, roughly square. Most important, the Omnibus Act provided an $80,000 appropriation to begin land purchases, instead of relying on the uncertainties of an exchange with the forest service.[7]

The state acquired enough land during the later 1960s to permit the usual development of such amenities as roads, trails, picnic area, and utilities in the next few years. By 1971 Lake Maria was a functioning state park.[8]

At an early stage in the planning process, the parks people had decided that a regular automobile campground would be inappropriate and had proposed instead a few scattered walk-in campsites in remoter parts of the park. Before they could implement this plan, however — indeed, before they could develop the trails that would lead to these sites — they had to acquire a 222.38-acre parcel of land located near the center of the park, with frontage on Bjorkland Lake. The 1971 legislature granted the DNR the right of eminent domain in reference to this piece of land.[9]

Once this land had been acquired, development went forward. A combination trail center and interpretive center, an attractive building that serves as a warming house in winter, was constructed; more trails were laid out in the southern section of the park; eleven walk-in campsites, accessible from these trails, were added; and the entrance road was blacktopped as far as the trail center.[10]

Though the park was compact in shape, with roads serving as boundaries on the east and south sides, its planners thought that it would benefit from expansion on the north and west, particularly in the area fronting on what was now called Maria Lake, where state ownership of the entire lakeshore was deemed desirable. When these proposals for expansion were aired in the spring of 1977 at public meetings on the management plan, they drew fire from local residents, especially those who owned land in the area to be added to the park. Nonetheless, the 1980 legislature authorized an expansion of some 360 acres, which would place the whole of Maria Lake (though not of Silver Lake) within the park and make a township road its western boundary.[11]

The management plan classified Lake Maria as a natural state park, in which protection of the natural setting would be given precedence over recreational use. So long as camping is restricted to the walk-in sites, it should be possible to achieve this goal. In spite of its comparative nearness to the Twin Cities, Lake Maria is not heavily used. Hiking, boating, horseback riding, and fishing are possible in summer, cross-country skiing in winter. Horses tend to scar the trail surface, but otherwise these activities are not harmful to the park. If more people discover the park, the thirteen miles of trails provide quite a bit of space in which they can be dispersed. That amount of trail mileage means, of course, that the trails are sometimes rather close together, so much so that hikers on adjacent trails can see one another in the leafless season. That is perhaps a small price to pay for the opportunity to explore a fragment of the Big Woods only forty-five miles from Minneapolis.

## *Forestville*

Forestville State Park, another member of the "Class of '63," was originally authorized in 1949, with the stipulation that land should be acquired through exchange with the USFS. As in the case of Lake Maria, Forestville's primary function was to preserve a tract of hardwood forest, but it was also historically significant as the site of the pre–Civil War town of Forestville, once a contender for the seat of Fillmore County. Forestville had its inception in 1853, when Robert M. Foster came there from Illinois and opened a store in conjunction with two boyhood friends, William J. and Felix Meighen. Soon afterward they were joined by Forest Henry, for whom the town was named. Henry, in partnership with his brother-in-law, William Renslow, built a sawmill and gristmill on the South Branch of the Root River. In 1855 the brothers-in-law laid out the town of Forestville on the south side of the river, and about the same time Foster and the Meighens platted "North Forestville" just across the stream. A post office was established the same year, and Forestville was fairly launched.[12]

At its peak in the later 1850s Forestville had at least a dozen business places and was a station on two important stage lines. Farmers from a fifty-mile radius brought their grain to the gristmill and traded at the fine brick store that Foster and the Meighens had built in 1857 to replace the original double log building. But as time passed they found more convenient trading points. When the railroads missed Forestville, the village was left isolated and began a long decline. By 1900 its only business place was the Meighen store, operated by Felix's son, Thomas J., who locked up the building one May evening in 1910, leaving its stock intact.[13]

Until his death in 1936 Thomas Meighen carefully guarded the woods his father and uncle had acquired in the early days of settlement. In response to his inquiry as to the possibility of making the area a state park, the forestry division in 1934 sent Harold Ostergaard to inspect the woods. Despite a highly favorable report on the

*Forestville State Park, 1975*

"dense hardwood forests, spring fed creeks, steep limestone cliffs, springs and possibly some caverns," and despite considerable newspaper publicity in that year and in 1935, the state was apparently unable to pay the price the Meighen heirs demanded, and the park proposal got nowhere. Director Harold Lathrop remained interested in the project, however, and "Forestville Woods" continued to appear on lists of tracts of land considered desirable for future parks.[14]

During the revival of interest in new state parks following World War II, the Forestville proposal surfaced once more. Various local organizations and individual citizens began agitating for the establishment of a park. When the concrete proposal was advanced too late for action by the 1947 legislature, conservation commissioner Chester Wilson proposed that the land-exchange de-

vice attempted in connection with Nerstrand Woods and the unnamed Wright County park be tried at Forestville when the legislature next met. During the interval state officials, including Wilson
and parks director Lew Fiero, made two visits to Forestville and
were reportedly impressed with the woods as a potential state park.
Fiero recommended a park of 720 to 800 acres — somewhat less
than the proposal two years earlier of 1,000 to 1,200 acres.[15]

On January 24, 1949, three southeastern Minnesota state senators introduced a bill drafted by the parks division and patterned
after the Wright County park bill of the previous session. The bill
passed both houses without difficulty and was signed by Governor
Youngdahl on April 4. It called for the establishment of a state park
(not named) of not more than 850 acres, in Fillmore County, the
lands to be acquired by exchange with the federal government.
This scheme met with the same lack of success that had characterized it at Lake Maria, and in the meantime the legislation did not
deter the owners from cutting timber as a means of getting some income from the land on which they were paying taxes.[16]

In the 1963 legislative session a Forestville park bill was again
introduced in each house, this time as part of the spate of new park
proposals. The companion bills were later superseded by the Omnibus Act, which retained most of their language but deleted a reference to the use of eminent domain. With Governor Rolvaag's signa-
ture on May 20 the bill became law, and the thirty-year effort to
create a park in the Meighen Woods was ended.[17]

Like Lake Maria, the Forestville State Park established in 1963
was both larger and more adequately provided for by the legislature than the one proposed earlier. The external boundaries enclosed an area of 2,440 acres — two or three times the size of the
earlier park proposals — and the legislature appropriated $122,000
for land acquisition and an additional $20,865 for capital improve-
ments. Both because limited staff was available to do appraisal
work and because the owners were scattered and reluctant to sell,
land acquisition proceeded slowly for the first two years. In 1965
the legislature restored the right of eminent domain, and thereafter
the owners were more cooperative. Soon 1,380 acres, owned by two
Meighen heirs, were purchased; together with another tract of 205
acres, this land provided a nucleus for development, including as

it did the old brick Meighen store and the land desired for use as campground and picnic areas.[18]

Although Thomas Meighen had closed the store in 1910, he had over the years frequently opened it for the benefit of visitors. According to a 1935 newspaper article, he had made a practice of giving away to such visitors items that they expressed a special interest in. Consequently, when Kenneth B. Sander of the parks division began taking an inventory of the store's contents, he had to describe them as the "dregs of a once well stocked store." Still, the "dregs" included such relics of the nineteenth century as side-saddles, a horse's straw hat, ox yokes, a spinning wheel, a Civil War drum, phonograph records and horn, and a profusion of patent medicines. People from the Minnesota Historical Society assisted with the inventory, and in 1977 the store and its immediate environs were turned over to the society.[19]

Except for the store and its attached dwelling, a livery stable across the road, and Foster's long-empty brick house, none of the buildings associated with old Forestville had survived. With the aid of old plats and other records, however, it was possible to determine the sites of the gristmill, distillery, first and second schoolhouses, and other buildings, as well as an early cemetery on a hill north of the village. The streets shown on the town plat were located and identified by means of conventional street signs.[20]

Besides restoring the vanished town to some degree of visibility, development involved creating a picnic area on the south bank of the Root River, just upstream from the store, and constructing a campground farther upstream and on the left bank. Trails were also laid out, some of them along old logging roads, others using portions of two township roads that were closed off to reduce the number of entrances to the park. In the late 1970s a small interpretive center and a campfire circle were added. Although most of the land within the statutory limits of the park has been acquired, a few small parcels remain in private ownership. In 1969 a small expansion was authorized, bringing the total area to more than 2,500 acres. The park was opened to the public in 1968, though not formally dedicated until May 21, 1972.[21]

In its short history the park has been threatened by both human and natural forces. A Corps of Engineers scheme for a dam that would have inundated most of the park met with so much opposition from state officials and the general public that it was abandoned. Periodic floods repeatedly washed out two small footbridges over the Root River and Canfield Creek that provided trail access to the southern end of the park. In 1982 they were replaced by a sturdier steel-and-concrete bridge over the Root, below the mouth of the creek.[22]

From 1973 to 1986 local people sponsored a Fine Arts Festival in the park some time in May or early June. Arts and crafts of local manufacture were displayed, and an effort was made to recreate the atmosphere of the old village. In 1990 the Minnesota Historical Society began intensive planning for a full-scale interpretive program at the Meighen store.[23]

Forestville is one of Minnesota's major parks. Project 80 proposed retaining it and classifying it as a natural state park. Apart from its historical interest, its significance derives from the degree to which it represents a particular landscape type: the stream-dissected region of southeastern Minnesota. Forestville does not lie in the driftless (unglaciated) part of the state, but erosion has been the principal agent in determining its topography. Botanically it is probably richer than Lake Maria, and this comparative richness is reflected in its animal life. If one wants to establish a record for the number of wildflower species seen in a single day at one place, the trails of Forestville would be a good place to try. Birders discovered the Forestville woods long before the park was established, and the presence of the park does not seem to have diminished its potential in this respect. Minnesotans waited a long time for Forestville State Park, but it was worth waiting for.[24]

Administered as part of Forestville State Park is Mystery Cave, about five miles (by road) west of the park. The state's largest known natural limestone cave, with at least twelve miles of passages, Mystery Cave had been used for commercial tours since 1935. When the owners put it up for sale just a half-century later, DNR officials, local business people, and cave enthusiasts ("spelunkers") became interested in acquiring it for the state. In 1987 the legislature authorized its purchase and addition to Forestville State Park. Although the parks people conduct tours of the cave, they are mindful of its scientific value and of the fragility of its formations. They see it as an ecosystem in need of protection as well as a valuable educational tool, and further development of the cave will try to balance these objectives.[25]

---

## Glacial Lakes

Companion bills to establish Glacial Lakes were introduced on January 31, the first date on which any of the park bills of that session were introduced. Representative Edward E. Barsness of Glenwood, moving spirit behind the proposal, had said in 1962 that he had favored the area as a park site ever since his first visit, some fifty years earlier. The area under consideration was a 1,400-acre tract in Blue Mounds Township, five miles south of Starbuck, in Pope County. It consisted mostly of rolling, moorlike prairies that had been grazed to some extent but never plowed, but also included a small oak forest, one 56-acre lake surrounded by hills, and several smaller ponds and marshes. Its chief advantage was its comparatively pristine condition, harboring a rich prairie flora.[26]

After working on the park project for over a year, in August 1961 Barsness brought parks director U. W. Hella, park planner Bernard Halver, and the NPS's Evan A. Haynes out to inspect the site. All were impressed, and Hella invited Barsness to begin taking options on at least 1,000 acres. When this had been accomplished, Hella revisited the area and told the Starbuck Lions Club, "This site has everything." In December 1962 he gave a "glowing report" on it before the Minnesota Council of State Parks.[27]

Naming the proposed park presented somewhat of a problem. The township name, of course, had already been preempted by another park. After considering such possibilities as Signalness Hills, a county committee early in January 1963 settled on Glacial Lakes.[28]

So efficiently had Barsness done his job that he had options on more than 1,400 acres by the time the Omnibus Act, into which the Glacial Lakes bills had been incorporated, was approved. It included a $98,220 appropriation for land acquisition, to which the 1965 legislature added another $7,500, plus $15,000 for capital improvements. Since nearly all the necessary land was purchased almost immediately, development began without delay. By the time of the 1965 MORRC report, the map of Glacial Lakes showed a

*Glacial Lakes State Park, 1977*

park headquarters, a swimming area, and two picnic areas. A circle trail over the moors had also been laid out. Subsequent development included a campground on the north side of Signalness Lake, later renamed Mountain Lake. The campground has two parts: the main area, intended chiefly for trailers and other recreational vehicles, and the Oak Grove extension, designed mainly for tent camping. In recent years several walk-in sites have been developed along the peripheral trail that begins at the Oak Grove parking lot. Provision has also been made for horseback riding in summer and snowmobiling in winter, and the trail system has been developed to cover every section of the park except the marshy southeastern and southwestern portions.[29]

Glacial Lakes is preeminently a wildflower park. From the first pasqueflowers in spring to the last downy gentians, goldenrods, and asters of the fall, the moors display a continuous parade of prairie flowers. On a day in August one can see several kinds of goldenrod and sunflowers, coneflowers, prairie clover, blazing star, leadplant, asters, gentians, and still more. Although all the trails lead past a representative sampling of flowers, perhaps the best one is that which goes around the outside of the trail system, past the walk-in campsites, past the highest point in the park (1,352 feet) — from which one can see a small lake on the eastern border — and back past the horse corral to the main picnic area. Between there and the campground a trail crosses a marsh, part of the distance on a boardwalk, where water-loving flowers like swamp milkweed and green-headed coneflower are in evidence (and where the hiker is most vulnerable to mosquitoes and deer flies). Glacial Lakes preserves a special kind of landform, a fact Project 80 recognized, proposing to retain it as a state park, even though the scenery is not especially striking. In 1987 the legislature authorized a 500-acre addition to the park, including some land previously purchased by The Nature Conservancy and another parcel obtained from the U.S. Fish and Wildlife Service in exchange for state-owned land in the Minnesota River valley. This expansion gives Glacial Lakes an area of nearly 1,900 acres — substantially more than even U. W. Hella had suggested when the park was first being considered for addition to the system.[30]

---

## Upper Sioux Agency

After the Minnesota Dakota had sold their ancestral lands in 1851, they were placed on a long, narrow reservation on the upper Minnesota River; the old St. Peters Agency, which had been at Fort Snelling, was reestablished on the reservation. For administrative convenience it was divided into a Lower, or Redwood, Agency, serving the Mdewakanton and Wahpekute bands, collectively known as the Lower Sioux, and an Upper, or Yellow Medicine, Agency for the Sisseton and Wahpeton bands, referred to as the Upper Sioux. During the Dakota War of 1862 the Dakota burned both agencies, but at each site one building, later converted into a farmhouse, survived. At the Upper Agency a brick duplex, greatly altered over the years, seemed worth preserving for its historical significance.[31]

In the summer of 1962 Charles Kelehan, whose grandparents had been among the early white settlers in the vicinity, set about arousing local support for a state park at the Upper Sioux Agency site. He assembled a group of people, including members of the county historical society, state legislators, and candidates for the legislature, and took them over the ground. Apparently people in the parks division had been thinking along similar lines, for at a meeting in St. Paul in December the site was revealed to be one of thirty-eight being considered for state park status.[32]

With assistance from the Granite Falls newspaper, the county historical society took the lead in drumming up support for the park proposal. Members got an appraisal on the 320.4-acre property on which the building stood and learned that the owners wanted $30,000 for it. When companion bills were introduced in the legislature on January 31 and February 11, the society provided delegates to attend hearings and speak in favor of the park proposal. When the Omnibus Act was passed, it included a provision for the creation of Upper Sioux Agency State Park and a $30,000 appropriation for land acquisition. Two years later the legislature provided $5,000 for capital improvements.[33]

The first developments were necessarily modest: an entrance road, a picnic area, and a seasonal residence and shop. The Minnesota Historical Society, to which the agency site was transferred in 1969, conducted archaeological investigations that revealed the locations of other buildings, which were duly identified by markers. The duplex was restored to its original appearance, a building much more severe than the multi-gabled farmhouse had been.[34]

The 1969 and 1971 legislatures authorized large additions to the park, bringing the statutory acreage to 1,280, nearly all of which has been acquired. The expansion was designed to incorporate more of the Yellow Medicine River — the mouth of the river to the east and segments above the old agency — into the park. With the additions, the park included the site of a steamboat landing on the Minnesota, an old wagon road, and the route used by John Other Day in leading sixty-two white settlers to safety during the Dakota conflict.[35]

Meanwhile, development continued. Some of the improvements originally planned were later scrapped. A 1965 map of the park shows a campground to be located just east of the agency site. This campground has never been completed. Camping has been permitted, though not encouraged, both on this site and in a picnic area adjoining the boat landing on the Minnesota, reached by a rather steep, narrow road. On the other hand, plans for an interpretive center have been carried out, and on June 27, 1976, dedication ceremonies were held for a fine new building overlooking the Minnesota River valley near the park entrance. Since an emphasis on the historical features of the park would only duplicate the Minnesota Historical Society's work at the agency site, the designers of the interpretive center elected to confine its displays largely to reflections of the natural setting — the topography, the vegetation, the bird and animal life to be found there.[36]

The trail system at Upper Sioux Agency provides access to the various life zones: the prairie that covers most of the higher portions of the park, the oak-elm forest that clothes the steeper north-facing slopes, and the cottonwood-ash woodland that predominates on the bottomlands along the rivers. Beyond a low-water crossing of the Yellow Medicine, a trail ascends to the bluffs overlooking the valley of that river from the south. Picnicking is possible at the main picnic grounds between the interpretive center and the agency site, at the boat landing on the Minnesota, and at the mouth of the Yellow Medicine, reached by a winding dirt road.

Like most of the parks, Upper Sioux Agency has its share of problems. In 1985 and 1986 high water on the Minnesota River flooded the lower level and left a layer of mud on the picnic area and boat landing. As elsewhere in the system, the people who were instrumental in getting the park established feel a proprietary interest in it and resent any decisions the park personnel do not clear in advance with them. This attitude surfaced in 1977, when the parks people attempted to prohibit camping along the river and to close a toboggan run nearby; a regional administrator in New Ulm predicted "an overwhelming anti-DNR reaction in the Granite Falls area" if the plan was carried out. And there is a visibility problem at the turnoff from Trunk Highway 67, though traffic and park visitation are both normally light enough so that the problem has not become acute. Upper Sioux Agency (which some have proposed renaming Yellow Medicine State Park), however, has enough historical and natural attractions to give it an important role to play in its region.[37]

## Sakatah Lake

Before the arrival of the whites, most of the countryside between Mankato and Faribault was covered with trees — the southern end of the Big Woods. When railroads came through and towns were established, the forest went down before the axe and saw, until by the early twentieth century the area was dotted with farms, scattered over what looked to the casual observer like original prairie. Here and there patches of forest survived, however, preserved as farm woodlots or spared from the loggers by difficult access. One of these remnant woodlands occupied a strip of land, bisected by a railroad, between Upper Sakatah Lake and Trunk Highway 60, just east of Waterville.[38]

Early in 1962 the conservation department did a study of this area to determine its potential as a state park, and about the same time the Waterville Commercial Club and several individual citizens began taking an interest in the park project. The state proposed acquiring all the land between the lake and the highway, from the eastern edge of Waterville to approximately a mile east of the Le Sueur–Rice county line. Besides the forest, predominantly elm, basswood, aspen, oak, and walnut, the park would include some areas of wet and dry prairie. For the park to constitute a manageable unit and provide space for development, however, it would be necessary also to include some land then being actively farmed.[39]

All through 1962 the commercial club conducted a publicity campaign and negotiated with landowners for options on the land needed as a nucleus for the proposed park. Members of the club also met with the Minnesota Council of State Parks, with representatives of the conservation department, and with local lawmakers, who promised to introduce a Sakatah Lake State Park bill in the next session of the legislature. By February 1, 1963, when the usual companion bills were introduced, more than 400 acres were under

*The shore of Sakatah Lake in Sakatah Lake State Park*

option, and the local committee was negotiating with owners for the remaining 350 acres seen by the parks division as necessary for establishment of the park. When the Omnibus Act, into which the Sakatah Lake bills had been incorporated, became law on May 20, the *Waterville Advance* carried banner headlines: "State Park Bill Given Approval."[40]

Sakatah Lake received $175,000 for land acquisition — the most any of the new parks got — and $50,000 more in 1965, plus $10,000 for capital improvements that year and $20,000 in 1967. Development began in 1965, when the park received a road to the shoreline, a well, picnic tables, toilets, a rough campground, and a seasonal residence. Opened to the public on a limited basis in 1966, the park was formally opened the next year, when some features were still rather primitive. By 1968 attendance totaled 58,000, not including Boy Scouts and school conservation groups.[41]

The most important development at Sakatah Lake during the

1970s was the 1973 inauguration of a nature center. Occupying a large cottage, it started with a projector and a few chairs and soon added an aquarium and other displays. Two resident naturalists offered programs every day but Tuesday and Wednesday that summer. The next summer, with the aid of volunteer naturalists, evening programs included slide showings and singing, and often ended with a hike along the lake without flashlights. When the moon was dark, an astronomy program was added. This extensive nature program reflected regional naturalist Sidney Smith's view that strictly recreational development had gone as far as it ought to, and that resources should now be shifted to interpretation. In 1989 the original nature center was replaced by one more centrally located near the campground, in what was formerly the manager's residence.[42]

As the park matured, a few problems arose. When the state was unable to buy some of the optioned land immediately, the owner sold it, and the new owner threatened to develop it. There were also 137 acres in life estates within the boundaries, and these tracts continued to be farmed. About 1976 the Dutch elm disease began to make inroads. During the winters of 1977–78 and 1978–79 a logging company removed over twelve hundred trees, altering the appearance of the park considerably. The railroad running the length of the park might have proved distracting, but fortunately there was little traffic on the line. When it was abandoned in 1976, the grade became part of the Sakatah Singing Hills Trail, one of several corridor trails authorized by the legislature (to be discussed in chapter nine).[43]

Sakatah Lake State Park also has its own trails, which take the hiker or skier to nearly every corner of the park and are usually more interesting than the nearly straight, dead-level abandoned railroad grade. A pioneer camp is located on a tract of land added by the 1965 legislature, the only boundary change in the park's history.[44]

Project 80 would have relegated Sakatah Lake to the status of a recreation area but would have continued it under state management. This proposal does not appear to have been taken very seriously by the parks people, who seem willing to let Sakatah Lake remain a state park. Not one of Minnesota's great parks, Sakatah Lake now has an area of 842 acres, and there is little likelihood of expansion. But the park provides many people, most from the local area and the Twin Cities, with an opportunity to fish, swim, hike, and camp in summer and enjoy the standard winter activities at that season. Although a visitor does not escape the sound of cars on Trunk Highway 60 or motor boats on the lake, the park offers a visual illusion of being deep in the primeval hardwood forest that has been removed from most of southern Minnesota.[45]

## Little Elbow Lake

Little Elbow Lake was proposed by the parks division itself, not so much because of intrinsic merit or strong local support, but because it might take pressure off Itasca, which by the early 1960s was said to be receiving more than a million visitors annually and was expected to draw two million by the year 2000. Located in southeastern Mahnomen County, near the center of the White Earth Indian Reservation, Little Elbow Lake's chief strength was that it was entirely undeveloped, a pleasant bit of second-growth forest with several attractive lakes.[46]

Little Elbow Lake's legislative history parallels that of the other parks created by the Omnibus Act. It was given a statutory area of 3,360 acres, of which nearly two-thirds consisted of Ojibway tribal lands. The state proposed to acquire these through exchange, a device that had not worked elsewhere and was not to work here. Eventually more than 900 acres were obtained, including a great deal of tax-forfeited land, enough to permit construction of a campground, a picnic area, and a boat landing; the state also got an easement for an entrance road over Ojibway lands. That is all the development accomplished in the park's twenty-five-year history.[47]

Project 80 did not recommend the retention of Little Elbow Lake in the state park system, but proposed its reclassification as a state forest day-use and campground area. The White Earth tribe's reluctance to enter into a land-exchange agreement, coupled with the fact that the park did not seem to attract many campers away from Itasca — the manager referred to it as Minnesota's least-known park — gave it somewhat the status of a white elephant in the system. Finally, in 1989 the legislature transferred the land to the tribe.[48]

## Rice Lake

By contrast, the next park, Rice Lake, had strong local support and has had heavy use, mainly by people from the immediate vicinity. In another part of the state, this lake would scarcely be noticed, but natural lakes are hard to find in the southeastern counties. On the eastern edge of Steele County, lapping over into Dodge County, Rice Lake is at the southeast limit of Minnesota's glacier-produced lake country. It is situated on the watershed separating the Zumbro River and Straight River drainage systems. In the late nineteenth century, mill owners along the Zumbro, wishing to increase the amount of water reaching them, constructed dams and dikes to channel more water in their direction, and thereby deprived Maple Creek, a tributary of the Straight, of its normal flow. As a result, the lake, which may have been as much as fifty-five feet deep at one time, began filling up, not so much with upland soil as with decomposing plant matter; the dissolved nutrients running off surrounding fields stimulated abundant growth of algae and other plants. When it seemed possible that a state park would be established in the area, many local residents hoped that the state would take the lead in deepening the lake by dredging.[49]

Because it was the only natural lake for miles around, Rice Lake had a long history of recreational use. The Izaak Walton League owned land on the lake; it and the Rice Lake Rod and Gun Club both developed recreational facilities of one sort or another there. When highway construction took land from Kaplan Woods State Park, public interest in the Owatonna area shifted to Rice Lake. Initially, however, the impetus for a state park came from the Dodge County town of Claremont, east of the lake, where Dana A. Hinckley, editor of the *Claremont News*, became its most vocal proponent. From the fall of 1961, when Hinckley began talking up the idea, civic groups showed an increasing interest in it. Local legislators worked with parks division officials to draft a park bill in May of the next year. At Hinckley's instigation, a Rice Lake State Park Association was formed; it sent delegates to the December 14 meeting with state officials and the Minnesota Council of State Parks at which plans were made for the upcoming legislative session. The Izaak Walton group, whose land would form the nucleus of the proposed park, was also represented.[50]

In the early months of 1963 companion bills calling for the establishment of Rice Lake State Park were introduced, hearings were held at which members of the local park association presented their case, and the substance of the bills was incorporated into the Omnibus Act. The park was to include the entire shoreline of the lake and have a land area of about 1,020 acres. To begin land acquisition, the legislature appropriated $100,000, to which it added $35,000 in 1965, along with $13,000 for capital improvements.[51]

As in most cases, land acquisition moved too slowly to satisfy local park supporters. Negotiators for the state did not reach an agreement with the Izaak Walton League until September 1964, and actual development, mainly on that property, did not begin until the spring of 1967. By the following November picnic and camping facilities were in place, though stumps and other evidence of recent work gave the park a decidedly raw appearance. The state owned about 600 acres by then, including the 50 acres bought from the Izaak Walton League.[52]

After the major purchases in the middle 1960s, land acquisition ground to a near-halt. Additions had brought the park's statutory acreage to 1,056, of which only 692 acres, or about 65 percent, had been acquired by the end of 1976. In order to encircle the lake, the parks division had drawn the original boundaries in such a way that some productive farmland, whose owners were reluctant to sell, was included. Moreover, two brothers opened the Enchanted Forest Camp Ground, on the south shore of the lake opposite the Izaak Walton tract, about two weeks before the Omnibus Act was approved and the park was established. It was some time before the state was able to purchase this land, and even then it was accessible only through other privately owned land. The parks people had always hoped to construct a hiking trail all the way around the lake, but this remained impossible so long as the state did not own a continuous band of shoreline.[53]

Rice Lake State Park encountered other problems. One of the points park supporters had made was that the Owatonna swimming pool was crowded and that the park would relieve some of the pressure on it. Unfortunately, algae, leeches, and mud made Rice Lake a less desirable place to swim than had been expected. A related problem was the continuing siltation of the lake. Only five or six feet deep in normal years, the lake was much less than that

during the drought years in the middle 1970s. It receded so much
that one could walk dry-shod on caked mud far out from the normal shoreline. Joseph F. Cummins, a retired Soil Conservation Service scientist, commented in 1979 that "not much of anything we
are doing now will save the lake." He doubted that dredging it
would be economically feasible.[54]

With all Rice Lake's defects, however, the people of Steele and
Dodge counties wanted to keep their state park. Project 80 proposed reclassifying it as a recreation area under some type of
regional administration. When this proposal came up during discussions of the park division's management plan in 1981, it met
with strong resistance. One of the park's defenders sent parks director Donald Davison twelve letters from people outside the
Owatonna area, asking that Rice Lake be retained as a state park.
Although it is no doubt used most heavily by local people, its proximity to U.S. Highway 14 enables it to attract some travelers following that route. Besides, such parks as Sakatah Lake, Myre–Big
Island, and Sibley also depend greatly on a regional patronage.[55]

In spring Rice Lake offers a varied wildflower display, and it
is a good place to see birds, particularly shorebirds such as sand-
pipers, snipes, killdeer, Virginia rails, and great blue herons. The
causes of the lake's siltation have increased its attractiveness to some
forms of bird life. Prehistoric people came to Rice Lake to harvest
wild rice, so important to their diet; some of them may have maintained permanent residence on the lake. Archaeological investigations have not yet been extensive, but knowledge of pre-European
habitation in a place adds a dimension to at least some visitors' enjoyment. With all these features of interest, Rice Lake can justify
its continued status as a state park.

---

## Lake Louise

Another southern Minnesota park, Lake Louise, has also been
the subject of some argument about its status. A tract of woodland
and old fields at the confluence of the Upper Iowa and Little Iowa
rivers, the park lies just north of Le Roy, in the southeast corner of
Mower County. The park's central feature is an artificial body of
water, originally a millpond, impounded behind a dam just below

*Lake Louise State Park, about 1982*

the junction of the two rivers. The millpond area had been the site of the original village of Le Roy, platted in 1857 but superseded a decade later by the present town when the railroad passed a mile to the south. Of the original village, only a gristmill and a dozen houses survived into the twentieth century.[56]

After the mill finally closed, the village took over the millpond and 28 acres of land surrounding it and transformed the area into a park locally called Wildwood. Nearby was a small tract of hardwood forest, a comparatively rare commodity in heavily agricultural Mower County. When the parks division was inventorying the state for potential park sites, local interest in the Wildwood area led to a visit by U. W. Hella, Evan Haynes, and Bernard Halver early in August 1961. A few months later Hella and Halver wrote to the Le Roy village clerk, outlining the procedure for getting a state park established and suggesting that donation of the city-owned parcel of land might serve in lieu of a monetary contribution.[57]

The Omnibus Act contained a provision for Lake Louise State Park, with an area of nearly 1,100 acres. Besides Wildwood Park, a considerable amount of pasture and cultivated fields and several roads were included. The legislature provided a generous appropriation of $175,000 for land acquisition (as much as Sakatah Lake's appropriation and more than any other park's); another $35,040 was appropriated in 1965, along with $19,500 for capital improvements.[58]

Despite this auspicious beginning, development of the park proceeded too slowly for local people. They began to feel that they had lost more than they had gained by the transformation of their city park into a state park, entry to which would require a vehicle permit. Even after development got under way in 1966, the permit requirement continued to rankle. Eventually, however, relations improved between the parks division and the people of Le Roy. A group of private citizens called the Lake Louise State Park Association assists with the preservation and betterment of the park and annually sponsors Old Wildwood Days. With the assistance of a separate citizens' committee, the state operates a small historic site called the Hambrecht Historical Cottage and Museum.[59]

Project 80 would have relegated Lake Louise to the status of a regional recreation area, presumably on grounds that it is of less than state park calibre and is used primarily by people from the region, if not the locality. A survey published there revealed that 80 percent of the visitors to both Lake Louise and Rice Lake were from a fifty-mile radius — the largest percentage of local use for any park except Camden. Moreover, except for the swimming beach, Lake Louise has few attractions for visitors. Trails along both banks of the Little Iowa, through the woods, and across the old fields do not take the hiker to anything of special interest. Lake Louise does have a good wildflower display, both of the spring ephemerals and of the late summer composites. Except for wild turkeys, which have been introduced, the wildlife is pretty much that of the surrounding countryside. All in all, though Lake Louise is certainly worth preserving, there is some question as to whether it ought to be a state park. Perhaps the time will come when Le Roy or Mower County will be in a position to assume management of it.[60]

---

## Banning

The next state park established in 1963, Banning, encompasses land bordering a ten-mile stretch of the turbulent Kettle River, flowing through a logged-over, burned-over northern forest. Interest in the establishment of a park in this area goes back at least to 1934, when an organization was formed to promote "a woodland park and forest reserve . . . along the Kettle River." Officials in the conservation department were approached and a survey was made in 1935. When the proposal reached Harold Lathrop's desk, he responded with an essentially negative recommendation. Since the land was not classified as submarginal, it could not be purchased for park purposes under existing law. Besides, with Jay Cooke State Park and the St. Croix Recreational Demonstration Area nearby, another park was not deemed necessary. "The purchase of it," added Lathrop, "would deprive the county of tax paying lands." Thus ended the first attempt to establish a park in the Banning area.[61]

The idea surfaced again in 1959, when the president of the Pine County Historical Society wrote the Department of Conservation, inquiring about the possibility of acquiring the Banning townsite for historical purposes. The Banning townsite was almost all that remained of a thriving town that grew up around a stone quarry in the 1890s, when Kettle River sandstone was in heavy demand for use in public buildings. After reaching a peak about 1900, the town declined when the advent of structural steel reduced the demand for stone. By 1918, when a railroad spur was taken up and the plat was vacated, there was practically nothing left of it. Soon not even a road led to the abandoned townsite and quarry.[62]

The county historical society was interested in preserving this ghost town, but no doubt the scenic attractions of the Kettle River also figured in people's thinking. Bernard Halver, who had investigated several other potential park sites, visited Banning and reported that the area had "high historic as well as scenic interest"

*Banning State Park, 1963*

and that a state park of several thousand acres was possible. His favorable report, coupled with local interest on the part of the Sandstone Chamber of Commerce and the Sandstone Rod and Gun Club, provided the necessary impetus to a Banning State Park bill in February 1963. Like the other individual park bills, it became law as part of the Omnibus Act, which provided $107,482 for land acquisition and $29,700 for development. Two years later the legislature added $16,000 more for land acquisition and $25,000 for capital improvements.[63]

Although representatives of the Sandstone and Pine county organizations had been active in lobbying before the legislature, they had not gone out and taken options on the land. As a result, land acquisition proceeded very slowly, and the addition of some key parcels, such as the village site, was long delayed. Development did not really get under way until 1967, when enough land had been purchased so that campgrounds, a picnic area, trails, and other necessities could be put in place. The picnic area and boat landing are located at the head of Hell's Gate, which historian James Taylor Dunn describes as "a wild, two-mile stretch of racing chutes, cascades, and rapids with a gradient of forty feet in one mile." Shooting the rapids, which have individual names like Blueberry Slide, Mother's Delight, and Dragon's Tooth, in a canoe or kayak is a thrilling experience, but only the adventurous (and skilled) need apply. The great majority of park visitors should enjoy Hell's Gate from the shore, where a trail closely parallels the river and gives access to the ruins of a powerhouse and crusher and to the old quarry. The campground is well away from the river, at the head of a trail that leads to Wolf Creek Falls, a pretty little sheet of water whose impressiveness depends largely on how much water is flowing in the creek.[64]

As originally established, Banning State Park had an area of 5,246 acres. Additions made in 1965, 1967, and 1971 brought the statutory acreage to 5,877 and extended the boundaries to include a stretch of the Kettle west of Interstate 35 and another south almost to the gates of the Sandstone Federal Correctional Institution. Another expansion in 1986 brought the park's area to 6,237 acres. Even though much land remains to be acquired, Banning is a large park. The northern two-thirds of the segment of the Kettle included in the park is not accessible by trail; much of this can be reached by canoe, however, for the rapids upstream are less formidable than those in Hell's Gate.[65]

It should come as no surprise to learn that Project 80 recommended that Banning remain a state park. Some may be surprised, however, to learn that the authors of that document gave it a rating of 1 + — a distinction shared with only three other parks then in the system, Beaver Creek Valley, Itasca, and St. Croix. Except for the unspoiled Kettle River with its rapids, Banning is not markedly superior to such parks as Jay Cooke, Gooseberry Falls, or Judge C. R. Magney. But it is definitely of state park calibre, and no one worries nowadays, as Harold Lathrop apparently did in 1935, that it is too close to other units of the system. In fact, three more parks — Savanna Portage, Moose Lake, and St. Croix Wild River — have been created in this region, and all six seem to do a thriving business.[66]

## Maplewood

The largest park established in 1963 — and fifth largest in the system — is Maplewood, located in northwestern Otter Tail County, about halfway between Fergus Falls and Detroit Lakes. Besides being a park of exceptional beauty, Maplewood is noteworthy because it is to a large extent a human artifact. Instead of setting aside a semiwilderness area for protection, the state acquired a largely agricultural block of land, duly equipped with roads, rural schools, churches, and such, and proposed returning it to its presettlement condition. Portions of the park lands still were in forest and had never been cultivated, and farming was a declining activity in the rest, but a 1936 map of Otter Tail County reveals fifty-five dwellings, four school buildings, two churches, and a town hall within the present limits of the park. Maplewood is a clear case of *making* a park in response to a recognized need.[67]

The idea of establishing a park in the vicinity of Lake Lida goes back at least to 1923, when State Auditor Ray Chase included it among the park proposals he submitted to the legislature. Much later, a land-use study conducted by the University of Minnesota concluded that some 9,000 acres of hilly, lake-dotted terrain was better suited to recreation than to farming. In 1959 the NPS published a study of current and future recreational needs in the Missouri River drainage and some adjacent areas such as the valley of the Red River of the North. Among its recommendations for Minnesota was a "sizable area (from 2,000 to 3,000 acres) located in the Fergus Falls, Detroit Lakes, and Wadena region," the most densely populated section of the Red River drainage, "with no existing public areas to serve the people." The accompanying map showed a proposed park in the northwestern part of Otter Tail County.[68]

By that time Evan Haynes, of the NPS, and others had been investigating an area including the south arm of Lake Lida and the adjacent woodlands. Locally, interest in the site was sparked by Dr. Norman H. Baker, a Fergus Falls physician and conservationist, who played a leading role in the establishment of the park. He consulted the Soil Conservation Service to get information on the least disturbed area with park potential in that part of the state. After an aerial survey in June 1960, attention centered on Maplewood Township and adjoining parts of Lida Township. Some frontage on Lake Lida proper would be desirable, thought Haynes, but private development was rapidly expanding there. He proposed a park of 5,920 acres, including 1,210 acres of water.[69]

On December 31, 1960, a group of six men, chaired by Dr. Baker, met to discuss the proposed park. A Maplewood State Park Association was formed, and soon its members began soliciting contributions to a fund for the purchase of lands to be donated to the state upon establishment of the park. The association seems to have been broadly based. An early list of officers includes the names of two men from Maplewood Township and people from Pelican Rapids and Fergus Falls. There seems to have been remarkably little opposition to the park plan, considering the great amount of private property and the number of owners involved.[70]

The original intention had been to introduce a park bill in the 1961 session of the legislature, but it was postponed until February 1963, when companion bills were introduced to authorize Maplewood State Park, last of the original thirteen to be proposed. The Omnibus Act, into which all these bills were incorporated, created a park of approximately 5,600 acres and appropriated $100,000 for land acquisition. The 1965 legislature added another $75,000, together with $12,000 for capital improvements, and the 1967 legislature contributed another $80,000. After reassuring a few worried landowners that eminent domain would not be used (an eminent domain provision had been deleted from the final bill) and that both parties must agree upon the selling price, the parks people concentrated on getting lakeshore property on Lida and Beers lakes as quickly as possible and consolidating the state-owned land between these areas. Land acquisition proceeded rapidly enough so that much of the desired nucleus had been obtained by 1965.[71]

As development got under way, park planner Milt Krona waxed lyrical about Maplewood. "The more I see of this area," he wrote Hella, "the more enthused I get of the possibility of having a really great park in this area. The series of lakes, the hills with the long overlooks and the open meadows are almost ideal." As more land was added, the necessary facilities were provided. Two picnic areas, one including a swimming beach, were located on Lake Lida; a campground was laid out on the northeast side of Grass Lake. Later another public campground was developed on the opposite side of the lake, and a primitive group camp was laid out on the southwest end of Beers Lake. Boat landings were provided on both Lida and Beers lakes. The parks and forestry divisions worked out a cooperative demonstration woodland to give the public a chance to view selected forestry management practices in a northern hardwood forest.[72]

Although the creation of a state park out of former farmland proceeded smoothly enough, some problems arose. One was the questions of what to do with the existing road network. As long as some owners were still actively farming, access roads had to be retained; this meant that the park could be entered from various places. The parks people have always preferred a single entrance so that they can exert a measure of control over traffic. At Maplewood part of the road system was incorporated into the network of park roads, and one township road still crosses the park and provides access for landowners. Public roads extend along the north, south, and west boundaries of the park, but most of the roads leading in from these have been blocked off.[73]

Like most of the other parks established in 1963, Maplewood has been expanded significantly since then. Small additions were made in 1965, and much more extensive ones in 1971, when several sections of land along the eastern and southern sides of the park were added, to bring its statutory acreage to about 9,250. Not all of this has been acquired — by 1978 the state owned 7,234 acres — but the proportion of private inholdings is smaller than at Banning, for example.[74]

When Maplewood State Park was formally dedicated, on September 30, 1973, a plaque was unveiled honoring Dr. Norman Baker, who had died the previous year. The principal speaker was Robert L. Herbst, commissioner of natural resources. Present also were U. W. Hella and his successor as director of the Division of Parks and Recreation, Donald Davison, as well as many local people who had assisted in getting the park started. They must have agreed that the effort had been worthwhile. In the face of increasing private development a park had been created in an area where a few years later it would no longer have been possible to do so. All the parks established in 1963 had their distinctive merits; some, like Forestville, Glacial Lakes, and Banning, were outstanding. But Maplewood was the best of all — more than 9,000 acres of hardwood forest, lakes, wetlands, and old fields in a part of Minnesota where recreational facilities were especially needed.[75]

Mainly because of its size, Maplewood is not quickly explored. The topography is varied enough so that something new is always around the next corner. In the northwestern part is a steep, isolated hill, densely wooded all the way to the top. The official map of the park shows fifty-six bodies of water, most of them small and nameless but a few large enough to afford boating and fishing. The twenty-five miles of hiking trails, fifteen miles of which are open to horseback riding, take visitors to almost every corner of the park. A hiker in a remote section may come upon the crumbling remains of old farm buildings left from a time when people tried to practice agriculture on land better suited to forest. In winter much of the trail system is available for snowmobiling and cross-country skiing.

As might be expected of a park carved out of farmlands, alien plants such as Canada thistles were firmly established when development began. With some help, however, the native flora is reasserting itself. The forested sections contain a number of large individual trees, such as the largest known ironwood in the state. The native wildlife is also making a comeback. The park's location in the transition zone between woodland and prairie means that it harbors animals representative of both regions. Deer are common, beavers less noticeable but decidedly present, and a visitor might see raccoons, squirrels, chipmunks, and rabbits. Bird life is numerous and varied; nearly 150 species nest in the park, not to mention those that pass through during migration.

Even though some of the park roads were blacktopped in 1981 and other improvements are going on continuously, Maplewood will be developed only to render its attractions more accessible to those who appreciate them. The management plan drawn up in 1978 proposed that a large area, at least a third of the park, be classified as a "primitive zone," where visitors might "experience solitude and remoteness . . . insulation from human contact and associated activities." Besides trails, the only development in this zone would be hike-in picnic and campsites near unspoiled Fladmark Lake and the Kettle Moraine area east of Twenty-one Lake. Belonging to all the people of Minnesota as part of their heritage, this land will not be lost to the kind of commercial development that is sweeping over other areas once considered as potential state parks. Maplewood was saved in time.[76]

## Soudan Underground Mine

If Maplewood is in a sense a human artifact, Soudan Underground Mine State Park is even more so, for its central feature is Minnesota's oldest and deepest iron mine. Opened in 1884, the Soudan Mine was operated until 1962. Early the next year the owner, United States Steel Corporation, offered it to the conservation department as a state park. Parks director Hella and members of his staff, accompanied by officials of the mining company, promptly made a reconnaissance survey and soon afterward recommended acceptance of the offer. Although the earlier park bills had already been combined, companion bills authorizing Tower Soudan State Park were introduced late in February. These were added to the Omnibus Act, and Tower Soudan came into being at the same time as the other parks proposed earlier in the legislative session.[77]

In addition to the mine, with all its operating equipment, the state received free of charge some 1,300 acres of wild forested land and three and a half miles of lakeshore. No great amount of development was required, because the state did not intend to dupli-

*Underground tour at Soudan Underground Mine State Park, about 1982*

cate the recreational facilities of more typical state parks. A picnic area was provided and a few trails were laid out, but Tower Soudan remains one of the few parks without campgrounds. The transfer of the property and certain limited improvements were accomplished in time for the park to be dedicated July 1, 1965. No boundary changes have occurred, but the 1988 legislature changed the name to Soudan Underground Mine State Park in order more accurately to describe the unit.[78]

Whatever its name, it is assuredly like no other Minnesota state park. Its major attractions are underground — 2,400 feet underground. An elevator takes visitors down to the twenty-seventh level of the mine in three minutes; then they are taken by train some three-fourths of a mile, where they climb thirty-two steps in a spiral staircase to the Montana stope. Another tour explores the mine's surface facilities, from which visitors get a view of the town of Soudan far below. It is possible also to look down into an open-pit mine, used in the early years before the major operations went underground. Such things as a restored ore car donated by the Duluth, Missabe and Iron Range railroad contribute to the visitor's knowledge of an important phase of the state's history. [79]

Some people have questioned the appropriateness of a state park consisting almost entirely of an abandoned iron mine. For a time the Iron Range Resources and Rehabilitation Board maintained that the mine ought to be removed from the park system and turned over to that body. After a series of meetings, an agreement was worked out for joint management of the park, which would remain within the system, with the mine itself operated by the IRRRB. [80]

Soudan Underground Mine is unquestionably a success as a tourist attraction. During the summer, the mine tours are usually booked well in advance. Except in terms of visitation, it cannot be compared with other parks, for the kind of experience it offers is unlike those provided by the others.

---

## Summary

Tower Soudan was the last of the eleven parks brought into being by the Omnibus Act — the largest number ever created by one piece of legislation. Those who drafted the act must have realized that this was the last chance they were to have to effect such a swift expansion of the park system. True, there were passing references to the need for thirty or thirty-five new parks in the next ten years; when the Project 80 report was issued nearly a decade later, it contained recommendations for several new parks. But by that time the climate of public opinion had changed, and the DNR was definitely on the defensive when proposals for creation of new parks or expansion of old ones were made.

Besides spawning a flock of new parks, the Omnibus Act provided for additions to seventeen old ones. The expansions varied from negligible, in the cases of Lake Shetek and Savanna Portage, to proportionately immense, in such parks as Helmer Myre, which was expanded from 120 acres to 967, and John A. Latsch, which grew (on paper) from 322 acres to 1,467. Further additions were made to these seventeen and to other parks in 1965 and 1967. Except for newly established parks, very little expansion of the state park system has occurred since then. In fact, some parks, such as Camden and Whitewater, have had their acreage reduced by recent legislation.[81]

Of the ten articles in the Omnibus Act, only four bear directly on the parks. Article V is the big one, providing for new parks and authorizing additions to some of the old ones. Article IV increases the cigarette tax and provides that 12.5 percent of the revenues shall be deposited in a natural resources fund. Article VI deals specifically with Tower Soudan, whose case was sufficiently different from the rest to call for separate treatment. Article VIII provides specific sums for land acquisition, as well as $472,000 for capital improvements. The remaining articles pertain to the establishment and function of the Minnesota Outdoor Recreation Resources Commission and to matters unrelated to the park system.[82]

But the most important contribution of the Omnibus Act was the establishment of a baker's dozen of new parks (including Grand Mound and O. L. Kipp) at one stroke. No such sudden expansion of the system had ever happened before; nor is it likely ever to happen again. In a way, it resembles President Jimmy Carter's proclamation of seventeen Alaskan national monuments on December 1, 1978. That action, however, was intended to grant interim protection to certain areas in the face of congressional deadlock and inaction, whereas the Omnibus Act was the result of efforts by both the legislative and executive branches and enjoyed widespread grassroots support from park users. In sharp contrast to the manner in which parks had been established prior to the 1930s, site selection for new parks was not haphazard. Local interest was important, to be sure, but professionals in the parks division were now available to evaluate proposals advanced by local supporters and to offer proposals of their own. The result was a qualitative as well as quantitative improvement in the state park system.[83]

# CHAPTER NINE

# *Rounding Out the System 1964-1990*

BECAUSE of some unfinished business left over from the Omnibus Act, and also because of a few windfalls of one sort or another, at least one new park unit emerged from each legislative session from 1965 through 1973, and another — an important one — followed in 1979. Moreover, the Minnesota Outdoor Recreation Resources Commission (MORRC), created by the Omnibus Act, submitted a valuable study of the parks in 1965; six years later another analysis, sponsored jointly by the Department of Natural Resources and the State Planning Agency, offered an evaluation of the existing park system and a number of suggestions for future expansion. Partly as a result of these studies, the 1975 legislature passed a comprehensive Outdoor Recreation Act, which mandated several policy changes.

The MORRC report was more descriptive than prescriptive; most of its space was given to maps of all the parks and waysides, showing how much land remained to be acquired within the statutory boundaries of each unit. The maps also showed what roads, campgrounds, and other improvements were in place and what additional facilities were planned. The report presented comparative statistics on park use and gave a brief history of the system. It was basically a compendium of information on the park system as of 1965.

The report did not wholly omit recommendations, however. For one thing, it offered suggestions regarding park expansion. Relatively large acreage increases were recommended for parks that had not benefited from the Omnibus Act or that had inadequate increases under the legislation. For one park, Big Stone Lake, the report proposed a *reduction* in size of more than 1,100 acres. It also favored the transfer of six small parks to local agencies, as had already been done with four others. On the other hand, it proposed a number of additions, three of which were made in the next few years. Finally, it recommended several changes in park policy and management and, as might have been expected, stressed the need for increased appropriations, both for land acquisition and for capital improvements.[1]

The years immediately following the Omnibus Act were a time of stocktaking for the parks division, a time to concentrate on developing the newly established parks. Although park proposals continued to enter the legislative hopper, few of them originated with the parks people, and very few reached the governor's desk. The more modest the proposal, the better its chances of being enacted into law. The first addition made to the system after the Omnibus Act was extremely modest.

---

## Flood Bay

Motorists driving up the North Shore of Lake Superior may scarcely notice the first of fourteen units of the park system along or near U.S. Highway 61 between Duluth and the Canadian border. If they do notice it, they may take it for a mere rest stop along the highway a few miles beyond Two Harbors. As a matter of fact, that is what the Flood Bay State Wayside originally was and what it may again become. When the Lake County Board of Commissioners asked the Department of Conservation to assume responsibility for the Flood Bay area, then under the jurisdiction of the highway department, a small tract of land (18.65 acres) was transferred, and on May 21, 1965, a bill was approved creating the Flood Bay Wayside Park, as it was at first called.[2]

Flood Bay has only minimum facilities: a parking area, a few picnic tables, a trash can or two, and pit toilets. Since it is not a park and offers little by way of recreation, there is no apparent reason why the Division of Parks and Recreation should administer it. But when some land was deleted from the wayside in 1984, a condition was attached specifying that "this area be developed and operated in a manner consistent with the continued operation and preservation of the remaining portions of the Flood Bay State Wayside." This suggests that the DNR intends to retain the wayside as a unit of the state park system.[3]

## Franz Jevne

Flood Bay was the only addition the 1965 legislature made to the system. In 1967, two units, both on the far northern border of the state, were added. The first of these was a gift, a fact that made it more palatable to the legislature. After conducting an NPS survey of the Rainy River between International Falls and Baudette, Evan Haynes submitted a report in 1961, recommending a park of about 1,300 acres, to include some land owned by the family of Franz Jevne, who had been a lawyer in International Falls and later in Minneapolis. No action was taken at that time, but late in 1966 Jevne's son, Franz Jevne, Jr., wrote to park planner Milt Krona, offering on behalf of himself and his brother Robert to donate 117.83 acres to the state for use as a park, on condition that it be named for their father, then almost eighty-four, whom he described as a true pioneer of northern Minnesota.[4]

This small tract was a far cry from the 1,300-acre park Haynes envisioned, but it was more scenic than most of the land along the Rainy River. Krona thought of acquiring it as one of a series of waysides along the river, with little development. This plan suited the Jevnes. According to Franz, Jr., the site was already a public park for all practical purposes, and perhaps Koochiching County could maintain it temporarily.[5]

With parks division approval, a bill to create Franz Jevne State Wayside Park was introduced in the 1967 legislative session. Encountering no opposition, it passed both houses unanimously and was signed into law by Governor Harold LeVander on May 24. In 1969, when a degree of uniformity was imposed on the nomenclature of the various units in the system, the word "wayside" was deleted. It would have been more appropriate if the word "park" had been, for it was more of a wayside — smaller, in fact, than such waysides as Cross River, Devils Track Falls, or Old Crossing Treaty.[6]

As Krona wished, development at Franz Jevne has been held to a minimum. It has a ten-site campground, equipped with the usual pit toilets, fire rings, picnic tables, and garbage cans; the water supply is a short distance away, in the picnic area. The park is used chiefly by anglers, though now and then a traveler on Trunk Highway 11 may use it as a rest stop (it is about a mile off the highway) or as an overnight campsite. Thus far, none of the other tracts of land that Krona suggested might be acquired has been added to the parks division's domain, and Franz Jevne remains a small, isolated park, little used except by local people, in a part of the state deficient in recreation areas. (Zippel Bay, the nearest, is more than fifty miles to the northwest.) Yet with a change of name to identify it more accurately, Franz Jevne could continue to serve the people of Minnesota.

---

## Hayes Lake

Back in the 1930s Lake Bronson and Old Mill state parks had been established to fill a recreational void in the far northwestern corner of the state. But neither they nor the much later Zippel Bay completely met the needs of the population. Surveys conducted in 1959 revealed a good site for a park on the North Fork of the Roseau River, southeast of the town of Roseau. Among the advantages of the Hayes Creek site, as it was then called, was that the river had its source in a bog and therefore was not contaminated by agricultural pollutants. Moreover, much of the land was already owned by the state. Finally, the location would fit the proposed route of the Great River Road, which, as projected, would go far beyond the source of the Mississippi, all the way to Winnipeg.[7]

After a favorable staff evaluation of the site in 1964, citizen support was organized at the suggestion of Albert Marshall, then president of the Minnesota Council of State Parks, and lobbying began. Although a "Hayes state park" bill introduced in the 1965 legislature bogged down in committee, the legislators did authorize a feasibility study. Carried out by Brauer and Associates, Inc., this study in 1966 recommended a park of 2,993 acres, including an artificial lake of 187 acres. Besides the advantages noted earlier, the adjacent wilderness bog provided habitat for game animals not found in or near any other state park. Les Blacklock, naturalist and nature photographer, assisted in the survey and offered a more subjective evaluation of the site. After several days in the area, he wrote,

> Conditions were miserable. It was unbearably hot; you could wring the moisture from the air; voracious mosquitoes gave my OFF! a strong test; three-quarter inch bull flies (that's what the natives call them) tried to knock me over and were constantly getting tangled in my hair; it rained about an inch and a half in several thunderstorms; ticks hiked over me in good numbers — and I enjoyed every minute of it!

About 1,694 acres of public lands were available; for the purchase of the 1,298 acres of privately owned lands, the study recommended an appropriation of $49,600, along with $34,250 for initial development of the park.[8]

Companion bills calling for the establishment of Hayes Lake State Park were introduced in the 1967 session of the legislature. Though neither came up for a vote, their provisions were embodied in the general parks bill that emerged from that session. The park as described would be a long, narrow tract of land, on both sides of the Roseau River; the central part would be widened enough to allow for a substantial buffer along the proposed lake.[9]

When work did not begin immediately, local people who had expected an instant park began deluging the parks division with complaints. But a dam had to precede almost any other development, and its construction was delayed, with resulting cost overruns. (Eventually a contractor was found who did the job for $467,000 — well over the original estimate of $300,000.) By August 1971 about all that was in place at the park was the entrance sign. Lettered stakes indicated where various facilities were going to be, and the area looked rather like a logging camp. It was hard to believe that a state park would ever take shape in this wounded wilderness. But the work went ahead, the reservoir filled up behind the dam, and in mid-July of 1973 Hayes Lake State Park was formally dedicated.[10]

When the Outdoor Recreation Act of 1975 mandated a management plan for each state park, it required that a park whose central feature was an artificial lake be classified as a recreational park. Local people would have preferred to see Hayes Lake classified as a natural park; some wanted to bar motorboats on the lake. The compromise that finally emerged restricted the use of motorboats to those with electric motors.[11]

Hayes Lake State Park is a worthy addition to the system, but it has yet to be discovered by any appreciable number of people. Located at the end of the bituminous-surfaced portion of a county road, it is not likely to attract many long-distance travelers in search of a place to spend the night. Nor is it a probable destination for people from other parts of the state, where there are natural lakes. This artificial lake, however, does not suffer from the drawdown problems that afflict recreational areas on reservoirs intended for irrigation, flood control, or other purposes that produce widely varying levels at different times. The shoreline is extremely irregular, wooded nearly everywhere, and therefore aesthetically more pleasing than the regular, largely open shoreline at Lake Bronson. Recent park leaflets show twelve miles of foot trails — almost as many as at Lake Bronson and far more than at Old Mill. Hayes Lake has much to attract the visitor and only one defect: its remoteness from centers of population.

## Minnesota Valley Trail

The 1969 legislative session produced two major additions to the state park system: the Minnesota Valley Trail and a new park on the St. Croix. Because land acquisition problems delayed the opening of Afton State Park until 1982, the Minnesota Valley Trail, with its six park-sized waysides, will be considered first.

In 1979 a departmental reorganization led to the creation of a Trails and Waterways Unit within the DNR structure, and the Minnesota Valley Trail (though not the waysides that it connected) was transferred from the Division of Parks and Recreation to the new body. Recreational development in the Minnesota River valley has been carried out by means of a cooperative effort by the DNR, the federal Fish and Wildlife Service, and various counties and municipalities in the region.

The lower Minnesota River valley — the segment from Le Sueur to the mouth of the river — had long been recognized for its recreational and historical potential, and at least as early as 1939 an NPS study had recommended the establishment of a state park there. The 1965 MORRC report had also offered such a recommendation, with the area around the village of Carver as the focus of attention. The parks division had in mind an 18,000-acre park, on both sides of the river, between Carver and Belle Plaine. In the 1967 legislative session bills calling for a study of such a park were introduced but failed to pass. Two years later the same fate awaited a bill to establish a Carver State Park and another to establish a Minnesota Valley Trail. The substance of the latter, however, was incorporated into the general parks bill, which was signed into law by Governor LeVander on May 29, 1969.[12]

Trails were "in" that year. In the mid-1960s the state of Wisconsin had acquired a stretch of abandoned Chicago & North Western railroad track and converted it into a recreational trail. A year or so later Minnesota had purchased a similar segment of abandoned track, between Pipestone and Lake Wilson, for use as a wildlife management area. Seeing no necessary conflict between this function and the presence of a recreational trail, the 1967 legislature established the Casey Jones State Trail on this land. Trails suddenly became popular; in the 1969 legislative session there were eight trail proposals. Only one other than the Minnesota Valley bill was enacted into law, and that trail has not been developed. All but two of the others, however, were reintroduced in later sessions and then passed.[13]

The Minnesota Valley Trail legislation should be seen against this background. Besides being more successful than the others in getting through the legislature, the Minnesota Valley bill differed in that it provided for a series of six waysides, the smallest of which was larger than such parks as Carley, Temperance River, and Franz Jevne. The trail was to run from Fort Snelling to Le Sueur, and the waysides were spaced at fairly equal intervals along the river, all but one on the right, or southeast, bank. Starting from Fort Snelling, they were Rice Lake, 585 acres; Carver Rapids, between Shakopee and Jordan, 481 acres; Lawrence, between Jordan and Belle Plaine, 1,063 acres; Belle Plaine, adjacent to the community of that name, 2,386 acres; Blakeley, five or six miles above Belle Plaine, 238 acres; and Rush River, which incorporated a Sibley County park a mile or so west of the river, 693 acres.[14]

Not only were most of these waysides large enough to be developed into respectable parks, but three of them — Carver Rapids, Lawrence, and Belle Plaine, with a total of nearly 4,000 acres — were within the boundaries of the proposed park for which the parks division had requested funds for a study in 1967. It was later charged that the DNR, unable to get the park it wanted by direct action, had resorted to more devious means. This allegation was hardly fair, for the 4,000 acres now sought was a far cry from the 18,000 acres proposed earlier. Later, however, more land was acquired below Carver Rapids and within the area of the original park proposal, as well as elsewhere.[15]

So ambitious a plan as the Minnesota Valley Trail was certain to be the object of criticism, both from people whose land was sought and from those whose money was used to buy it. In 1974 the *Minneapolis Tribune* carried an article titled "Riverside land acquisition by DNR questioned," the thrust of which was that the DNR was buying too much land with little recreational value and paying too much of the taxpayers' money for it. The author of the article, Steven Dornfeld, thought the DNR, instead of buying whole farms, should have confined itself to buying a strip of land along the river.[16]

Parks and recreation director Donald Davison replied that often owners refused to sell only a strip, or else set the price for it as high as for the entire holding. Moreover, in an area so close to the Twin Cities the DNR sometimes had to move quickly in order to forestall private developers, who might be willing to pay more than the DNR had been authorized to pay for a particular tract. Davison did not mention it, but here as elsewhere in the park system a buffer was needed between the truly scenic land and privately owned land used for residences, businesses, or industry. Besides, if visitors were to see a wide variety of plant communities, they needed to hike the hillsides and bluffs as well as the floodplain.[17]

Another kind of complaint came from people who would be dispossessed from their homes if the entire plan should materialize. Vigorous opposition to the Blakeley wayside came from the township as well as from individuals. The DNR was unable to find any willing sellers, and there was some question as to whether the site chosen was the most desirable. Eventually the DNR found another site that it regarded as preferable, and the legislature in 1984 authorized a substitution.[18]

Apart from Rush River, where the usual facilities were already in place when the county park was acquired, the first wayside to be developed extensively was Lawrence, where more than 700 acres had been obtained by 1972. Some trail mileage was available for use by that time, and an entrance sign had been erected. In the years that followed, the trail system at Lawrence was enlarged, a picnic area was laid out, and eventually the wayside was equipped with a campground boasting twenty-five regular sites and eleven walk-in sites. With a group camp adjacent to the picnic area, Lawrence has most of the facilities of a full-fledged state park. Besides offering a cross-section of Minnesota valley plant and animal communities, it includes the site of the long-vanished pioneer settlement of St. Lawrence and three charming old stone houses, two of which are now in state ownership.[19]

Before much development had taken place along the Minnesota Valley Trail, a movement to establish a national wildlife refuge in the valley had got under way. It received congressional authorization in 1976, and since then the state and federal governments have cooperated in administering the lands the respective agencies have acquired. For example, the Carver Rapids wayside is really an enclave in the Louisville Swamp unit of the Minnesota Valley National Wildlife Refuge, with federally owned lands surrounding it on three sides and the Minnesota River forming its western boundary; the wayside is accessible on the landward side only by trail. Informational signs use the same format in both jurisdictions; the only way one knows which agency owns a particular tract of land is to observe the boundary markers. With the formation of the Trails and Waterways Unit in 1979, a dual jurisdiction also began operating on the state-owned lands. In both cases of joint management (state-federal and state park–state trail) the cooperative effort seems to be working. At least the casual visitor sees no evidence of jurisdictional problems.[20]

Problems of other sorts are present, however. Perhaps the most serious is unavoidable, given the nature of the landforms. The floodplain, on which most of the Minnesota Valley Trail is located, is susceptible to periodic flooding, and this necessarily interferes with the trail system. The Louisville Swamp is more or less permanently inundated, and boardwalks have been laid down in especially wet places. Elsewhere the situation is less serious but can create difficulties, as it did in the spring and early summer of 1983. The Minnesota and its tributaries were out of their banks more than once, and the main corridor trail, which follows the river, was unusable for many weeks and difficult to use for an even longer time. Much the same thing happened in 1984.

Development of the Minnesota Valley Trail is an ongoing process. By 1990 it was possible to hike, ski, or ride without interruption from just west of Shakopee to Belle Plaine — about a third of the distance from Fort Snelling to Le Sueur. Each year more land is acquired, and the trail is extended. Conceivably it may even some day be extended beyond Le Sueur. The 1969 legislation authorized a study of a potential extension all the way to Big Stone Lake. Fragments of public land here and there, including some large county parks on the north bank in Renville County, might be incorporated into such an extension. Even if hiking or riding the entire length of the valley is never possible, one can already canoe the whole river. Perhaps by a combination of hiking and canoeing, real devotees will eventually be able to travel from Big Stone Lake to Fort Snelling.

## Other State Trails

Although the Minnesota Valley Trail was the only one of the trail proposals advanced in the 1969 legislature to be enacted into law that year and developed, the next session did much better. Besides Casey Jones and Minnesota Valley, which were given official status by this legislation, five other trails were authorized: Countryview Bicycle Trail, Glacial Lakes Trail (originally proposed in 1969), Root River Trail (also a second try), and two new ones, Douglas Trail (from Rochester to Pine Island) and Sakatah Singing Hills Trail (from Mankato to Faribault). The last two were specifically authorized to use abandoned railroad rights-of-way, as was the Luce Line Trail, which followed in 1973. Since that time the

*Willard Munger State Trail near Duluth, about 1988*

Heartland Trail, using old railroad grades between Park Rapids and Cass Lake, the Minnesota-Wisconsin Boundary Trail (renamed the Willard Munger Trail in 1988), the North Shore Trail, the Taconite Trail, the Hinckley Fire Trail, and the Paul Bunyan Trail have been established and, to varying degrees, developed. The Root River Trail has also been partly developed, though not precisely on its original route, and the DNR has acquired a stretch of abandoned Soo Line grade in Ramsey and Washington counties, which, after a lengthy legal battle, finally became the state's to develop like the others.[21]

Many other trails were proposed, but landowner opposition, coupled with the increasing cost of acquiring and developing such trails, has made most of them unfeasible. Railroad abandonment speeded up during the 1970s and early 1980s, but the intense controversy that erupted over the DNR's effort to acquire part of the Milwaukee Road's line from La Crescent to Ramsey for the Root River Trail led to the decision to concentrate on the development of the trails already securely in state ownership. It had become more and more evident that without an abandoned railroad grade to build on, trails through heavily farmed countryside had no chance of materializing. The Glacial Lakes Trail, for example, will in all likelihood never be built; it has been dropped from maps showing the state's corridor trail system.

---

## Afton

The one real state park established by the 1969 legislature was created in response to the continuing need for more recreational facilities in the Twin Cities metropolitan area. Perhaps the most scenic area within a fifty-mile radius was the St. Croix valley, where the last state park, William O'Brien, established nearly a quarter-century earlier, was heavily overused, despite sizable increases in its area. It was generally thought that there were no unspoiled tracts of land left along the lower St. Croix, but in 1967 Chester Wilson, once conservation commissioner, told Samuel Morgan, of the Minnesota Council of State Parks, that land containing the last remaining beach on the Minnesota side of the river was on the market; Wilson urged Morgan to move quickly before it was sold for

*Perry Vining with Minnesota Viking celebrity guests "smooching"*
*at the Minne'soda Classic, Afton State Park, 1985*

residential development. As it happened, the Minnesota Parks
Foundation had just been formed to work with the DNR in acquiring land for state parks and was looking for a specific project. Morgan and his confreres immediately began negotiating for the
lakeshore property of Roy Dosé and his son Donn, and in the summer of 1968 they reached agreement and signed a contract.[22]

By that time the members of the Foundation had convinced
parks director U. W. Hella of the merits of the area surrounding the
Dosé property, in Afton and Denmark townships, Washington
County. At the beginning they had in mind an area of about 2,300
acres (later scaled down to 1,669) of rolling, partly wooded countryside, with about three miles of frontage on the St. Croix, here
expanded to form Lake St. Croix. Some of it had been farmed, but
for the most part the topography was rough, with deep ravines and
an intermittent stream called Trout Brook leading down to the
river. Near the middle of the property was a skiing enterprise called
Afton Alps, a going concern that was extremely unlikely to sell to
the state and thus presented a defect in the area's potential as a state

park. A less serious blemish was a railroad track that extended though the whole area, from north to south, along the river. Despite the nearness to the Twin Cities, little residential development had occurred.

Although two studies of the area had already been conducted, during the 1969 legislative session opponents of the park demanded yet another. (The resolution calling for the study was introduced by a local real estate agent.) The study was carried out in the space of three weeks, and the results were presented to the legislature a few days after the first of two companion bills was introduced for the establishment of Afton State Park. After intense lobbying by both proponents and opponents of the park, both chambers passed the house bill just before the end of the session. Though urged by those hostile to the park to veto the bill, Governor LeVander signed it on June 6.[23]

Afton State Park had a legal existence as of that date, but thirteen years were to pass before it would be formally opened to the public. More than the usual number of problems, most of them connected in some way with land acquisition, cropped up in the course of its development. In order to obtain federal funds for land acquisition, the state was required to compensate displaced residents for their relocation and moving expenses, and it took time to evaluate each case and arrive at an agreement. In addition, development of the park was delayed by difficulties in obtaining a key parcel of land, on which it was proposed to locate a visitor center, a parking area, the main picnic ground, and part of the entrance road. Not until 1979, when the legislature authorized eminent domain proceedings, was this tract acquired.[24]

By that time the state had already spent $1.8 million on development in other parts of Afton. A temporary entrance was designated at the north end of the park. The road there was rough, narrow, and winding, but it ended at a former farmhouse, now used as temporary park headquarters, where there was a well and where a few other facilities were installed. From this point one could hike or ski along a number of trails that led by various routes to the shore of the St. Croix. Picnic tables and other facilities were provided in a pleasant open area near the river. An old township road was now used as a service road, and to prevent park visitors' use of it, a gate was placed across it.[25]

Local residents were opposed to a permanent park entrance at the north end, and they and the DNR found themselves at odds over several other issues as well. Through their advisory committee, residents resisted efforts to build a road deep into the park, arguing that instead visitors should have to hike or bike into the interior. They were also concerned about the snowmobile traffic, which by the winter of 1973–74 had become quite controversial. A local resident wrote Commissioner Robert Herbst that snowmobiles were taking over the park:

> This leads to the conclusion that, by default, the Afton State Park will be given over to the land-damaging motorized sportsmen who maintain the strongest lobby and speak with the most strident voice. The nature-lovers and the followers of the less environmentally destructive sports will be denied enjoyment of the park simply through being crowded out. And the land itself, extremely fragile, by reason of steep slopes and thin soil cover, will inevitably deteriorate.

Eventually, when the park was formally opened, snowmobiles were excluded.[26]

After passage of the Outdoor Recreation Act of 1975, the parks people drew up a management plan for Afton. Unlike most of the plans in that series, the one for Afton described improvements that did not yet exist, so at the public meetings citizens had more opportunity to influence the direction of that development. A number of concerns were voiced at these meetings, but most of the really important issues had been confronted earlier and solutions had been worked out. In general, the plan was carefully crafted and took into account concerns local people had previously expressed.[27]

Perhaps the most innovative feature in the plan for Afton State Park, one that set it apart from most other parks in the system, was that it would have no automobile campground. Camping would be permitted, but on a hike-in basis only. Campsites would be scattered over an area of relatively stable soils, deep in the interior of the park. Besides a major picnic area accessible by automobile, walk-in picnic facilities would be laid out at various locations within the park. The trail system being planned would be extensive, reaching every portion of the park, but some trails would be restricted to hikers.[28]

Construction finally got under way in 1981, and the park was opened in the summer of 1982, though not everything was completed by that time. The visitor center, surely one of the finest in the park system, was opened in 1983. A smooth but winding entrance road, bituminous surfaced, leads in two miles from the arresting entrance sign and ends in a spacious parking lot near the visitor center. From there trails lead down to the St. Croix, where other paths follow the river or wind up the ravines to the interior of the park. Everywhere the goal has been to make the development harmonize with the landscape. The long-range plan is to restore the oak savanna, which was largely destroyed by farming operations, so that the park visitor will get an idea of what the countryside was like before the intrusion of Europeans.

The discovery of the land now embraced in Afton State Park in the late 1960s was an important event in the history of the Minnesota park system. Here, only about twenty miles from downtown St. Paul, in the scenic St. Croix valley, was a sizable tract of relatively unspoiled land. It was not a wilderness, to be sure, but in the part of Minnesota first opened to white settlement, this area still retained enough of its presettlement character to be returned to something like that condition in the space of a few years. It is heavily used, as its sponsors expected it to be. But if the park planners have done their work properly, and if damage by users can be held to a minimum, Afton State Park will satisfy the urban dweller's need for frequent exposure to outdoor experience in a natural setting — and go on satisfying it, not for tomorrow or next year but for the indefinite future.

## O. L. Kipp

The 1971 legislature relocated one park and accepted the transfer of some land for another. O. L. Kipp State Park has the distinction of having been established in one location and later "moved" to another. In its original form it was a product of the Omnibus Act of 1963. The Mississippi River Parkway Commission of Minnesota had recently adopted a resolution asking the legislature to establish a state park on the bluffs near Dresbach, just upriver from La Crosse, Wisconsin. The idea appealed to the planners in the parks

*On Queen's Bluff at O. L. Kipp State Park, 1976*

division, who felt the need for a park near the point where many visitors coming from the east entered Minnesota. Only two parks lay along the Mississippi below the Twin Cities. Frontenac was in the early stages of development then, and John A. Latsch, though it included three bluffs, had the disadvantage that the summit could be reached only by a steep trail.[29]

As with other parks established in 1963, separate companion bills for O. L. Kipp were introduced by state senators and representatives from the district where the park would be located. Although they were the last of the park bills introduced at that session — later even than Tower Soudan — they were incorporated into the Omnibus bill, which became law on May 20. No appropriation was included, because it was thought that federal funds would be available for land acquisition under a twenty-year-old law for the preservation of scenic and historic roadside areas. When this expectation proved unfounded, the 1965 legislature appropriated $96,000 — more than for any other park that year. Members of the highway department suggested the name; Orin Lansing Kipp had joined the department in 1916 and had risen to the position of assistant commissioner and chief engineer by the time of his retirement in 1955. The department wanted to honor him by having a roadside park named for him, and the original O. L. Kipp State Park was not much more than that.[30]

As established by the 1963 law, the park was a long, narrow strip of land, some six miles long and only a quarter of a mile wide at its narrowest point. For most of its length it was bounded on the east by U.S. Highways 14 and 61, which follow the Mississippi, and on the west by a county road, which roughly parallels the highway but is on the bluffs some 600 feet higher. The park, which extended most of the way from La Crescent to Dresbach, was planned to be about 1,350 acres in size. A campground and picnic area were to be laid out along the county road; the extreme narrowness would make extensive development impossible, confined as it would have to be to the blufftops.[31]

Apparently the state never acquired any land at the Dresbach site. Not only did federal funds prove to be unavailable, but land-owners in the area of the park refused to sell their choice lots over-looking the river at the price the state was prepared to pay. Mean-while, however, the forestry division of the DNR had been buying up lands since 1962 for inclusion in the Minnesota Memorial Hard-wood State Forest (later renamed the Richard J. Dorer Memorial Hardwood State Forest) at a site several miles up the Mississippi, between Dakota and Lamoille. This tract, roughly triangular in shape, with its longest side fronting the river, was definitely of state park calibre. Among other attractions, it included the scenically and botanically significant King's and Queen's bluffs. Its compact shape would make it easier to administer than the Dresbach site, and, most important, the DNR already owned more than 1,000 acres there.[32]

After an unsuccessful attempt to relocate the park in the 1969 legislative session, its supporters had better luck two years later. The Queen's Bluff site, somewhat enlarged since 1969, was sub-stituted for the Dresbach site as part of a complex piece of legisla-tion. What began as a simple bill for the expansion of Maplewood State Park snowballed, to wind up containing provisions for addi-tions to ten other parks, boundary changes at Lake Bronson, a land exchange at Interstate, the establishment of the Moose Lake State Recreation Area, the use of eminent domain at five parks, expansion of the Minnesota Valley Trail, the establishment of several other trails — and the relocation of O. L. Kipp.[33]

Despite some controversy, 1,073.36 acres of land was transferred from the DNR lands and forestry division to the parks and recreation division. Now O. L. Kipp State Park could finally be developed. One problem was created, however, by the two DNR agencies' different objectives. The lands and forestry division's aim was to restore the soil and retard erosion by planting trees, including both nonnative species, such as red pine, and species that were native to the region but not to the sites on which they had been planted, such as white pine, walnut, and ash. The parks division's goal was, as at Afton, to restore the presettlement vegetation as far as possible. What to do with a fifteen-year-old stand of red pine? Ultimately the decision was to harvest these trees as they reached maturity and to replace them with indigenous hardwoods. Other trees would be transplanted to locations more like those in which they were naturally found.[34]

O. L. Kipp State Park also has problems resulting from its topography. Most of the park area consists of rough, broken terrain, unsuited to intensive use. The roads and other developments are located along narrow ridges separated by deep valleys. These ridges were at one time cultivated, and erosion became a serious problem. This threat has been alleviated since the land went out of cultivation, but it could recur with excessive use. The steep slopes — locally called "goat prairies" — are too fragile for any kind of use, even foot trails, so the trail system has been confined to the ridges.[35]

Botanically the most significant feature of the park is a relict community of northern white cedar near the tip of Queen's Bluff. Far south of its usual range, this small stand is a survival from glacial times. Because of the need to protect it, The Nature Conservancy (TNC) purchased a 20-acre tract that it named the Jean Lundberg Teeter Memorial. When the park was relocated, there was some concern about the continued protection of this area. Professor Calvin R. Fremling, of Winona State College, wrote Hella that classes from the University of Minnesota and other institutions had been going there for over fifty years. Fear of damage had led TNC to buy it; now Fremling feared that, surrounded by a state park, the tract might be in danger. Hella replied that protection of the area had been one of the reasons for establishing the park and that the parks division's concern antedated TNC's.[36]

Other concerns also have led the parks people to discourage hikers from going out on Queen's Bluff. In March 1976, only a few weeks before the official opening of the park, a Wisconsin woman fell to her death while trying to climb down the face of the bluff. All of the bluffs present some danger, and trails have been routed as far as possible from the sheer cliffs. Railed-in platforms have been erected at most of the overlooks to minimize the hazard; warning signs advise adults to keep close watch over children at these points.[37]

Development at O. L. Kipp went on through the early 1970s. In July 1976 the picnic area opened, and two months later the campground followed. The picnic area is unusual in that the tables are scattered around the gentle slope, each one separated from the rest by bushes or small trees. Plans call for the construction of camping and picnic areas in more suitable locations less subject to erosion; modern sanitation buildings will replace the present pit toilets. The building now used as park headquarters and manager's residence will eventually become an interpretive center.[38]

The 1977 management plan classified O. L. Kipp as a natural state park. The terrain, it was felt, could not withstand heavy recreational use; with proper precautions, however, the park could tolerate a normal amount of use. Thus far not many people have discovered the park. Despite being within sight of Interstate 90, it does not attract a great many overnighters traveling that highway. Even so, those people make up about half the campers who stay at O. L. Kipp; the other half consists mostly of people from La Crosse, Winona, and other nearby communities.[39]

The chief activity at the park is hiking to the seven or eight overlooks, most of which offer views of the Mississippi, with its barge traffic, pleasure craft, and wooded islands. Although no official trail leads out to the point of Queen's Bluff, a trail goes part way out on King's Bluff; the tip of the bluff is still privately owned, as are several other important parcels of land. Because the state has been unable to acquire a large tract along the approach road, the visitor must enter the park by way of a narrow, winding gravel road that passes two farmsteads. Some valley land in the southeastern corner of the park is also still in private hands.

With a statutory acreage of 2,835, O. L. Kipp will be large enough to contain a great variety of landforms and vegetative communities. About one-fourth of its area is covered by what is known botanically as the Big Woods, which consists chiefly of red and pin oak, green ash, basswood, elm, and shagbark hickory. About 17 percent is classified as Northern Hardwoods — much the same species except for the absence of shagbark hickory and the presence of sugar maple. Nearly one-fourth of the park's statutory acreage is in agricultural land, much of it not yet acquired. Smaller areas are in open brush, open woods, and dry prairie. The north- and east-facing bluffs are forested, while the south- and west-facing slopes are in "goat prairies."[40]

O. L. Kipp fulfills a need for a bluff-top park along the Mississippi. With no immediate prospect that John A. Latsch will expand to its statutory limits, Kipp is, except for Frontenac, the only sizable unit in the system to provide the experience of looking down on the great river and the Wisconsin shore. Definitely of state park quality (as Project 80 recognized), it provides a good introduction to Minnesota for travelers from the east coming into the state on Interstate 90. Its usable area is much too limited, however, for the kind of intensive use that parks like Whitewater and Sibley receive. Carefully developed, so as to minimize human impact on its fragile environment, it can continue serving its special purpose far into the future.

## Moose Lake

A lesser unit of the state park system came into being the same year that the location of O. L. Kipp was finally settled. The Moose Lake State Hospital farm, a 965-acre tract of land near the town of Moose Lake, was transferred from the Department of Public Welfare to the DNR and designated a state recreation area.

As early as 1962 people in the locality had been agitating for a state park, mainly as a means of increasing the amount of camping space in the vicinity. In reply to one such appeal, Hella pointed out that campgrounds were only incidental to state parks, which were established for quite different reasons. He continued to discourage the idea, saying that the aims of the park advocates could be better achieved by private enterprise or a county park; the legislature, he thought, would be unlikely to consider a state park so near Jay Cooke and Banning.[41]

In 1965, however, Milt Krona surveyed the site and recommended that it be acquired for outdoor recreation purposes, mainly group camping. For a time some thought was given to using the land for a tent and trailer campground capable of accommodating up to 24,000 campers at one time, but local sentiment continued to favor a park. In 1971 the legislature authorized the transfer to the DNR, with the site to be administered like other state recreation areas.[42]

Development at Moose Lake has not been extensive. By August 1977 a picnic area was in place on the north shore of Echo Lake. Over the next few years other facilities were added, including a small family campground on an elevated terrace overlooking the lake. The first hiking trail laid out was less than a mile long and led from the campground to the picnic area and swimming beach; since then modest additions have been made. For winter use by snowmobilers and cross-country skiers, an extensive trail system traverses nearly every accessible portion of the park. The scenery is attractive, especially in late summer, when the goldenrod contrasts with the intense blue of the lake; but it is not exceptional.[43]

Recreation areas are, in general, less scenically outstanding or historically significant than other state parks. Hence some activities restricted or prohibited in parks can, under certain circumstances, be permitted in recreation areas. The parks and recreation division has been adamant — and rightly so — in forbidding the use of trail bikes and other all-terrain vehicles (ATVs) on park trails. The DNR decided, however, to permit their use at Moose Lake as a pilot project. The proposal stirred up a great deal of opposition, including that of Les Blacklock, who had studied the effects of ATVs and did not like what he saw. Despite Hella's reassurances that due care would be taken to ensure that no harm would be done, the controversy went on for several months and finally ended in the DNR's decision to ban ATVs from Moose Lake, as from other units of the system.[44]

The area has some historical significance. A settlement named Moosehead Lake, which was a stagecoach stop on the run from St. Paul to Superior in the 1860s, had a hotel, a few horse barns, and a small Indian village. When the railroad came through, the settlement was moved to a new location, where it was nearly destroyed by the forest fire of 1918. No effort has been made to capitalize on this history, and Moose Lake State Recreation Area remains pretty much what it was intended to be: a convenient camping place for travelers on Interstate 35 and a place for local people to fish and swim. Whether it should be a part of the state park system is debatable.[45]

## St. Croix Wild River

For many years the Northern States Power Company (NSP) had considered a plan by which the company would donate to the state a strip of land it owned along the St. Croix River in northern Chisago County. Judge Clarence Magney had discussed the possibility with NSP officials in the 1930s, and the idea was revived in the 1950s, by Magney, by people in the conservation department, and by Theodore A. Norelius, the editor of the *Chisago County Press*. In 1962 NSP officials took the initiative and contacted Clarence Prout, then conservation commissioner, about the best use of the company's lands on the St. Croix.[46]

None of these efforts bore fruit, but in 1968, as a result of the work of a task force representing the National Park Service and the states of Minnesota and Wisconsin, the upper St. Croix was included in the National Wild and Scenic Rivers System and designated as a scenic river by act of Congress. With this designation providing needed impetus, companion bills to make a park out of the NSP holdings were introduced in the 1969 state legislature. Said to have been drawn up hastily, and defective in several ways, the bills died in committee. Two years later similar but much improved bills were introduced but were defeated by what one supporter of the park called a "vocal uninformed minority." Besides a few who were adamantly opposed to the park in any form, a larger number were concerned about the loss of tax revenues from the NSP lands and other privately owned land that would be needed to round out the park.[47]

The third try at establishing a park in Chisago County came in 1973, and this time it was successful. Several changes may have

*St. Croix Wild River State Park*

contributed to its passage. For one thing, the name was altered. Earlier versions had proposed calling the park "Sunrise," for a river whose mouth would be included. For reasons not clear, there was local opposition to this name. Dale D. Rott, one of the most vocal advocates of the park, had referred to a "Wild Rivers Park" in a 1969 letter, and now that name, modified to "St. Croix Wild River," was adopted — an awkward name, to say the least, and one fraught with potential for confusion with St. Croix State Park, St. Croix Islands State Recreation Area, and St. Croix State Forest.

More important, the area of the park was scaled down from the 11,530 acres originally proposed in 1969 to not more than 6,000 acres, as the 1973 bill specified. Of this total, NSP would donate 4,497 acres, leaving a smaller proportion of private land for the state to acquire.[48]

A provision for reimbursement to the county for lost taxes was retained from the 1971 bill; in the first year the county would be paid 90 percent of what it would have received had the state not acquired the land, in the second year 80 percent, and so forth, until the tenth year, when the state would pay nothing in lieu of taxes. The county was also granted $200,000 for the construction or improvement of access roads. Two amendments may also have made the bill more palatable than its predecessors. One prohibited the state's use of eminent domain; the other provided for residents to continue to occupy their homes for up to twenty-five years, if the land was not needed for the "proper administration" of the park. In its amended form the bill passed both houses and was signed by Governor Wendell Anderson on May 24. Minnesota had its fifth state park on the St. Croix.[49]

Besides the provisions designed to make the park more acceptable to Chisago County, the act establishing St. Croix Wild River State Park differed in other respects from most earlier parks legislation. In a sense it might be called prescriptive, in that it spelled out how the park was to be developed and for what purposes. The plan definitely had an environmental quality. One paragraph clearly states what the park should and should not be, as summarized in this sentence: "Park use shall be primarily for aesthetic, cultural, and educational purposes, and [it] shall not be designed to accommodate all forms or unlimited volumes of recreational use." This directive certainly lays it on the line and suggests that the park's sponsors wanted to avoid creating simply another place for miscellaneous outdoor recreation.[50]

NSP transferred its lands to the state by increments, 316 acres in 1972, another 368 in 1975, 1,025 in 1976, and the rest in 1977. The NSP donation was matched in value by federal funds under the Land and Water Conservation Fund Act of 1965. Before the state could buy up private lands adjacent to the NSP property, prices rose sharply, and the state wound up paying more than it would have had to pay if the park had been established earlier. In some cases The Nature Conservancy was able to act more quickly than the state and thus buy in advance of the price increase, but sometimes speculators managed to sell the land to TNC for as much as 70 percent more than they had paid for it a few days earlier.[51]

Development of the park did not really get under way until 1976, when enough land was available to begin construction of buildings, utilities, trails, and other facilities. For the first time, the parks division started with enough funds to develop a whole park at once, so that the buildings could reflect a single coordinated plan. The entrance station and interpretive center were finished with rough, sawn cedar and redwood battens and roofed with cedar shingles; even the entrance sign was built of cedar planks. Enough had been accomplished by the fall of 1978 that the new park could be dedicated September 25. The next season it had 160,000 visitors, a number that has been rising steadily since then. People discovered the campground in short order. Unlike the other new parks near the metropolitan area, Wild River had facilities for family camping, and these were soon heavily used.[52]

On the map, Wild River is a strangely shaped park, resembling a snake with an outsized head and an enlarged tail. The most highly developed area is the eastern end, where state land extends for more than a mile inland from the river; the entrance station, campground, and main picnic area, as well as the McElroy Interpretive Center, are located there. Another picnic area, together with a boat landing, is located at the mouth of the Sunrise. A strip of varying width connects the two, with a horseback and hiking trail along the river. Twenty pack-in or canoe campsites are scattered through the park. The tail of this reptile is the largely undeveloped area upstream from Sunrise Landing.

Wild River has both historical and natural attractions. It includes the sites of two important early fur trading posts and a segment of the military road that extended from Point Douglas, at the mouth of the St. Croix, to Superior, Wisconsin. The shrunken town of Sunrise, just outside the park, marks the site of the prosperous community that called itself Sunrise City. Amador, a paper city that never amounted to much on the ground, lies within the park boundaries. During the heyday of the lumbering industry a large wooden dam was constructed to control the water on the St. Croix so that logs could be "flushed" down the river. Built in 1889–90, it lasted until 1954, long after the demise of lumbering as a major industry. A short hike from the main picnic area will take the visitor to the damsite.[53]

The linear shape of the park makes it less of a wildlife haven than the much larger St. Croix State Park to the north, but the river and its adjacent marshes provide good habitat for waterfowl and shorebirds. Upland game birds make use of the brushlands inland from the river, and eagles, hawks, and owls hunt along the river. White-tailed deer, red and gray squirrels, cottontail rabbits, otters, and other small mammals make the park their home. The wildflowers found at other St. Croix valley parks are seen in this second-growth forest with its open glades. A complex network of trails near the interpretive center provides access to the various plant communities, from the riverside to old fields and pastures.

Wild River is at the heart of a large recreational complex. To the north lies the Chengwatana State Forest; across the river are forest areas in Wisconsin; and the river itself has been included in the St. Croix National Scenic Riverway, a unit of the national park system. Whichever way a visitor looks, there is much to do and see, at every season of the year.

## Tettegouche

After Wild River it was six years before the legislature authorized another state park, and then the furor the bill aroused and the compromises that had to be made to secure its passage were enough to discourage the legislature and the DNR from further attempts in the immediate future. For a number of years the parks people had had their eyes on a tract of land just west of the undeveloped Baptism River State Park. Logged over between 1895 and 1905 by Alger, Smith and Company, about 1,000 acres had been bought in 1911 by the Tettegouche Club, a group of Duluth sportsmen who managed the land as if it were a park, allowing no hunting, even by members. When the club was dissolved in 1921, one of its members, Clement K. Quinn, purchased the property, and he protected it for the next half-century and added adjacent land until he had a truly baronial estate.[54]

*Netting a fish at the mouth of the Baptism River, about 1910*

The Department of Conservation showed an interest in the Tettegouche land at least as early as 1962, but there seemed no special urgency then about acquiring it. Five years later F. Rodney Paine, who had been active in the establishment of Jay Cooke State Park more than fifty years earlier, conveyed Hella's idea to Quinn: the Tettegouche land, together with some adjoining public land, could be made into a park of 10,000 to 15,000 acres, to relieve the pressure on other North Shore parks. Quinn replied that he would be "glad to think it over" but did not commit himself any further than that. In 1971, when he was eighty-five and no longer able to live the hardy outdoor life he had enjoyed for so many years, he sold Tettegouche to John deLaittre, former president of Farmers and Mechanics Savings Bank, who extended the same kind of protection to the land that Quinn had.[55]

In 1974 the DNR learned that deLaittre planned to sell the property and decided to act to preclude the transfer of the land to someone who might develop it. The first attempt to establish Tettegouche State Park, the following year, ran into strong opposition from Lake County residents, some of whom, fearing the loss of tax revenues, organized as the Northeastern Minnesota Environmental and Economic Council (NEMEEC). Even though various concessions were made, including a reduction in the size of the proposed park from over 10,000 acres to under 8,000, the effort failed.[56]

Although the local population's hostility was symptomatic of a changing attitude toward parks throughout the state, special circumstances operated in the northeastern counties. As R. Newell Searle explains in his analysis of the resistance to consolidating the roadless areas in the Superior National Forest in the late 1930s and 1940s, the counties had expanded their services to attract more residents; when the tax base dwindled as a result of increasing public ownership of land, they found themselves in a bind and responded negatively, sometimes irrationally, to proposals for further expansion of state and federal ownership. County officials wanted to be reimbursed for tax losses, on the theory that if Lake County were going to be the playground of outsiders, then those people should share the cost of running the county.[57]

Many people now saw the proposed Tettegouche State Park as yet another threat to the solvency of Lake County, in which the proportion of publicly owned land was claimed to be 80 or 90 percent. Before a meeting of DNR representatives and members of NEMEEC, the latter issued an announcement that two men from the state government had "accepted the challenge of supporting" the park proposal. In capital letters the announcement urged: "Join NEMEEC and help us fight the harrasement [*sic*] and discrimination forced upon us by the federal and state bureaucracies." The reverse side of the announcement carried an advertisement from Lake Country Realty, listing properties for sale.[58]

Anticipating eventual passage of a Tettegouche State Park bill, the DNR again enlisted the aid of The Nature Conservancy, which arrived at an agreement with deLaittre to buy his property by June 30, 1979. Although the appraised value of the land was nearly $1.3 million, TNC was able to purchase it for $880,000. Before another park bill was introduced, TNC made some use of the land on which it held an option: in July 1978 the Minnesota chapter had a field trip to Tettegouche, which otherwise was not open to the public.[59]

The proposal for a Tettegouche State Park surfaced again in 1979, as an amendment to a bonding bill. Representative David Battaglia of Two Harbors tried to eliminate the amendment but failed, and the bill passed the house by a vote of 87 to 43. The margin of victory, though impressive enough, is a far cry from the unanimous votes commonly given to park measures in earlier years. The bill passed the senate by 59 to 2 and was signed by Governor Albert H. Quie on May 31. The Tettegouche clause contained an appropriation of $880,000 to reimburse TNC, plus $10,000 to cover part of TNC's costs (real estate taxes, caretaker's salary, legal fees, and the like). Like the Wild River bill, it also provided for the state to pay the county money in lieu of taxes, on a diminishing scale.[60]

The bill also provided that any tax-forfeited land within the boundaries of the park would be transferred to the state, the transfer to be effective only after the state paid the county an amount equal to the fair market value of the land. Finally, the DNR commissioner was to sell a quantity of state-owned lands in Lake County equal in value to the price paid for the Tettegouche property. Lake County had driven a hard bargain and had secured a remarkably good deal, because of course it also stood to benefit from the increased tourist traffic that Tettegouche would bring.[61]

Before the park would officially come into existence, a hearing had to be held, and time was running out on TNC's option. The hearing was held on June 22, and the formal transfer of the property was made on June 29, one day before the option was due to expire. The DNR's Joseph N. Alexander on that occasion made a statement that no doubt delighted people on the North Shore; the *Ely Miner* quoted him as telling a group of local residents: "This will be the last new state park in the program." A few days later the *Duluth News-Tribune* reported that he had restated his position, that "Tettegouche will be the last state park created while he is commissioner." From now on the department would concentrate on the management, maintenance, and development of the existing parks.[62]

Whatever the people of Lake County may have thought of the final agreement hammered out with the DNR, they were going to be given a voice in planning the new park. A task force was formed, whose membership included such people as Ruth Ericson, president of NEMEEC, who advocated a minimum of development.

*Palisade Head viewed from Shovel Point, 1960*

That suited the DNR, for it wanted to preserve the central area by a buffer zone; it hoped to restrict fishing and to ban canoeing entirely on the inland lakes. One condition of the agreement was fulfilled in June 1980, when the DNR held an auction of 2,623 acres of state land. All but one of the sixty-nine parcels were sold, for a total of $1,365,000; the appraised value was $935,000. Local people were not wholly pleased with the result, however, for many of the buyers were Twin Cities residents.[63]

The development of Tettegouche State Park began almost immediately and had been substantially completed by 1990, at least in its more visible forms. A combination entrance station and information center was built on the south side of U.S. Highway 61 near the Baptism River bridge. Separate parking lots were provided for park visitors and for motorists who merely wished to stop at the Baptism River rest area, from which trails lead to Shovel Point and other overlooks, as well as upstream to Baptism (or High) Falls. A family campground was opened early in 1988, by which time the principal trails (some of which antedate the park) were laid out. The trails are well signed and easier to follow than those at George H. Crosby Manitou State Park. Still in the planning stage are an interpretive and trail center at the present trailhead parking lot, expansion of the campground, some additional trails, and other amenities.

The park that finally resulted from the various compromises is much smaller than the original 10,000-plus-acre proposal: 4,691 acres, of which 3,385 were purchased from deLaittre. The 706-acre Baptism River State Park has been incorporated into it; the remaining land consists of tax-forfeited and privately owned tracts.

Tettegouche is surely one of Minnesota's great parks. With its four inland lakes in a setting of rugged hills, with its frontage on Lake Superior, including the magnificent view of Palisade Head from Shovel Point, and with its waterfalls on the Baptism River, it is everything Geoffrey Barnard of TNC credited it with being when he called it the "crown jewel" of the North Shore parks. It is the most scenic park in the most scenic section of the state, and one hopes that it will be developed in such a way as to make it accessible without impairing the qualities that led to its addition to the park system.[64]

## Hill Annex Mine

Nearly a decade was to pass before another addition was made to the system. The 1988 legislature authorized the transfer of the Hill Annex Mine, near Calumet in Itasca County, from the Iron Range Resources and Rehabilitation Board to the DNR and its establishment as a state park, to be managed as a satellite to Soudan Underground Mine State Park. Unlike the Soudan Mine, Hill Annex, operated from 1914 to 1978, was an open-pit mine. Hence it would complement rather than duplicate the former unit. The underground tours at Soudan had always been popular, and Hill Annex, under IRRRB management, had shown steadily rising attendance figures through 1987, when it had over 27,000 visitors.[65]

The new park entered the system with one serious liability: it was partly filled with water and destined to receive even more water when a neighboring mine filled and began overflowing into it. The act establishing the park included a $298,000 appropriation to purchase and install an improved pumping system. It also gave the IRRRB $200,000 to operate the park until 1991. It will be interesting to see how Hill Annex compares with the Soudan Mine in popularity after enough time has elapsed for the public to find out about it.[66]

## Grand Portage

The 1989 legislature authorized Grand Portage State Park, along the Pigeon River near the extreme eastern tip of Minnesota's Arrowhead region. For years people familiar with the area had recognized its scenic potential, especially the state's highest waterfall, 130-foot Pigeon Falls (also called High Falls) and 30-foot Middle Falls. Ontario had long protected the Canadian side of the river in Middle Falls Provincial Park, and in 1985 the Minnesota Council of Parks formed a Pigeon Falls Committee to work for establishment of a park on the Minnesota side. Late in 1987, when Lloyd K. Johnson, the owner of land adjoining the two waterfalls, offered to sell about 130 acres and donate another 80 acres, the council secured an option on the land and set about raising the purchase money. Several foundations and individuals made contributions, and the Sigurd F. Olson Fund for a Park at Pigeon Falls was established to complete the job.[67]

Following negotiations among representatives of the DNR, the Minnesota Council, the Grand Portage Band of Chippewa, and Cook County, the 1989 legislature acted to establish a state park on the Pigeon River. The senate environment and natural resources committee introduced it as an amendment to House File No. 450, which abolished Little Elbow Lake State Park and made additions to several other parks. At that stage the legislation called for the establishment of a "High Falls State Park," but later in the session

*High Falls of the Pigeon River, about 1955*

Senator Douglas J. Johnson proposed an amendment changing the name to Grand Portage State Park. In this form the bill was passed unanimously by both houses and signed by Governor Rudolph G. Perpich on May 25.[68]

Besides a clause providing for payments to Cook County in lieu of taxes (similar to those in the laws establishing Wild River and Tettegouche), the Grand Portage bill had several provisions recognizing the Grand Portage Band's interest in the park. Lands purchased from private owners were to be transferred to the band, which agreed in turn to lease them to the state for park purposes at a nominal fee. The law also provided for an advisory committee to consist of a member of the band, a state citizen designated by the band, a citizen of Cook County, and, for the first five years, a member of the Minnesota Parks and Trails Council & Foundation; the commissioner of natural resources or the commissioner's representative would chair the committee.[69]

A small park as now constituted, Grand Portage embraces only 277.83 acres. This figure includes some federal lands adjacent to the Johnson property but does not include a 48-acre life estate also donated by Johnson. The park will be developed primarily for day use, with trails and overlooks at the waterfalls, picnic areas, and other basic facilities. The main objective will be to protect the falls and the river and to make them accessible to the public. Adjacent to the U.S.–Canadian border crossing and customs offices, it will be popular with people from both countries and will complement existing recreational facilities, on public and private lands, including such tourist attractions as the Witch Tree, Minnesota's oldest living thing, on Hat Point.[70]

---

## Summary

In the quarter-century from 1964 to 1989 the park system was influenced by state and federal legislation, as well as by internal changes in the DNR. The Land and Water Conservation Fund (LAWCON) Act of 1965 provided a new source of funding for the parks. The law specified that revenues from entrance and other user fees from various federally owned recreation areas, from surplus property sales, and from the motor boat fuels tax should be paid into a special fund, from which payments to the states would be made, on a matching basis, for planning, land acquisition, and development of parks.[71]

Coming as it did just after the massive expansion of the park system in 1963, LAWCON proved a great boon to the state. Much of the development that took place over the next few years would have been hard to implement without LAWCON funds. Besides calling for a comprehensive recreation plan, the law had a few strings attached, none of them onerous. Moneys paid into the fund had to be appropriated within the next fiscal year, or they would be transferred to the miscellaneous receipts of the U.S. Department of the Treasury. Property acquired with these payments could not be converted to other uses without the approval of the secretary of the interior.[72]

The state legislature passed a piece of legislation in 1969 that introduced greater consistency into the nomenclature of the various units of the park system. Over the years units had been established whose names included words like *historical, scenic,* or *memorial* (for example, Fort Snelling State Historical Park and McCarthy Beach State Memorial Park), and the word *state* was absent from several names (Hinckley Monument and Inspiration Peak Park). Some bore a double burden (Ray Berglund State Scenic Memorial Park and Father Hennepin State Memorial Wayside Park). Now there would be only four categories: state parks, state recreation areas (formerly "recreation reserves"), state waysides, and state monuments.[73]

The 1969 legislature also established "Project 80 — study of the total environment," providing $50,000 for the study in the "Natural Resources Acceleration" section of the appropriations bill. With the aid of matching funds from federal sources, the DNR's Bureau of Planning and the State Planning Agency's Environmental Planning Section studied Minnesota's projected recreational needs and the ways in which the state park system would meet those needs through 1980. The results were published in 1971 in a document titled *Minnesota Resource Potentials in State Outdoor Recreation.* Although the DNR has not adopted all of Project 80's recommendations, the Outdoor Recreation Act of 1975 reflected the findings of the project's report, which therefore merits attention.[74]

The Project 80 staff was assigned to determine the current and future recreational needs of the state in order to provide the legislature with guidelines to aid in making appropriations for parks and other recreational facilities. In carrying out this responsibility Project 80 first sought to inventory the state's recreational resources, both in and out of parks. Then it set about evaluating each of the 133 sites, 83 of which were units of the park system. In order to minimize individual subjectivity, it developed twenty-nine criteria, which fell under six main headings: accessibility, relative cost and availability, surrounding environment, essential services, characteristics, and significance. Not all criteria were of equal importance; "unique characteristics" ranked much higher, for example, than "conditions of existing access roads." Next, each site was subjected to a computer analysis, first to determine which "component" (park, recreation area, historic area, or scientific and natural area) it was best suited for, and second to discover how it ranked in comparison to others in the same component.[75]

Existing parks were divided into four quartiles, the top one being identified by the number 1, the lowest by number 4. If a park ranked in the top or bottom 10 percent of its component, a plus or minus was given after the number. The only parks given ratings of "1 + " as parks were Banning, Beaver Creek Valley, Itasca, and St. Croix; others in the first quartile were Forestville, Gooseberry Falls, Maplewood, Interstate, Savanna Portage, and Scenic. Other parks given high ratings as recreation areas were Afton, Frontenac, Mille Lacs Kathio, Lake Maria, and William O'Brien. Historical areas rated high were Fort Snelling, Fort Ridgely, Split Rock Lighthouse, Tower Soudan, and Upper Sioux Agency. Few units were classified as scientific and natural areas, but of those that were, Inspiration Peak, John A. Latsch, and Nerstrand Woods got the highest ratings.[76]

In recommending which component each unit ought to be placed in, the Project 80 team took into account other factors, such as current acreage and potential for expansion, the significance of the unit, the kind of use it could tolerate, and its primary user population (people from a fifty-mile radius or others). As a result, the final list of twenty units that warranted being classified as state parks included some that had not ranked very high in the computer analysis. For example, Buffalo River and Old Mill had been assigned to only the third quartile, but because they represented landscape regions not found elsewhere in the system, they were placed in the top twenty. On the other hand, Savanna Portage, which had received a very high computer rating as either a park or a recreation area, was classified as a historical area. Interstate was not included, pending further study of the St. Croix valley.[77]

The most controversial aspects of the Project 80 report centered on its excluding from state park status two-thirds of the units then so classified. There might be fairly wide agreement that Little Elbow Lake and Monson Lake ought not to enjoy that status, but when such popular parks as Lake Bemidji, Lake Carlos, Lake Shetek, McCarthy Beach, and Sibley were downgraded to recreation areas, a storm of protest went up from the regions of the state in which they were located. Likewise, the recommendation that Camden, Flandrau, Helmer Myre, Kilen Woods, Rice Lake, and others be transferred to regional administration (as recreation areas) did not sit well with those parks' supporters. The Project 80 staff anticipated such objections and commented, "Many citizens will continue to feel that the State has the primary responsibility for satisfying the requirements for local recreation facilities," but added that if the state were to discharge its responsibilities most effectively, "it must concentrate its limited funds to those units which truly merit State ownership and administration."[78]

Some among the Project 80 staff believed that less emphasis should be given to natural scenery in determining the location of state parks. They wanted parks to be chosen to represent as many as possible of the seventeen "landscape regions" into which the state was divided, such as the North Shore, the Big Woods Moraine, and the Stream-dissected Region. (The term landscape region, defined as "a geographic area, with generally homogenous natural characteristics, that exemplifies the slow processes which have carved and shaped the landscape of Minnesota and clothed it with plant and animal life," has since been replaced by "biocultural region" to give greater emphasis to the human impact on the system.)[79]

Not only did the stress on landscape regions influence the estimates of existing parks, but it also determined the preferences for recommended additions to the system. Several areas were considered of state park calibre; the five ranked highest by Project 80 were Collegeville, in Stearns County; Giant's Ridge, in St. Louis County; Glacial Ridge, in Kandiyohi County; Trout Lake, in Itasca County; and Park Region, in Douglas County. Collegeville, a wooded, lake-studded area south of Avon, provided a better example of the Big Woods Moraine than the already existing parks in that region. If it could be established, said the report, Lake Maria could be reclassified as a recreation area. The same proviso was suggested in the case of Sibley and the proposed Glacial Ridge State Park. Much of the land around Giant's Ridge, a wooded formation of ancient rocks along the northern edge of the Mesabi Iron Range, was already owned by the state. Trout Lake, nearly surrounded by the Chippewa National Forest, had the attraction of being a deep, unspoiled lake. Park Region, southwest of Alexandria, would supplement the heavily used Lake Carlos.[80]

Except for Sunrise (Wild River) and O. L. Kipp, none of the recommended parks has been authorized by the legislature, but many other recommendations contained in the Project 80 report were embodied in the Outdoor Recreation Act (ORA) of 1975. This legislation underwent massive changes before it emerged in its final form. One of these was that the categories of "state parks" and "state recreation areas" were replaced by "natural state parks" and "recreational state parks," presumably to placate those citizens who strongly opposed the downgrading of their favorite parks to recreation areas. Passed by a comparatively narrow margin in the house, after amendment the bill did better in the senate, and it was signed by Governor Wendell Anderson on June 4.[81]

The ORA was more sweeping than any previous law having to do with the state parks. In content and language it reflected the recommendations of Project 80 in modified form. For example, Project 80's definition of "landscape region" was taken over almost verbatim. The eleven components of the recreation system were adopted, with some minor changes in nomenclature. The law went beyond Project 80 in establishing criteria for each type of unit, though here again the influence of the earlier study is apparent. A "natural state park," for example, was defined as one that "exemplifies the natural characteristics of the major landscape regions of the state . . . in an essentially unspoiled or restored condition." Such a park had to be capable of attracting people from throughout the state and large enough to permit successful protection of the features that gave it its special quality.[82]

An important provision of the ORA stipulated that "no construction of new facilities or other development of an authorized unit, other than repairs and maintenance, shall commence until the managing agency has prepared . . . a master plan for administration of the unit." The law provided for the general public's review and participation in the process of preparing such master plans and also stipulated that the plans must be approved by the State Planning Agency before being implemented. As noted earlier, master plans for twenty existing parks were drawn up in 1977; the public meetings on these were often characterized by heated exchanges between members of the DNR planning staff and citizens who had strong feelings, either positive or negative, about certain parks. It is ironic that in all the years in which public sentiment overwhelmingly favored the establishment of new parks, no institutionalized means existed for that sentiment to play a part in determining park policy; but in the 1970s, when widespread hostility replaced the earlier attitude, the mechanics were available for its translation into action or at least verbal expression.[83]

Before the ORA's passage, a major internal change within the Division of Parks and Recreation had occurred. After twenty years of service as director, U. W. Hella retired in the summer of 1973. He had been director longer than either of his predecessors and had served under six commissioners. He had witnessed almost exponential growth in the park system and had been responsible, directly or indirectly, for much of that growth. Hella was succeeded by Donald D. Davison, who had long experience with the DNR. After attending St. Olaf College and the University of Minnesota, Davison had become a registered land surveyor and had begun work with the conservation department in 1949. In 1967 he had been appointed director of its Bureau of Engineering. Davison retained the office of parks director until 1987, when he resigned; after a brief interregnum, William H. Morrissey, who had previously been administrator of the DNR's southeast region, replaced him.[84]

Two laws passed in the early 1980s had considerable bearing on the present and future of the park system. The more important of these was the "Landowners' Bill of Rights," passed at the 1980 legislative session. Some provisions of this act merely restated or clarified existing laws, but sections 5 ("Owner's Rights") and 6 ("State's Responsibilities") spelled out the conditions of land acquisition in such a way that each party would know what to expect of the other in such transactions.

Some provisions were expressed in general terms: the landowner had the right "to be paid a fair price" and the state had the responsibility to "deal fairly and openly with the landowner in the purchase of property." Others were more specific. The owner, for example, was explicitly granted the rights to accompany the state's appraiser on inspections of the land and to have an independent appraisal conducted at the state's expense if the land was subsequently sold to the state. Other clauses specified the maximum length of options, the method of payment for land purchased, the right to continued occupancy of the property until payment was made, and similar technical matters. The final section of the bill of rights provided that when the state proposed to buy lands, the landowner should be given a written statement of these rights and responsibilities "in layman's terms" and be required to sign an acknowledgment that he or she had been so informed.[85]

The other piece of legislation stemmed from the need to reconcile the ORA's recommendations as to park size with the presence of units in the system that did not meet these specifications. Although no definite acreage was specified, a 500-acre minimum had been mentioned as early as the 1930s and was presumably still regarded as the ideal. Several parks, such as Carley, Charles A. Lindbergh, Father Hennepin, Interstate, Kilen Woods, and Temperance River, fell far below this minimum and were unlikely ever to be so expanded as to reach it. The 1984 legislature, therefore, included in its park legislation a clause to "grandfather in" these small units. It specified that "All other state parks which, though not meeting the resource and site qualifications contained in [the ORA], were in existence on January 1, 1984," should continue to be administered as parts of the outdoor recreation system.[86]

This act gave the smaller parks a measure of security that they had not enjoyed for nearly a decade. It also represented something of a setback to the DNR's efforts to enlarge them to what were perceived as more satisfactory dimensions. By 1984 it was clear that the climate of public opinion was not receptive to any proposal for park expansion that would involve taking productive farmland and converting it to recreational use. The changed attitude, hostility replacing the welcome most communities had earlier given to state parks, was one of the most singular developments in evidence a century after the first legislation to establish a state park in Minnesota.

# CHAPTER TEN

# The State Parks
# and the Public

A HUNDRED YEARS after the creation of the first state park in Minnesota, two recent developments stand out: the amount and nature of interaction between the professionals and the public, and the trend away from recreation per se and toward preservation. The two are closely intertwined, of course, for in the future park development will follow a course that represents a compromise between the professionals' and the public's demands, to the extent that these are in conflict. And if the parks people pursue their educational function successfully, they will be able to influence what the public asks for.

## Interaction of Public and Professionals

Public influence on the parks has always existed, sometimes informally and sometimes formally, by advisory committees or boards. In the early decades, before a Division of State Parks was created, such citizens' groups often managed the parks, not invariably in the best interests of those lands. The groups often resulted from a transitory enthusiasm and tended to die out as the original membership passed from the scene, if not sooner (for example, the Sibley advisory group came and went over the years). Although new advisory bodies formed during the great period of park expansion of the 1930s, most of them became inactive during World War II. In the decades after the war, when many new parks were established, such organizations were the exception rather than the rule. In the fall of 1983 a Minnesota Council of State Parks survey revealed that out of forty-four questionnaires returned by park managers (sixty-four were sent), only seventeen indicated the existence of active park support groups. Nine advisory committees that had once existed had become inactive, while eighteen parks had never had such advisory bodies.[1]

It was partly because of these advisory boards' short lives and partly because of the felt need for a statewide citizens' group that conservation commissioner Chester Wilson in the fall of 1954 called for the establishment of such an organization. The Minnesota Council of State Parks was formed on September 19 at Douglas Lodge, where the Itasca State Park advisory board adopted a resolution calling for a statewide organization; at a formal organizational meeting at the State Office Building on December 3 the name was adopted. (In 1984 it was changed to Minnesota Council of Parks in recognition of its broadened role in the promotion of county and regional parks.) The council had no statutory authority or government connection. There were no bylaws, and the membership was originally limited to sixteen; delegates from local advisory committees were automatically members. Later the number was increased to fifty, and eventually membership was opened to the public at large. Among the founders were Judge Clarence R. Magney, Red Wing newspaperman Albert Marshall, and F. Rodney Paine, who had supervised Jay Cooke State Park in its earliest days. From the beginning the council worked closely with parks director U. W. Hella, who often spoke at its meetings.[2]

In December 1962 an extraordinary meeting was called to plan strategy for the coming legislative session, at which the Omnibus bill was to be introduced. At that time Hella listed several areas that he thought warranted state park status and mentioned several older parks for which additions were recommended. The subsequent legislation very closely followed his recommendations, which the council had in large part adopted. On June 24, 1963, the council's executive committee met, at chairman Marshall's suggestion, to consider expanding its purposes to include the promotion of foot, horse, bicycle, and canoe trails. Later a trails committee was established with Marshall as chairman. The development of state trails, starting in 1967, owes much to the endeavors of this committee. In

1967 the council organized the Minnesota Parks Foundation to serve as a vehicle for the receipt of gifts of money, stocks, bonds, and land. The foundation has played an important role in the establishment of the more recent parks and the expansion of earlier ones. On January 1, 1987, the council and the foundation merged under the cumbersome name of the Minnesota Parks and Trails Council & Foundation — which was changed to the Minnesota Parks & Trails Council late in 1990.[3]

In a sense, the Minnesota Council has constituted a sort of "third house," together with the legislature and the DNR. Its members, most of whom are not parks professionals, have offered knowledgeable advice from outside the bureaucracy. It would not be quite accurate to say that they represent the public at large, for their interest in the parks is more informed than the public's and, in many cases, more than the legislature's as a group. Many individual legislators, of course, through the years have displayed a serious interest in the parks and have welcomed the advice and suggestions of council members.

If the Minnesota Council of Parks and the various advisory committees have usually agreed with the professionals' goals and supported their efforts before the legislature, not all residents of the state have been so sympathetic to the parks people's aims, nor have they confined their objections to constructive criticism. Except for temporary coalitions of landowners opposed to the expansion of a particular park, however, they have not acted collectively in the pursuit of their aims, which have usually been negative. Earlier chapters have provided samples of such complaints, commonly aired in letters to the director of parks or to newspapers. During the series of public meetings initiated in 1977 as part of a legislatively mandated preparation of management plans, the Department of Natural Resources actively solicited the opinions of people living in the vicinity of state parks. As we have seen, the result was often a strident attack on the DNR, devoid of any positive suggestions and reflecting mainly a paranoid hostility toward "big government" in any of its manifestations.[4]

Yet even such acrimonious exchanges led to beneficial results; the DNR was made aware of the need to improve its public image. In some cases joint committees were formed, composed of disparate elements and charged with the task of hammering out a compromise. This device was employed with good results in the dispute over the Root River Trail in 1981 and 1982. Opponents of the trail, after failing to prevent its establishment, continued to fight it every way they could. Eventually a Citizens Advisory Group, composed of people who might have been expected to disagree on everything from the shape of the table to more substantive issues, was appointed in December 1981. It did its work so well that by August 1983, when a meeting concerning the trail was held at Lanesboro, a hotbed of opposition, there was scarcely a hint of dissension.[5]

Absence of overt opposition at a public meeting does not necessarily prove that a universally satisfactory compromise has been reached; it may only indicate that one side or the other has given up the struggle as futile. In the case of the Root River Trail it was the opponents of the project who, after extracting all the concessions they could from the DNR, resigned themselves to the prospect that the trail was, after all, going to be built. Other proposals broached about the same time, such as those for trails between Mankato and Rapidan and between Faribault and Zumbrota, ran into so much hostility that the DNR finally abandoned its effort to acquire the necessary land. The same type of conflict arose over park expansion, and the same kinds of resolution eventuated. Sometimes opponents were able to halt the project in its tracks, and sometimes the DNR was able to get most of what it wanted.[6]

## Recreation and Preservation

Besides the outright opposition from landowners who stand to lose some of their property as a result of park expansion, the DNR has had to contend with hostility almost as strong from people who oppose the way the DNR is running the parks — for example, the storm of protest that went up when the golf course at Whitewater was closed and the land allowed to return to something like its presettlement condition. The issue was not over whether a park should be established or expanded but over what should be done with a long-established park, which people in surrounding towns had come to think of as their own to do with as they pleased. The conflict, reduced to its essentials, was between recreation and preservation. Should a state park be a place to play golf or a "home for prairie dogs"?

On etymological grounds alone, the advocates of recreation would win the argument hands down. Alfred Runte, in a valuable book on the national parks, cites a dictionary definition of *park* as "an enclosed piece of ground stocked with beasts of the chase, held by prescription or by the king's grant." As he points out, until the establishment of the great western national parks, the word traditionally meant a playground. Moreover, even when such early parks as Yosemite, Yellowstone, Sequoia, and Mount Rainier came into being, it was their "grand, monumental scenery" that justified their being made into national parks — that and the belief that the land was worthless for any other purpose. Not until the authorization of Everglades in 1934 was a park seen as a place where certain plant and animal species could be protected, nor was it recognized until then that an area might be considered as of national park calibre even though it was devoid of "great mountains, deep canyons, and tumbling waterfalls."[7]

The "monumentalism" that Runte identifies as essential to a national park had its reflections on the state level. Such early parks as Itasca, Interstate, and Minneopa, as well as later ones like Gooseberry Falls, were created to protect some geological or topographical attraction. Not until many years later was consideration given to preserving a sample of the presettlement vegetation and its attendant animal life. Just as proponents of a "Prairie National Park" have consistently failed to persuade Congress of the propriety of preserving an unmodified tract of tallgrass prairie, so until recently it has been left to The Nature Conservancy to acquire scattered fragments of prairie that had somehow escaped the plow. Although considerable emphasis has been given in recent years to the grasslands surviving in such parks as Buffalo River, Camden, and Blue Mounds, those grasslands were not the reason the parks were established in the first place. Those who saw the former golf course at Whitewater growing up to "weeds" were in the mainstream of American opinion in their distress at what the DNR was doing to the park. Most people driving past one of The Nature Conservancy's prairie preserves would, if they bothered to look at it at all, probably characterize it as "wasteland."

In the context of this widespread attitude toward nature in its less spectacular forms, the DNR's efforts to preserve or restore bits and pieces of the natural landscape as it existed before white settlement are bound to generate opposition, just as on another level the removal of playground equipment from a state park is likely to evoke resentment. Ultimately the question is: whose parks are they? If the answer has to be that they belong to the public, which pays most of the cost of their development and maintenance, then what business does a group of professional park managers have running them in ways that a majority of park users do not approve? The average voter and taxpayer probably sees the parks people as empire builders, like the members of any other bureaucracy intent on justifying their existence, responsive (if at all) to a small minority of preservationists who want to reverse the whole direction of American history by restoring the landscape to its presettlement condition.

Another contemporary student of the national parks, Joseph L. Sax, argues the preservationist case quite cogently so far as it is reflected in current policies being followed by the NPS. Some of his arguments have a certain relevance to the state parks also. What the preservationist wants is what the rest of the population ought to want, too, but it is necessary to convince the public of that. "The preservationist is not an elitist who wants to exclude others," he writes; "he is a moralist who wants to convert them." In this respect the preservationist's status is similar to a doctor's: the patient with abdominal pain does not demand an appendectomy, but merely asks the doctor to make him well. In other words, says Sax, a patient gives up some personal autonomy to "let someone else decide in the particular what is good for him," though in a general way he knows what he wants. Libraries, universities, and public broadcasting are all founded on the same principle: that the people who run them know better than the public what is good for it in detail. It is the business of the preservationists, in and out of the park service, to "encourage the public increasingly to internalize its capacity to wring satisfaction out of experience," both while in the parks and after leaving them.[8]

According to Sax, although the NPS carries out the mandates of Congress, "It has its own sense of mission, an internal conception of what it ought to be doing." Nonetheless, "no bureaucracy behaves simply according to its own sense of mission. It lives in a political milieu, with constituencies of users and neighbors who impose strong, and at times irresistable [*sic*], pressures on it." So preservationists, especially those involved in the administration of parks, must get at least the "passive support" of the public, and this means somehow persuading the public that the parks are good for something other than picnics and swimming, that even contemplating dramatic features like waterfalls is not the highest use we can make of them.[9]

The most obvious, and probably most effective, way in which the people who run our state parks are trying to "convert" the public, to use Sax's word, is through the medium of the interpretive program. Even in the national parks, the first museums and interpretive programs appeared only in the 1920s, and they came along later still in the state parks. For the most part, such programs have been started since World War II. Some park users, says author and activist Edward Abbey, ask three questions upon arriving in a national park: "(1) Where's the john? (2) How long's it take to see this place? (3) Where's the Coke machine?" But the growth of interpretive programs in recent years suggests that enough people use them to justify their continuation and even expansion. Each summer the DNR publishes leaflets listing special programs and interpretive services offered by the system. More detailed descriptions are available for specific parks. The more people, adults as well as children, who can be induced to involve themselves in these activities, the more widely the DNR can spread the message that a state park is a place where people can extend and expand their knowledge of nature and thus supplement the more traditional forms of recreation with what Sax calls "contemplative" or "reflective" recreation.[10]

The greatest benefits to be obtained from the state parks, however, reside not in the interpretive program but in the encounter with nature itself. After three and a half centuries of trying to destroy the original wilderness, during the past twenty or thirty years the American people have been having a belated love affair with the remnants of it.

*Wilderness*, of course, is a relative term. As environmental historian Roderick Nash says, "One man's wilderness may be another's roadside picnic ground. The Yukon trapper would consider a trip to northern Minnesota a return to civilization while for the vacationer from Chicago it is a wilderness adventure indeed."[11]

If we accept this much latitude in our definition of the word, then it is quite possible to have a wilderness experience in a Minnesota state park. And it is not necessary to seek out the back country of Itasca or the remoter reaches of Savanna Portage, George H. Crosby Manitou, or Judge C. R. Magney. If we define "wilderness" broadly enough, it can be experienced in a southern Minnesota park. This definition assumes the legitimacy of what has been called "retread wilderness" — land once cultivated or otherwise modified by Euro-Americans but allowed to revert to a semblance of its presettlement condition. Such wilderness is what the hiker finds in Shenandoah National Park and elsewhere in the East. In any event, whether a natural area is called wilderness or not, the visitor is able to enjoy a relationship to nature not possible in a modern city or town or even on a modern farm. Such a relationship may serve as a necessary bridge for the city dweller who is not yet ready for the challenge of true wilderness — the kind of primitive environment to which purists would restrict the use of the term.

The standard forms of recreation — swimming, camping, picnicking, and nature study in its less sophisticated forms — will continue to attract great numbers of visitors, who will probably not distinguish sharply between "natural" and "recreational" state parks but will continue to pursue their own interests in whatever parks are most conveniently located for them. Some of these people, especially the young, may, through exposure and education, eventually develop a taste for relatively unmodified natural landscapes. Whatever visitors' reasons for coming to the parks, so long as their objectives are legitimate, they can find what they seek in the wealth of varied settings that the Minnesota state park system offers after a century of growth.

# Minnesota's State Park System, 1991

| Park | County or Counties | Year Established | Acreage |
|------|--------------------|-----------------|---------|

## State Parks and Recreation Areas

| Park | County or Counties | Year Established | Acreage |
|------|--------------------|-----------------|---------|
| Afton | Washington | 1969 | 1,699 |
| Banning | Pine | 1963 | 6,237 |
| Bear Head Lake | St. Louis | 1961 | 4,384 |
| Beaver Creek Valley | Houston | 1937[1] | 1,214 |
| Big Stone Lake | Big Stone | 1961 | 1,118 |
| Blue Mounds | Rock | 1937[1] | 2,028 |
| Buffalo River | Clay | 1937[1] | 1,240 |
| Camden | Lyon | 1935 | 1,712 |
| Carley | Wabasha | 1949 | 211 |
| Cascade River | Cook | 1957 [1934][2] | 2,813 |
| Charles A. Lindbergh | Morrison | 1931 | 328 |
| Crow Wing | Cass, Crow Wing, Morrison | 1959 | 2,042 |
| Father Hennepin | Mille Lacs | 1941 | 316 |
| Flandrau | Brown | 1937[1] | 805 |
| Forestville | Fillmore | 1963 [1949][3] | 2,691 |
| Fort Ridgely | Nicollet, Renville | 1911 | 584 |
| Fort Snelling | Dakota, Hennepin, Ramsey | 1961 | 3,300 |
| Franz Jevne | Koochiching | 1967 | 118 |
| Frontenac | Goodhue | 1957 | 1,754 |
| George H. Crosby Manitou | Lake | 1955 | 3,400 |

# Minnesota's State Park System, 1991 (continued)

| Park | County or Counties | Year Established | Acreage |
|------|-------------------|-----------------|---------|
| Glacial Lakes | Pope | 1963 | 1,940 |
| Gooseberry Falls | Lake | 1937[1] | 1,662 |
| Grand Portage | Cook | 1989 | 278 |
| Hayes Lake | Roseau | 1967 | 2,950 |
| Helmer Myre | Freeborn | 1947 | 1,600 |
| Hill Annex Mine | Itasca | 1988 | 635 |
| Interstate | Chisago | 1895 | 293 |
| Itasca | Becker, Clearwater, Hubbard | 1891 | 32,000 |
| Jay Cooke | Carlton | 1915 | 8,813 |
| Judge C. R. Magney | Cook | 1957 | 4,514 |
| Kilen Woods | Jackson | 1945 | 228 |
| Lac qui Parle | Lac qui Parle | 1959 [c. 1938][2] | 530 |
| Lake Bemidji | Beltrami | 1923 | 1,688 |
| Lake Bronson | Kittson | 1937[1] | 2,983 |
| Lake Carlos | Douglas | 1937[4] | 1,250 |
| Lake Louise | Mower | 1963 | 816 |
| Lake Maria | Wright | 1963 [1947][3] | 1,580 |
| Lake Shetek | Murray | 1937 [1929][1] | 1,175 |
| Maplewood | Otter Tail | 1963 | 9,250 |
| McCarthy Beach | St. Louis | 1945 | 2,566 |
| Mille Lacs Kathio | Mille Lacs | 1957 | 10,585 |
| Minneopa | Blue Earth | 1905 | 1,145 |
| Minnesota Valley Trail | Carver, Dakota, Hennepin, Le Sueur, Scott, Sibley | 1969 | 8,000 |
| Monson Lake | Swift | 1937[1] | 187 |
| Moose Lake | Carlton | 1971 | 1,215 |
| Nerstrand Woods | Rice | 1945 | 1,280 |
| O. L. Kipp | Winona | 1963 [1971][5] | 2,835 |
| Old Mill | Marshall | 1951 [1937][6] | 287 |
| Rice Lake | Dodge, Steele | 1963 | 1,060 |
| St. Croix | Pine | 1943 | 34,037 |
| Sakatah Lake | Le Sueur, Rice | 1963 | 842 |
| Savanna Portage | Aitkin, St. Louis | 1961 | 15,818 |
| Scenic | Itasca | 1921 | 2,922 |

# Minnesota's State Park System, 1991 (continued)

| Park | County or Counties | Year Established | Acreage |
|------|--------------------|-----------------|---------|
| Schoolcraft | Cass, Itasca | 1959 | 295 |
| Sibley | Kandiyohi | 1919 | 2,926 |
| Soudan Underground Mine | St. Louis | 1963 | 1,300 |
| Split Rock Creek | Pipestone | 1937[1] | 400 |
| Split Rock Lighthouse | Lake | 1945 | 1,872 |
| Temperance River | Cook | 1957 [c. 1936][2] | 200 |
| Tettegouche | Lake | 1979[7] | 4,691 |
| Upper Sioux Agency | Yellow Medicine | 1963 | 1,280 |
| Whitewater | Winona | 1919 | 2,862 |
| Wild River | Chisago | 1973 | 7,000 |
| William O'Brien | Washington | 1947 | 1,330 |
| Zippel Bay | Lake of the Woods | 1959 | 2,946 |

## *Waysides*[8]

| Park | County or Counties | Year Established | Acreage |
|------|--------------------|-----------------|---------|
| Caribou Falls | Lake | 1947 | 89 |
| Cross River | Cook | 1961 | 2,520 |
| Devils Track Falls | Cook | 1961 | 240 |
| Flood Bay | Lake | 1965 | 19 |
| Inspiration Peak | Otter Tail | 1931 | 82 |
| John A. Latsch | Winona | 1925 | 389 |
| Joseph R. Brown | Renville | 1937 | 3 |
| Kodonce River | Cook | 1947 | 130 |
| Ray Berglund | Cook | 1951 | 50 |
| St. Croix Islands | Washington | 1943 | 39 |
| Sam Brown | Traverse | 1929 | 1 |

1. Although established formally in 1937, these parks had been developed earlier, from 1933 on. See chapter five; for Lake Shetek, see page 89.

2. Although formally established later, these three parks were all developed in the 1930s. See chapter five.

3. Lake Maria and Forestville were first established in 1947 and 1949, respectively. No land was acquired then, however, and they were reestablished in 1963. Mystery Cave was added to Forestville in 1987. See pages 214 and 217.

4. No specific legislation created Lake Carlos, but lands were acquired in 1937. See page 130.

5. O. L. Kipp was established in 1963, but the location was changed in 1971. See page 262.

6. Old Mill was developed as Middle River State Park in the 1930s. The name was changed and the park formally established in 1951. See page 132.

7. Tettegouche incorporated Baptism River State Park, established in 1945. See pages 156 and 273.

8. When the Minnesota Valley Trail was established in 1969, it consisted of six waysides: Belle Plaine, Blakeley, Carver Rapids, Lawrence, Rice Lake, and Rush River. The Rice Lake wayside was abolished in 1987, and the Bell Plaine wayside was combined with Lawrence. The remaining waysides are now designated as "units." Thompson Ferry and Trail Site Number 2 are also sometimes referred to as waysides. All these are included in what is now unofficially called "Minnesota Valley Trail State Park."

# Notes

Abbreviations

DNR . . . . . . . . . . . . . . . . Minnesota Department of Natural Resources
DNR Files . . . . . . . . . . . State Parks, Waysides, and Monuments Files, DPR,
DNR, St. Paul. For more information, see p. 339.
DOC . . . . . . . . . . . . . . . . Minnesota Department of Conservation
DOC Records . . . . . . . . DOC Records, Minnesota State Archives, MHS
DPR . . . . . . . . . . . . . . . . Division of Parks and Recreation, DNR
DSP . . . . . . . . . . . . . . . . Division of State Parks, DOC
FFPD . . . . . . . . . . . . . . . Forestry and Fire Prevention Division, State Parks
Correspondence, DOC Records
*House Journal* . . . . . . . . Minnesota, House of Representatives, *Journal*
*Laws* . . . . . . . . . . . . . . . . Minnesota, *Laws*
*Legislative Manual* . . . . . Minnesota, Secretary of State, *Legislative Manual*
MHS . . . . . . . . . . . . . . . . Minnesota Historical Society, St. Paul
MORRC . . . . . . . . . . . . . Minnesota Outdoor Recreation Resources Commission
MPTCF . . . . . . . . . . . . . Minnesota Parks and Trails Council & Foundation
NPS . . . . . . . . . . . . . . . . National Park Service
PRD . . . . . . . . . . . . . . . . Parks and Recreation Division, DOC Records
*Senate Journal* . . . . . . . . Minnesota, Senate, *Journal*

## Chapter 1. *The Beginnings: 1885–1895*

1. *St. Paul Pioneer Press*, December 28, 1884, p. 4, 6.
2. *Laws*, 1885, p. 117–21.
3. Theodore Wirth, *Minneapolis Park System, 1883–1944: Retrospective Glimpses into the History of the Board of Park Commissioners of Minneapolis, Minnesota, and the City's Park, Parkway, and Playground System* (Minneapolis: The Park Board, 1946), 49–51; Isaac Atwater, ed., *History of the City of Minneapolis, Minnesota*, 2 vols. (New York: Munsell & Company, 1893) 1:412; Rhoda J. Green, "Division of State Parks: An Informational Review," *Conservation Volunteer* (DOC) 8 (September–October 1945): 48–51.

4. Wirth, *Minneapolis Park System*, 51; *Laws*, 1889, p. 183–85. A reservation attached to section 1 specified that the park should be designated "'Minnehaha State Park,' and not otherwise." Minneapolis evidently had its eye on Minnehaha State Park from the moment of the park's inception. According to Atwater, the original bill was prepared by the secretary of the Minneapolis park board, and Loring later served as chairman of the commission appointed by the governor. See Atwater, ed., *Minneapolis*, 412.

5. Freeman J. Tilden, *The State Parks: Their Meaning in American Life*, foreword by Conrad L. Wirth (New York: Alfred A. Knopf, 1962), 47–48; Roderick Nash, *Wilderness and the American Mind*, rev. ed. (New Haven, Conn.: Yale University Press, [1973]), 119. As a matter of fact, the preserve was created on May 15, more than two months after the act of the Minnesota legislature.

6. *Laws*, 1889, p. 520–21; 1893, p. 381; June Drenning Holmquist and Jean A. Brookins, *Minnesota's Major Historic Sites: A Guide* (St. Paul: MHS, 1963), 109–10. Subsequent citations are to the revised, second edition (1972); the first edition gives more extended treatment to Camp Release.

7. *Laws*, 1901, p. 629–30; 1903, p. 433; 1905, p. 538; 1907, p. 763; 1909, p. 439; 1915, p. 517; 1919, p. 572; 1921, p. 948; 1923, p. 695; 1925, p. 732; 1927, p. 659. Apparently nothing at all was provided in 1911, 1913, or 1917.

8. L[udvig] R. Lima to Grover M. Conzet, March 7, 1928, May 23, 1929 — both in Camp Release File, FFPD, DOC Records; *Laws*, 1929, p. 672; 1931, p. 518; 1933, p. 812; 1935, p. 583; 1937, p. 549. In 1939 the legislature adopted a policy of appropriating a lump sum for the maintenance and improvement of the state parks, leaving to the discretion of the department of conservation the apportionment of the amount among the various units.

9. DOC, *Statistical Report: Biennium Ending June 30, 1940* (hereafter *Fifth Biennial Report*), 253–54.

10. *Laws*, 1975, p. 1162.

11. Brower, "Itasca State Park: An Illustrated History," *Minnesota Historical Collections* 11 (1904): 74–75, 77.

12. John Dobie, *The Itasca Story* (Minneapolis: Ross & Haines, 1959), 67–68; Brower, "Itasca State Park," 79–80; *St. Paul Pioneer Press*, January 22, 1890, p. 4.

13. Minnesota, Geological and Natural History Survey, *Eighteenth Annual Report, for the Year 1889*, by Winchell, 5–6.

14. *United States Statutes at Large* 17:32–33.

15. Dobie, *Itasca*, 68–69; *Laws*, 1891, p. 137–39; Brower, "Itasca State Park," 87–89.

16. Dobie, *Itasca*, 72–73, 75; *United States Statutes at Large* 27:347; *Laws*, 1893, p. 111–12; Brower, "Itasca State Park," 89–90, 105, 117.

17. Dobie, *Itasca*, 76, 78–79; *Laws*, 1893, p. 397; 1895, p. 233–36; Brower, "Itasca State Park," 145; *Melrose Beacon*, April 27, 1916, p. 1.

18. Dobie, *Itasca*, 81–82, 84, 86, 93; *Laws*, 1899, p. 383–85; 1901, p. 56, 573–74.

19. Dobie, *Itasca*, 95–96, 99; *Laws*, 1907, p. 104; 1911, p. 151–60.

20. Dobie, *Itasca*, 96–98, 103–4, 105–6; *Laws*, 1909, p. 251–52; 1919, p. 324–25.

21. Dobie, *Itasca*, 85, 87, 88–90, 100, 102.

22. Brower, "Itasca State Park," xxxi, 155; Dobie, *Itasca*, 84, 91; *Laws*, 1903, p. 649.

23. *Laws*, 1907, p. 104; Dobie, *Itasca*, 96, 110, 159; A. C. Hodson, *History of the Lake Itasca Biology Sessions* (Occasional Papers, Field Biology Program, no. 1;

[Minneapolis: University of Minnesota, 1979]), 8–9, 49–50. Dobie devotes a chapter (p. 155–63) to the later history of the forestry school and biological station.

24. *Laws*, 1901, p. 628–29; 1903, p. 432; 1909, p. 439; 1911, p. 391; 1915, p. 516; 1919, p. 573–74; 1921, p. 948; 1923, p. 694; 1925, p. 731–32; 1927, p. 658–59; 1929, p. 670–71.

25. Dobie, *Itasca*, 111, 114, 115–16.

26. Dobie, *Itasca*, 116.

27. Dobie, *Itasca*, 110; DOC, *Third Biennial Report: Fiscal Years 1935–1936*, 255, 266.

28. Dobie, *Itasca*, 114.

29. Dobie, *Itasca*, 114; DOC, *Eighth Biennial Report: Biennium Ending June 30, 1946*, 314.

30. DNR, *Itasca State Park: Summer Trails* (1988), copy of leaflet in author's possession; "Visitors Find Improvements at Itasca State Park," *Minnesota Volunteer* (DNR) 47 (May–June 1984): 62.

31. *Laws*, 1893, p. 381–82.

32. William Watts Folwell, *A History of Minnesota*, 4 vols., rev. ed. (St. Paul: MHS, 1956–69) 2:386–89; *Laws*, 1895, p. 776–77. Folwell devoted five pages to the Birch Coulee controversy and, in the course of his discussion, summarized the history of the monument itself up to 1924, the volume's original publication date.

33. Folwell, *Minnesota* 2:390–91. At some undetermined date before 1923 the state had acquired six acres on the actual battlefield, for in his report to the legislature that year State Auditor Ray P. Chase referred to both parcels and suggested that the monuments be moved to the larger one. See Chase, *Statement to the Nineteen Hundred Twenty-three Legislature* ([St. Paul, 1923]), 29.

34. *Laws*, 1929, p. 77–79; 1931, p. 519; 1935, p. 585; J. R. Landy to O[scar] H. Smith, December 27, Landy to Ray P. Chase, December 10 — both 1926 and in Birch Coulee File, FFPD, DOC Records. In the legislation concerning the park the name is variously spelled "Coulie," "Cooley," and "Coulee." The third spelling is used here because it has acquired general acceptance, though the township in which the park is located is still called Birch Cooley.

35. DOC, *Third Biennial Report*, 249, *Annual Report 1938 and Fourth Biennial Report (for Biennium Ending June 30, 1938)* (hereafter *Fourth Biennial Report*), 245; *Laws*, 1976, p. 254. The act transferring jurisdiction to the historical society renamed the park the Birch Coulee Battlefield State Historic Site. In January 1976 Eliza Marguth, widow of the veteran, Christian Marguth, was interred at Birch Coulee by special dispensation of Donald D. Davison, parks and recreation director. See Rene Marguth to Davison, Davison to Bob Nelson (funeral director, Redwood Falls), photocopy — both January 15, 1976, Birch Coulee File, DNR Files.

36. *Legislative Manual*, 1897, p. 233; 1903, p. 256, 259; 1907, p. 203; Hazzard, comp., *Lectures, Laws, Papers, Pictures, Pointers: Interstate Park, Dalles of the St. Croix, Taylors Falls, Minn., St. Croix Falls, Wis.* ([St. Paul?], 1896), 3–4; Josephine Blanich to Davison, August 22, October 21, 1974, DNR. For more on the park's establishment, see Ward Moberg, "Interstate Park Protects the Dalles," *Dalles Visitor* 13 (1981): 1, 8, 9, 20, 21, 26, and "1890s Fight Created Dalles Parks," *Dalles Visitor* 14 (1982): 1, 13, 14, 24, 25.

37. Hazzard, comp., *Interstate Park*, 3; *Laws*, 1895, p. 379–82; *House Journal*, 1895, p. 358, 575, 657–58.

38. Hazzard, comp., *Interstate Park*, 4; *Legislative Manual*, 1903, p. 256; 1907, p. 203; 1909, p. 194; "Narrative Report of Areas Not Covered in Survey," 1935,

State Parks-Miscellaneous File, FFPD, DOC Records; Wisconsin, Department of Natural Resources, *Visitor's Guide to Wisconsin's State Parks, Forests and Other Recreation Lands* (1988), copy in author's possession. In 1963 Roos's son requested a free entrance permit to the park on the strength of his father's donation. See Alford Roos to Commissioner of State Parks, August 16, 1963, Interstate File, DNR Files.

39. *Legislative Manual*, 1899, p. 251; 1903, p. 259-60.

40. *Laws*, 1901, p. 630; 1903, p. 437; 1905, p. 557; 1907, p. 764; 1909, p. 439; 1911, p. 371; 1913, p. 582; 1915, p. 516; 1921, p. 949; 1923, p. 694; 1925, p. 732; 1927, p. 659; 1929, p. 672; 1931, p. 518; 1933, p. 812; 1935, p. 583; 1937, p. 549; DOC, *Third Biennial Report*, 254-55; *Fourth Biennial Report*, 251. WPA labor provided picnic and camping facilities, two parking areas, a refectory-shelter, and other conveniences.

41. *Laws*, 1909, p. 439.

42. *Laws*, 1895, p. 579. Identical phraseology, except for the state name, appears in the Wisconsin law. See Hazzard, comp., *Interstate Park*, 88.

43. *Legislative Manual*, 1907, p. 204-5.

44. Conzet to James Seed (amusement park operator), July 6, carbon, Charles W. Truesdell (park superintendent) to Conzet, July 23 — both 1931 and in Interstate File, FFPD, DOC Records; Harold W. Lathrop to Lew E. Fiero, August 26, 1946, MORRC File, PRD, DOC Records. The letter from Lathrop to Fiero is a detailed description of conditions at the parks, written by the outgoing director to his successor.

45. DOC, *Third Biennial Report*, 255.

46. Duane Eilertson (park manager) to Milton E. Krona, December 21, 1981, Interstate File, DNR Files; *Laws*, 1977, p. 1146.

47. Roger L. Hartman (chairman, Minnesota-Wisconsin Boundary Area Commission) to Udert W. Hella, July 27, Hella to Hartman, August 3, carbon — both 1970, Interstate File, DNR Files; *Laws*, 1987, p. 909-10.

48. Wisconsin, Department of Natural Resources, *Visitor's Guide;* U.S., Department of the Interior, NPS, *Ice Age National Scientific Reserve* (1984), copy of leaflet in author's possession.

## Chapter 2. *Slow Expansion: 1895-1915*

1. Holmquist and Brookins, *Minnesota's Major Historic Sites*, 133-37.

2. *Senate Journal*, 1895, p. 283, 452, 563, 798; *Laws*, 1895, p. 775; Holmquist and Brookins, *Minnesota's Major Historic Sites*, 180.

3. Hopkins to Grover M. Conzet, December 15, 1925, Fort Ridgely File, FFPD, DOC Records; *Laws*, 1907, p. 763-64.

4. *House Journal*, 1911, p. 244; *Laws*, 1911, p. 481-82; 1913, p. 582; "Narrative Report," State Parks-Miscellaneous File, FFPD, DOC Records; Chase, *Statement*, 26, 31-33.

5. *Olivia Times*, March 18, 1926, p. 1.

6. Frank Hopkins to Conzet, June 22, 1927, Charles Hopkins to Conzet, December 15, 1925, Harold W. Lathrop to Conzet, February 1, 1935, Harold Ostergaard (assistant) for Conzet to C. W. Heinmann, May 27, 1935, carbon — all in Fort Ridgely File, FFPD, DOC Records; Holmquist and Brookins, *Minnesota's Major Historic Sites*, 137. In 1914 another state monument, to the Ojibway leader, Mouzoomaunee, and the loyalty of the Ojibway during the Dakota War, was added.

7. *Laws*, 1915, p. 516–17; 1919, p. 572; 1921, p. 948; 1923, p. 694; 1925, p. 732; 1927, p. 659; 1929, p. 671; 1931, p. 518; 1933, p. 812; 1935, p. 583; 1937, p. 548; Frank Hopkins to Conzet, March 16, Hopkins to Ray P. Chase, Conzet, and J. F. Gould, April 3 — both 1928 and in Fort Ridgely File, FFPD, DOC Records; *Fairfax Standard*, December 10, 1942, p. 1.

8. DOC, *Fifth Biennial Report*, 253.

9. DOC, *Third Biennial Report*, 252, *Fourth Biennial Report*, 248–49, *Fifth Biennial Report*, 241.

10. "Narrative Report," State Parks — Miscellaneous File, FFPD, DOC Records; DOC, DSP, *State Parks of Minnesota* (St. Paul: The Department, 1948), 38; Minnesota, Legislature, Outdoor Recreation Resources Commission, *Parks and Recreation in Minnesota*, report no. 12 (hereafter MORRC report; [St. Paul?: The Commission, 1965]), 36; *Laws*, 1963, p. 1355–56; 1965, p. 1278; 1969, p. 2079–80.

11. Holmquist and Brookins, *Minnesota's Major Historic Sites*, 137; *Laws*, 1969, p. 1880; "New Exhibits Dedicated at Fort Ridgely," *Minnesota History News* (MHS) 16 (June 1975): 2.

12. *Zumbrota News*, July 14, 1982, p. 5; *Home Magazine* (Mankato), February 13–19, 1979, copy of shoppers' publication in author's possession.

13. *Laws*, 1899, p. 136; 1915, p. 524; Holmquist and Brookins, *Minnesota's Major Historic Sites*, 180.

14. *Laws*, 1929, p. 252–53.

15. Of the twenty-three state monuments erected with public funds, only fifteen (including Birch Coulee) were at any time units of the state park system: four at Fort Ridgely, one each at Lake Shetek State Park and Sam Brown State Wayside, the rest as separate units. The other eight, mostly located in cemeteries, were never incorporated into the state park system. *Legislative Manual*, 1939, p. 157; *Laws*, 1969, p. 909–11; 1975, p. 1162; DOC, *Fourth Biennial Report*, 223–27.

16. Holmquist and Brookins, *Minnesota's Major Historic Sites*, 117–20.

17. *Senate Journal*, 1905, p. 120, 960, 1003, 1048; *Laws*, 1905, p. 185; 1915, p. 516. James H. Baker and Thomas Hughes of Mankato had been appointed two years earlier by the MHS to investigate Traverse des Sioux and induce the next legislature to appropriate funds for a monument. See *Mankato Review*, August 11, 1903, p. 5.

18. Thomas Hughes, *Old Traverse des Sioux . . . A History of Early Exploration, Trading Posts, Mission Station, Treaties, and Pioneer Village*, edited by Edward A. Johnson (St. Peter, Minn.: Herald Publishing Company, 1929), 117, 120; *St. Peter Tribune*, June 17, 1914, p. 1.

19. *Laws*, 1919, p. 572; 1921, p. 948; 1923, p. 695; 1925, p. 732; 1927, p. 659; 1929, p. 672; Moll to Conzet, July 7, Conzet to Moll, July 8, carbon, September 11, carbon, Edward A. Johnson to Conzet, September 28 — all 1931 and in Traverse des Sioux File, FFPD, DOC Records; *St. Peter Herald*, July 3, 10, 17, 22, 24, 1931 — all p. 1, July 31, 1931, p. 8.

20. *Laws*, 1937, p. 199; *St. Peter Herald*, June 21, August 30, September 13, 1962 — all p. 1: Josie P. (Mrs. M. E.) Stone (president, Nicollet County Historical Society) to Russell W. Fridley, June 6, 1962, Traverse des Sioux File, DNR Files.

21. *Laws*, 1963, p. 1354, 1360; *St. Peter Herald*, March 19, May 28, 1964 — both p. 1; MORRC report, 86.

22. *St. Peter Herald*, June 13, 1968, p. 1; Donald D. Davison to Files, July 26, 1972, Traverse des Sioux File, DNR Files. That spring the water reached the 762-foot level, as it had done last in 1881. There had been eleven years since 1881, how-

ever, in which it had reached 750 feet or more — not a reassuring statistic for proponents of the park.

23. *St. Peter Herald*, June 13, November 14, 28, 1968, February 5, 1970 — all p. 1; Ron E. Miles to Milton E. Krona, January 12, 1976, Traverse des Sioux File, DNR Files; *Laws*, 1980, p. 408–11; *Free Press* (Mankato), March 19, 1980, p. 8; *St. Peter Times Herald*, June 18, 1981, p. 1. Four days after the legislation abolishing Traverse des Sioux State Park, another law was passed reestablishing Traverse des Sioux State *Monument* on the 109 acres belonging to the MHS and the Department of Transportation. See *Laws*, 1980, p. 728.

24. Thomas Hughes, *History of Minneopa State Park* ([St. Paul?]: DOC, Division of Forestry, 1932), 15–16. A contemporary account paints a somewhat different picture. The second issue of the *Mankato Record* reported on July 12, 1859 (p. 2) that, except for "rude steps" leading to the base of the lower falls and a temporary footbridge over the stream, the grounds were "as yet entirely unimproved."

25. *Mankato Record*, July 12, 1859, p. 2; Hughes, *Minneopa State Park*, 15–16.

26. *Mankato Review*, January 17, p. 6, April 11, p. 1, May 12, p. 6 — all 1885.

27. *Mankato Review*, September 29, 1885, p. 7; *St. Paul Pioneer Press*, October 10, 1909, sec. 2, p. 6; Hughes, *Minneopa State Park*, 18–19; *Laws*, 1905, p. 444–45.

28. *Laws*, 1905, p. 444–45.

29. *Mankato Review*, February 13, 1906, p. 1, August 7, 1906, p. 4, December 4, 1906, p. 7, January 8, 1907, p. 5, March 19, 1907, p. 7; *St. Paul Pioneer Press*, October 10, 1909, sec. 2, p. 6; Hughes, *Minneopa State Park*, 19, 21; *Laws*, 1909, p. 488–89; 1917, p. 235–36; "Narrative Report," State Parks — Miscellaneous File, FFPD, DOC Records.

30. Hughes, *Minneopa State Park*, 21; *Mankato Review*, January 8, 1907, p. 5.

31. Palmer to Conzet, October 19, 1927, Minneopa File, FFPD, DOC Records. Palmer was writing mainly to find out how soon the trees would mature.

32. *St. Paul Pioneer Press*, October 10, 1909, sec. 2, p. 6.

33. *Mankato Review*, August 24, 1915, p. 5.

34. Hughes, *Minneopa State Park*, 23; *Laws*, 1919, p. 572; 1935, p. 582; *Mankato Review*, June 3, 1919, p. 4.

35. DOC, *Third Biennial Report*, 259, *Fourth Biennial Report*, 255, *Fifth Biennial Report*, 248.

36. Hughes, *Minneopa State Park*, 26–28; "Narrative Report," State Parks — Miscellaneous File, FFPD, DOC Records. An exchange was negotiated in 1947 by means of which the park added 3.3 acres. See *Laws*, 1947, p. 372–73.

37. *Laws*, Ex 1961, p. 1600; *Mankato Free Press*, July 7, 1967, p. 9–10.

38. *Mankato Free Press*, April 21, 1967, p. 1, July 7, 1967, p. 9–10; MORRC report, 65.

39. *Laws*, Ex 1967, p. 1613–14, 2309; *Mankato Free Press*, August 2, 1967, p. 13, 15, March 6, 1968, p. 17, December 20, 1968, p. 1, 3, December 31, 1968, p. 20, September 16, 1969, p. 11, October 9, 1969, p. 17.

40. *Mankato Free Press*, November 10, 1967, p. 15, June 25, 1969, p. 26, July 7, 1970, p. 17, December 28, 1972, p. 11.

41. *Mankato Free Press*, January 30, 1957, p. 9, April 21, 1967, p. 1, July 7, 1970, p. 14, December 28, 1972, p. 11.

42. *Mankato Free Press*, June 22, 1972, p. 1, June 26, 1972, p. 15; *Free Press*, October 14, 1976, p. 14; report from Ken Sander, March 9, 1971, DNR.

43. *Mankato Free Press*, May 29, 1969, p. 11; *Free Press*, January 22, 1977, p. 9, June 21, 1980, p. 9.

44. *Free Press*, April 24, p. 1, April 26, p. 1, May 19, p. 15, September 29, p. 2 – all 1976.

45. *Free Press*, April 24, p. 1, April 26, p. 1, October 13, p. 19 – all 1976.

46. DNR, *Management Plan Summary (Draft): Minneopa State Park* (St. Paul: DNR, 1977); *Free Press*, April 2, 1977, p. 7, May 26, 1977, p. 1, June 1, 1977, p. 17, December 22, 1978, p. 15, 24.

47. *Laws*, 1907, p. 459; 1909, p. 441; June Drenning Holmquist, Sue E. Holbert, and Dorothy Drescher Perry, comps., *History Along the Highways: An Official Guide to Minnesota State Markers and Monuments*, Minnesota Historic Sites Pamphlet Series, no. 3 (St. Paul: MHS, 1967), 41.

48. *Laws*, 1909, p. 441; Holmquist et al., comps., *History Along the Highways*, 41.

49. *Laws*, 1915, p. 524; Holmquist et al., comps., *History Along the Highways*, 42. By contrast, in 1971 the legislature authorized a state monument to honor the "Dakota Indians who fought and died for the freedom of their people in 1862." See *Laws*, 1971, p. 1121. O tempora! O mores!

50. *Laws*, 1911, p. 358; *Legislative Manual*, 1913, p. 205–7; DOC, DSP, *State Parks of Minnesota*, 8.

51. *Laws*, 1911, p. 359; 1921, p. 948; DOC, *Third Biennial Report*, 246, 249, *Fourth Biennial Report*, 244, *Fifth Biennial Report*, 238.

52. *Laws*, 1957, p. 274–75.

53. *Laws*, 1913, p. 509–11; *Legislative Manual*, 1915, p. 229; Warren Upham, *Minnesota Geographic Names: Their Origin and Historic Significance* (1920; reprint, St. Paul: MHS, 1969), 363.

54. *Laws*, 1915, p. 517; 1919, p. 572; 1921, p. 948; 1923, p. 694; 1925, p. 732; 1927, p. 659; 1929, p. 671; DOC, *Third Biennial Report*, 254.

55. Nelson, "Notes on State Parks," June 24, 1930, State Parks – Miscellaneous File, FFPD, DOC Records; *Legislative Manual*, 1939, p. 156; *Laws*, 1949, p. 716–17. See also DOC, DSP, *The Minnesota State Park and Recreational Area Plan* ([St. Paul], 1939), 121.

56. *Jay Cooke State Park, Carlton County, Minnesota* (ca. 1921–31), leaflet, F. Rodney Paine to Attorney General [Clifford L. Hilton], "Attention Mr. Gurney [William H. Gurnee, assistant attorney general]," September 18, 1928, carbon – both in Jay Cooke File, FFPD, DOC Records.

57. *Laws*, 1915, p. 517; "Narrative Report," State Parks – Miscellaneous File, FFPD, DOC Records.

58. [F. Rodney Paine?], "Jay Cooke State Park," (1920; enclosed with Paine to Udert W. Hella, October 17, 1957), Paine, "Jay Cooke State Park: Report for the Fiscal Years: July 1, 1923 to June 30, 1925: Use of the Park by the Public," photocopy, A[lbert Marshall] to Hella, June 11, 1981 – all in Jay Cooke File, DNR Files.

59. Paine, "Report for the Fiscal Years," 1923–25, Jay Cooke File, DNR Files.

60. [Paine?], "Jay Cooke State Park" and Paine, "Report for the Fiscal Years," 1923–25, both in Jay Cooke File, DNR Files; *Jay Cooke State Park*, (leaflet), Jay Cooke File, FFPD, DOC Records.

61. Paine, "Report for the Fiscal Years," 1923–25; transcript of presentation by Krona to National Trails Symposium, August 30, 1979 (based on information contained in Paine to L. D. Hartson, October 17, 1957, carbon) – all in Jay Cooke File, DNR Files.

62. Paine to Attorney General, September 18, 1928, Conzet to Attorney General [Henry N. Benson], August 24, 1931, carbon – both in Jay Cooke File, FFPD, DOC Records.

63. Appellant's Brief, 31, *Minnesota Power & Light Company v. State*, 177 Minn. 343 and 225 N.W. 164–67.

64. "Jay Cooke State Park Master Plan," September 6, 1933, Jay Cooke File, FFPD, DOC Records; DOC, DSP, *State Parks of Minnesota*, 17; DOC, *Third Biennial Report*, 257, *Fourth Biennial Report*, 253, *Fifth Biennial Report*, 245; John H. Martin (assistant) for Lew E. Fiero to Norman E. Nelson, Jr., August 28, 1950, carbon, Jay Cooke File, DNR Files.

65. *Laws*, 1951, p. 1223; 1967, p. 1615–16; *Duluth News-Tribune*, September 2, 1976, p. 24; Krona presentation, August 30, 1979, Jay Cooke File, DNR Files. *Mille Lacs Kathio State Park: Summer Trails*, a 1990 DNR leaflet (copy in author's possession), described the park as Minnesota's fourth largest and credited it with over 10,000 acres.

66. Thomas F. Waters, *The Streams and Rivers of Minnesota* (Minneapolis: University of Minnesota Press, 1977), 30.

67. Holmquist and Brookins, *Minnesota's Major Historic Sites*, 158–63.


Chapter 3. *The Rudiments of a Park System: 1915-1925.*

1. *Senate Journal*, 1917, p. 140; *Legislative Manual*, 1921, p. 237.

2. *Senate Journal*, 1919, p. 252, 403; 1921, p. 274, 287–88, 369–70; *Laws*, 1919, p. 573; 1921, p. 46.

3. DOC, *Third Biennial Report*, 263, *Fourth Biennial Report*, 259, *Fifth Biennial Report*, 251; DOC, DSP, *State Parks of Minnesota*, 38; *Laws*, 1965, p. 1280; Nelson, "Notes on State Parks," State Parks — Miscellaneous File, FFPD, DOC Records.

4. *Senate Journal*, 1917, p. 293, 330; *Laws*, 1919, p. 573; DNR, *Management Plan Summary (Draft): Whitewater State Park* (St. Paul: DNR, 1977); Warming, comp., *The Paradise of Minnesota: The Proposed Whitewater State Park* ([St. Charles, Minn.], 1917).

5. *Senate Journal*, 1921, p. 267, 289, 960; *Laws*, 1921, p. 230–31; [Fred] Bateman to Harold Ostergaard, received on June 28, 1932, Park Histories File, FFPD, DOC Records; DNR, *Management Plan Summary: Whitewater*; John H. Martin to Mrs. Milo J. Hyland, August 18, 1965, carbon, Whitewater File, DNR Files. Some sources give the acreage of Latsch's donation as 165.67.

6. Eugene Miller to Oscar H. Smith, December 19, 1926, Dr. F. H. Rollins et al. to Smith, December 20, 1926, Fred Bateman to Grover M. Conzet, July 1, 1931, Ostergaard for Conzet to Bateman, August 23, 1934, carbon, M. J. McGrath to C. C. Rieger, April 28, 1931 — all in Whitewater File, FFPD, DOC Records; C. W. Crippen to Conzet, August 18, 1925, carbon, Jay Cooke File, FFPD, DOC Records.

7. Conzet to Alex Rodgers, February 20, carbon, Rodgers to Dear Sir [Conzet], March 2, Albert Blankenberg to Conzet, March 9 — all 1931 and in Whitewater File, FFPD, DOC Records; DNR, *Management Plan Summary: Whitewater*.

8. DOC, *Third Biennial Report*, 264, *Fourth Biennial Report*, 259, *Fifth Biennial Report*, 252.

9. DNR, *Management Plan Summary: Whitewater*. One popular trail had to be closed — permanently, it would seem — in the early 1970s, and the trail to Coyote Point, even more popular, is hazardous to all but the most cautious of climbers.

10. *St. Charles Press*, June 9, 1977, p. 2. This information is contained in a long

letter from Charles L. McCarthy, chairman of the Whitewater River Association, a landowner group.

11. Conzet to Jno. Reiland, April 19, 1934, carbon, Whitewater File, FFPD, DOC Records; Robert S. Story to M. J. ("Mac") McCauley, July 17, 1976, Whitewater File, DNR Files; *St. Charles Press*, January 1, 1976, p. 3. The state legislature had also questioned the use of funds for such purposes, presumably on grounds that only local people would benefit.

12. *St. Charles Press*, August 5, September 2, 9, 1976, May 22, 1980 — all p. 2. After an informal public meeting at which Mayor McCready and the DNR's Dennis Thompson disagreed on the issue, Robert Althoff, a candidate for county commissioner, asked, "What more can we do to convince the DNR that we want a golf course instead of a home for prairie dogs or a swamp?" See *Press*, September 16, 1976, p. 1.

13. DNR, *Management Plan Summary: Whitewater*.

14. *St. Charles Press*, June 23, 1977, p. 1.

15. *St. Charles Press*, June 15, September 7, 14, 21, November 30, 1978 — all p. 1; October 19, 1978, p. 1, 3.

16. *St. Charles Press*, January 18, April 19, May 17, December 20, 1979 — all p. 1; September 27, 1979, p. 9; Donald D. Davison to Phil[ip J.] Olfelt, February 12, 1980, carbon, Whitewater File, DNR Files; *Laws*, 1980, p. 407–8.

17. Victor E. Lawson, ed., *Illustrated History and Descriptive and Biographical Review of Kandiyohi County, Minnesota* ([Willmar, Minn.]: The Author & J. Emil Nelson, 1905), 133.

18. J[ames] F. Gould to Conzet, June 15, 1927, enclosing undated letter (carbon) from Victor E. Lawson, Sibley File, FFPD, DOC Records; *House Journal*, 1919, p. 944; *Senate Journal*, 1919, p. 814; *New London Times*, January 25, 1917, p. 5; "Sixty Years: A History of Sibley State Park," by Barbara Mossberg, a Comprehensive Employment and Training Act (CETA) worker at the park, *New London–Spicer Times* (New London), August 5, 1976, p. 7.

19. *Laws*, 1919, p. 572–73; *New London Times*, April 23, 1931, p. 1.

20. Karl Thurn and Helen Thurn, *Round Robin of Kandiyohi County, Minnesota: Centennial Year 1858–1958* (Raymond, Minn.: Press, 1958), 171; Mossberg, "Sixty Years," 7–8.

21. Ed Erickson (game warden) to Conzet, July 15, Lawson to Ray P. Chase, Conzet, and George W. McCollough [McCullough], August 15 — both 1929 and in Sibley File, FFPD, DOC Records; *New London Times*, March 14, 1929, April 23, 1931 — both p. 1; *Laws*, 1931, p. 346; 1933, p. 813; 1935, p. 585; 1937, p. 550. The state auditor had expended small sums, mainly for salaries, in the fiscal years 1930, 1931, and 1932. See Minnesota, State Auditor, *Biennial Report*, 1929/30, p. 395; 1931/32, p. 329, 478.

22. O. A. Nelson (secretary) to William T. Cox, January 16, Victor E. Lawson to Conzet, July 24, Conzet to Lawson, July 27, carbon — all 1933 and in Sibley File, FFPD, DOC Records; Thurn and Thurn, *Kandiyohi County*, 172.

23. *Willmar Weekly Tribune*, July 10, 1935, p. 1; DOC, *Third Biennial Report*, 262–63, *Fourth Biennial Report*, 258.

24. *Willmar Weekly Tribune*, July 10, p. 1, September 11, p. 4 — both 1935.

25. *Willmar Weekly Tribune*, October 9, p. 2, October 16, p. 3, October 23, p. 1 — all 1935.

26. Thurn and Thurn, *Kandiyohi County*, 173–74. A flagstaff had been erected on this site soon after the park was established. See *Legislative Manual*, 1921, p. 236.

27. Nelson to Cox, January 16, Ostergaard for Conzet to Nelson, February 15, carbon — both 1933 and in Sibley File, FFPD, DOC Records; *Willmar Weekly Tribune,* October 16, p. 3, September 11, p. 4 — both 1935; DOC, DSP, *State Parks of Minnesota,* 31. The bill establishing the park merely authorized the game and fish commissioner to select lands in two sections, section 35 of Colfax Township and section 2 of Lake Andrew Township, and gave no clear directive concerning the future acquisition of lands. At times the parks people acted upon the assumption that any other lands in these two sections could be acquired without special legislation, but at other times they treated the matter as though the statutory boundaries of the park enclosed only what had already been acquired.

28. *Laws,* 1957, p. 76–77; 1959, p. 1929; Ex 1961, p. 1600–1601; 1963, p. 1357; 1965, p. 1277; 1967, p. 1614; 1969, p. 1639.

29. *House Journal,* 1973, p. 1098, 1858, 2145–46, 3574–75; *Senate Journal,* 1973, p. 2374, 2992; *Laws,* 1973, p. 1503; 1974, p. 757; 1980, p. 406–7; "Environmental Assessment — Sibley State Park," 1976–77, Sibley File, DNR Files.

30. Chase, *Statement,* 47.

31. *Senate Journal,* 1921, p. 236, 431.

32. *Senate Journal,* 1921, p. 692, 1096–97; *Laws,* 1921, p. 525–26.

33. "Narrative Report," State Parks — Miscellaneous File, FFPD, DOC Records; *Laws,* 1923, p. 694; 1935, p. 582.

34. Udert W. Hella to Mrs. C. F. Gilbertson, February 2, 1956, carbon, Scenic File, DNR Files; *Laws,* 1927, p. 659; 1929, p. 671; 1931, p. 518; 1933, p. 812; 1935, p. 582; 1937, p. 549; DOC, *Third Biennial Report,* 260.

35. Hella to Gilbertson, February 2, 1956, Scenic File, DNR Files.

36. Hella to Gilbertson, February 2, 1956, Scenic File, DNR Files; DOC, *Third Biennial Report,* 260, 262, *Fourth Biennial Report,* 257.

37. *Laws,* 1925, p. 732; Geo[rge] H. Herreid to Rines, September 20, typescript copy, Rines to Herreid, September 24, carbon — both 1925 and in Scenic File, FFPD, DOC Records. Herreid, a member of the state house of representatives, had introduced a bill paralleling McGarry's senate bill in 1921. A resident of Deer River, he long took an active interest in Scenic State Park.

38. DOC, *Fifth Biennial Report,* 250.

39. *House Journal,* 1921, p. 404, 432, 574, 1269; *Laws,* 1921, p. 878–79; 1923, p. 694; 1925, p. 732; 1927, p. 659; 1935, p. 582; 1937, p. 550.

40. *Legislative Manual,* 1923, p. 213; *Laws,* 1965, p. 1280; Nelson, "Notes on State Parks," State Parks — Miscellaneous File, FFPD, DOC Records; DOC, *Third Biennial Report,* 263, *Fourth Biennial Report,* 258.

41. *House Journal,* 1919, p. 935; *Senate Journal,* 1919, p. 816; 1921, p. 59, 344, 431, 454, 589, 717, 874.

42. *Senate Journal,* 1921, p. 59, 199, 414, 1132; 1923, p. 187, 1176–78, 1350, 1351, 1386; *House Journal,* 1921, p. 73, 388; 1923, p. 281, 1553; *Laws,* 1923, p. 695; *Bemidji Sentinel,* July 20, 1921, p. 1, February 9, 1923, p. 2; Chase, *Statement,* 55–64.

43. *Laws,* 1923, p. 695; Mildred Simmons, "A History of Lake Bemidji State Park, 1923–1979" (research paper prepared for English course, Bemidji State University, 1979?), copy in author's possession from John Fylpaa, naturalist, Lake Bemidji State Park.

44. John H. Nelson to Ostergaard, December 14, 1932, Park Histories File, FFPD, DOC Records; Minnesota, State Auditor, *Report to the 1925 Legislature Covering Minnesota State Parks* ([St. Paul: Riverside Press, 1925]).

45. George T. Baker to Conzet, September 29, Conzet to Baker, October 13, carbon — both 1926 and in Lake Bemidji File, FFPD, DOC Records.

46. Ostergaard for Conzet to Nelson, March 26, carbon, Conzet to Nelson, August 3, carbon, Nelson to Conzet, April 12 — all 1932 and in Lake Bemidji File, FFPD, DOC Records.

47. Conzet to John H. Nelson, March 4, 1931, carbon, Lake Bemidji File, FFPD, DOC Records; "State Parks Write Up for Bi-ennial Report," October 1, 1934, State Parks Miscellaneous Correspondence File, FFPD, DOC Records; *Laws*, 1931, p. 346; 1933, p. 813; 1935, p. 584; 1937, p. 549.

48. DOC, *Third Biennial Report*, 258, *Fourth Biennial Report*, 254, *Fifth Biennial Report*, 246.

49. *Laws*, 1945, p. 632.

50. DOC, DSP, *State Parks of Minnesota*, 23; MORRC report, 3; *Laws*, 1955, p. 1177; 1971, p. 1694.

51. Sauer to Davison, December 15, 1973, Lake Bemidji File, DNR Files.

52. Frank Svoboda to Davison, February 2, Jerry Bachman to Davison, March 7, carbon — both 1977 and in Lake Bemidji File, DNR Files.

53. "Summary and Disposition of Comments Received at the Public Information Meeting on 2/21/77 Regarding the Lake Bemidji State Park Management Plan," accompanying Jim Dustrude and Franklin Svoboda for Davison to Citizens Interested in the Management Plan for Lake Bemidji State Park, September 26, 1977 — copies in author's possession.

54. Samuel H. Morgan to Davison and All Trustees and Honorary Trustees, Minnesota Parks Foundation, July 12, 1978, photocopy, Lake Bemidji File, DNR Files; *Minneapolis Tribune*, June 20, 1978, p. 2B, 8B. The 41.68-acre parcel on the east shore of Lake Bemidji remains a detached portion of the park. There is also a 28.5-acre tract on the north shore, now occupied by the Northwest Regional Office of the DNR.

55. DNR, *[Lake] Bemidji State Park Interpreter* (1977) copy of information sheet in author's possession.

56. *Legislative Manual*, 1925, p. 228; DOC, *Third Biennial Report*, 252.

57. DOC, *Third Biennial Report*, 252, *Fifth Biennial Report*, 241; *Laws*, 1935, p. 585; 1937, p. 550; 1961, p. 238–39.

58. Field notes describing land donated by John A. Latsch (1929) in John A. Latsch File, and John A. Latsch material in Park Histories File — both in FFPD, DOC Records; *Laws*, 1929, p. 672. Latsch also donated land for the establishment of Perrot State Park in Wisconsin. See Samuel H. Morgan, "Our Citizens and State Parks," *Conservation Volunteer* 30 (May–June 1967): 29.

59. *Laws*, 1929, p. 672; 1933, p. 812; 1935, p. 584; 1937, p. 549; *Winona Republican-Herald*, October 1, 1929, p. 5; Conzet to John [A.] Latsch, September 20, 1929, carbon, Fugina to Jean W. Wittich, August 22, 1932, carbon, Wittich to Fugina, September 1, 1932, carbon, Fugina to Conzet, January 20, 1934 — all in John A. Latsch File, FFPD, DOC Records. The park received $750 a year until 1937, when the amount was increased to $850.

60. F. J. Fugina to Ostergaard, July 12, 1933, Ostergaard for Conzet to John R. Foley, August 23, 1933, carbon, D. E. Tawney to Armand D. Brattland, April 22, 1935, carbon — all in John A. Latsch File, FFPD, DOC Records; DOC, *Third Biennial Report*, 258, *Fourth Biennial Report*, 253, *Fifth Biennial Report*, 245.

61. *Legislative Manual*, 1925, p. 228; R[euben] A. Skogland (NPS) to Second District Officer, February 4, carbon, F. J. Fugina to Conzet, April 8 — both 1934

and in John Latsch File, FFPD, DOC Records; *Winona News,* January 20, 1963, p. 10.

62. *Winona News,* January 20, 1963, p. 10; *Laws,* 1963, p. 1356; MORRC report, 47.

63. Martin to Hella, November 7, 1968, and DNR, DPR, "Profile: John A. Latsch: Winona County," September 18, 1973 – both in John A. Latsch File, DNR Files; *Laws,* 1969, p. 1074; 1975, p. 1144–46; DNR, Bureau of Planning, and State Planning Agency, Environmental Planning Section, *Minnesota Resource Potentials in Outdoor Recreation,* Project 80, Staff Report no. 1 (hereafter Project 80 report; [St. Paul?, 1971]), 150; *Republican Eagle* (Red Wing), November 23, 1965, p. 4. A story current at the Parks and Recreation Division holds that the intent of the 1969 law was to retain John A. Latsch as a park and Franz Jevne as a wayside but that through a clerical error the two were reversed.

64. *Rochester Post-Bulletin,* September 7, 1972, p. 5.

65. John A. Latsch material, Park Histories File, FFPD, DOC Records.

66. Chase, *Statement,* 6–7.

67. Chase, *Statement,* 6, 8, 21, 24–25, 31–32, 53.

68. Chase, *Statement,* 7.

69. Chase, *Statement,* 55–66. Chase also advocated parks at or near Leech Lake, Lake Okabena, Lake Benton, St. Cloud, and elsewhere. Some of these sites were proposed later for state parks but rejected by the legislature; a few eventually became county parks.

70. *Laws,* 1923, p. 641–44; Chase, *Statement,* 76.

## Chapter 4. *Under the Conservation Commission: 1925–1935*

1. *Laws,* 1925, p. 764–65.

2. *Legislative Manual,* 1933, p. 476; University of Minnesota, *General Catalogue of the University of Minnesota,* compiled for the University and General Alumni Association ([Minneapolis?: R. L. Polk & Company], 1916), 164.

3. *Laws,* 1931, p. 206–8, 211.

4. *Legislative Manual,* 1933, p. 478; University of Minnesota, *General Catalogue,* 160.

5. *Laws,* 1935, p. 620–21.

6. *Senate Journal,* 1925, p. 163; 1927, p. 96; 1929, p. 79; *Laws,* 1929, p. 252.

7. Holmquist and Brookins, *Minnesota's Major Historic Sites,* (first ed.; see chapter 1, note 6), 105; *Laws,* 1933, p. 813; 1935, p. 584; 1937, p. 549; 1975, p. 1162.

8. Federal Writers' Project, Minnesota, *Minnesota: A State Guide,* American Guide Series (New York: Viking Press, 1938; reprinted as *The WPA Guide to Minnesota* [St. Paul: Minnesota Historical Society Press, Borealis Books, 1985]), 340; Holmquist and Brookins, *Minnesota's Major Historic Sites,* 179.

9. *Senate Journal,* 1927, p. 339; *House Journal,* 1929, p. 475; *Laws,* 1929, p. 493–94.

10. Paul to Commissioner of Conservation, July 21, John H. Martin for Udert W. Hella to Paul, August 3, carbon, Hella to Paul, November 28, carbon, Paul to Martin, September 1 – all 1966, Sam Brown File, DNR Files; "1977 Legislative Report," *Minnesota History News* 18 (June 1977): 1. The park was demoted to a wayside in 1969. See *Laws,* 1969, p. 910.

11. *Laws,* 1905, p. 531–32; 1921, p. 948.

12. *Senate Journal*, 1923, p. 561, 948; 1929, p. 78, 219; *Laws*, 1923, p. 171; 1929, p. 319-20; *House Journal*, 1929, p. 173, 449; Holmquist and Brookins, *Minnesota's Major Historic Sites*, 180.

13. DOC, *Third Biennial Report*, 258-59, *Fourth Biennial Report*, 255, *Fifth Biennial Report*, 246.

14. *Laws*, 1937, p. 819-21; 1947, p. 604-5; 1963, p. 1357; 1965, p. 1279-80; 1967, p. 1613; DOC, DSP, *State Parks of Minnesota*, 25; MORRC report, 3; DNR, Project 80 report, 116.

15. Sidney A. Frellsen to Sigvald Lervaag, September 19, 1952, carbon, Martin for Hella to Mrs. H. L. Matson, September 14, 1955, carbon, Milton E. Krona to Hella, March 4, 1969, Martin to Krona, April 25, 1973 — all in Lake Shetek File, DNR Files.

16. Ludwig to Hella, August 27, 1962, Lake Shetek File, DNR Files.

17. DNR, Project 80 report, 116, 149.

18. Holmquist and Brookins, *Minnesota's Major Historic Sites*, 72-77.

19. Holmquist and Brookins, *Minnesota's Major Historic Sites*, 75-76; *Senate Journal*, 1931, p. 51, 177, 481; *Laws*, 1931, p. 51-52; H. W. Austin to Grover M. Conzet, July 9, M[artin] A. Engstrom to Conzet, September 20 — both 1931 and in Charles A. Lindbergh File, FFPD, DOC Records.

20. Engstrom to Conzet, September 20, 1931, Lindbergh File, FFPD, DOC Records; DOC, *Third Biennial Report*, 251, *Fourth Biennial Report*, 247, *Fifth Biennial Report*, 240; *Laws*, 1969, p. 1860; "1973 Historic Sites Season Opens: Two New Centers Added to Roster," *Minnesota History News* 14 (May 1973): 1.

21. Holmquist and Brookins, *Minnesota's Major Historic Sites*, 113-16.

22. *Senate Journal*, 1931, p. 485; *Laws*, 1931, p. 519.

23. *Laws*, 1933, p. 813; 1935, p. 584; 1937, p. 549; DOC, *Fifth Biennial Report*, 246; Holmquist and Brookins, *Minnesota's Major Historic Sites*, 116; DOC, DSP, *State Parks of Minnesota*, 22; *Madison Independent Press*, June 27, 1941, p. 6, August 15, 1941, p. 1, June 12, 19, July 10, 1942 — all p. 1; Jon Willard, *Lac qui Parle and the Dakota Mission* (Madison, Minn.: Lac qui Parle County Historical Society, 1964), 260-61.

24. DOC, DSP, *State Parks of Minnesota*, 22; *Laws*, 1973, p. 454-55.

25. *Senate Journal*, 1931, p. 563, 965; *House Journal*, 1931, p. 1226; *Laws*, 1931, p. 519-20.

26. Elmer E. Adams to Conzet, June 20, 1931, Inspiration Peak File, FFPD, DOC Records; *Parkers Prairie Independent*, October 15, 1931, p. 1.

27. Conzet to William T. Cox, October 6, 1931, Harold Ostergaard for Conzet to Anton Rots, May 27, 1935, carbon — both in Inspiration Peak File, FFPD, DOC Records; *Laws*, 1933, p. 813; 1935, p. 585; 1937, p. 550; DOC, *Third Biennial Report*, 254, *Fourth Biennial Report*, 250.

28. Holmquist and Brookins, *Minnesota's Major Historic Sites*, 164-66.

29. Holmquist and Brookins, *Minnesota's Major Historic Sites*, 166; DOC, *Third Biennial Report*, 260, *Fourth Biennial Report*, 256; *Laws*, 1987, p. 257-58.

30. *Laws*, 1935, p. 586-87.

31. DOC, *Third Biennial Report*, 258, *Fourth Biennial Report*, 253, *Fifth Biennial Report*, 245; Harold W. Lathrop to Lew E. Fiero, August 26, 1946, MORRC File, PRD, DOC Records.

32. *Laws*, 1963, p. 830-32.

33. *Senate Journal*, 1925, p. 537, 708; 1927, p. 551, 697; 1929, p. 344. Carlton Lake is a small body of water near the Minnesota River, just south of Montevideo.

34. *Senate Journal*, 1927, p. 87, 500, 1079, 1229. Many areas suggested for state parks did not even reach the legislative halls. A wooded area on Lake Shaokatan, in Lincoln County, which had been proposed in the 1929 session, was still alive as a private idea three years later. Among other areas suggested at one time or another were a 13-acre tract on Lake Osakis and some property near Granite Falls. See *Senate Journal*, 1929, p. 91; Ostergaard for Conzet to Nicholas Erschens, July 14, August 19, 1932, carbons, Mrs. Elmer Bundy to Governor [Floyd B.] Olson, June 24, 1933, Ostergaard for Conzet to Cox, August 19, 1932, carbon — all in Proposed State Parks File, FFPD, DOC Records.

35. Robert A. Murray, *A History of Pipestone National Monument, Minnesota* ([Pipestone, Minn.?]: Pipestone Indian Shrine Association, 1965), 42, 44.

36. Murray, *Pipestone National Monument*, 46; *Senate Journal*, 1925, p. 126, 771; *House Journal*, 1925, p. 138; *Laws*, 1925, p. 99; *Legislative Manual*, 1927, p. 149.

37. Murray, *Pipestone National Monument*, 49–51.

38. Rines to Conzet, November 16, 1927, carbon, Sleepy Eye Lake File, FFPD, DOC Records.

39. Nelson, "Notes on State Parks," State Parks — Miscellaneous File, FFPD, DOC Records.

## Chapter 5. *Professionalism and Expansion: 1935–1945*

1. DOC, *Third Biennial Report*, 244.

2. DOC, *Third Biennial Report*, 244, *Fourth Biennial Report*, 238.

3. DOC, *Third Biennial Report*, 247–48; *Laws*, 1925, p. 756. In the two years from July 1, 1934, to June 30, 1936, for example, the state contributed $285,566.02, the federal government, $1,825,706.78.

4. DOC, *Third Biennial Report*, 225–27, 236.

5. DOC, *Third Biennial Report*, 237, 240–41.

6. DOC, *Third Biennial Report*, 228–29, *Fourth Biennial Report*, 223.

7. Waters, *Streams and Rivers*, 290–91, 295; John H. Martin, "A History of Camden State Park," *Conservation Volunteer* 21 (March–April 1958): 54; DNR, *A Management Plan for Camden State Park* (draft; St. Paul: DNR, 1977), 12, 16–17.

8. DNR, *Management Plan: Camden*, 17; Martin, "History of Camden State Park," 54–55; Torgny Anderson, *The Centennial History of Lyon County, Minnesota* (Marshall, Minn.: Henle Publishing Company, 1970), 40, 101–4; Arthur P. Rose, *An Illustrated History of Lyon County, Minnesota* (Marshall, Minn.: Northern History Publishing Company, 1912), 231; *Prairie Schooner* (Marshall), December 24, 1874, p. 1.

9. Martin, "History of Camden State Park," 56; [John H. Martin?], "Camden State Park: Background and History," n.d., Camden File, DNR Files.

10. Martin, "History of Camden State Park," 57; [Martin?], "Camden: Background and History," R[euben] A. Skogland, "Master Plan Report: Camden State Park, Lynd, Minnesota," 1937? — both in Camden File, DNR Files; Whitney to Grover M. Conzet, received on March 30, Conzet to Whitney, March 31, carbon, Harold Ostergaard to Conzet, July 10, carbon–all 1933 and in Proposed State Parks File, FFPD, DOC Records; *Marshall Messenger*, August 1, 1934, p. 1, 3.

11. DOC, *Second Biennial Report: Fiscal Years 1933–1934*, 10; Martin, "History of Camden State Park," 57; [Martin?], "Camden: Background and History,"

Skogland, "Master Plan Report" — both in Camden File, DNR Files; DNR, *Management Plan: Camden*, 19.

12. *Laws*, 1935, p. 585–86; DOC, *Third Biennial Report*, 250, *Fourth Biennial Report*, 246, *Fifth Biennial Report*, 240; John H. Martin to Udert W. Hella, May 19, 1970, Camden File, DNR Files.

13. Norman Reitan to Hella, June 19, George A. Selke to Orville L. Freeman, June 24, carbon — both 1957 and in Camden File, PRD, DOC Records; Don Olson to Harold LeVander, August 12, 1969, photocopy, Camden File, DNR Files; *Laws*, 1963, p. 1355; 1965, p. 1279, 1826–27; 1967, p. 1612; MORRC report, 25 (map).

14. DNR, Project 80 report, 124.

15. Common Council of the City of Marshall, Lyon County, Resolution No. 1132, "Resolution Opposing Return of Camden State Park to the County of Lyon," May 1, 1972, Hella to Sam Pomantz, June 5, 1972, carbon — both in Camden File, DNR Files.

16. *Lyon County Independent* (Marshall), June 6, 9, 1975 — both p. 4; DNR, *Management Plan: Camden*, 57.

17. Ed[ward J.] Cushing to Ned [Edmund C.] Bray, October 1, 1971, photocopy, Camden File, DNR Files.

18. DNR, *Management Plan: Camden*, 23.

19. DNR, *Management Plan: Camden*, 62–65. Legislation passed in 1980 deleted some land at the north and south ends of the park. See *Laws*, 1980, p. 400–401.

20. Grace Lee Nute, "Gooseberry Falls State Park: Its History and Natural History," pt. 1, *Conservation Volunteer* 10 (May–June 1947): 27–30.

21. Nute, "Gooseberry Falls State Park," 28–30.

22. Nute, "Gooseberry Falls State Park," 30; DOC, *Second Biennial Report*, 102; DNR, *A Management Plan for Gooseberry Falls State Park* (St. Paul: DNR, 1979), 17.

23. DOC, *Second Biennial Report*, 102–3, *Third Biennial Report*, 253, *Fourth Biennial Report*, 249.

24. DOC, *Third Biennial Report*, 241, *Fourth Biennial Report*, 249, *Fifth Biennial Report*, 241–42.

25. *Laws*, 1937, p. 824.

26. *Laws*, 1955, p. 1032; 1967, p. 1612; 1971, p. 1694; *Two Harbors Chronicle and Times*, December 14, 1972, p. 1; *Silver Bay News*, March 14, 1973, p. 4.

27. Waters, *Streams and Rivers*, 53, 61.

28. *Laws*, 1937, p. 815–19; *New Ulm Journal*, April 23, 1965, p. 2

29. DOC, *Third Biennial Report*, 251–52, *Fourth Biennial Report*, 248, *Fifth Biennial Report*, 240; *New Ulm Journal*, April 23, 1965, p. 2.

30. DOC, *Seventh Biennial Report: Biennium Ending June 30, 1944*, 259; Kenneth Carley, *The Sioux Uprising of 1862*, 2d ed. (St. Paul: MHS Press, 1976), 34–39; *Laws*, 1945, p. 96.

31. Henry N. Somsen, Jr., to Wayne H. Olson et al., April 23, Somsen to Hella and Sidney A. Frellsen, April 27, Hella to Olson, May 12, photocopy, Frank P. Bourgin to Chester J. Moeglein, October 11 — all 1965 and in Flandrau File, PRD, DOC Records; *New Ulm Journal*, July 9, 1947, April 12, 16, 21, 1965, February 6, 1966 — all p. 1.

32. Hella to Jerome H. Kuehn, July 8, 1969, carbon, Flandrau File, DNR Files.

33. Chase, *Statement*, 59; "Mound Springs State Park," 1961?, and DOC, DPR, "Profile: Blue Mounds State Park — Rock County," April 6, 1970 — both in Blue Mounds File, DNR Files; DOC, *Third Biennial Report*, 260.

34. DOC, *Third Biennial Report*, 260, *Fourth Biennial Report*, 256; "Profile: Blue Mounds State Park," Blue Mounds File, DNR Files; *Laws*, 1955, p. 1033; 1961, p. 240; Ex 1961, p. 1600; 1963, p. 1354–55; 1965, p. 1278.

35. Donald D. Davison to Charles P. Reinert, August 20, 1974, carbon, Blue Mounds File, DNR Files; letter in *Rock County Star-Herald* (Luverne), August 21, 1974, p. B2.

36. *Worthington Globe*, July 18, 1974, p. 1, 3; Blanich to Davison, August 22, October 21, 1974 — both in Blue Mounds File, DNR Files.

37. *Rock County Star-Herald*, August 21, 1974, p. B2, July 7, 1976, p. 1; *Worthington Globe*, April 18, 1977, p. B1; *St. Paul Pioneer Press*, April 21, 22, 1977 — both p. 23.

38. *Rock County Star-Herald*, November 9, 1961, p. 1; *Minneapolis Star*, November 1, 1978, p. 1B.

39. Gary W. Hudak, "Notes on the Archaeology: Blue Mounds State Park," Blue Mounds File, DNR Files; letter in *Worthington Globe*, November 3, 1975, p. 3.

40. DNR, Project 80 report, 124.

41. *Laws*, 1937, p. 828; DOC, *Third Biennial Report*, 263, *Fourth Biennial Report*, 259, *Fifth Biennial Report*, 251.

42. *Laws*, 1969, p. 911.

43. DNR, *A Management Plan for Split Rock Creek State Recreation Area* (St. Paul: DNR, 1981), 60–61; *Laws*, 1982, p. 581–82.

44. Martin to Bruce Hitzman, August 19, 1968, carbon, and DNR, DPR, "Profile: Monson Lake State Park: Swift County," September 26, 1973 — both in Monson Lake File, DNR Files; DOC, *Third Biennial Report*, 259, *Fourth Biennial Report*, 255, *Fifth Biennial Report*, 248.

45. DOC, *Fifth Biennial Report*, 248; *Laws*, 1965, p. 1280.

46. *Laws*, 1937, p. 822–23; 1965, p. 1280; DOC, *Third Biennial Report*, 260, *Fourth Biennial Report*, 257, *Fifth Biennial Report*, 250.

47. DNR, *A Management Plan for Lake Bronson State Park* (draft; St. Paul: DNR, 1977), 20.

48. DNR, *Management Plan: Lake Bronson*, 20–21; J. Merle Harris, "Lake Bronson, Old Mill, Old Crossing," *Conservation Volunteer* 19 (September–October 1956): 43; DOC, *Third Biennial Report*, 263, *Fourth Biennial Report*, 259.

49. DNR, *Management Plan: Lake Bronson*, 21; *Kittson County Enterprise* (Hallock), April 21, 1937, p. 1; *Laws*, 1937, p. 823–24; 1945, p. 99; Alan H. Patera and John S. Gallagher, *The Post Offices of Minnesota* (Burtonsville, Md.: The Depot, 1978), 101.

50. *Laws*, 1937, p. 823–24; 1961, p. 783–84; 1965, p. 1828; 1967, p. 1612; 1969, p. 1639; 1977, p. 1145–46; DNR, *Management Plan: Lake Bronson*, 15, 25, 147.

51. DNR, *Management Plan: Lake Bronson*, 24, 96; Harris, "Lake Bronson," 44; DNR, Project 80 report, 124.

52. DOC, *Third Biennial Report*, 265, *Fourth Biennial Report*, 246; *Sunday Fargo Forum, Daily Tribune and Moorhead News* (Fargo, N. Dak.), July 24, 1960, p. C10.

53. *Laws*, 1937, p. 814–15; 1961, p. 1599; 1967, p. 1611; 1969, p. 1638; O. A. Stevens to Department of Conservation, January 9, 1962, photocopy, Jerry Bachman to Mert[on V.] Christian, October 20, 1976, carbon — both in Buffalo River File, DNR Files.

54. R. Newell Searle, *Gardens of the Desert: Minnesota's Prairie Parks*, Minnesota State Park Heritage Series, no. 5 ([St. Paul?]: Minnesota Parks Foundation, 1983), 44–45.

55. DOC, *Third Biennial Report*, 249; Georgina Lommen and Helen Steffen, "Come See Our State Parks," *Minnesota Journal of Education* 33 (September 1952): 32.

56. *Caledonia Journal*, June 6, July 18, 25, 1935, July 23, 1936 — all p. 1.

57. *Caledonia Journal*, July 23, 1936, July 21, 1938 — both p. 1; *Laws*, 1937, p. 813-14; "Beaver Creek Valley State Park: Abstract of Lands acquired by the State of Minnesota," February 18, 1970, Beaver Creek Valley File, DNR Files; DOC, *Fourth Biennial Report*, 245; DOC, DSP, *State Parks of Minnesota*, 10.

58. "Beaver Creek Valley," May 11, 1959, Beaver Creek Valley File, DNR Files; *Laws*, 1955, p. 1033; 1963, p. 1354; 1967, p. 1611; 1969, p. 1637; DNR, *A Management Plan for Beaver Creek Valley State Park* (St. Paul: DNR, 1980), 8.

59. *Caledonia Argus*, February 24, March 10, 17, May 5, September 15, 1977, October 5, 1978 — all p. 1; *Senate Journal*, 1977, p. 774, 1640, 1682, 2703, 3136; *House Journal*, 1977, p. 1776, 1779, 2306-7, 2405-8, 2924-31, 3230-35.

60. DNR, *Management Plan: Beaver Creek Valley*, 101-2.

61. DNR, Project 80 report, 96-98.

62. DNR, *Management Plan: Beaver Creek Valley*, 44-45.

63. *Caledonia Argus*, March 17, June 30, 1977 — both p. 1.

64. DNR, *Management Plan: Beaver Creek Valley*, 7.

65. DOC, *Fourth Biennial Report*, 256; *Fifth Biennial Report*, 250; *Laws*, 1965, p. 1280.

66. Martin for Hella to Lorayne Larson, May 11, 1965, carbon, Lake Carlos File, DNR Files.

67. Martin for Hella to Larson, May 11, 1965, Larson to Martin, May 12, 1965 — both in Lake Carlos File, DNR Files; *Park Region Echo* (Alexandria), August 5, September 2, October 14, 1937 — all p. 1.

68. *Park Region Echo*, October 7, 21, December 9, 1937; January 27, 1938 — all p. 1; DOC, *Fourth Biennial Report*, 254, *Fifth Biennial Report*, 246.

69. *Park Region Echo*, October 7, 14, 1937 — both p. 1; DOC, DSP, *State Parks of Minnesota*, 24; *Laws*, Ex 1961, p. 1599; 1963, p. 1356-57; 1967, p. 1612-13.

70. U[dert] W. Hella, "History of Old Mill State Park," May 28, 1958, Old Mill File, DNR Files; *Warren Sheaf*, June 6, 1934, p. 1, 4, June 13, 20, July 25, 1934 — all p. 1.

71. *Warren Sheaf*, February 13, 20, 27, March 20, April 3, May 1, 1935 — all p. 1, September 23, 1936, p. 1, 10; Hella, "History of Old Mill State Park," J. B. Carter (NPS), "Inspection Report on the Proposed State Park Recreational Grounds, Marshall County, Minnesota," April 22, 1935, Harold W. Lathrop to L. P. Zimmerman, May 5, 1936, carbon, Lathrop to A[rnold] A. Trost, May 26, 1936, carbon, S. L. Stolte for Victor Christgau to J. B. Kovarik, November 24, 1936, carbon — all in Old Mill File, DNR Files.

72. "Dedication of the Restored Old Mill: Sunday, June 1, 1958" (program), Martin for Lew E. Fiero to H. F. Hedquist, January 24, 1952, carbon — both in Old Mill File, DNR Files; *Warren Sheaf*, September 5, 1951, p. 1.

73. *Warren Sheaf*, May 9, July 18, September 5, 1951 — all p. 1, June 4, 1958, p. 1, 6, September 29, 1971, p. 11; Martin and Fiero to Hedquist, January 24, 1952, Bill [William W.] Weller to Joe Ludwig, July 5, 1974, photocopy — both in Old Mill File, DNR Files; *Laws*, 1951, p. 312-13.

74. Richard W. Fitzsimons to Davison, August 2, 1974, Old Mill File, DNR Files; DNR, Project 80 report, 124.

75. Holmquist and Brookins, *Minnesota's Major Historic Sites*, 130.

76. Holmquist and Brookins, *Minnesota's Major Historic Sites*, 131–32; *Renville Star-Farmer*, October 13, 1955, p. 1; *Laws*, Ex 1937, p. 154–55.

77. *Laws*, Ex 1937, p. 154–55; DOC, *Fourth Biennial Report*, 253; Martin for Fiero to Tom and Amy Reinertson, March 29, 1950, carbon, Joseph R. Brown File, DNR Files; *Renville Star-Farmer*, October 13, 1955, p. 1; Holmquist and Brookins, *Minnesota's Major Historic Sites*, 132.

78. "1977 Legislative Report," *Minnesota History News* 18 (June 1977): 1.

79. DOC, *Fourth Biennial Report*, 185; *United States Statutes at Large* 49:1583, 50:917–19.

80. DOC, *Third Biennial Report*, 251, *Fourth Biennial Report*, 185, 229–31; *Watson Voice*, June 8, 22, 1939, August 15, 1940 – all p. 1; *Madison Independent Press*, May 12, 1939, p. 1; *Laws*, 1939, p. 1084.

81. DNR, DPR, "Profile: Lac qui Parle State Park: Lac qui Parle County," March 31, 1972; Dave Vesall to Bernie Halver, July 8, 1964, carbon, Watson File, PRD, DOC Records; DOC, *Fifth Biennial Report*, 246, 251; *Laws*, 1957, p. 1016–17; 1959, p. 485–86.

82. DNR, *Lac qui Parle State Park: Summer Trails* (1987), copy of leaflet in author's possession.

83. DOC, *Second Biennial Report*, 108, 111.

84. Federal Writers' Project, *Minnesota*, 286; DOC, DSP, *State Park and Recreational Area Plan*, 97; *Laws*, 1957, p. 511–13.

85. DOC, DSP, *State Park and Recreational Area Plan*, 95.

86. DNR, Project 80 report, 124.

87. "Narrative Report, State Parks — Miscellaneous File, FFPD, DOC Records; *Laws*, 1957, p. 513; Waters, *Streams and Rivers*, 58. Information on Temperance River is singularly sparse. It is said to have been acquired in 1930 by the department of highways and opened to public use in 1934.

88. James Taylor Dunn, *State Parks of the St. Croix Valley: Wild, Scenic, and Recreational*, Minnesota State Park Heritage Series, no. 4 ([St. Paul?]: Minnesota Parks Foundation, 1981), 47–49; DOC, DSP, *State Park and Recreational Area Plan*, 103.

89. *United States Statutes at Large* 56:326–27; *Laws*, 1943, p. 404; DNR, Division of Parks, *A Guide to Minnesota's State Park and Recreation System* (St. Paul: DNR, n.d.) 6, 10 (copy in author's possession).

90. DOC, *Seventh Biennial Report*, 239–40; Lathrop to Fiero, August 26, 1946, MORRC File, PRD, DOC Records. Although the St. Croix Islands Recreation Area is not closely associated with St. Croix State Park, it perhaps should be mentioned here as one of the units of the system whose origins are obscure. Entirely undeveloped, it consists of five small islands with a total area of about 38 acres, in the St. Croix River a short distance above Stillwater. The islands had been forfeited to the state for nonpayment of taxes and were declared conservation lands by the county board and offered to the parks division about 1943. No specific legislation established this unit; in *Minnesota Statutes* the authority cited is the 1935 law establishing the DSP and granting the director the power of acquiring land for park purposes. Valuable as a wildlife habitat, the St. Croix Islands are used only as a place for canoeists to land and rest on their way down river. They are at present leased to the federal government as part of the St. Croix National Scenic Riverway and are no longer listed as a unit of the state park system.

91. *Legislative Manual*, 1937, p. 492–93.

92. DOC, *Second Biennial Report*, 110–11, *Third Biennial Report*, 236, *Fifth Biennial Report*, 215, *Seventh Biennial Report*, 232–33. Conzet listed thirty-three

units in his 1933/34 report. This figure, however, included Camden, Gooseberry Falls, Cascade River, and St. Croix, and it omitted Garvin Heights. The figure for 1940 is taken from Lathrop's 1939/40 report and does not include Cascade River, St. Croix, or the so-called Chippewa Mission Wayside. If these are included and Temperance River added, there were fifty-one units in 1940.

93. DOC, *Fourth Biennial Report*, 221, *Fifth Biennial Report*, 234, 237; DOC, DSP, *State Park and Recreational Area Plan*, 135.

94. *Laws*, 1937, p. 548–50; 1939, p. 511; DOC, *Fifth Biennial Report*, 255.

95. DOC, DSP, *State Park and Recreational Area Plan*, 128, 137. The report specified areas where land should be acquired (see p. 125, 126, 128). Some of them (such as Lac qui Parle) were soon to be obtained, while others eventually became units of the system. Among those to be mentioned later in this account were Nerstrand Woods (a high-priority item), Frontenac, Mille Lacs Lake, two or three parks in the southern tier of counties, one in the Wright County area, another along the Minnesota River, and, for its historical value, the Ignatius Donnelly homesite near Hastings, which was never acquired. The Cascade River and St. Croix areas should, said the report, be transferred to the parks division as soon as possible.

96. DOC, DSP, *State Park and Recreational Area Plan*, 51, 56, 120, 146.

97. DOC, DSP, *State Park and Recreational Area Plan*, 121, 145–46.

98. DOC, DSP, *State Park and Recreational Area Plan*, 146–50, 152.

99. DOC, *Second Biennial Report*, 23.

100. DOC, DSP, *State Park and Recreational Area Plan*, 60.

## Chapter 6. *Years of Slow Growth: 1942–1952*

1. DOC, *Seventh Biennial Report*, 230.

2. DOC, *Seventh Biennial Report*, 229–30.

3. *Legislative Manual*, 1941, p. 510; 1947, p. 472.

4. *Legislative Manual*, 1947, p. 473.

5. DOC, *Ninth Biennial Report: 1947–48*, Section 5, *Division of State Parks* (hereafter *Ninth Biennial Report*), 8, 12; Harold W. Lathrop to Lew E. Fiero, August 26, 1946, MORRC File, PRD, DOC Records.

6. DOC, *Eighth Biennial Report*, 290, *Ninth Biennial Report*, 10, *Tenth Biennial Report: 1949–50*, Section 5, *Division of State Parks* (hereafter *Tenth Biennial Report*), 33.

7. DOC, *Ninth Biennial Report*, 29.

8. Chase, *Statement*, 63; Harry T. Bergman to Guy W. Cravens (deputy commissioner), January 25, Cravens to Bergman, January 31, carbon — both 1938 and in Father Hennepin File, PRD, DOC Records; *Laws*, 1941, p. 985; *Mille Lacs Messenger* (Isle), May 1, 1941, p. 1; John H. Martin for Udert W. Hella to John A. Humphrey, August 2, 1960, carbon, Father Hennepin File, DNR Files.

9. *House Journal*, 1941, p. 960, 1374.

10. *Laws*, 1955, p. 1034; 1961, p. 1599; 1963, p. 1355; 1965, p. 1277; 1967, p. 1612; 1971, p. 1698; DNR, *A Management Plan for Father Hennepin State Park* (St. Paul: DNR, 1978), 7.

11. *Laws*, 1941, p. 986; *Mille Lacs Messenger*, May 15, 1941, p. 1; Lathrop to Fiero, August 26, 1946, MORRC File, PRD, DOC Records; DOC, *Ninth Biennial Report*, 49.

12. DNR, *Management Plan: Father Hennepin*, 6, 7, 17, 62. The apparent in-

crease in visitor-days is probably due in part to more sophisticated methods of counting visitors by 1975.

13. *Northfield News*, March 8, p. 4, April 12, p. 1 — both 1935; *Kenyon News*, October 24, 1934, p. 1; Kenyon Junior Chamber of Commerce to Conservation Commission, September 11, 1934, "Portion of minutes of meeting of Conservation Commission . . . September 13 and 14, 1934," "A portion of the minutes of the meeting of the Conservation Commission . . . October 11 and 12, 1934," Lathrop to L. P. Zimmerman, January 16, 1935, carbon — all in Nerstrand Big Woods File, DNR Files; Ken Morrison, "A Report on Nerstrand Woods: Acquisition is Nearly Completed," *Conservation Volunteer* 5 (March 1943): 30.

14. [Hilman H. Mielke] to L. P. Zimmerman, October 13, 1934, carbon, R. J. Wolfangle (SERA), to S. L. Stolte (SERA), February 18, 25, March 11, May 28, 1935, carbons, Lathrop to Zimmerman (SERA), March 7, 1935, carbon, Norman Knutson (Kenyon Junior Chamber of Commerce) to Lathrop, April 26, 1935 — all in Nerstrand Big Woods File, DNR Files.

15. Lathrop to Weicht, April 19, 1938, carbon, Weicht to Lathrop, May 7, 1938, Weicht to H[erman] C. Wenzel, April 6, 1938 — all in Nerstrand Big Woods File, DNR Files.

16. Elmer A. Benson to Lathrop, October 25, 1938, Wenzel to E. T. Tufte, November 1, 1938, carbon, Wenzel to Webster Lumber Company, St. Paul, December 6, 1938, carbon, Paul D. Webster to Wenzel, December 10, 1938, L[aurence] M. Gould to Lathrop, April 21, 1939, March 15, 1940 — all in Nerstrand Big Woods File, DNR Files; *House Journal*, 1939, p. 540, 696, 1239; 1941, p. 244, 956, 1829–30; *Senate Journal*, 1939, p. 401; 1941, p. 179; *Northfield News*, April 6, 1939, p. 1.

17. *Legislative Manual*, 1939, p. 29; Morrison, "Nerstrand Woods," 29–30. The constitutional amendment, adopted November 8, 1938, provided for a Land Exchange Commission, consisting of the governor, the attorney general, and the auditor.

18. DOC, *Seventh Biennial Report*, 259, *Tenth Biennial Report*, 26; Harold W. Lathrop, "Our Newest State Parks: Baptism River Is Spectacular Addition," *Conservation Volunteer* 9 (July–August 1946): 32.

19. *Senate Journal*, 1945, p. 165, 321; *House Journal*, 1945, p. 346, 900–901; *Laws*, 1945, p. 234–35; *Northfield News*, February 8, March 1, April 12, 1945 — all p. 1.

20. Lathrop to Fiero, August 26, 1946, MORRC File, PRD, DOC Records; Lathrop, "Our Newest State Parks," 32; DOC, DSP, *State Parks of Minnesota*, 30; DOC, *Tenth Biennial Report*, 26; *Laws*, 1955, p. 1033; DOC, DPR, "Profile: Nerstrand Woods State Park — Rice County," April 16, 1968, Nerstrand Big Woods File, DNR Files.

21. *Laws*, 1971, p. 1698; DNR, DPR, "Profile: Nerstrand Woods State Park: Rice County," January 11, 1974, "Nerstrand Woods State Park — Environmental Assessment" [1976–77] — both in Nerstrand Big Woods File, DNR Files.

22. "Profile: Nerstrand Woods State Park," April 16, 1968, Jim Bloemendal for Hella to Mr. and Mrs. Michael Kolling, March 20, 1973, carbon — both in Nerstrand Big Woods File, DNR Files. The Kollings had written to "Mr. Ledein" (Donald Ledin) late in 1972, complaining of the snowmobile regulations.

23. C[larence] R. Magney, "Saved from Private Ownership: Our Newest State Park — Baptism River," Harold W. Lathrop, "And Who Saved Baptism River State Park? It Was Associate Justice C. R. Magney" — both in *Bulletin* (Izaak Walton

League of America, Minnesota Division), Third Quarter 1945, p. 5, 6; *House Journal*, 1945, p. 207; Morgan, "Our Citizens and State Parks," 29–31.

24. *House Journal*, 1945, p. 517; *Senate Journal*, 1945, p. 1111; *Laws*, 1945, p. 436–37; Lathrop, "Our Newest State Parks," 31.

25. Lathrop, "Our Newest State Parks," 31; *Laws*, 1969, p. 1637; 1979, p. 664; DNR, DPR, "Profile: Baptism River State Park: Lake County," June 20, 1975, Baptism River File, DNR Files. Pigeon Falls, shared with Canada, is the highest.

26. *Laws*, 1945, p. 436–37; 1967, p. 1609–10; "Split Rock Lighthouse State Park: Chronology of Split Rock Coast Guard Light Station," April 27, 1971, and DNR, DPR, "Profile: Split Rock Lighthouse State Park: Lake County," August 31, 1979 – both in Split Rock Lighthouse File, DNR Files.

27. Glenn Sandvik, "A Brief History of the Split Rock Lighthouse," Split Rock Lighthouse File, DNR Files. Sandvik also wrote a pamphlet that was described as part of a longer manuscript on the Split Rock complex; see *A Superior Beacon: A Brief History of Split Rock Lighthouse* ([Two Harbors, Minn.: The Author, 1972]; copies in Split Rock Lighthouse File, DNR Files, and MHS Reference Library). See also *Duluth Herald*, March 1, 1967, p. 2; *St. Paul Pioneer Press*, January 7, 1969, p. 1.

28. Resolution of the Lake County Board of Commissioners, February 10, 1969, Clifford M. Harding to Harold LeVander, December 20, 1969, photocopy, Hella to Jarle B. Leirfallom, January 9, 1970, carbon, LeVander to Jeffrey P. Hillelson (General Services Administration), January 19, 1970, photocopy, "Split Rock Lighthouse: Chronology," Sandvik, "Brief History," Architectural Resources, Inc., Duluth, *A Master Plan for Split Rock Lighthouse Historic Site* – all in Split Rock Lighthouse File, DNR Files; *Duluth News-Tribune*, May 2, 1971, p. 1; R. Newell Searle, *State Parks of the North Shore*, Minnesota State Park Heritage Series, no. 3 ([St. Paul?]: Minnesota Parks Foundation, 1979): 37–38; DNR, *Split Rock Lighthouse State Park: Summer Trails* (1989), copy of leaflet in author's possession; *Laws*, 1976, p. 253–54.

29. "New Recreation Facilities for North-Shore Park," *Minnesota Volunteer* 47 (July–August 1984): 62; *Newsletter* (Minnesota Council of Parks), May, p. 4, September, p. 1 – both 1984.

30. *Senate Journal*, 1945, p. 211, 884; *House Journal*, 1945, p. 996, 1530; *Laws*, 1945, p. 907–8.

31. *Cottonwood County Citizen* (Windom), January 24, 1945, p. 1.

32. DNR, *Kilen Woods State Park Management Plan* (draft; St. Paul: DNR, 1980), 113–14; DNR, *A Management Plan for Kilen Woods State Park* (St. Paul: DNR, 1980), 73, 91–94; Lathrop to Fiero, August 26, 1946, Interstate File, PRD, DOC Records; *Laws*, 1951, p. 798–99; 1955, p. 1034; *Cottonwood County Citizen*, April 7, 1948, p. 1; *Lakefield Standard*, April 22, 1948, p. 1, January 6, 1949, p. 1, 3.

33. DNR, *Management Plan: Kilen Woods*, 73.

34. DNR, *Kilen Woods Management Plan*, 40, 114.

35. Friendly Garden Club to Robert L. Herbst, April 13, 1977, Kilen Woods File, DNR Files; DNR, *Kilen Woods Management Plan*, 112, 117.

36. DNR, *Kilen Woods Management Plan*, 117–19.

37. DNR, *Kilen Woods Management Plan*, 120–22, 129–30; *Jackson County Pilot* (Jackson), April 23, 1980, p. 1, 8; Rosenow to files, April 28, 1980, photocopy, Kilen Woods File, DNR Files.

38. Howard F. Krosch to Mark Bezdicek, photocopy received on August 13, 1980, Kilen Woods File, DNR Files.

39. Lowell Jaeger, "Annual Report for Kilen Woods State Park: 1977," February 28, 1978, Kilen Woods File, DNR Files.

40. *Laws*, 1945, p. 915–16; Leona Train Rienow, "Something to Remember Us By," *Nature Magazine* (American Nature Association) 38 (December 1945): 538; *St. Louis County Independent* (Hibbing), January 8, 1943, p. 1; *Hibbing Tribune*, January 5, 1943, p. 1; *Hibbing City Directory . . . 1940–1941*, p. 208.

41. Rienow, "Something to Remember Us By," 538; *Senate Journal*, 1945, p. 605, 1378; *House Journal*, 1945, p. 1587, 1639; *Laws*, 1945, p. 915–16; DOC, *Eighth Biennial Report*, 296.

42. "Statement," n.d. (1951?), McCarthy Beach File, DNR Files; DOC, *Ninth Biennial Report*, 49.

43. "McCarthy's Beach State Park," September 19, 1950, "Statement," July 12, 1950, "Statement" (1951?) — all in McCarthy Beach File, DNR Files; *Hibbing Tribune*, July 14, 1962, p. 3.

44. *Laws*, Ex 1961, p. 1900; 1969, p. 1639; 1971, p. 320–21; 1977, p. 1144; DNR, DPR, "Profile: McCarthy Beach State Park: St. Louis County," May 17, 1972, "Profile: McCarthy Beach State Park: St. Louis County," July 5, 1977, Peg McCabe to Hubert [H.] Humphrey, May 10, 1977, photocopy, Michael C. O'Donnell to Humphrey, June 14, 1977, carbon — all in McCarthy Beach File, DNR Files.

45. "Profile: McCarthy Beach State Park," July 5, 1977, McCarthy Beach File, DNR Files.

46. Folwell, *Minnesota* 1:109–11; Holmquist et al., *History Along the Highways*, 10–11; *Senate Journal*, 1945, p. 138, 859, 934; *House Journal*, 1945, p. 1507; *Laws*, 1945, p. 1007–8.

47. "125th Anniversary: Count Giacomo Constantino Beltrami: Memorial Dedication: Program," August 22, 1948, Joe Ludwig to Donald D. Davison, November 19, 1974, photocopy, miscellaneous lease, December 11, 1974 — all in Count Beltrami File, DNR Files; *Laws*, 1976, p. 178.

48. *Senate Journal*, 1947, p. 84, 240; *House Journal*, 1947, p. 94, 352–53; *Laws*, 1947, p. 29; *Blackduck American*, January 30, February 20, 27, 1947 — all p. 1; "Pine Tree State Wayside — Beltrami," n.d., Pine Tree File, PRD, DOC Records.

49. *Laws*, 1963, p. 1357; 1965, p. 1280; "Pine Tree State Wayside," Pine Tree File, PRD, DOC Records.

50. *House Journal*, 1947, p. 249, 738–39; *Senate Journal*, 1947, p. 364; *Laws*, 1947, p. 325–26; 1969, p. 909–10; MORRC report, 26, 52; Upham, *Minnesota Geographic Names*, 144; Federal Writers' Project, *Minnesota*, 285.

51. Harold W. Lathrop, "New Park on the St. Croix Is Gift of Miss Alice O'Brien," *Conservation Volunteer* 9 (May–June 1946): 43–44; *St. Paul Pioneer Press*, November 4, 1945, sec. 2, p. 1.

52. Lathrop, "New Park on the St. Croix," 43–44; *Laws*, 1947, p. 431–32; *House Journal*, 1947, p. 827, 1331; *Senate Journal*, 1947, p. 1318.

53. "History of Wm O'Brien State Park: Land Acquisition," n.d., Elmer L. Andersen to Greenberg, June 19, 1961, photocopy, Samuel H. Morgan to Herbst, Hella, Milton E. Krona et al., January 21, 1973, photocopy, Donald M. Carlson to Herbst, July 8, 1976, photocopy, Davison to James Taplin, July 19, 1976, Bill [William] Weir to Davison, November 1, 1976, Davison to Wayland K. Porter, November 5, 1976 — all in William O'Brien File, DNR Files; *Laws*, 1955, p. 1033–34; Ex 1959, p. 1929; 1963, p. 1357; 1973, p. 1072–73; 1986, p. 708; *St. Paul Dispatch*, July 29, 1958, p. 17.

54. Jim Ettema, "William O'Brien State Park," July 9, 1970, Jerry Sullivan to Bill [William] Weir, February 26, 1979 — both in William O'Brien File, DNR Files.

55. Martin to Conservation Commissioner [Chester S. Wilson], January 24, 1947, carbon, Myre–Big Island File, DNR Files.

56. Martin to Wilson, January 24, 1947, Fiero to Helen E. Jensen, April 19, 1948, carbon — both in Myre–Big Island File, DNR Files; *Senate Journal*, 1947, p. 457, 1535–36; *House Journal*, 1947, p. 526; *Laws*, 1947, p. 623–24. The bill did not pass entirely without difficulty. Later, Representative Talle told the Albert Lea Lions Club of the senate finance committee's effort to cut the appropriation to $8,000. Senator Myre "did some fast talking" and restored the original figure. See *Albert Lea Tribune*, May 2, 1947, p. 7.

57. *Albert Lea Tribune*, July 2, 10, 1947 — both p. 1; "Articles of Association of Big Island State Park Founders Association of Albert Lea, Minnesota," July 1947, Martin for Fiero to Gladys Bruno, August 2, 1950, carbon, Irvin M. Talle et al. to Wilson, January 5, 1952 (dated 1951), carbon — all in Myre–Big Island File, DNR Files; DOC, *Tenth Biennial Report*, 23; *Laws*, 1953, p. 17–18.

58. *Albert Lea Tribune*, January 11, 1963, p. 7; *Laws*, 1963, p. 1356; Ex 1967, p. 2309; MORRC report, 43.

59. Mr. and Mrs. Lloyd Mellang to Herbst, November 9, 1974, Davison to Herbst, November 20, 1974 — both in Myre–Big Island File, DNR Files.

60. Davison to Carol Thompson, November 26, 1974, carbon, Davison to Herbst, November 20, 1974, Robert E. Hansen to Davison, June 25, 1975 — all in Myre–Big Island File, DNR Files; *Laws*, 1975, p. 1367.

61. Al Spranger to File, July 23, 1975, photocopy, Davison to Files, August 1, 1975, photocopy, Davison to Files, October 30, 1975, carbon, "Proposed News Release: Helmer Myre State Park," April 9, 1976 (marked "Not Released"), Wayland K. Porter to Davison, May 6, 1976, Morgan to Herbst, May 7, 1976, photocopy, Davison to C. Paul Faraci, July 16, 1976, carbon, Davison to Files, July 29, 1976, Davison to Faraci, August 4, 11, 1976, carbons, Davison to Files, August 31, 1976, Donald J. Paquette to Herbst, November 22, 1976, Davison to Gene Gere, December 17, 1976, carbon — all in Myre–Big Island File, DNR Files.

62. *Minneapolis Tribune*, June 5, 1978, p. 2B; DNR, *A Management Plan for Helmer Myre State Park* (St. Paul: DNR, 1980), 76, 83; "Bequest to the State of Minnesota for Helmer Myre State Park" from Owen Johnson, July 31, 1972, Myre–Big Island File, DNR Files.

63. *Plainview News*, December 2, 1948, January 13, 1949, March 22, 1962, May 14, September 24, 1964, March 25, 1965 — all p. 1, May 27, 1965, p. 7; *House Journal*, 1949, p. 1175, 1460–61; *Senate Journal*, 1949, p. 1013, 1477; *Laws*, 1949, p. 571–72; DOC, *Tenth Biennial Report*, 24; DOC, DPR, "Profile: Carley State Park — Wabasha County," June 6, 1968, Carley File, DNR Files.

64. *Laws*, 1951, p. 277–78; 1969, p. 1639; *St. Paul Pioneer Press*, October 25, 1959, sec. 2, p. 6; Fiero to William Gitts, August 12, 1952, carbon, Ray Berglund File, DNR Files.

## Chapter 7. *A Time of Change: 1953–1962*

1. Chase, *Statement*, 76; *Laws*, 1923, p. 643.

2. *Laws*, 1933, p. 664; 1937, p. 648–49; DOC, *Fifth Biennial Report*, 256.

3. *Laws*, 1953, p. 552–53; 1959, p. 40.

4. *Laws*, Ex 1961, p. 1598, 1601. Previously the short-term stickers were sold in lots of twenty-five or more, mainly to organized groups using a park for special

occasions. *Laws*, 1969, p. 1760; 1976, p. 1380, 1388; 1981, p. 1940–41; 1985, p. 2218–19; 1987, p. 1184.

5. "New Director for State Parks," *Conservation Volunteer* 16 (March–April 1953): 21–22; U[dert] W. Hella, *Quest for Excellence: A History of the Minnesota Council of Parks, 1954 to 1974* ([St. Paul]: Minnesota Parks Foundation, 1985), 41–42; DOC, DSP, *Minnesota Park, Parkway and Recreational Area Study* (1938), copy in MHS Reference Library.

6. *Duluth News-Tribune*, April 25, 1954, p. 1; Crosby to Burnquist, January 11, 1954, John Fritzen to Chester S. Wilson, January 22, 1954 — both in George H. Crosby Manitou File, DNR Files; *Senate Journal*, 1955, p. 221–22, 328; *House Journal*, 1955, p. 851; *Laws*, 1955, p. 213–15.

7. March 28, 1971, p. H5, Ron Schara, "4,700 wild acres for backpackers," August 5, 1973, p. 1F, 4F — both *Minneapolis Tribune*.

8. Searle, *State Parks of the North Shore*, 39–40.

9. Kenneth E. Lunzer to Ms. [Ruth] Husom, September 30, 1975, George H. Crosby Manitou File, DNR Files.

10. *House Journal*, 1957, p. 153, 1539; *Senate Journal*, 1957, p. 1790–91, 1985; *Laws*, 1957, p. 726; *Cook County News-Herald* (Grand Marais), April 4, 1957, p. 1.

11. Searle, *North Shore*, 44–45.

12. *Cook County News-Herald*, April 4, 1957, p. 1; resolution by Minnesota Council of State Parks on death of C. R. Magney, n.d., Correspondence: Minnesota Council of State Parks File, PRD, DOC Records; *Laws*, 1963, p. 356; *Duluth News-Tribune*, September 28, 1964, p. 6.

13. MORRC report, 49; *Laws*, 1965, p. 1280; DNR, DPR, "Profile: Judge C. R. Magney State Park: Cook County," July 15, 1980, Judge C. R. Magney File, DNR Files.

14. *Onamia Independent*, November 3, 1960, p. 1; *N. W. Ayer & Son's Directory: Newspapers and Periodicals 1956* (Philadelphia: N. W. Ayer & Son, 1956), 521; *Mille Lacs County Times* (Milaca), April 4, p. 1, May 30, p. 5 — both 1957; *House Journal*, 1957, p. 657, 1722, 1810–11; *Senate Journal*, 1957, p. 1939; *Laws*, 1957, p. 876–77.

15. *Laws*, 1957, p. 876; *Mille Lacs County Times*, April 4, p. 1., October 10, p. 3 — both 1957; John H. Martin, "Mille Lacs Kathio State Park," *Conservation Volunteer* 21 (November–December 1957): 29.

16. Fridley to Udert W. Hella, March 4, 1957, Mille Lacs Kathio File, DNR Files; Holmquist and Brookins, *Minnesota's Major Historic Sites*, 63–67.

17. Holmquist and Brookins, *Minnesota's Major Historic Sites*, 66; Johnson to Hella, July 8, 1965, April 9, 1973 — both in Mille Lacs Kathio File, DNR Files.

18. Merle DeBoer to Donald D. Davison, August 20, 1973, photocopy, Milton E. Krona to Robert L. Herbst, November 7, 1973, carbon — both in Mille Lacs Kathio File, DNR Files; DNR, *Mille Lacs Kathio: Summer Trails* (1988), leaflet in author's possession.

19. Holmquist and Brookins, *Minnesota's Major Historic Sites*, 91–93.

20. "Calendar of Principal Events Leading to the Establishment of Proposed Frontenac State Park" (January 18, 1957?), John S. McLaughlin (NPS) to Hella, May 25, 1954 — both in Frontenac File, DNR Files; Harold W. Lathrop to C. A. Rasmussen, January 29, 1935, carbon, Hayes A. Redmond to Lathrop, January 29, 1935, Ordner T. Bundlie to Harry M. Peterson, January 22, 1936, carbon, Victor Christgau to August H. Andresen, March 16, 1936, carbon, Lathrop to J. F. Gould, June 7, 1935 — all in Frontenac File, PRD, DOC Records.

21. Wilson to Nell Mabey, June 3, 1953, carbon, Wilson to C. Elmer Anderson, May 12, 1954, carbon — both in Frontenac File, PRD, DOC Records; Marshall, "Frontenac State Park," *Minnesota Naturalist* 7 (March 1956): 14–15; *Republican Eagle*, January 7, 20, 1954 — both p. 1; *Winona Republican-Herald*, May 5, 1954, p. 5, 9.

22. *Lake City Graphic*, July 8, 1954, p. 4, January 20, February 3, 1955 — both p. 1; Marshall, "Frontenac State Park," 15; *House Journal*, 1955, p. 136; *Senate Journal*, 1955, p. 96.

23. Marshall, "Frontenac State Park," 15; Hella to George A. Selke, November 30, 1955, Frontenac File, PRD, DOC Records.

24. *Lake City Graphic*, November 17, December 15, 1955 — both p. 1; *Republican Eagle*, November 17, 1955, p. 1; Marshall, "Frontenac State Park," 15.

25. *Republican Eagle*, May 24, 1956, p. 1; *Lake City Graphic*, May 24, November 15, 1956 — both p. 1.

26. *Lake City Graphic*, January 24, 31, February 21, 1957 — all p. 1; *Senate Journal*, 1957, p. 247; *House Journal*, 1957, p. 418; E[dward] S. Hall to Hella, April 8, 1957, Frontenac File, PRD, DOC Records.

27. *Lake City Graphic*, February 21, 1957, p. 1; Hall to Hella, April 8, 1957, Frontenac File, PRD, DOC Records.

28. *Senate Journal*, 1957, p. 756–57, 1062, 1159–60; *House Journal*, 1957, p. 1442, 2463–66, 2500; *Lake City Graphic*, May 2, 1957, p. 1.

29. *Laws*, 1957, p. 1066–68; 1961, p. 922–23; "Explanation of Frontenac State Park Bill: House File No. 1786, Senate File No. 1481," Frontenac File, DNR Files.

30. Martin, "Frontenac Land Negotiation: Randall Tract," n.d., "Frontenac State Park (a report on land acquisition to date)," January 10, 1962 — both in Frontenac File, DNR Files; *Senate Journal*, 1961, p. 885, 1981; *House Journal*, 1961, p. 1163; *Laws*, 1961, p. 919–23.

31. *Minneapolis Tribune*, January 14, 1966, p. 5; *Republican Eagle*, November 23, 1965, p. 4.

32. *Laws*, 1965, p. 1278; 1969, p. 1638–39; 1971, p. 1694; 1986, p. 707; *Rochester Post-Bulletin*, July 23, 1971, p. 12; DNR, *Management Plan Summary (Draft): Frontenac State Park* (St. Paul: DNR, 1977).

33. DNR, *Management Plan Summary: Frontenac;* DNR, Project 80 report, 149.

34. *House Journal*, 1959, p. 312, 400; *Senate Journal*, 1959, p. 285, 392; *Laws*, 1959, p. 90–91; 1961, p. 1601; MORRC (revised by DSP), "Profile: Zippel Bay Recreation Reserve: Lake of the Woods County," July 7, 1966, Zippel Bay File, DNR Files.

35. MORRC, "Profile: Zippel Bay Recreation Reserve"; DNR, *Zippel Bay State Park: Summer Trails* (1987), copy of leaflet in author's possession.

36. *Cass County Independent* (Walker), June 26, 1964, p. 1; *Laws*, 1959, p. 139–40; *House Journal*, 1959, p. 413, 733–34; *Senate Journal*, 1959, p. 330, 465, 545.

37. MORRC (revised by DSP), "Profile: Schoolcraft State Recreation Area — Cass County," July 7, 1966, Schoolcraft File, DNR Files; *Cass County Independent*, June 26, 1964, p. 1; *Grand Rapids Review*, June 24, 1976, p. 1.

38. DNR, *Schoolcraft State Park* (1990), copy of leaflet in author's possession.

39. *Minneapolis Star*, August 19, 1957, p. 11A, July 10, 1959, p. 23; Holmquist and Brookins, *Minnesota's Major Historic Sites*, 71.

40. *Laws*, 1959, p. 1929–30; *Minneapolis Star*, July 10, 1959, p. 23; Hella to Selke, October 15, 1957, carbon, John A. Humphrey to Hella, October 22, 1959 — both in Crow Wing File, PRD, DOC Records.

41. *St. Paul Pioneer Press*, April 29, 1960, p. 5.

42. Hella to Milton Knoll, July 5, 1962, carbon, Ken Sander to Hella, February 11, 1969, photocopy — both in Crow Wing File, DNR Files; Holmquist and Brookins, *Minnesota's Major Historic Sites*, 71.

43. *Newsletter* (American Civil Liberties Union, Minnesota Branch), July 1960, p. 1–2; *Minneapolis Star*, July 10, 1959, p. 2B; Gaston D. Cogdell to Harold LeVander, August 2, 1968, LeVander to Cogdell, October 18, 1968, carbon, Thomas J. Ryan, to Director, Parks and Recreation Division, November 10, 1977, Davison to Ryan, December 2, 1977, carbon — all in Crow Wing File, DNR Files.

44. *Laws*, 1963, p. 1355; 1965, p. 1277; 1971, p. 1694; "Environmental Assessment: Crow Wing State Park," received on November 1, 1975 or 1976, John Sauers to Curt Bernd, November 4, 1971, photocopy — both in Crow Wing File, DNR Files.

45. DNR, Project 80 report, 124, 150.

46. Holmquist and Brookins, *Minnesota's Major Historic Sites*, 158–63; *Senate Journal*, 1961, p. 50, 918; *House Journal*, 1961, p. 88, 1076, 1470; *Laws*, 1961, p. 372; *Aitkin Independent Age*, April 13, 1961, p. 1.

47. *Aitkin Independent Age*, August 10, 1961, p. 12; *Owatonna People's Press*, May 1, 1963, p. 1; Warren Johnson and Hazel A. Sorensen to Hella, September 27, 1967, Hella to Johnson, October 4, 1967, carbon, *News from the Minnesota Department of Conservation* (news release), September 21, 1967, "Environmental Assessment: Savanna Portage State Park" (1976–77) — all in Savanna Portage File, DNR Files; DNR, *Savanna Portage State Park: Summer Trails* (1989), copy of leaflet in author's possession.

48. Lawson to Hella, December 14, 1959, Selke to Hella, September 3, 1959, Zaffke to Mr. [John H.] Martin, August 15, 1960, Hella to Zaffke, September 8, 1960, carbon — all in Bear Head Lake File, PRD, DOC Records.

49. *House Journal*, 1961, p. 266, 501, 1508–9; *Senate Journal*, 1961, p. 225, 392, 1212; *Laws*, 1961, p. 591–92; *Ely Miner*, February 16, 1961, p. 1.

50. DNR, DPR, "Profile: Bear Head Lake State Park: St. Louis County," July 5, 1977, Hella to Ted Wynn, May 14, 1962, carbon, Wynn to Hella, May 11, 1962 — all in Bear Head Lake File, DNR Files; *Ely Miner*, October 26, 1961, p. 1; *St. Paul Pioneer Press*, October 29, 1961, *Sunday Pictorial Magazine*, 7.

51. *Laws*, 1963, p. 1354.

52. Holmquist and Brookins, *Minnesota's Major Historic Sites*, 1–8; Robert P. Patterson (U.S. secretary of war) to Omar N. Bradley (Veterans Administration), May 17, 1946, "copy," Commanding General (HQ, Fifth Army, Chicago) to Commanding Officer (Fort Snelling), September 27, 1946, telegram — both in Fort Snelling File, DNR Files.

53. Marilyn Ziebarth and Alan Ominsky, *Fort Snelling: Anchor Post of the Northwest*, Minnesota Historical Sites Pamphlet Series, no. 4 (St. Paul: MHS, 1970), 31–33; DNR, *A Management Plan for Fort Snelling State Park* (draft; St. Paul: DNR, 1978), 24–25; Holmquist and Brookins, *Minnesota's Major Historic Sites*, 6–7.

54. Ben [H. Thompson] (NPS) to Hella, February 29, 1956, photocopy, Fort Snelling File, DNR Files; Ziebarth and Ominsky, *Fort Snelling*, 33–34; DNR, *Management Plan: Fort Snelling*, 25.

55. Nichols to Hella, April 29, 1960, carbon, Fort Snelling File, DNR Files.

56. Floyd J. Maynard to Department of Conservation, October 11, 1960, Fort Snelling File, DNR Files; DNR, *Management Plan: Fort Snelling*, 25–26; *St. Paul Dispatch*, January 19, 1961, p. 17.

57. *Senate Journal*, 1961, p. 132, 1013, 1628–29, 2015; *House Journal*, 1961, p. 158, 1896, 2138–39; *Laws*, 1961, p. 1027; *St. Paul Dispatch*, January 25, 1961, p. 13.

58. *South St. Paul Reporter*, June 1, 1962, p. 9; *St. Paul Pioneer Press*, October 18, 1964, p. 11; *Round Tower* (newsletter, Fort Snelling State Park Association), July 15, 1965.

59. Raymond D. Black and Samuel H. Morgan to Hubert H. Humphrey (vice president), Orville L. Freeman (secretary of agriculture), and Minnesota congressional delegation, December 12, 1967, enclosing "Summary Data and Plans Pertinent to Historic Monument Status of Federal Surplus Land within Fort Snelling State Historic Park, Minnesota," "Minutes of directors' meeting, Fort Snelling State Park Association," December 14, 1967, Hella to Richard B. Dunsworth, January 22, 1969, carbon — all in Fort Snelling File, DNR Files; *St. Paul Dispatch*, March 6, 1971, p. 8, 17. It had been hoped that the 141.39-acre tract could be acquired without cost, as the original 320 acres were, but some question arose over its historical significance. The GSA decided that it had to be classified as a recreational area and purchased by the state at 50 percent of its appraised value. The issue dragged on through the remainder of the Johnson administration and into the Nixon administration, complicated by the change of top personnel at the GSA.

60. Walfred Boberg to Hella, October 7, 1971, "Fort Snelling State Park Memorial Chapel," December 16, 1971 — both in Fort Snelling File, DNR Files.

61. "Minutes of directors meeting, Fort Snelling State Park Association," January 16, 1969, Harold H. Raak (park planner), "Biennial Compliance Report," February 7, 1974 — both in Fort Snelling File, DNR Files; *Laws*, 1969, p. 1878–80.

62. *St. Paul Dispatch*, July 30, 1970, sec. 2, p. 1.

63. "Interpretive Plan for the Development and Operation of the Fort Snelling Nature Center on Pike Island," n.d., Howard Teague to Donald Carlson, July 8, 1975 — both in Fort Snelling File, DNR Files; *Minneapolis Star*, April 13, 1968, p. 5A.

64. *Ortonville Independent*, January 5, 1961, p. 1; Selke to Everett Holtz, February 11, 1957, carbon, Hella to Selke, October 4, 1957, C. J. Benson to Selke, September 12, 1960, carbon — all in Big Stone Lake File, PRD, DOC Records; B[ernard] A. Halver, "Big Stone Lake State Park: Big Stone County: Plan Narrative," n.d., Big Stone Lake File, DNR Files.

65. *Senate Journal*, 1961, p. 143, 1151–52; *House Journal*, 1961, p. 2208–9; *Laws*, 1961, p. 705–7.

66. MORRC report, 19, 20, 21; *Laws*, 1963, p. 1354.

67. *Laws*, 1965, p. 906; 1971, p. 1693; DNR, Division of Parks, *A Guide to Minnesota's State Park and Recreation System*, (St. Paul: DNR, [1981]), 4 (copy in author's possession).

68. Elden Johnson, "A Proposal for a Big Stone Lake Park Museum," accompanying Johnson to Hella, July 9, 1968, Johnson to Krona, October 29, 1971, carbon — both in Big Stone Lake File, DNR Files.

69. DNR, Project 80 report, 149–50.

70. *Senate Journal*, 1961, p. 62, 319, 736; *House Journal*, 1961, p. 101, 167–68; *Laws*, 1961, p. 97; *Cook County-News Herald*, February 2, p. 6, February 9, p. 1, May 18, p. 4 — all 1961. Introduced the same day were similar bills calling

for the establishment of Flood Bay State Wayside. The house bill passed that body but got no further in that session. Reintroduced in 1965, it is treated in Chapter 9.

71. Federal Writers' Project, *Minnesota*, 287; Waters, *Streams and Rivers*, 57; *Laws*, 1961, p. 97.

72. MORRC report, 29. The boundaries have been revised to exclude the forty acres in the southeast corner — the only part of the wayside touching U.S. 61. This tract included residences and the only cafe in the town of Schroeder, whose residents were able to have it deleted from the wayside in 1977. See Doris Lamb to Willard M. Munger, April 4, 1977, Davison to Lamb, May 2, 1977, photocopy — both in Cross River File, DNR Files; *Laws*, 1977, p. 1146.

73. *House Journal*, 1961, p. 209, 1929; *Senate Journal*, 1961, p. 192, 1688; *Laws*, 1961, p. 1601.

74. "Justification for a Devils Track Falls State Park," n.d., Devils Track Falls File, DNR Files; Waters, *Streams and Rivers*, 60–61.

75. *Cook County-News Herald*, May 18, 1961, p. 4; Jerry Bachman to Milt Stenlund, March 9, 1976, carbon, Devils Track Falls File, DNR Files.

76. *Ortonville Independent*, January 5, 1961, p. 1.

## Chapter 8. *The Omnibus Act: 1963*

1. "The History of Chapter 790, Minnesota Laws of 1963: The Omnibus Natural Resources and Recreation Act of 1963," p. 2–3, accompanying F. Robert Edman to Udert W. Hella, March 10, 1964 — both in MORRC File, PRD, DOC Records.

2. "History of Chapter 790," p. 1, 4, 6, MORRC File, PRD, DOC Records.

3. *Laws*, 1969, p. 1880–81.

4. *House Journal*, 1947, p. 426–27, 1794; *Senate Journal*, 1947, p. 390, 1530–31, 1918; *Laws*, 1947, p. 615.

5. *Laws*, 1947, p. 615; *Monticello Times*, May 1, 1947, p. 1.

6. *Senate Journal*, 1963, p. 193; *House Journal*, 1963, p. 190; *Laws*, 1963, p. 1352.

7. *Laws*, 1963, p. 1352, 1359.

8. DNR, DPR, "Profile: Lake Maria State Park: Wright County," January 11, 1974, Donald D. Davison to Steve Sokolik, September 6, 1974, carbon — both in Lake Maria File, DNR Files.

9. *Laws*, 1971, p. 1698.

10. Davison to Sokolik, September 6, 1974, Lake Maria File, DNR Files; DNR, *Management Plan Summary (Draft): Lake Maria State Park* (St. Paul: DNR, 1977).

11. Dorene H. Scriven to Davison, October 7, 1977, Lake Maria File, DNR Files; *Monticello Times*, October 6, 1977, p. 1; *Laws*, 1980, p. 404.

12. Roy W. Meyer, "Forestville: The Making of a State Park," *Minnesota History* 44 (Fall 1974): 86–87.

13. Meyer, "Forestville," 87.

14. Meyer, "Forestville," 88–89; Ostergaard, "Excerpt from Report to Conservation Commission," November 1934, Forestville Woods Area File, General Correspondence, Commissioner's Office, DOC Records; Hella to Mary E. Healy, October 10, 1956, Forestville File, DNR Files; DOC, DSP, *State Park and Recreational Area Plan*, 128.

15. Meyer, "Forestville," 89–90; Chester S. Wilson to John A. Johnson, April 25, 1947, John H. Martin for Lew E. Fiero to Wilson, January 12, 1949, carbon — both in Forestville File, DNR Files.

16. Meyer, "Forestville," 90; *Senate Journal*, 1963, p. 106, 887, 1498; *Laws*, 1949, p. 469–70.

17. Meyer, "Forestville," 90–91; *Senate Journal*, 1963, p. 180–81; *House Journal*, 1963, p. 365; *Laws*, 1963, p. 1350.

18. Meyer, "Forestville," 91; *Laws*, 1963, p. 1359; 1965, p. 1280–81; *Spring Valley Tribune*, September 15, 1966, sec. 2, p. 1.

19. Meyer, "Forestville," 92; R. C. Emery, "Pioneer Store is Sentry of the Past," *Austin Daily Herald*, April 6, 1935, magazine section, p. 8; Sander to Hella, Martin, and Milton E. Krona, March 8, 1967, carbon, Forestville File, DNR Files; Ruth Rogers, "A New Park Opens in Area," *Winona News*, May 12, 1968, p. 18A; *Laws*, 1977, p. 799.

20. Meyer, "Forestville," 92.

21. Meyer, "Forestville," 92; *Rochester Post-Bulletin*, April 4, 1968, p. 12; *Laws*, 1969, p. 1638.

22. Meyer, "Forestville," 93.

23. Meyer, "Forestville," 93.

24. DNR, Project 80 report, 124; Dwain W. Warner, "Summer Bird Life of Carimona Woods, Filmore County, Minnesota," *The Flicker* (Minnesota Ornithologists' Union) 22 (June 1950): 27–34.

25. Mark White, "Explore Minnesota's Mystery Cave," *Minnesota Volunteer* 52 (May–June 1989): 37–43; *Laws*, 1987, p. 3203–4.

26. *Starbuck Times*, May 17, 1962, p. 1; *Pope County Tribune* (Glenwood), May 17, 1962, p. 8; *Senate Journal*, 1963, p. 181; *House Journal*, 1963, p. 170.

27. *Starbuck Times*, May 17, 1962, p. 1; *Pope County Tribune*, August 24, 1961, p. 2, May 17, 1962, p. 8, September 20, December 20, 1962 – both sec. 2, p. 1.

28. *Pope County Tribune*, June 20, 1963, p. 1, 8. The Blue Mound in Rock County is a massive rock outcropping, whereas the "blue mounds" of Pope County are rolling hills, the rocks deeply buried under a layer of glacial till.

29. "Justification for a Bill Establishing Glacial Lakes State Park, in Pope County near Starbuck, Minnesota," n.d., Joseph R. Brown File, DNR Files; *Pope County Tribune*, February 7, sec. 2, p. 1, March 21, p. 1, May 23, p. 1 – all 1963; *Laws*, 1963, p. 1359; 1965, p. 1281, 1283; MORRC report, 39. That these conveniences were not all in place at that time is suggested by the fact that the map of Glacial Lakes shows the swimming beach in the wrong place, though other features are shown correctly.

30. DNR, Project 80 report, 124; DNR, DPR, "Profile: Glacial Lakes State Park: Pope County," September 26, 1979, Glacial Lakes File, DNR Files; *Laws*, 1987, p. 256, 258.

31. Folwell, *Minnesota* 1:353–54; MHS, *Upper Sioux Agency* (1978), *Lower Sioux Agency and Interpretive Center* (1972), copies of leaflets in author's possession. At the Lower Agency the walls of a new stone warehouse survived, to be subsequently transformed into a farmhouse. For many years historically minded people thought that the state should acquire it. Finally, in 1967, it was purchased by the MHS, which built an interpretive center nearby.

32. *Granite Falls Tribune*, October 11, 1962, p. 1, 8, December 20, 1962, p. 1; Carl Narvestad and Amy Narvestad, *A History of Yellow Medicine County, Minnesota: 1872–1972* (Granite Falls, Minn.: Yellow Medicine County Historical Society, 1972), 639.

33. *Granite Falls Tribune*, December 20, 1962, January 10, February 21,

March 21, May 2, 1963 — all p. 1; *Senate Journal*, 1963, p. 185; *House Journal*, 1963, p. 265; *Laws*, 1963, p. 1360; 1965, p. 1284.

34. MORRC report, 89.

35. *Laws*, 1969, p. 2080; 1971, p. 1695; *Granite Falls Tribune*, April 27, 1972, p. 1; DNR, DPR, "Profile: Upper Sioux Agency State Park: Yellow Medicine County," November 14, 1979, Upper Sioux Agency File, DNR Files.

36. MORRC report, 89; "Profile: Upper Sioux Agency State Park," Upper Sioux Agency File, DNR Files.

37. Krona to Maynard Nelson, February 25, 1977, photocopy, Nelson to Krona, April 6, 1977 — both in Upper Sioux Agency File, DNR Files.

38. "Justification for a bill establishing Sakatah Lake State Park in LeSueur [*sic*] and Rice counties near Waterville, Minnesota," n.d., Sakatah Lake File, DNR Files.

39. Waterville Commercial Club, *Planning the future . . . Sakatah State Park* (undated leaflet), Sakatah Lake File, DNR Files; *Waterville Advance*, May 17, 1962, p. 1.

40. *Waterville Advance*, December 20, 27, 1962, January 3, 24, May 23, 1963 — all p. 1; *Senate Journal*, 1963, p. 191; *House Journal*, 1963, p. 181.

41. *Waterville Advance*, May 23, 1963, February 4, May 27, 1965, May 9, November 21, 1968 — all p. 1; *Waseca Herald*, April 22, 1966, p. 1; *Laws*, 1963, p. 1360; 1965, p. 1282, 1284; 1967, p. 2287.

42. *Lake Region Life* (Waterville), July 19, 26, 1963, July 12, 1973, August 8, 1974 — all p. 1; *Free Press*, July 3, 1974, p. 9.

43. Jerry Bachman to Davison, March 11, 1977, carbon, "Environmental Assessment: Sakatah Lake State Park" (1976–77), Frank Knoke to Davison, September 3, 1976, photocopy — all in Sakatah Lake File, DNR Files; *Lake Region Life*, February 9, 1978, p. 1, April 20, 1979, p. 12; Minnesota, Department of Transportation, Office of Railroads and Waterways, "Railroad Abandonments in Minnesota," January 20, 1990, photocopy of computer printout in author's possession.

44. James W. Buchanan, *A Guide to Hiking and Cross-Country Skiing in the Pioneer Region*, vol. 5, *Minnesota Walk Book* (Minneapolis: Nodin Press, 1979), 47; *Laws*, 1965, p. 1277.

45. DNR, Project 80 report, 149.

46. "Justification for a bill to establish Little Elbow Lake State Park, Mahnomen County," n.d., Little Elbow Lake File, DNR Files.

47. *Senate Journal*, 1963, p. 200; *House Journal*, 1963, p. 222; *Laws*, 1963, p. 1359; 1965, p. 1284; "Justification . . . Little Elbow Lake State Park," Little Elbow Lake File, DNR Files.

48. DOC, DPR, "Profile: Little Elbow Lake State Park — Mahnomen County," May 16, 1968, Little Elbow Lake File, DNR Files; DNR, Project 80 report, 124; *Laws*, 1989, p. 876.

49. *Owatonna People's Press*, August 5, 1979, p. 1A–2A; *Claremont News*, December 21, 1962, January 25, 1963 — both p. 1.

50. *Owatonna People's Press*, August 5, 1979, p. 1A–2A; *Claremont News*, January 12, May 4, October 5, November 30, December 7, 14, 21, 1962 — all p. 1.

51. *Claremont News*, December 7, 14, 21, 1962, February 15, March 8, 22, April 5, 12, 1963 — all p. 1; *Senate Journal*, 1963, p. 235; *House Journal*, 1963, p. 191; *Laws*, 1963, p. 1360; 1965, p. 1282, 1284.

52. *Claremont News*, September 11, 1964, p. 1; *Rochester Post-Bulletin*, July 26, 1967, p. 42.

53. *Claremont News*, January 25, May 10, 1963 — both p. 1; "Environmental Assessment, Rice Lake State Park" (1976–77), Rice Lake File, DNR Files.

54. "Environmental Assessment," Rice Lake File, DNR Files; *Owatonna People's Press*, August 5, 1979, p. 1A–2A.

55. DNR, Project 80 report, 125; Judi Kurth to Davison, November 9, 1981, Rice Lake File, DNR Files.

56. Franklyn Curtiss-Wedge, comp., *The History of Mower County, Minnesota* (Chicago: H. C. Cooper, Jr., 1911), 396.

57. DOC, DPR, "Profile: Lake Louise State Park — Mower County," April 15, 1968, Halver for Hella to Grant Hawkins (village clerk, Le Roy), March 7, 1962, carbon — both in Lake Louise File, DNR Files.

58. *Senate Journal*, 1963, p. 248; *House Journal*, 1963, p. 180; *Laws*, 1963, p. 1351–52, 1359; 1965, p. 1282, 1284.

59. Martin to Hella, November 16, 1965, DOC, "Profile: Lake Louise State Park," Ruth E. Bohlen to Hella, October 7, 1969, photocopy, Lake Louise File, DNR Files; *Le Roy Independent*, June 3, 10, 1982 — both p. 1; DNR, DPR, *Hambrecht Historical Cottage and Museum* (undated leaflet), copy in author's possession.

60. DNR, Project 80 report, 116–17, 124.

61. *Askov American*, December 27, 1934, p. 1; Alvie Johnson to Floyd B. Olson, December 19, 1934, carbon, Director [Grover M. Conzet] to Harold W. Lathrop, February 14, 1935, carbon, P. W. Swedberg to Conzet, March 4, 1935, "copy," Conzet to [E. V.] Willard, March 7, 1935, carbon — all in Proposed State Parks File, FFPD, DOC Records; Lathrop to Willard, March 19, 1935, Banning File, DNR Files.

62. Mrs. A. E. Borchart (president, Pine County Historical Society) to Department of Conservation, December 4, 1959, Hella to Borchart, December 23, 1959, carbon, "Application for Federal Lands: Sandstone Federal Correctional Institution," July 20, 1971 — all in Banning File, DNR Files; John C. Randall, "A Plea for a New Park," *Conservation Volunteer* 26 (March–April 1963): 57–59; Jo Ann N. Nelson, "Banning — A Minnesota Ghost Town," *Conservation Volunteer* 21 (January–February 1958): 37; *St. Paul Pioneer Press*, November 27, 1896, p. 2.

63. Joe Gimpl to Hella, July 31, 1962, Hella to Gimpl, August 6, 1962, carbon — both in Banning File, DNR Files; *House Journal*, 1963, p. 219; *Senate Journal*, 1963, p. 290; *Laws*, 1963, p. 1359; 1965, p. 1281, 1283.

64. *Laws*, 1967, p. 2286; *Pine County Courier* (Sandstone), May 20, August 29, 1963 — both p. 1; "Quitclaim Deed," October 8, 1971, Banning File, DNR Files; Dunn, *State Parks of the St. Croix Valley*, 43.

65. *Laws*, 1965, p. 1278–79; 1967, p. 1610–11; 1971, p. 1693.

66. DNR, Project 80 report, 97, 124; Appendix B, 17.

67. Maplewood Township, about half of which, together with a strip of Lida Township, was taken to form the park, had a population of 726 in 1940. U.S., *Census*, 1940, *Population* 1:546.

68. "Park Association's Final Donation," *Minnesota Volunteer* 48 (January–February 1985): 63–64; U.S., Department of the Interior, NPS, *Recreation Today and Tomorrow: A Survey of the Recreation Resources of the Missouri River Basin* ([Washington, D.C., 1959]), 85–86.

69. Haynes to Hella, October 6, 1960, Maplewood File, DNR Files.

70. *Fergus Falls Daily Journal*, January 3, 1961, p. 3, November 6, 1963, p. 1; *Pelican Rapids Press*, February 7, June 13, 1963 — both p. 1.

71. *Senate Journal*, 1963, p. 386; *House Journal*, 1963, p. 412; *Laws*, 1963,

p. 1359; 1965, p. 1282, 1284; 1967, p. 2287; *Pelican Rapids Press*, June 13, 1963, p. 1; *Fergus Falls Daily Journal*, December 2, 1963, p. 9.

72. Krona to Hella, December 8, 1966, photocopy, "Maplewood Demonstration Woodland," n.d., Krona to Hella, November 26, 1968, photocopy, Hella to Virgil Mueller, May 27, 1969, carbon – all in Maplewood File, DNR Files; MORRC report, 63.

73. DNR, *Maplewood State Park: Summer Trails* (1990), copy of leaflet in author's possession. More recent maps no longer show the road crossing the park.

74. *Laws*, 1965, p. 1277; 1971, p. 1694; DNR, DPR, "Profile: Maplewood State Park: Ottertail [*sic*] County," May 16, 1978, Maplewood File, DNR Files.

75. Davison to Robert L. Herbst, July 17, 1973, Davison to Files, October 1, 1973, carbon – both in Maplewood File, DNR Files; *Pelican Rapids Press*, September 27, October 4, 1973 – both p. 1.

76. DNR, *A Management Plan for Maplewood State Park* (St. Paul: DNR, 1978), 29, 32 (map), 117 (map), 130, 134.

77. Michael Eliseuson, *Tower Soudan – The State Park Down Under*, Minnesota State Park Heritage Series, no. 1 ([St. Paul?]: Minnesota Parks Foundation, 1976), 8–22; Bureau of Engineering for DSP, DOC, "Tower Soudan State Park Feasibility Study," September 3, 1964, [C. F. Beukema] to Clarence Prout, January 14, 1963, photocopy, "A Proposed Tower Soudan State Park: Minnesota's First Iron Ore Mine," 1963 – all in Soudan Underground Mine File, DNR Files. It is not certain where the initiative for this offer came from; it is said that the citizens of the towns of Tower and Soudan proposed that the mine be preserved by being made into a state park. Herman T. Olson, town clerk at Tower, was credited with an important role in getting the park established. *House Journal*, 1963, p. 535; *Senate Journal*, 1963, p. 496; *Laws*, 1963, p. 1358.

78. "Justification: A Bill for an Act to Establish a New State Park Located in St. Louis County to be Known as Tower Soudan State Park," n.d., "Interpretive Plan for Tower Soudan State Park," n.d. – both in Soudan Underground Mine File, DNR Files; "Introducing: The State Park 'Down Under,' " *Conservation Volunteer* 28 (July–August 1965): 21–24; *Laws*, 1987, p. 257.

79. "News from the Minnesota Department of Natural Resources, August 8, 1972," Soudan Underground Mine File, DNR Files.

80. Marvin Lamppa to Krona et al., July 28, 1970, Soudan Underground Mine File, DNR Files.

81. MORRC report, 3.

82. *Laws*, 1963, p. 1344–63. Specific amounts are also earmarked for land acquisition and capital development at Savanna Portage and Fort Snelling and for "maintenance, operation, and improvement" at Tower Soudan.

83. *United States Statutes at Large* 93:1446–75 (1979); "17 National Monuments Proclaimed," *Living Wilderness* 42 (October–December 1978): 16.

## Chapter 9. *Rounding out the System: 1964–1988*

1. MORRC report, 1, 3, 9.

2. Resolution of the Board of Commissioners of the County of Lake, August 22, 1961, John H. Martin to Udert W. Hella, August 25, 1961 – both in Flood Bay File, DNR Files; *House Journal*, 1965, p. 773, 1954, 2083–84; *Senate Journal*, 1965, p. 2002–3; *Laws*, 1965, p. 812.

3. *Laws*, 1965, p. 812; 1984, p. 1398–99.

4. U.S., Department of the Interior, NPS, "Inventory of Existing and Potential Areas," April 25, 1961, Franz Jevne, Jr., to Milton E. Krona, November 15, 1966 — both in Franz Jevne File, DNR Files.

5. Krona to Hella, December 9, 1966, carbon, Jevne to Jarle B. Leirfallom, April 7, 1967, photocopy — both in Franz Jevne File, DNR Files.

6. *Senate Journal*, 1967, p. 1199, 1758–59; *House Journal*, 1967, p. 3090; *Laws*, 1967, p. 1441; 1969, p. 907. See also chapter 3, note 63.

7. Hella to William [J.] O'Brien, August 26, 1964, carbon, "Proposed Hayes Creek [*sic*] State Park," September 4, 1964 — both in Hayes Lake File, DNR Files.

8. Address by C. B. Buckman (DNR) at Hayes Lake State Park dedication, July 14, 1973, Brauer and Associates, Inc., Edina, Minn., *Hayes Lake State Park Feasibility Study*, August 31, 1966, p. A1 — both in Hayes Lake File, DNR Files; *House Journal*, 1965, p. 1245; *Laws*, 1965, p. 1286.

9. *Senate Journal*, 1967, p. 815; *House Journal*, 1967, p. 935; *Laws*, 1967, p. 1610.

10. Dwight Roll to Hella, September 5, 1969, Merlin H. Berg to Hella, November 30, 1970, Buckman address, July 14, 1973 — all in Hayes Lake File, DNR Files.

11. Jim Dustrude to Files, June 15, 1976, photocopy, Hayes Lake File, DNR Files; "Summary and Disposition of Comments Received at the Public Information Meeting on 2/22/77 Regarding the Hayes Lake State Park Management Plan," September 26, 1977, accompanying Dustrude and Franklin Svoboda for Donald D. Davison to Citizens Interested in the Management Plan for Hayes Lake State Park, September 26, 1977 — copies in author's possession.

12. *Legislative Manual*, 1979–80, p. 301; Lawrence E. Samstad, "A Plan for Recreational Trails in the Minnesota River Valley," January 29, 1969, Minnesota Valley File, DNR Files; Steven Dornfeld, "Riverside land acquisition by DNR questioned," *Minneapolis Tribune*, August 11, 1974, p. A1; *House Journal*, 1967, p. 1917, 3252; 1969, p. 478, 954, 2366–68, 2445–46, 3462–63; *Senate Journal*, 1967, p. 1411; 1969, p. 423, 680, 1806; *Laws*, 1969, p. 1644; *Jordan Independent*, April 24, October 30, 1969 — both p. 1.

13. "Wisconsin's Whistle-stop Nature Trail," *Audubon* 69 (May–June 1967), 78–79; Albert Marshall, "Railways to Pathways," *Parks and Recreation* 1 (December 1966): 978, 985; *Laws*, 1967, p. 1229; 1969, p. 1439; *Senate Journal*, 1969, p. 423, 425, 802, 1003–4, 1087. Each of these bills had a house companion. Besides the Minnesota Valley Trails, there were a Cannon River Trail, to run from Cannon Falls to near the mouth of the river; a Chief Red Iron Trail, from the Twin Cities to Clara City (later to be revived as the Luce Line Trail); a Crooked Creek Trail, to extend from Beaver Creek Valley State Park to the mouth of Crooked Creek; a Moraine Trail, to connect Sibley, Glacial Lakes, and Lake Carlos state parks; a Root River Trail, from Chatfield to the mouth of the Root River; a Minnesota-Wisconsin Boundary Trail; and an Iron Range Trail, to be located on the "Vermilion, Mesabi, and Cuyuna iron ranges and at related points on Lake Superior."

14. *Laws*, 1969, p. 1640–42; *Jordan Independent*, October 30, 1969, p. 1.

15. DNR, Project 80 report, 125; Dornfeld, "Riverside land acquisition," A10.

16. Dornfeld, "Riverside land acquisition," A1, A10, A11.

17. Dornfeld, "Riverside land acquisition," A11.

18. *Jordan Independent*, November 27, 1975, p. 1; *Minneapolis Tribune*, December 4, p. A6, November 27, p. B13 — both 1975; *Laws*, 1983, p. 1398.

19. DNR, *Minnesota Valley Trail: Summer Trails* (1990), copy of leaflet in author's possession; *Jordan Independent*, December 10, 1971, October 12, 19, 1972 all p. 1.

20. *United States Statutes at Large* 90:1992–96; *Jordan Independent*, January 1, 1976, p. 1, January 29, 1976, p. 8, January 13, 1977, p. 1, November 24, 1977, p. 8, November 8, 1979, p. 1; *Free Press*, June 18, 1981, p. 35.

21. *Laws*, 1971, p. 1698–1701; 1973, p. 1861–63; 1974, p. 761–62; 1975, p. 365–66; 1985, p. 2379–80; *Minneapolis Tribune*, March 14, p. C7, September 1, p. B3 — both 1980; Samuel H. Morgan and Peter Seed, "The Saga of the Soo Line: An Unfinished Story," *Newsletter* (MPTCF), Fall 1988, p. 1–2.

22. DNR, *A Management Plan for Afton State Park* (draft; St. Paul: DNR, 1977), 15; Morgan, "The Story of Afton Park," August 25, 1980, Afton File, DNR Files.

23. *St. Paul Pioneer Press*, March 6, 1969, p. 33; *Stillwater Gazette*, March 10, 1969, p. 5; Samuel H. Morgan to Carl R. Dale, March 8, 1969, photocopy, Morgan to Robert O. Ashbach, April 14, 1969, photocopy, Morgan, "Afton Park," Morgan to Hella, June 4, 1969, telegram — all in Afton File, DNR Files; *Senate Journal*, 1969, p. 2765, 2931; *House Journal*, 1969, p. 1402, 2368, 3572–73, 3714; *Laws*, 1969, p. 1957–58. In all fairness it should be mentioned that another real estate agent opposed it, saying, "All the land on the river shouldn't rest with the rich."

24. Martin possibly to Raymond L. Blomgren, November 12, 1970, Davison to Mert Christian, August 31, 1978, Morgan to Roger McGrath, February 3, 1978, Davison to Joseph P. Alexander, June 6, 1979 — all in Afton File, DNR Files.

25. Davison to Alexander, June 6, 1979, Davison to C. Paul Faraci, November 1, 1979, carbon — both in Afton File, DNR Files; *Laws*, 1969, p. 245; *Minneapolis Tribune*, June 7, 1979, p. B2.

26. Grace B. (Mrs. John R.) Stoltze to Robert L. Herbst, January 1, 1974, Afton File, DNR Files.

27. "Summary and Disposition of Comments Received at the Public Information Meeting on 6/9/77 Regarding the Afton State Park Management Plan," July 7, 1977, accompanying Jim Dustrude and Franklin Svoboda for Davison to Citizens Interested in the Management Plan for Afton State Park, July 15, 1977 — copies in author's possession.

28. DNR, *Management Plan: Afton*, 143, 145–53.

29. Harold Olson to James C. Marshall, March 12, 1963, carbon, O. L. Kipp File, DNR Files; DNR, *A Management Plan for O. L. Kipp State Park* (draft; St. Paul: DNR, 1977), 12.

30. *Senate Journal*, 1963, p. 842; *House Journal*, 1963, p. 942; *Laws*, 1963, p. 1353–54; 1965, p. 1282; *Legislative Manual*, 1955, p. 120; *Minneapolis Star*, April 25, 1964, p. 10A; Olson to Marshall, March 12, 1963, "Biography," n.d. — both in O. L. Kipp File, DNR Files.

31. MORRC report, 69.

32. *Winona News*, October 19, 1975, p. 6B; DNR, *Management Plan: O. L. Kipp*, 12; DNR, Division of Forestry, *Richard J. Dorer Memorial Hardwood Forest: A Forest for Everyone* (St. Paul: The Division, [1979]), 3.

33. *House Journal*, 1969, p. 1054, 2412–13; *Senate Journal*, 1969, p. 681; 1971, p. 288, 1872–75, 2479–80.

34. DNR, *Management Plan: O. L. Kipp*, 33, 35, 37–38.

35. DNR, *Management Plan: O. L. Kipp*, 32–33, 37, 75, 77.

36. Fremling to Hella, September 29, 1971, photocopy, Hella to Fremling, October 5, 1971, carbon — both in O. L. Kipp File, DNR Files; R. Newell Searle and Mark E. Heitlinger, *Prairies, Woods and Islands: A Guide to the Minnesota Preserves of The Nature Conservancy* (Minneapolis: The Nature Conservancy, Minnesota Chapter, 1980), 72–73.

37. Arol McCaslin to Bob Johnston, March 20, 1976, photocopy, O. L. Kipp File, DNR Files.

38. *Winona News*, October 19, 1975, p. 6B; John W. Wilzbacher, "O. L. Kipp State Park: 1977: Annual Report," January 27, 1978, O. L. Kipp File, DNR Files.

39. DNR, *Management Plan: O. L. Kipp*, 16, 80; Wilzbacher, annual report, O. L. Kipp File, DNR Files.

40. DNR, *Management Plan: O. L. Kipp*, 35.

41. Floyd Henspeter and Gordon Peterson to Hella, July 13, 1962, Hella to Henspeter, July 19, 1962, carbon, Peterson to Hella, February 18, 1963, Hella to Peterson, February 27, 1963, carbon, J. R. Burkholder to Wayne H. Olson, January 21, 1965, photocopy, Hella to Olson, January 27, 1965, carbon, Herbst to Burkholder, August 10, 1966, carbon — all in Moose Lake File, DNR Files.

42. Louis F. Dahlmeier to Herbst, December 5, 1966, Krona to Hella, December 8, 1966, Les Blacklock to Leirfallom, February 10, 1967, carbon, Richard T. Hart, Jr., to Hella, September 12, 1967 — all in Moose Lake File, DNR Files; *Laws*, 1971, p. 1703–4.

43. Hella to Herbst, May 5, 1972, carbon, Moose Lake File, DNR Files.

44. Blacklock to Hella, July 12, 1971, Hella to Blacklock, September 10, 1971, carbon, Krona to Editor, *St. Paul Dispatch*, n.d., photocopy — all in Moose Lake File, DNR Files; *St. Paul Dispatch*, April 27, p. 43, April 28, p. 10, May 26, p. 30 — all 1972.

45. DNR, DPR, "Profile: Moose Lake Recreation Area: Carlton County," June 20, 1975, Moose Lake File, DNR Files.

46. Theodore A. Norelius to Richard [J.] Doer [Dorer], December 24, 1953, carbon, "St. Croix Wild River State Park" (probably an address by Governor Wendell R. Anderson at signing ceremony, May 24, 1973) — both in St. Croix Wild River File, DNR Files.

47. *United States Statutes at Large* 82:906–18; *Senate Journal*, 1969, p. 508; 1971, p. 1119; *House Journal*, 1969, p. 1154; 1971, p. 1326; Dale D. Rott to Thomas O. Savage, June 16, 1969, photocopy, Rott to Jerald C. Anderson and Krona, March 14, 1973, photocopy — both in St. Croix Wild River File, DNR Files.

48. *Senate Journal*, 1973, p. 619; *Chisago County Press* (Lindstrom), March 27, 1969, p. 1, 2; Rott to Hella, June 16, 1969, Chester S. Wilson to Herbst, March 3, 1975, carbon, Davison to Wilson, March 18, 1975, carbon — all in St. Croix Wild River File, DNR Files. After reaffirming the acreage limitation in 1977, the legislature three years later authorized a substantial addition to the park. According to official figures, Wild River now has about 7,000 acres.

49. *East Central Minnesota Post-Review* (Rush City), March 8, 1973, p. 1; *Senate Journal*, 1973, p. 937–38, 2195–96; *House Journal*, 1973, p. 1822, 3598–99; *Laws*, 1973, p. 1273.

50. *Laws*, 1973, p. 1265–73.

51. *Chisago County Press*, November 6, 1974, p. 1, 5, November 13, 1974, p. 1, 5, August 31, 1977, p. 1, 3; DNR, DPR, "Profile: St. Croix Wild River State Park: Chisago County," July 9, 1981, St. Croix Wild River File, DNR Files.

52. *Chisago County Press*, August 31, 1977, p. 1, 3; "Profile: St. Croix Wild River State Park," St. Croix Wild River File, DNR Files.

53. Dunn, *State Parks of the St. Croix Valley*, 40–41.

54. "Proposed Tettegouche State Park," Tettegouche File, DNR Files; R. Newell Searle, "Crown Jewel of North Shore Parks," *Minnesota Volunteer* 42 (September–October 1979): 50, 52–53. Members of the Smith family, which had ties to New Brunswick, had given Micmac Indian names to the four lakes that constitute

the centerpiece of the area: Tettegouche, Nicado, Nipisiquit, and Micmac (as they are now spelled). In northeastern New Brunswick there are rivers named Tetagouche and Nipisiguit and a village named Nigadoo.

55. "Proposed Tettegouche State Park," F. Rodney Paine to Clement K. Quinn, January 9, 1967, Quinn to Paine, January 11, 1967, Hella to Paine, January 16, 1967 — all in Tettegouche File, DNR Files; Searle, "Crown Jewel," 53. DeLaittre was a grandson of the earlier John De Laittre.

56. Searle, "Crown Jewel," 53; *Minneapolis Tribune*, March 9, 1980, *Picture* magazine, 4–5, 8–10, 14–16, 19–20; *Lake County News Chronicle* (Two Harbors), March 19, 1975, p. 1; "Proposed Tettegouche State Park," Tettegouche File, DNR Files.

57. R. Newell Searle, *Saving Quetico-Superior: A Land Set Apart* (St. Paul: MHS Press, 1977), 110, 152–56. One can argue, of course, that if the counties had fewer people, they would need fewer services. Ernest C. Oberholtzer thought that they should be consolidated as a means of effecting savings in administration. According to this line of thinking, northeastern Minnesota would be better off if it had fewer people and more timber wolves, though one would be hesitant about expressing such sentiments in Two Harbors.

58. Announcement of NEMEEC annual meeting, February 11, 1979, Tettegouche File, DNR Files.

59. Searle, "Crown Jewel," 53; *Newsletter* (The Nature Conservancy, Minnesota Chapter), Spring 1978, p. 2–3.

60. *Senate Journal*, 1979, p. 531, 1906–9, 2563–65; *House Journal*, 1979, p. 902, 2401–5, 2539–40, 2544–49; *Laws*, 1979, p. 663–67.

61. *Laws*, 1979, p. 663–65.

62. Searle, "Crown Jewel," 55; *Ely Miner*, June 27, 1979, p. 3; *Duluth News-Tribune*, June 30, 1979, p. 1. An editorial in the *Minneapolis Tribune* (July 6, 1979, p. 6A) strongly favorable to Tettegouche said that Alexander had conceded the justice of some of the criticism leveled at the DNR, which he said "had better quit looking at new parks and start looking at better managing our existing parks."

63. *Minneapolis Tribune*, March 9, 1980, *Picture* magazine, 4–5, 8–10, 14–16, 19–21; *Duluth News-Tribune*, May 23, 1980, p. 1, 9; *St. Paul Pioneer Press*, June 22, 1980, Metro/Region section, 1.

64. DNR, *A Summary of the Tettegouche State Park Management Plan* (St. Paul: DNR, 1981), 7.

65. "Hill Annex Mine," March 14, 1988, Hill Annex Mine File, DNR Files; "Legislative Wrap-Up," *Newsletter* (MPTCF), Spring 1988, p. 1.

66. "Hill Annex Mine," Hill Annex Mine File, DNR Files; *Newsletter* (MPTCF), Spring 1988, p. 1; DNR, *Operations Report: Hill Annex Mine State Park*, 4 vols. (St. Paul: DNR, 1990), copy in DNR Library.

67. *Newsletter* (MPTCF), Winter 1988, p. 2, Winter 1989, p. 5; Judith L. Erickson to the author, July 16, 1990.

68. *Newsletter* (MPTCF), Summer 1989, p. 1; *House Journal*, 1989, p. 278, 524, 6341, 9121; *Senate Journal*, 1989, p. 2134–36, 3700, 3747; *Laws*, 1989, p. 876–78. The name change, of course, leaves the park open to confusion with Grand Portage National Monument, Grand Portage State Forest, and the Grand Portage Band — all in the immediate vicinity.

69. *Laws*, 1989, p. 877–78.

70. *Newsletter* (MPTCF), Summer 1989, p. 1. In 1988 the Witch Tree was reported to be in danger, and an organization, Friends of the Witch Tree, was

formed to acquire the land on which the tree stands and donate it to the Grand Portage Band. See *Newsletter*, Spring 1988, p. 2.

71. *United States Statutes at Large* 78:897–904.

72. *United States Statutes at Large* 78:899, 901, 902.

73. *Laws*, 1969, p. 906–11. A few parks were demoted to waysides (e.g., Kodonce River and Caribou Falls), and at least one wayside (Camp Release) was reclassified as a monument.

74. *Laws*, 1969, p. 2460; DNR, Project 80 report, 1; Herbst and Gerald W. Christenson to Thomas W. Newcome, September 2, 1970 (photocopy of letter attached to copy of Project 80 report in DNR Library).

75. DNR, Project 80 report, 1, 93–96. The same criteria were used to evaluate all sites, but they were not given the same weight for different components. For example, "appropriateness of water for water-based recreational activities" was considered a much more important criterion for judging recreational areas than for judging parks.

76. DNR, Project 80 report, 96–98.

77. DNR, Project 80 report, 149–50. The other parks considered worthy of continued park status were Afton, Baptism River (as expanded), Bear Head Lake, Blue Mounds, Frontenac, George H. Crosby Manitou, Glacial Lakes, Jay Cooke, Judge C. R. Magney, and Whitewater.

78. DNR, Project 80 report, 123–25, 149–50.

79. DNR, Project 80 report, 25, 63.

80. DNR, Project 80 report, 99, 126, 128–29; Appendix A, 11–14.

81. *Senate Journal*, 1975, p. 115, 599–604, 912, 2250–52, 2522–23; *House Journal*, 1075, p. 213, 565, 1531 56, 2433 34, 2084 86; *Laws*, 1075, p. 1130–62. Besides the four components specifically treated in the Project 80 report, seven others were suggested, all of which already existed in some form: state trails, wilderness areas, forests, wildlife management areas, water access sites, wild and scenic waterways, and rest areas. The Project 80 staff considered detailed analysis of these beyond its purview, given the time constraints imposed on it. All eleven types of recreational unit appeared, however, in the law that grew directly out of this study, the Outdoor Recreation Act of 1975.

82. DNR, Project 80 report, 25; *Laws*, 1975, p. 1141. If the language of the ORA often reflects that of Project 80, in certain respects it is reminiscent of the federal Wilderness Act of 1964. For example, a state wilderness area was defined as a unit that "appears to have been primarily affected by the forces of nature, with the evidence of man being substantially unnoticeable or where the evidence of man may be eliminated by restoration." See *Laws*, 1975, p. 1146.

83. *Laws*, 1975, p. 1151–52.

84. "To Be Discovered . . . "; "Judge, Vi, Deer, Finland . . ." — in *Minnesota Volunteer* 36 (July–August 1973): 67; 36 (September–October 1973): 65; *Legislative Manual*, 1975–76, p. 342; *St. Paul Pioneer Press Dispatch*, May 27, 1987, p. 2C.

85. *Laws*, 1980, p. 296–98.

86. *Laws*, 1975, p. 1142; 1984, p. 1400.

## Chapter 10. *The State Parks and the Public*

1. *Newsletter* (Minnesota Council of Parks), January–February 1984, p. 4.

2. Hella, *Quest for Excellence*, 11–12; minutes of first meeting, Minnesota

Council of State Parks, December 3, 1954, Correspondence: Minnesota Council of State Parks File, PRD, DOC Records.

3. Hella, *Quest for Excellence*, 12, 29, 45; "Merger Announced: New Officers Elected," *Newsletter* (MPTCF), Winter 1988, p. 1. The foundation also sponsored a series of pamphlets on individual parks or groups of parks in a particular region of the state. The first in this Minnesota State Park Heritage Series was Eliseuson's *Tower Soudan* (1976). It was followed by Searle's *Whitewater — The Valley of Promise* (1977) and *State Parks of the North Shore* (1979), Dunn's *State Parks of the St. Croix Valley* (1981), and Searle's *Gardens of the Desert* (1983).

4. As early as 1941 a columnist writing under the name of "Poison Ivy" in the *Watson Voice* (June 19 and July 24, both p. 3) blasted the parks administration for requiring that visitors to Lac qui Parle leave their cars in a $50,000 parking lot, where the sun would blaze down on them all day, instead of allowing people to drive into the shade nearer to the picnic grounds. Director Harold W. Lathrop replied a few weeks later, first assuring his readers that no parking lot in the system had cost even 20 percent of the $50,000 figure and then pointing out that cars damage vegetation.

5. *Root River Trail Newsletter* (DNR), November 1981, January, February 1982 — all p. 1–3, copies in author's possession; *Minneapolis Tribune*, February 4, 1982, p. 1B.

6. *Free Press*, July 1, 1978, p. 2, August 3, 1978, p. 1, August 23, 1978, p. 14, April 7, 1979, p. 3, August 21, 1979, p. 19; *Minneapolis Tribune*, September 25, 1979, p. 2B, 9B; *Faribault News*, May 10, 1979, p. 1; *Zumbrota News*, May 16, 1979, p. 1; *Kenyon Leader*, May 17, 1979, p. 1.

7. Alfred Runte, *National Parks: The American Experience* (Lincoln: University of Nebraska Press, 1979), 2, 5, 55, 108.

8. Joseph L. Sax, *Mountains Without Handrails: Reflections on the National Parks* (Ann Arbor: University of Michigan Press, 1980), 14, 54, 75.

9. Sax, *Mountains Without Handrails*, 105. For a critical analysis of the various pressures, legislative and other, that operate on the NPS, see Ronald A. Foresta, *America's National Parks and Their Keepers* (Washington, D.C.: Resources for the Future; [Baltimore]: Distributed by Johns Hopkins University Press, 1984). Much of what Foresta says about the national park system applies also, with some modifications, to a state park system.

10. Runte, *National Parks*, 111; Edward Abbey, *Desert Solitaire: A Season in the Wilderness* (New York: Ballantine Books, 1971), 52.

11. Nash, *Wilderness and the American Mind*, 1.

# Select Bibliography

## Manuscripts

Department of Conservation Records. Minnesota State Archives, Minnesota Historical Society, St. Paul.

Simmons, Mildred. "A History of Lake Bemidji State Park, 1923–1979." Research paper prepared for English course, Bemidji State University, 1979?; copy in author's possession.

State Parks, Waysides, and Monuments Files. Minnesota Department of Natural Resources, Division of Parks and Recreation, St. Paul. Items in these files are currently being used by division staff.

## Government Publications

Hughes, Thomas. *History of Minneopa State Park.* [St. Paul?]: Minnesota Department of Conservation, Division of Forestry, 1932.

Minnesota. Department of Conservation. *Biennial Report.* 1933/34 through 1949/50.

——. Division of State Parks. *The Minnesota State Park and Recreational Area Plan.* [St. Paul], 1939.

——. Division of State Parks. *State Parks of Minnesota.* St. Paul: The Department, 1948.

Minnesota. Department of Natural Resources (DNR). *Kilen Woods State Park Management Plan.* Draft. St. Paul: DNR, 1980.

——. *A Management Plan for Afton State Park.* Draft. St. Paul: DNR, 1977.

——. *A Management Plan for Beaver Creek Valley State Park.* St. Paul: DNR, 1980.

——. *A Management Plan for Camden State Park.* Draft. St. Paul: DNR, 1977.

——. *A Management Plan for Father Hennepin State Park.* St. Paul: DNR, 1978.

——. *A Management Plan for Fort Snelling State Park.* Draft. St. Paul: DNR, 1978.

——. *A Management Plan for Gooseberry Falls State Park.* St. Paul: DNR, 1979.

——. *A Management Plan for Helmer Myre State Park.* St. Paul: DNR, 1980.

——. *A Management Plan for Kilen Woods State Park.* St. Paul: DNR, 1980.

——. *A Management Plan for Lake Bronson State Park.* Draft. St. Paul: DNR, 1977.

——. *A Management Plan for Maplewood State Park.* St. Paul: DNR, 1978.

——. *A Management Plan for O. L. Kipp State Park.* Draft. St. Paul: DNR, 1977.

——. *A Management Plan for Split Rock Creek State Recreation Area.* St. Paul: DNR, 1981.

——. *Management Plan Summary (Draft): Frontenac State Park.* St. Paul: DNR, 1977.

——. *Management Plan Summary (Draft): Lake Maria State Park.* St. Paul: DNR, 1977.

——. *Management Plan Summary (Draft): Minneopa State Park.* St. Paul: DNR, 1977.

——. *Management Plan Summary (Draft): Whitewater State Park.* St. Paul: DNR, 1977.

——. *Operations Report: Hill Annex Mine State Park.* 4 vols. St. Paul: DNR, 1990.

——. *A Summary of the Tettegouche State Park Management Plan.* St. Paul: DNR, 1981.

Minnesota. Department of Natural Resources, Bureau of Planning, and State Planning Agency, Environmental Planning Section. *Minnesota Resource Potentials in State Outdoor Recreation.* Project 80, Staff Report no. 1. [St. Paul?, 1971.]

Minnesota. Department of Natural Resources. Division of Parks. *A Guide to Minnesota's State Park and Recreation System.* St. Paul: DNR, [1981].

Minnesota. Geological and Natural History Survey. *Eighteenth Annual Report, for the Year 1889,* by N[ewton] H. Winchell.

Minnesota. House of Representatives. *Journal.* 1895 through 1979.

Minnesota. *Laws.* 1885 through 1989.

Minnesota. Legislature. Outdoor Recreation Resources Commission (MORRC). *Parks and Recreation in Minnesota.* Report no. 12. [St. Paul?: The Commission, 1965.]

Minnesota. Secretary of State. *Legislative Manual.* 1897 through 1987/88.

Minnesota. Senate. *Journal.* 1895 through 1979.

Minnesota. State Auditor. *Biennial Report.* 1929/30 through 1931/32.

——. *Report to the 1925 Legislature Covering Minnesota State Parks.* [St. Paul: Riverside Press, 1925.]

United States. Department of the Interior. National Park Service. *Recreation Today and Tomorrow: A Survey of the Recreation Resources of the Missouri River Basin.* [Washington, D.C., 1959.]

## Books and Pamphlets

Abbey, Edward. *Desert Solitaire: A Season in the Wilderness.* New York: Ballantine Books, 1971.

Anderson, Torgny. *The Centennial History of Lyon County, Minnesota.* Marshall, Minn.: Henle Publishing Company, 1970.

Atwater, Isaac, ed. *History of the City of Minneapolis, Minnesota.* 2 vols. New York: Munsell & Company, 1893.

Buchanan, James W. *A Guide to Hiking and Cross-Country Skiing in the Pioneer Region.* Vol. 5, *Minnesota Walk Book.* Minneapolis: Nodin Press, 1979.

Carley, Kenneth. *The Sioux Uprising of 1862.* 1961. 2d ed. St. Paul: Minnesota Historical Society Press, 1976.

Chase, Ray P. *Statement to the Nineteen Hundred Twenty-three Legislature.* [St. Paul, 1923.]

Curtiss-Wedge, Franklyn, comp. *The History of Mower County, Minnesota.* Chicago: H. C. Cooper, Jr., 1911.

Dobie, John. *The Itasca Story.* Minneapolis: Ross & Haines, 1959.

Dunn, James Taylor. *State Parks of the St. Croix Valley: Wild, Scenic, and Recreational.* Minnesota State Park Heritage Series, no. 4. [St. Paul?]: Minnesota Parks Foundation, 1981.

Eliseuson, Michael. *Tower Soudan — The State Park Down Under.* Minnesota State Park Heritage Series, no. 1. [St. Paul?]: Minnesota Parks Foundation, 1976.

Federal Writers' Project, Minnesota. *Minnesota: A State Guide.* American Guide Series. New York: Viking Press, 1938. Reprinted as *The WPA Guide to Minnesota* (St. Paul: Minnesota Historical Society Press, Borealis Books, 1985).

Folwell, William Watts. *A History of Minnesota.* 4 vols. Rev. ed. St. Paul: Minnesota Historical Society, 1956–69.

Foresta, Ronald A. *America's National Parks and Their Keepers.* Washington, D.C.: Resources for the Future; [Baltimore]: Distributed by Johns Hopkins University Press, 1984.

Hazzard, George H., comp. *Lectures, Laws, Papers, Pictures, Pointers: Interstate Park, Dalles of the St. Croix, Taylors Falls, Minn., St. Croix Falls, Wis.* [St. Paul?], 1896.

Hella, U[dert] W. *Quest for Excellence: A History of the Minnesota Council of Parks, 1954 to 1974.* [St. Paul]: Minnesota Parks Foundation, 1985.

Holmquist, June Drenning, and Jean A. Brookins. *Minnesota's Major Historic Sites: A Guide.* 2d ed., rev. St. Paul: Minnesota Historical Society, 1972.

Holmquist, June Drenning, Sue E. Holbert, and Dorothy Drescher Perry, comps. *History Along the Highways: An Official Guide to Minnesota State Markers and Monuments.* Minnesota Historic Sites Pamphlet Series, no. 3. St. Paul: Minnesota Historical Society, 1967.

Hughes, Thomas. *Old Traverse des Sioux . . . A History of Early Exploration, Trading Posts, Mission Station, Treaties, and Pioneer Village.* Edited by Edward A. Johnson. St. Peter, Minn.: Herald Publishing Company, 1929.

Ise, John. *Our National Park Policy: A Critical History.* Baltimore: Published for Resources for the Future by Johns Hopkins Press, 1961. Reprinted as *Our National Park Policy* (New York: Arno Press, 1961).

Lawson, Victor E., ed. *Illustrated History and Descriptive and Biographical Review of Kandiyohi County, Minnesota.* [Willmar, Minn.]: The Author & J. Emil Nelson, 1905.

Murray, Robert A. *A History of Pipestone National Monument, Minnesota.* [Pipestone, Minn.?]: Pipestone Indian Shrine Association, 1965.

Nash, Roderick. *Wilderness and the American Mind.* Rev. ed. New Haven, Conn.: Yale University Press, [1973].

Patera, Alan H., and John S. Gallagher. *The Post Offices of Minnesota.* Burtonsville, Md.: The Depot, 1978.

Rose, Arthur P. *An Illustrated History of Lyon County, Minnesota.* Marshall, Minn.: Northern History Publishing Company, 1912.

Runte, Alfred. *National Parks: The American Experience.* Lincoln: University of Nebraska Press, 1979.

Sandvik, Glenn. *A Superior Beacon: A Brief History of Split Rock Lighthouse.* [Two Harbors, Minn.: The Author, 1972.]

Sax, Joseph L. *Mountains Without Handrails: Reflections on the National Parks.* Ann Arbor: University of Michigan Press, 1980.

Searle, R. Newell. *Gardens of the Desert: Minnesota's Prairie Parks.* Minnesota State Park Heritage Series, no. 5. [St. Paul?]: Minnesota Parks Foundation, 1983.

——. *Saving Quetico-Superior: A Land Set Apart.* St. Paul: Minnesota Historical Society Press, 1977.

——. *State Parks of the North Shore.* Minnesota State Park Heritage Series, no. 3. [St. Paul?]: Minnesota Parks Foundation, 1979.

——. *Whitewater — The Valley of Promise.* Minnesota State Park Heritage Series, no. 2. [St. Paul?]: Minnesota Parks Foundation, 1977.

——, and Mark E. Heitlinger. *Prairies, Woods and Islands: A Guide to the Minnesota Preserves of The Nature Conservancy.* Minneapolis: The Nature Conservancy, Minnesota Chapter, 1980.

Thurn, Karl, and Helen Thurn. *Round Robin of Kandiyohi County, Centennial Year 1858–1958.* Raymond, Minn.: Press, 1958.

Tilden, Freeman J. *The State Parks: Their Meaning in American Life.* Foreword by Conrad L. Wirth. New York: Alfred A. Knopf, 1962.

Upham, Warren. *Minnesota Geographic Names: Their Origin and Historic Significance.* 1920. Reprint. St. Paul: Minnesota Historical Society, 1969.

Warming, L[udvig] A., comp. *The Paradise of Minnesota: The Proposed Whitewater State Park*. [St. Charles, Minn.], 1917.

Waters, Thomas F. *The Streams and Rivers of Minnesota*. Minneapolis: University of Minnesota Press, 1977.

Wirth, Theodore. *Minneapolis Park System, 1883–1944: Retrospective Glimpses into the History of the Board of Park Commissioners of Minneapolis, Minnesota, and the City's Park, Parkway, and Playground System*. Minneapolis: The Park Board, 1946.

Ziebarth, Marilyn, and Alan Ominsky. *Fort Snelling: Anchor Post of the Northwest*. Minnesota Historic Sites Pamphlet Series, no. 4. St. Paul: Minnesota Historical Society, 1970.

## Articles

Brower, J[acob] V. "Itasca State Park: An Illustrated History." *Minnesota Historical Collections* 11 (1904), 285 p.

Green, Rhoda J. "Division of State Parks: An Informational Review." *Conservation Volunteer* (Minnesota Department of Conservation) 8 (September–October 1945): 48–51.

Harris, J. Merle. "Lake Bronson, Old Mill, Old Crossing." *Conservation Volunteer* 19 (September–October 1956): 1–44.

"Introducing: The State Park 'Down Under.' " *Conservation Volunteer* 28 (July–August 1965): 21–24.

Lathrop, Harold W. "And Who Saved Baptism River State Park? It Was Associate Justice C. R. Magney." *Bulletin* (Izaak Walton League of America, Minnesota Division), Third Quarter 1945, p. 6.

———. "New Park on the St. Croix Is Gift of Miss Alice O'Brien." *Conservation Volunteer* 9 (May–June 1946): 43–44.

———. "Our Newest State Parks: Baptism River Is Spectacular Addition." *Conservation Volunteer* 9 (July–August 1946): 29–32.

Lommen, Georgina, and Helen Steffen. "Come See Our State Parks." *Minnesota Journal of Education* 33 (September 1952): 32–34.

Magney, C[larence] R. "Saved from Private Ownership: Our Newest State Park — Baptism River." *Bulletin* (Izaak Walton League of America, Minnesota Division), Third Quarter 1945, p. 5.

Marshall, Albert M. "Frontenac State Park." *Minnesota Naturalist* 7 (March 1956): 12–15.

Martin, John H. "A History of Camden State Park." *Conservation Volunteer* 21 (March–April 1958): 54–57.

———. "Mille Lacs Kathio State Park." *Conservation Volunteer* 21 (November–December 1957): 26–31.

Meyer, Roy W. "Forestville: The Making of a State Park." *Minnesota History* 44 (Fall 1974): 82–95.

Moberg, Ward. "1890s Fight Created Dalles Parks." *Dalles Visitor* 14 (1982): 1, 13, 14, 24, 25.

——. "Interstate Park Protects the Dalles." *Dalles Visitor* 13 (1981): 1, 8, 9, 20, 21, 26.

Morgan, Samuel H. "Our Citizens and State Parks." *Conservation Volunteer* 30 (May–June 1967): 24–31.

Morrison, Ken. "A Report on Nerstrand Woods: Acquisition Is Nearly Completed." *Conservation Volunteer* 5 (March 1943): 29–31.

Mossberg, Barbara. "Sixty Years: A History of Sibley State Park." *New London–Spicer Times* (New London, Minn.), August 5, 1976, p. 7–8.

Nelson, Jo Ann N. "Banning — A Minnesota Ghost Town." *Conservation Volunteer* 21 (January–February 1958): 36–38.

"New Director for State Parks." *Conservation Volunteer* 16 (March–April 1953): 21–22.

Nute, Grace Lee. "Gooseberry Falls State Park: Its History and Natural History." Parts 1, 2. *Conservation Volunteer* 10 (May–June; July–August 1947): 27–30; 7–11.

"Park Association's Final Donation." *Minnesota Volunteer* (Minnesota Department of Natural Resources) 48 (January–February 1985): 63–64.

Randall, John C. "A Plea for a New Park." *Conservation Volunteer* 26 (March–April 1963): 57–59.

Rienow, Leona Train. "Something to Remember Us By." *Nature Magazine* (American Nature Association) 38 (December 1945): 538–40.

Searle, R. Newell. "Crown Jewel of North Shore Parks." *Minnesota Volunteer* 42 (September–October 1979): 44–55.

"17 National Monuments Proclaimed." *Living Wilderness* 42 (October–December 1978): 16.

Warner, Dwain W. "Summer Bird Life of Carimona Woods, Filmore County, Minnesota." *The Flicker* (Minnesota Ornithologists' Union) 22 (June 1950): 27–34.

White, Mark, "Explore Minnesota's Mystery Cave." *Minnesota Volunteer* 52 (May–June 1989): 36–43.

"Wisconsin's Whistle-stop Nature Trail." *Audubon* 69 (May–June 1967): 78–79.

# Index

*345*

## Picture Credits

The illustrations in this book appear through the courtesy of the individuals and institutions listed below. Within the institutional collections, the names of the photographers, donors, or special collections, when known, are given in parentheses.